ON POLITICAL ECONOMY

ON

POLITICAL ECONOMY,

IN CONNEXION WITH THE

MORAL STATE & MORAL PROSPECTS

OF

SOCIETY,

BY

THOMAS CHALMERS

[1832]

REPRINTS OF ECONOMIC CLASSICS

AUGUSTUS M. KELLEY · PUBLISHERS
NEW YORK 1968

First Edition, 1832

(**GLASGOW**: *Printed for* William Collins; OLIVER
& BOYD, WM. WHYTE & CO. AND WM. OLIPHANT,
Edinburgh; W. F. WAKEMAN AND WM. CURRY, JUN.
& CO., *Dublin*; WHITTAKER, TREACHER & ARNOT,
HAMILTON, ADAMS & CO. AND SIMPKIN
& MARSHALL, *London*, 1832)

Reprinted 1968 by

AUGUSTUS M. KELLEY · PUBLISHERS

New York   New York   10010

Library of Congress Catalogue Card Number

67-19707

PRINTED IN THE UNITED STATES OF AMERICA
by SENTRY PRESS, NEW YORK, N. Y. 10019

ON

POLITICAL ECONOMY,

IN CONNEXION WITH THE

MORAL STATE AND MORAL PROSPECTS

OF

SOCIETY.

BY

THOMAS CHALMERS, D. D.
PROFESSOR OF DIVINITY IN THE UNIVERSITY OF EDINBURGH.

GLASGOW:

PRINTED FOR WILLIAM COLLINS;

OLIVER & BOYD, WM. WHYTE & CO. AND WM. OLIPHANT, EDINBURGH;
W. F. WAKEMAN, AND WM. CURRY, JUN. & CO. DUBLIN;
WHITTAKER, TREACHER, & ARNOT; HAMILTON, ADAMS, & CO.
AND SIMPKIN & MARSHALL, LONDON.

MDCCCXXXII.

PREFACE.

——

Political Economy, though not deemed an essen‑
tial branch of education for churchmen, touches
very closely, notwithstanding, on certain questions,
in which both the interest and the duty of eccle‑
siastics are deeply concerned. The questions of
Pauperism and of a Religious Establishment, though
no others could be specified, would, of themselves,
justify a reference to the lessons and principles of
this science, even in a theological course.

But there is one general application that might
be made of the whole subject, and which gives it,
in our judgment, its principal claim on the earnest
and respectful attention of a Christian philanthro‑
pist. Political economy aims at the diffusion of
sufficiency and comfort throughout the mass of the
population, by a multiplication or enlargement of
the outward means and materials of human enjoy‑
ment. Now, we hold it to be demonstrable, on its
own principles, that, vary its devices and expedi‑
ents as it may, this is an object which it never can
secure, apart from a virtuous and educated peasan‑
try. Our endeavour is to prove, that, in every
direction, there is a limit to the augmentation of

our physical resources; and that, in virtue of this, there must, especially in old countries, be a felt pressure and discomfort throughout every community, which has either outgrown the means for its Christian instruction, or, in any other way, renounced the habits and decencies of a Christian land. In other words, our object will be gained, if we can demonstrate, that, even but for the economic well-being of a people, their moral and religious education is the first and greatest object of national policy; and that, while this is neglected, a government, in its anxious and incessant labours for a well-conditioned state of the commonwealth, will only flounder from one delusive shift or expedient to another, under the double misfortune, of being held responsible for the prosperity of the land, and yet, finding this to be an element most helplessly and hopelessly beyond its control.

It is obvious of such a task as that which we have prescribed to ourselves, that it cannot fully be accomplished, without an extensive range and survey among the doctrines of political economy. More especially, the theory of wealth had to be examined in connexion with the theory of population; and the great resulting lesson is—the intimate alliance which obtains between the economical and the moral; insomuch, that the best objects of the science cannot, by any possibility, be realized, but by dint of prudence and virtue among the common people.

Some of the text in this volume was recently

delivered in Lectures to the Students of the Theological Hall in Edinburgh. We gladly transfer
them from the chair to the press, were it for no
other reason, than to relieve our academic work,
in all time coming, even from the semblance of
aught that is extra-professional.* We cannot,
however, bid adieu to political economy, without
an earnest recommendation of its lessons to all
those who enter upon the ecclesiastical vocation.
They are our churchmen, in fact, who could best
carry the most important of these lessons into practical effect. If sufficiently enlightened on the
question of pauperism, they might, with the greatest
ease, in Scotland, clear away this moral leprosy
from their respective parishes. And, standing at
the head of Christian education, they are the alone
effectual dispensers of all those civil and economical blessings which would follow in its train.

We are not sanguine either of a general or of
an instant reception for the doctrines of our work.
Its novelties may long be disregarded or derided
as paradoxes. And it is not the achievement of a
day, to overturn the principles of a reigning school.

---

* It may be right to mention, that all which we did deliver
upon this subject, was in a separate lectureship of one hour in
the week, distinct from the regular lessons of the Theological
course, though preparatory to our views on the treatment of
pauperism, and other questions in parish economics, which enter largely into the duties and attentions of the pastoral care.
It besides formed the natural precursor to another lectureship
which we have begun, on the methods and the machinery of
Christian education.

And if not very hopeful of an instant acquiescence in our principles, far less do we look for the instant adoption of our practical suggestions. The urgencies of the country may perhaps speed onwards the commutation of tithes, and the measure of a universal education. The commutation of taxes into a territorial impost, will be the work of a later age; though we should rejoice even now, did we witness a commencement however humble, an approximation however slow, to this great political and economical reform.

May God of his infinite mercy grant, that whatever the coming changes in the state and history of these nations may be, they shall not be the result of a sweeping and headlong anarchy; but rather, in the pacific march of improvement, may they anticipate this tremendous evil, and avert it from our borders. There is a general impression upon all spirits, that something must be done. But to be done well, it must not be by the hand of violence, but by the authority of legitimate power under the guidance of principle; by a government having both the wisdom and righteousness to direct, and the strength to execute. Amid the conflicts and agitations of our social state, it will be the heart's desire of every Christian, the fondest prayer of every true patriot, that Religion and Reason may ever preside over the destinies of our beloved land.

CONTENTS.

—

PAGE

CHAP. I.—On the Increase and Limit of Food, . . 1

CHAP. II.—On the Increase and Limit of Employment, 30

CHAP. III.—On the Increase and Limit of Capital, . 75

CHAP. IV.—On the Parallel between Population and Capital, both in respect of their Limits and their Powers of Expansion, ... 106

CHAP. V.—On the Possibility of Over-production, or of a General Glut, ... 137

CHAP. VI.—On the Limits of a Country's Foreign Trade, and its supposed Power to Furnish a People with Employment and Maintenance, ... 174

CHAP. VII.—The same subject continued, . . 216

CHAP. VIII.—On the supposed effect of Taxes in aggravating the condition of the Labouring Classes, with the converse effect which the Remission of Taxes is conceived to have on their Relief, and the enlargement of their Comforts, ... 241

CHAP. IX.—The same subject continued, . . 264

PAGE

CHAP. X.—On Tithes, ... 303

CHAP. XI.—On the Distinction made by Economists between Productive and Unproductive Labour, . 332

CHAP. XII.—On the Law of Primogeniture, . . 352

CHAP. XIII.—On Emigration, ... 378

CHAP. XIV.—On a Compulsory Provision for the Indigent, ... 398

CHAP. XV.—On the Christian Education of the People, 420

CHAP. XVI.—Conclusion, ... 450

APPENDIX.

On the Rent of Land, ... 459

On Machinery, ... 473

On Home Colonization, ... 479

On the National Debt, ... 490

On Profit, ... 509

On Free Trade, ... 517

On the Corn Laws, ... 523

On the gradual Reform of our Financial System, . 541

Synoptical View of the Political Economy of this Volume, 551

ON

POLITICAL ECONOMY,

IN CONNEXION WITH THE

MORAL STATE, AND MORAL PROSPECTS,

OF

SOCIETY.

———

CHAPTER I.

ON THE INCREASE AND LIMIT OF FOOD.

1. Each science has certain commanding positions, whence, if the observer look rightly around him, he may obtain an extensive view of important truths and important applications. Such a position, we think, has been recently gained in Political Economy, although full advantage has not yet been taken of it. We hold it the more interesting, that it includes within its range, certain unexplored places of the science; and, more especially, that department where the theory of wealth comes into contact with the theory of population, and where the two, therefore, might be examined in connexion.

2. The doctrine, or discovery, to which we re-fer, is that promulgated some years ago, and both at the same time, by Sir Edward West and Mr. Malthus. It respects the land last entered upon for the purposes of cultivation, and which yields no rent. It is obvious, that land of this inferior productiveness must mark the extreme limit of cultivation at the time—as land of still inferior quality could not be broken up without loss to the cultivator.

3. Any land, that is cultivated for food to human beings, must, at least, yield as much as shall feed the labourers who are employed in working it. But it must do more than this. These agricultural labourers require to be clothed and lodged, as well as fed. They must be upheld, not in food alone, which is the first necessary ; but in, what may be termed, the second necessaries of life. The people whose business it is to work up these, may, in contradistinction to the *agricultural*, be termed the *secondary* labourers of a country. It is evident, that the worst of cultivated land must, at least, be able to feed those who are directly employed upon the soil, and, moreover, those who prepare for the agricultural labourers all the other articles, beside food, which enter into their support or maintenance. Else the cultivation of it behoved to be abandoned. All that land which, by no possible improvement, either in the processes of husbandry or of manufacturing labour, could yield as much as would subsist the agricultural labourers

and their secondaries, is doomed, by nature, to everlasting sterility, and must always remain without the scope of cultivation.

4. The imagination is, that the land of greatest fertility was first occupied. Men would naturally settle on those soils which yielded the most plentiful return for their labour, or which enabled them to subsist with the least labour. It is farther conceived, that, after all the first-rate land had been cultivated, an increasing population flowed over, as it were, on the second-rate land; which, in virtue of its inferior quality, yielded a scantier return for the same labour. As mankind continued to multiply, a still further descent behoved to be made, through a gradation of soils, each of less fertility than the one before entered on; and so, either requiring a greater amount of labour to draw from it the same food, or yielding a smaller amount of food to the same labour. This process, it is evident, admits of being extended, till the produce of the soil last entered on shall, by the utmost labour which men will expend on it, be barely sufficient for the subsistence of its agricultural labourers, and of their secondaries.

5. In filling up this sketch, or *histoire raisonnée*, of the conjunct progress of culture and population, economists have given in to certain conceptions, which require to be modified. They sometimes describe the process, as if, at each successive descent to an inferior soil, the comfort and circumstances of the human race underwent deterioration;

or as if, under the impulse of a hard and hunger-
bitten necessity, men were driven, like so many
famishing wolves, to those intractable soils, whence
they could only force out a more stinted and penurious fare than before—and that, at a greater
expense of toil and of endurance. Agreeably to
this imagination, even economists and calculators
have, by a reverse process, found their way to a
golden age at the outset of the world—when men
reposed in the lap of abundance; and, with no
other fatigue than that of a slight and superficial
operation on a soil of first-rate quality, richly par-
took in the bounties of nature. But when all this
soil came to be occupied, and the race continued
to multiply, land of a second quality behoved to
be taken in—and the conception is, that, at every
such transition from a better to a worse land, a
heavier imposition of toil was laid upon workmen,
and a smaller amount of produce was yielded to
them in return for their industry. This, certainly,
represents to us the species in a course of deterioration, at least, in as far as the comfort of the labouring classes is concerned. They are pictured
to the eye, as if goaded on by hard and stubborn
necessity at every step of this movement, and going forth, in starving multitudes, from that better
land, which is now too narrow for them. At each
new stretch of cultivation, a more ungrateful soil
has to be encountered, on which it is thought that
men are more strenuously wrought, and more scan-
tily subsisted, than before—till, at the extreme

limit of this progression, a life of utmost toil, and
utmost penury, is looked to as the inevitable doom
that awaits the working classes of society.

6. Now, generally speaking, this is not accordant
with historical truth. We do read of extensive
emigrations, by men who felt themselves straitened
in their native land, and went forth in quest of a
settlement. But we do not witness, throughout
the various countries of the world, the successive
degradation of their peasantry. There may be
fluctuations in their economic state, from year to
year, or from generation to generation. But on
the survey and comparison of centuries, we should
rather say, that there had been a general march and
elevation in the style of their enjoyments. There
is a seeming incompatibility in this fact with the
process which has just been described—and this
has cast a suspicion over its reality. Men have
been at a loss to reconcile the descent of labourers
among the inferior soils, with the undoubted rise
which has taken place in their circumstances, or
in the average standard of their comfort. This
has darkened the whole speculation, and brought
on a controversy, which admits however, we think,
of a very obvious and easy adjustment.

7. For as the fresh soils that had to be successively entered on became more intractable, the
same amount of labour, by the intervention of tools
and instruments of husbandry, may have become
greatly more effective. The same labour which,
by a direct manual operation, could raise a given

quantity of subsistence from soil of the first quality,
might, with our present implements of agriculture,
raise as much from soil of the last quality that has
been entered on. If, from one generation to another, a descent had to be made on more stubborn and
impracticable soils, and which, therefore, required
a far more operose treatment, ere they could be
brought to yield as abundantly, as did their predecessor soils, in the career of agriculture—it should
be remembered that, by this time, the labour of
human hands might have been helped and facili-
tated, to the whole extent of the difference, by the
implements of labour. With the scraping and
stirring of first-rate land by the branch of a tree,
there might be as much of real muscular work required to obtain from it the same quantity of produce, as from second-rate land by means of a
wooden spade, or from third-rate land by means
of an iron one, or from fourth-rate land by means
of a plough, or lastly, from fifth-rate and following
lands, by means of those successive improvements
in the form of the plough, whereby it is made more
effective than before. We will not yet designate
the implements of husbandry by the name of capital—but, considering them merely as the products
of labour, it is enough at present to affirm, that
the whole labour, first, of making the plough,
and then of working it on the soil of the last and
latest quality, might fetch back as liberal a return
of food to the cultivators, as an equal quantity of
labour bestowed either directly by the hand, or

with the intervention of some rude and clumsy instrument on the land that was earliest entered on. It is thus that there may at once be a progress in agriculture, and yet, through all the gradations of it, the species be upheld in as great ease and sufficiency as at first. Instead of the strong impulse of population driving them helplessly and ungovernably onward, to those more inhospitable regions, where they are doomed to all the miseries of a more stinted provision than before,—they may, simply, and spontaneously, and without the pressure of any felt agony or violence, have entered on the possession of these regions, because now furnished by art with the means of extracting, even from the comparative barrenness of nature, as generous a remuneration for their toils as they before drew from nature's greatest fertility. We are not, therefore, to imagine of the great family of mankind, that as they grew in numbers, and spread themselves over upon tracks of greater sterility than before, they must necessarily sink down into a state of greater endurance, whether in the way of privation or fatigue. It is not always at the call of hunger or distress that these successive movements have been made. They are often made in another character —not in that of famishing hordes, making forcible descent on some untried region, in quest of that which might satiate their cravings; but in the higher character of dominant and devising men, walking forth with master step, and in the triumph of their new energies and acquisitions, to subdue some yet untrodden territory, and force from it as liberal subsistence, as any which their ancestors had ever gotten in more favoured climes.   We are not to suppose that every increase of cultivation is marked by an increase of wretchedness.   Through its whole process, from the first to the last of it, the species might be sustained on as high a level, and even be made to ascend higher than at the first.   And, as at the commencement of cultivation, there might have been impediments to be struggled with at the entrance upon the first land, such as the clearing it of wood,—so, on the extreme verge of our newest cultivation, there might have been helps to labour on the last and worst land, such as the perfection of our modern implements, which could ensure as generous a repayment for the same quantity of work, in the most recent, as in the most remote stages of this great process.

8. It follows not, that in the act of descending to an inferior soil, men have to put forth a greater quantity of labour for the same return,—because, it may have been some improvement in the modes or operations of husbandry, which has enabled them to make the descent, and to make the same labour as effective on the ground which they are now reclaiming from the waste, as on that which they had last brought within the domain of culti-vation.   When, therefore, we see the wilds of na-ture further broken in upon, we are not always to imagine, that it is from the pressure of a felt ne-cessity, by which men have been forced to submit

to a more painful endurance, and to put up with a scantier subsistence in return for it. It may have been the pacific, the prosperous result of some enlargement in the powers of agricultural labour ; and in consequence of which, men go spontaneously forth on an inferior soil, because now, for the same work, they earn the same recompense as they did on the soil immediately above it. It is thus a possible thing, that cultivation may be extended, without deterioration to the comfort of labourers ; and that along its last possible frontier, there might be stationed as high and well-conditioned a peasantry, as ever flourished in any olden or golden period on the lawns of Arcadia.

9. And cultivation may be extended by an improvement in manufacturing, as well as in agricultural labour. It may be conceived, of the land last entered, that in return for a certain quantity of labour, it yields the subsistence of a hundred families—and that the land next inferior to it cannot be profitably cultivated, because in return for the same labour, it yields the subsistence of only ninety families. Now, overlooking for the present, the element of profit, one might conceive these hundred families to be made up of seventy belonging to the agricultural, and of thirty belonging to the secondary class,—it being the employment of the latter to prepare, for the whole hundred, the second necessaries of life. It matters not whether there be such an improvement in agricultural labour, that sixty can do the work of seventy,

or such an improvement in manufacturing labour, that twenty can do the work of thirty. In either way, ninety labourers can do as much as a hundred did before; and whereas, formerly, land behoved to return for their labour the subsistence of a hundred families, ere it could be taken in, it may now be taken in, though of such inferior quality, as to return the subsistence of but ninety families. By the former improvement, the agricultural labourers necessary, for a given effect, became fewer than before,—by the latter improvement, though still as numerous, they would require the services of fewer secondaries than before. It is thus that a step of improvement in manufactures alone, can give rise to an onward step of extension in agriculture—and just because a method has been devised for the fabrication of as many yards of cloth, by fewer hands, soils of poorer out-field, than any that had yet been reached, may now be profitably entered upon. An improvement in the form of the stocking machine, may, as well as an improvement in the form of the plough, bring many an else unreclaimed acre within the reach of cultivation.

10. The actual and historical process that has taken place, we believe to be as follows. The labourers of our day, work harder than before, but live better than before. They put forth more strength, and receive more sustenance, than they wont to do. There has been an increase on both of these terms; or, such has been the change of habit among workmen, that while greatly more

industrious, they, at the same time, have become greatly more luxurious. They at once toil more strenuously, and live more plentifully—putting forth more strength, but withal, drawing the remuneration of a larger and more liberal sustenance. This we apprehend to be the actual change of habit and condition which has taken place, with artizans and labourers, in all the countries of civilized Europe,—so that while, on the one hand, we behold a harder working peasantry, we, on the other hand, behold them more richly upholden, both in the first and second necessaries of life.

11. Now, this may be either a deterioration or an improvement in their circumstances. One can imagine a day of slavish fatigue, followed by an evening of gross and loathsome sensuality,—as is often exemplified in the life of a London coal-heaver, whose enormous wage is absorbed in the enormous consumption, by which he repairs the waste and the weariness of an excessive labour. This surely is not a desirable habitude for the commonalty of any land—nor do we read the characteristics of a high or a well-conditioned peasantry in a state of existence, made up, first of drudgery to the uttermost of their strength, and then of grovelling dissipation to the uttermost of their means. They spend one part of their revolving day in the exercise of powers, which are merely animal; and the other part in the indulgence of enjoyments, which also are merely animal—like beasts of burden, who are better wrought than before, and, in

return for this, are better fed and lodged and lit-
tered than before.   They are now in better keep
than their forefathers; and this puts them into
heart for the greater work that is extracted out of
them.   Still it is conceivable of the work, that it
may be so very extreme, as, on the whole, to degrade and to depress these overdone children of
modern industry—and that, in spite of the greater
abundance wherewith their senses and their spirits
are coarsely regaled, during the intervals of their
sore bondage.

12. If this be the extreme to which the workmen of our present day are now tending, there is
an extreme opposite to this, from which men only
began to emerge at the outset of civilization, and
which is still realized among barbarous and demi-
barbarous nations.   We advert to the sordid condition of those, whom nought but the agonies of
hunger can impel to shake off an indolence that is
else unconquerable; and who, as soon as they have
satisfied its cravings, lapse again into the rooted and
habitual lethargy of their nature.   If they have
but enough of sleep, and enough of surfeiting, they
care for no higher gratification,—nor will they
make one effort, above that level to which they
subside, by the weight of their own constitutional
sluggishness.   Food of some description or other
they must have,—but having it, they are pleased
to live in filth and nakedness, and nearly in utter
want of all the secondary accommodations.   It is
obvious, of such a people, that so long as they

abide in this habit, the inferior soils of the earth never will be reached by them. It is even possible that they may stop short at the very first and most fertile of the land; and never taste of that abundance, which is within their reach, just because of their insuperable aversion to the labour of extracting it. It is thus that they might doze away their existence, on the surface of an earth, whose dormant capabilities they never enter upon,—and in vast territories, capable of sustaining millions over and above the few stragglers by whom they are occupied, both cultivation and population may, just because of this moral barrier, have been fixed and limited for many centuries.

13. So that, in reasoning on the causes which have led to the extension of agriculture among sterile and intractable soils, other things must be taken into account, beside the mere energy of the principle of population. We have already shown, how, without bringing this principle into collision with a taste for the enjoyments of life, there may, without any compromise of these enjoyments, and by a mere improvement in the powers of mechanical labour, be a descent among the inferior soils, and so an extension of agriculture, to afford the increasing population as large and liberal a subsistence as before. And it is evident, the very same thing would happen, with every increase that took place in the amount of manual labour, or in the industrious habits of the people. Certain it is, that, in climes and countries the most favourable to pro-

duction, we may often witness the squalid destitution of whole tribes, restrained, by the mere force
of indolence, from the enjoyment of that plenty,
which, with but a little effort, they could so easily
realize.   Now this proceeds, not from the principle
of population being of smaller strength there than
in other parts of the world, but from the counteractive force of indolence being there of greater
strength.   There is a lethargy, or love of ease, in
certain temperaments, which will even carry it over
the love of offspring ; so that shöuld it not prevent
early marriages, it will, at least, prevent a larger
proportion of the fruits of marriage from ripening
into maturity.   Of the many children who are
born, a few only will survive the sickliness and the
spare living to which they are exposed, from that
state of voluntary destitution, wherein their parents
will rather abide, than put forth those efforts of industry which they feel to be intolerable.   Just as
the taste for secondary enjoyments has not yet
aroused them to exertion, so neither might affection
for their famishing and misguided little ones arouse
them.   This accounts for the population being
stationary in many countries, where, as yet, the
first-rate soils have scarcely been entered upon—
and it should convince us, that something else than
the mere energy of this principle must be adverted
to, when we reason on that historical progress which
has conjunctly taken place, in the extension of
husbandry and in the numbers of mankind.

14. But if, by the strength of human indolence,

the process of cultivation may be arrested at an earlier stage in the scale of descending fertility, then, should this indolence, by some cause or other, be removed, or got the better of, the process may be again set at liberty. Now there is no influence by which man is more effectually roused to exertion, than the excitement of new desires, which require exertion ere they can be appeased. Let him, by any chance, come to have a greater number of wants than before; and, to supply these, he may be led to work a greater number of hours than before. His taste for idleness will give way to his taste for other things, when he comes to like these other things better than his idleness. If he will not be satisfied but with a certain style of dress and lodging, or with the enjoyment of certain luxuries, which his forefathers never dreamed of— then, rather than be without them, he will put forth a strenuous and sustained effort of regular industry, which his forefathers would have felt to be intolerable. This change of habit has actually taken place in modern Europe. Workmen both labour more, and live better, than their ancestors.

15. This is one important service which commerce has rendered to agriculture. It was the instrument of that great economic change which took place at the termination of the middle ages—when landlords dismissed their retainers, and expended the surplus produce of their estates on the purchase of those articles which trade and manufactures brought to their door. This great transition has

been well described both by Adam Smith and Dr.
Robertson,—but it should not be overlooked, that,
beside the reaction on landlords, there was also at
that time a strong reaction produced on the habit
of labourers. With their growing taste for the
new enjoyments which had been placed within their
reach, there was, in order to obtain them, a will-
ingness to forego the lounging and lazaroni life
which they formerly indulged in, and to brook the
restraints and the toils of regular industry. A
mighty extension must have arisen to agriculture
—not merely from the new power that has been
given to the implements of labour, but from the
new habit that has been given to the labourers
themselves. If they now work double of what they
did formerly—then, all other circumstances being
equal, the land last entered on, will, in return for
the same labour, only have to feed half of the number of agricultural labourers which it did formerly.
It affords room for an immense enlargement,
when, in virtue of this moral transition alone, the
cultivation which stopped short at the land that,
for a given amount of work, returned the subsistence
of twenty families, may now be carried downward
to a more barren and uncomplying soil, that, in return for the same work, yields but the subsistence
of ten families. In this way too, then, have trade
and manufactures widened the domain of cultivation—and the products of the former have stimulated and called forth in greater abundance the
products of the latter.

16. It is thus that, by a more strenuous industry, and a more effective machinery together, the poorer soils may, to a certain extent, be forced to yield an equal, or, perhaps, a more liberal subsistence to the labourer, than at earlier stages in the process of cultivation. Yet it must be quite evident that, whether in single countries, or in the whole world, it is a process which cannot go on indefinitely. The time may be indefinitely distant, and indeed may never come, when the absolute and impassable barrier shall at length be arrived at. But to be satisfied that there is such a barrier, one has only to look to the extent and quality of the land in any region of the earth. By labour we might grind even the naked rock into an arable soil,—but a soil thus formed never would return the expense of food bestowed upon the labourers. In every country there is an upland or outfield territory, which will always bid defiance to agriculture. And even though it were not so—though to its last acre it possessed a uniform richness—though the plough might be carried over the whole of the mighty continent, and should find an obstacle nowhere but at the margin of the sea; yet, as sure as that every country has its limit, and every continent its shore, we must acquiesce in it as one of the stern necessities of our condition, that the earth we tread upon, can only be made to yield a limited produce, and so to sustain a limited population.

17. It seems very generally admitted, that should it ever come to this, the population, brought to a

stand in respect of numbers, must either have to
encounter great positive distress, or must anticipate this distress by a preventive regimen.   In the
midst of all the minuter criticisms to which the
doctrine has been exposed, the great historical fact
remains unshaken—that, let the means of subsistence be increased however largely and suddenly,
this is sure to be followed by a corresponding increase of population.   Every state and country in
the world bears evidence to this truth—whether
in the steady augmentations of Europe, or in the
gigantic strides that are now making in the population of America.   The invariable connection, as
of antecedent and consequent, between a great extent of fertile and unoccupied land, and a great
multiplication of families, when once it is entered
upon, is too palpable to be obscured by any sophis-
try, or by the allegation of any mystic principle
whatever. Yet the power to support, and the power
to create a population, are just as distinct, the one
from the other, as the constitution of the external
world is distinct from the constitution or physiology
of human nature.   It is not an increase of the former power which gives rise to an increase of the
latter—it only gives situation and space for the development of its energies.   Should a population,
when every let and hindrance of a straitened subsistence is removed, be able to double itself in
fifteen years—it would still have the inherent ability
of doing so, after that every acre on the face of the
globe had been advanced to its state of uttermost

cultivation. The power of population would then be kept in perpetual abeyance—with a constant disposition to transgress beyond the limits of the world's food, and as constant a check on the expansion of the capabilities which belong to it.

18. All this is very generally allowed; but then the imagination of many is, that, not until the world be fully cultivated and fully peopled, shall we have any practical interest in the question. They seem to think of the doctrine of Malthus, that the consideration of it may, with all safety, be postponed, till the agriculture of every country and every clime have been carried to its extreme perfection; and that, meanwhile, the population may proceed as rapidly and recklessly as it may. When a household is straitened by its excessive numbers, or a parish is oppressed by its redundant families—they would bar every argument about the proximate causes of this inconvenience, by the allegation that there were still thousands of unreclaimed acres at home, or millions in distant places of the earth, though of as little real or substantial consequence to the suffering parties, as if the land were situated in another planet. They appear to conceive, that ere any body can be felt as an obstacle to our progress, it must have come to a dead stand—not aware that to act as a check or impediment, it has only to move more slowly, though in the same direction, than at the rate in which we are advancing ourselves. They proceed on the idea, that no shock or collision can be felt but by the stroke of an im-

pellent on a body at rest—whereas it is enough if the body be but moving at a tardier pace. In the one case, the strength of the collision would be estimated by the whole velocity—yet, in the other, there might still be a very hard collision, though estimated only by a difference of velocities. It is thus that, for the continued pressure of the world's population on its food, it is far from necessary that the food should have reached that stationary maximum, beyond which it cannot be carried. It is enough, for this purpose, that the limit of the world's abundance, though it does recede, should recede more slowly than *would* the limit of the world's population. A pressure, and that a very severe one, may be felt for many ages together, from a difference in the mere tendencies of their increase. The man, who so runs as to break his head against a wall, might receive a severe contusion, even to the breaking of his head, if, instead of a wall, it had been a slowly retiring barrier. And therefore we do not antedate matters, by taking up now the consideration of Malthus' preventive and positive checks to population. There is scarcely a period, even in the bygone history of the world, when the former checks have not been called for, and the latter have not been in actual operation. To postpone either the argument or its application till the agriculture of the world shall be perfected, is a most unpractical, as well as a most unintelligent view of the question—for long ere this distant consummation can be realized, and even now, may the obstacle of a slowly retiring limit begin to be felt.

The tendency of a progressive population to outstrip the progressive culture of the earth, may put
mankind into a condition of straitness and difficulty—and that for many generations before the
earth shall be wholly cultivated. We are not sure,
but it may have done so from the commencement
of the race, and throughout all its generations.
Certain it is, at all events, that the produce of the
soil cannot be made to increase at the rate that
population *would* increase. Neither mechanical
invention nor more intense manual labour is sufficient for this purpose. On the supposition that the
numbers of mankind were to increase up to their
natural capability of increase, no human skill or
human labour, though doing their uttermost, could
suffice for raising a produce up to the population—
nor will the mass of society ever be upheld in comfort, without the operation of certain other principles, by which to restrain the excess of the population over the produce.

19. The impotency of the one expedient, and
efficacy of the other, are no where more convincingly
exhibited than along what may be termed, the extreme margin of cultivation. It is there where the
land pays no rent;* and, laying aside for the present,

* We are aware of a certain modification and minuter sort
of controversy, to which the affirmation of the land absolutely
paying no rent has given rise. We shall not stop to offer any
adjustment on this matter, as it is in no way essential to the
validity of our argument. See Mr. Prinsep's note to his translation of Say's Political Economy, vol. II. p. 168.—and Dr.
Hamilton on the Progress of Society.

the consideration of profit, it is there where the
produce that is reared can do no more than feed
the labouring cultivators and their secondaries.
But let the population increase to the extent of its
own inherent power of increase, and it would force
the existing limit of cultivation; or, in other words,
flow over upon a soil inferior to that which had last
been entered on, or inferior to that which, at the
then rate of enjoyment, could do no more than
feed the labouring cultivators and their secondaries. The consequence of such a descent is inevitable. The rate of enjoyment must fall. The
agricultural workmen must either submit to be
worse fed than before; or, parting with so many
of their secondaries, they must submit to be worse
clothed, or lodged, or furnished than before. The
likelihood is, that they would so proportion their
sacrifices, as to suffer in both these ways—and so
there behoved to be a general degradation of comfort in the working classes of society. There is, to
be sure, another way in which they might possibly
extract from the more ungrateful soil, on which
they had just entered, the same plenty as before.
They may submit to harder labour, by putting forth
a more strenuous husbandry on the inferior land—
but this too is degradation. Whether by an increase of drudgery, or an increase of destitution,
there may, in either way, be a sore aggravation to
the misery of labourers.

20. If it be not possible, then, to sustain in comfort and sufficiency the working classes, by keeping

up the produce to the population, when suffered
to proceed according to its own spontaneous energies—there seems only to be another alternative
for the achievement of this great problem, that of
keeping down the population to the produce.   We
know of no right, or comfortable, or efficient way
of doing this, than by the establishment of a habit
and a principle among the labourers themselves.
If they will in general enter recklessly into marriage, it is not possible to save a general descent
in their circumstances.   By the operation of causes
already explained, a population may flow onward,
in the way of increase, from one age to another,
without any abridgment on the comforts of our
peasantry.   When these are trenched upon, it is
no longer a flow—but we should call it an overflow.
And the only way, we apprehend, of preventing
this overflow, with all its consequent wretchedness
and crime, is by the formation of a higher taste for
comfort and decency among the peasantry themselves.   Marriage is not necessarily the effect of a
headlong impulse; but may be a voluntary act,
in the determination of which, prudence and forethought have had an influential share.   It is evident, that the more we elevate man into a reflec-
tive being, and inspire him with self-respect, and
give him a demand for larger and more refined accommodations, and, in one word, raise his standard
of enjoyment—the more will the important step of
marriage become a matter of deliberation and delay.   There is the utmost difference, in this respect,

between the man who is content to live on potatoes,
and spend his days in a sordid hovel, and the man
who aspires, and, indeed, will not be satisfied without that style of food, and furniture, and dress,
which we find generally to obtain among a well-
conditioned peasantry.*   There is a sense of character, as well as a taste for comfort, connected with
this habit; and when these become general in a
land, there is, of consequence, a most sure and

* Mr. T. Perronnet Thomson, in his able Tract on the
" True Theory of Rent," has stated the effect of this difference
with laconic felicity and force. " A labourer in Ireland will
live and bring up a family on potatoes; a labourer in England
will see the world unpeopled first."—" Englishmen have the
physical capability of living on potatoes as much as other men,
but fortunately they have not the habit; and though it might
be wrong to say they would starve first in their own proper
persons, they will utterly refuse to multiply upon such diet,
the effect of which on population is ultimately the same."—
" The Englishman will not live and bring up a family on potatoes; because, though he may consent to live on them, when
he can positively procure nothing else,—habit, custom, the
opinion of those around him, have made it in his eyes con-
temptible, irrational, absurd, for a man to be living on potatoes,
when he has the opportunity of getting any thing better. In
his hours of prosperity, therefore, he will to a certainty solace
himself with bacon, and most probably venture upon beef; and
as this absorbs a greater portion of his income in what he views
as necessary to his individual existence, it proportionally reduces his disposition to burthen himself with new mouths. If
the Irishman had the prospect of all this bacon and beef, he
would view it as convertible into potatoes for a family like a
patriarch's. The Englishman thinks it but decency to swallow
all, and omits the family."

salutary postponement in the average date of matrimony.   In a newly settled country, where there
is much good land still unoccupied, the moral preventive check might not be called for.   In an old
country, where it is called for, but not observed,
we are sure to behold a wretched and degraded
peasantry.   There is no other method by which to
raise them above this level, or to prevent their
falling into it, than by the rigorous operation of
this check.   Our peasantry, it should be understood by all, have in this way, though in this way
only, their comfort and independence in their own
hands.   They are on high vantage-ground, if they
but knew it; and it is the fondest wish of every
enlightened philanthropist, that they should avail
themselves to the uttermost of the position which
they occupy.   It is at the bidding of their collective will, what the remuneration of labour shall be;
for they have entire and absolute command over the
supply of labour.   If they will, by their rash and
blindfold marriages, over-people the land, all the
devices of human benevolence and wisdom cannot
ward off from them the miseries of an oppressed and
straitened condition.   There is no possible help
for them, if they will not help themselves.   It is
to a rise and reformation in the habits of our peasantry that we would look for deliverance, and not
to the impotent crudities of a speculative legislation.   Many are the schemes of amelioration at all
times afloat.   We hold, that, without the growth
of popular intelligence and virtue, they will, every

one of them, be ineffectual. This will at length
save the country from the miseries of a redundant
population—and this, we apprehend, to be the
great, the only specific for its worst moral and its
worst political disorders.

21. It is not, however, by a direct promulgation
of the doctrines of Mr. Malthus, that the people
will be converted to the side of their own interest.
We can imagine nothing more preposterous than
the diffusion, for this purpose, of tracts on population among the families of the land.   The change
will be accomplished surely, though indirectly, and
by insensible progress, through the means of general instruction, or by the spread of common, and
more especially of sound Christian education over
the country.   There is an indissoluble connection
between the moral character and the economic
comfort of a peasantry ; and the doctrine of Malthus is the *vinculum* by which to explain it.   But
it is not necessary to point out the vinculum to
them.   To make good the effect, it is not at all
necessary that they should understand its dependence upon the cause.   It is enough, if in the
state of their own principles and feelings, they
present or provide the cause.   Let them only be
a well-taught and moralized people ; and, in that
proportion, will they mix prudence and calculation
and foresight, with every step in the history of their
lives.   The desirable effect will follow without any
theory, or any anticipation of theirs.   Let it, on
the average, be held disreputable to marry without

a fair and adequate prospect or provision ; and the
result would be a certain average of later marriages,
or a country less burdened with an excess of population.   It is thus, that half a century ago, in the
Lowlands of Scotland, the habit of a large preparation, that often required, for its accomplishment, the delay of years after the virtuous attachment was formed—this habit was nearly universal
among our well-schooled and well-ordered families.
And so, though poverty was not unknown, yet
pauperism was unknown ; and notwithstanding the
general barrenness of our soil, did the moral prevail over the physical causes, and uphold within
our borders, an erect and independent peasantry.
They exemplified the doctrine of Malthus, and
realized its benefits, long before that doctrine was
propounded to the world.

22. In the mechanism of human society, it needs
not, that, to effectuate a given result, the people,
who do in fact bring it about, should be able intelligently to view their own part in it.   This is
not more necessary in truth, than that, to fulfil the
beneficent end of the planetary system, its various
parts should be endued with consciousness—that
the satellites of Jupiter, for example, should understand and design their own movements.   The
multitude may be wholly innocent of economical
science themselves—yet may they exemplify, and
by their agency sustain, its most wholesome processes.   They may realize the full benefits of an
operation which they do not comprehend—though,

in very deed, they were themselves the operators.
We object not to the highest possible education of
the peasantry—yet it is not to the lessons of the
political, but to those of the moral and religious
school, that we look for the best and speediest instruments of their economic well-being.   Neither
teachers nor taught may understand this connection
—nor is it necessary they should.   The main object and the collateral good of Christianity may be
indissolubly conjoined—but there are thousands
who have verified this conjunction in experience,
though they have never viewed it in theory.   In
labouring for the good of their eternity, they have
reaped, by the way, those blessings which religion
so abundantly sheds over the pilgrimage that leads
to it.

23. All the remedies which have been proposed
against a state of general destitution in society, may
be classified under two descriptions.   By the first,
it is sought to provide the adequate means for the
increasing numbers of mankind.   By the second,
to keep down the numbers to the stationary, or,
comparatively speaking, to the slowly-increasing
means.   The first may, we think, be conveniently
designated the external remedies—insomuch that
their object is to equalize the means with the population, by an increase on the former term, or by
an increase and enlargement of the resources from
without.   The second may, perhaps, be contradis-
tinguished from the other, by viewing it in the light
of an internal remedy—insomuch as its object is to

maintain the equality of the two, by preventing an undue increase on the latter term, which can only be achieved, in a right way, by adding to the restraints of prudence and principle from within. It is our main design to demonstrate the insufficiency of one and all the remedies put together which belong to the first class—and to contrast, with their operation, the effect of the moral remedy, the prosperous economic state that will surely be realized through the medium of general intelligence and virtue, or by an action on the minds of the people themselves.

CHAPTER II.

ON THE INCREASE AND LIMIT OF EMPLOYMENT.

1. THE great and immediate demand is for the application of the external remedies; and, till these have done their uttermost, the feeling is, that the application of the internal is meanwhile uncalled for. So long, it is imagined, as there are still un-evoked any possible resources from without, it is yet time to think of a restraint from within. It is readily admitted, that, as cultivation is carried downward through the gradation of soils, the last which has been entered on does no more, in the existing state of our agriculture, than barely re-munerate the operations of its husbandry—or, lay-ing capital at present out of the account, than feed the agricultural labourers and their secondaries. And it is further granted, that, if the last possible limit is ever to be reached, the tendency of the population to increase must either be corrected by the positive, or kept in by the preventive checks; and that, were the operation of the moral preventive check sufficiently powerful, there might, even in the ultimate state of the world's agriculture, be as high, or a more highly-conditioned peasantry, than at any preceding stage of the world's history. But it is not seen, that, long anterior to this consumma-

tion, the moral preventive check may be imperiously called for, in order to sustain the comfort and circumstances of the working population. Nevertheless, this moral restraint is desirable *now*, as well as *then;* and that, just because the tendency to an increase in the number of labourers far outstrips the tendency to an increase in the productive powers of labour. It is quite true, that, by the inventions of machinery, and the improvements which are ever taking place, both in the methods of agriculture, and the implements of agricultural labour, the poorer soils may, for an indefinitely long period, be made to yield as much, in return for the same work, as did their predecessor soils in the series of cultivation. Yet there is nothing in this to supersede the moral restraint—and precisely because, with every possible enlargement, subsistence *will* not increase, so fast as population *would* increase. And therefore it is, that, notwithstanding all which may be alleged of the still unexhausted capabilities of the soil, either in this, or in any other country of the world, we cannot possibly be saved from the *present* and the perpetual miseries of a redundant population, but by a higher taste for the comforts and the decencies of life among the population themselves. This, by its controlling effect on the date of marriage, and so on the largeness and number of rising families, keeps up the price of labour, by keeping down the supply of it in the labour market. This we hold to be the great specific for ensuring a high average style of comfort

and enjoyment among our peasantry—nor do we
regard it as a less wise and beautiful connection in
the mechanism of society, that the most direct way
to establish it is through the medium of popular
intelligence and virtue—giving thereby a practical
importance to efficient Christian instruction, unknown to the most of economists, and which no
mere economist can possibly realize.

2. But though the progress of cultivation, and
the produce extracted by labourers from the last
and farthest margin of it, do truly represent both
the progress in numbers, and the state in respect to
comfort, of our operative population;* and though,
when viewed in this way, the conclusion seems
irresistible, that there is a slowly-receding limit to
the means of subsistence, on which population is
ever pressing, so that if it press too hardly, it must
straiten and depress the condition of labourers—
yet we hear of a thousand other expedients for an
amelioration in the state of the working classes of
society, beside the only effectual expedient of a
general principle and prudence in regard to marriages, which it is for the working classes of society,

---

* The produce extracted by that portion of our labourers
who are employed at the extreme margin of cultivation, will,
after a deduction for profit and taxes, truly represent and
measure the general state of comfort among the operative population at large; because an inferiority of condition cannot
long subsist between one class of labourers and another, there
being a constant tendency to equalization, by the free movements of individual labourers from the employment that is worse
remunerated to the employment that is better.

and them alone, to put into operation.　What gives plausibility to these expedients is, that society is so exceedingly complicated a thing ;* insomuch

---

* It has been well remarked by Malthus, in his Essay on Population, that the largeness and complication of a society tend to obscure the truth upon this subject :—

" Norway is, I believe, almost the only country in Europe where a traveller will hear any apprehensions expressed of a redundant population, and where the danger to the happiness of the lower classes of people, from this cause, is in some degree seen and understood.　This obviously arises from the smallness of the population altogether, and the consequent narrowness of the subject.　If our attention were confined to one parish, and there were no power of emigrating from it, the most careless observer could not fail to remark, that, if all married at twenty, it would be perfectly impossible for the farmers, however carefully they might improve their land, to find employment and food for those that would grow up; but when a great number of these parishes are added together in a populous kingdom, the largeness of the subject, and the power of moving from place to place, obscure and confuse our view.　We lose sight of a truth which before appeared completely obvious; and, in a most unaccountable manner, attribute to the aggregate quantity of land, a power of supporting people beyond comparison greater than the sum of all its parts."— " From the small number of people, and the little variety of employment, the subject is brought distinctly within the view of each individual ; and he must feel the absolute necessity of repressing his inclinations to marriage till a vacancy offer."— " In countries more fully peopled, this subject is always involved in great obscurity.　Each man naturally thinks that he has as good a chance of finding employment as his neighbour, and that if he fail in one place he shall succeed in some other. He marries, therefore, and trusts to fortune ; and the effect too frequently is, that the redundant population, occasioned in this manner, is repressed by the positive checks of poverty and dis-

that, when viewed in some one aspect, it holds out
a promise of improvement or relief, which, under
another or more comprehensive aspect, is seen to
be quite illusory.   For example, when one witnesses
the vast diversity of trades, or employments, in society, by each of which, or at least in the prosecution of which, so many thriving families are supported, then it is conceived, that the high-way for
the relief of the unprovided is to find them a trade,
to find them employment.   Or, when looking to

ease.   In Norway the subject is not involved in the same obscurity.   The number of additional families, which the increasing demand for labour will support, is more distinctly marked.
The population is so small, that even in the towns it is difficult
to fall into any considerable error on this subject; and in the
country, the division and improvement of an estate, and the
creation of a greater number of housemen's places, must be a
matter of complete notoriety.   If a man can obtain one of these
places he marries, and is able to support a family; if he cannot
obtain one, he remains single.   A redundant population is thus
prevented from taking place, instead of being destroyed after
it has taken place."—" There are no large manufacturing towns,
to take off the overflowing population of the country; and as
each village naturally furnishes from itself a supply of hands
more than equal to the demand, a change of place in search of
work seldom promises any success.   Unless, therefore, an opportunity of foreign emigration offer, the Norwegian peasant
generally remains in the village in which he was born; and, as
the vacancies in houses and employments must occur very
slowly, owing to the small mortality that takes place, he will
often see himself compelled to wait a considerable time before
he can attain a situation which will enable him to rear a family."
    These extracts are all taken from the chapter on the " Checks
to Population in Norway."

the connection between capital and labour, and perceiving that the office of the former is to maintain the latter—then, on the idea that capital may, by the operation of parsimony and good management, be extended *ad infinitum*, is it held, by almost every economist of high name, that every accumulation of capital carries an addition along with it to the subsistence of labourers. Or again, when one looks to the multitudes supported by foreign trade, in all its departments, the imagination is, that, as agriculture has its capabilities, so commerce has its distinct and additional capabilities; and that, whatever limit there may be to the power of the one for the maintenance of families, this is amply made up by the indefinite extension which might be given to the other. Again, we often hear taxation vaguely, though confidently talked of, as the great incubus on the prosperity of labourers; and that, if this were only lightened or removed, there would thenceforth ensue a mighty enlargement both of industry and comfort to the families of the working classes. And then, in the list of national grievances, we hear of the enormous and overgrown properties which are vested in the few—and a general abundance diffused among the many is figured to be the consequence that would result, if not from the spoliation and forcible division of this wealth, at least from the abolition of entails, and of the law of primogeniture. Or in the absence, perhaps the failure, of all these expedients, emigration is held forth as a sovereign specific for all the distresses of an over-crowded land. And, lastly, after every thing but the moral habit of labourers themselves has been thought of, there follows, in this list of artifices for their relief, a scheme, which no longer existing in fancy, has been bodied forth into actual operation, and is the one of all others most directly fitted to undermine the principle and prudence of labourers—even a compulsory tax on the wealthy for the relief of the destitute, so as to disarm poverty of its terrors, and proclaim a universal impunity for dissipation and idleness. Now that this last great expedient has been adverted to, we need scarcely advert to any of those lesser ones, which, though but the crudities of mere sentimentalism, have been proposed, each as a grand panacea, for all the disorders of the social state,—such as the cottage system, and the cow system, and the village economy of Mr. Owen, and the various plans of home colonization that have been thought to supersede the lessons of Malthus, or, at least, practically to absolve us from all regard to them for centuries to come.

3. Now the remedies we have just specified, may be regarded as belonging to the first class. They are all external remedies—and it will be our distinct aim, to demonstrate, in succession, the inefficacy of each of them. There is not one of them that will serve as a measure of permanent relief. In as far as they hold out the promise of an indefinite harbourage for an ever increasing population, they but practise a deceitful mockery on the hopes

of the philanthropist.   To whichever of the quarters now specified we may with fond expectation
turn ourselves, we shall speedily be met by a check
in every way as difficult to force as is the last limit
between cultivation and barrenness.   *To this limit,
in fact, one and all of them may be reduced*—and
just as really, though not so obviously, in Britain
as in Norway.   In every society of complicated
structure and widely diversified interests, many are
the distinct propositions that might be offered for
enlarging the sustenance and comfort of the human
species.   They can all, however apparently remote
and various among themselves, be brought to the
place at which husbandry ceases from her operations, because no longer profitable—and there the
merits of each may be tried and pronounced upon.
That is the place, in fact, though but recently adverted to in the science of political economy, where
many a question can be decided, which involves
the greatest earthly hopes and interests of society.

4. It may be thought, however, that, without
proceeding further in our argument, we might pronounce at once on the scheme of home colonization.
And we trust it is abundantly obvious, that it is
utterly incompetent to the end of providing indefinite sustenance for a population proceeding without restraint in the increase of its own numbers.
If there be any sanguine enough to imagine, that
cultivation may be so speeded forward beyond its
natural rate, under the auspices of government, as
to absorb all the redundancies of a population,

whom the scheme itself may have helped to eman-
cipate from the checks that would otherwise have
restrained them—we would appeal to the mighty
enlargement which has taken place in our own land
within these few years—the millions which have
been added to the inhabitants of Britain and Ireland within the lapse of a single generation.　The
progress of agriculture during this period, from individual enterprise alone, is quite obvious, and it
satisfactorily accounts for the commensurate increase that has taken place in the population.　And
yet though a larger, is it a more comfortable population than before?　Has the increase of food
wrought out any sensible increase on the average
sufficiency of families?　Have not the absolute
plenty in the land, and the relative poverty of the
people who live in it, kept pace the one with the
other?　And if this be all the result of that progress in our husbandry which has taken place under the enterprise of individuals, and has afforded
room for additional millions of human beings—can
we anticipate a more prosperous result from any
government enterprise, which at best will but afford
room and sustenance for as many additional thousands?　The history of the last thirty years may
well demonstrate, 'that with a mighty enlargement
in our means of subsistence, the population may retrograde, or at least be stationary, in point of comfort, notwithstanding.　It affords the clearest experimental proof of the little which can be done by
mere resources for an increasing population, with-

out restraints on the rate of their increase. There was nothing in the vast augmentation which has recently taken place of the one, that superseded the use or necessity for the other. And still less ought it to be superseded by any paltry augmentation of the means *ab extra*, which can be looked for from the scheme in question. The philosophy of Malthus, or rather the practical wisdom of families, ought not to be suspended, till home colonization have made full development of the capabilities which belong to it. A reckless population, made more reckless by the show and promise of such a relief, will shoot ahead of all that can possibly be achieved by it. The additional food that may have been created, will be more than overborne in the tide of an increasing population. The only difference will be a greater instead of a smaller number of wretched families—a heavier amount of distress, with less of unbroken ground in reserve for any future enlargements—a society in every way as straitened as before, yet nearer to the extreme limit of their resources than before— in short, a condition, at once of augmented hardship and diminished hope; with all the burden of an expensive and unprofitable scheme to the bargain.

5. We cannot complete our view of the system of home colonization, without the help of certain ulterior principles, which we shall afterwards apply to the further consideration of this scheme. We shall therefore enter immediately on the proper

subject of our present chapter, which is, the increase and limit of employment.

6. But before we commence this attempt, it will be necessary to premise a general view of the manner in which the distribution of the labouring classes is regulated by the state of landed property; and to show how a distinct class of labourers, additional to the agricultural, and secondary, arises in the progress of cultivation, and increases in number with every descent which it makes among the inferior soils. Hitherto we have only been attending to the limit of cultivation, where, at the soils last entered upon, the produce is barely adequate to the expenses of the husbandry,—or, abstracting still from the consideration of profit, where the produce could do no more than feed the agricultural labourers and their secondaries. But the produce of the superior soils is more than adequate to this object. The same improvement in agriculture, in virtue of which, we now draw a full subsistence for its labourers, from land that had long lain beyond the outskirts of cultivation, will enable us to draw from the fertile land, that had long lain within its boundary, a greater surplus of produce than before, over and above the expenses of the farm management. It is this surplus which constitutes rent,—which, generally speaking, is *measured* by the difference between the produce of a given quantity of labour on any soil, and the produce of the same labour on the soil that yields no rent. It goes in the shape of revenue to the land-

lord, who either receives it in kind, or receives in money the power of purchasing it—a power which, in the act of expenditure, he transfers in various parts throughout the year, to those who labour in his service, or who minister in various ways to his accommodation.*

7. Now, it is this expenditure on the part of landlords, which gives rise to another class of labourers, beside the two that we have already specified. Should the rent but enable the proprietor to provide himself with the necessaries of life—then that part of it, which goes to purchase the first necessaries, would but serve to subsist an idle man instead of a labourer; and that part of it which went to the purchase of second necessaries, would but serve to discharge additional maintenance, and so give additional extent to the secondary population. But such is the unequal distribution of landed property, and so large are the shares which fall in general to the possessors, that, in the vast majority of instances, the rent can do a great deal more than uphold the proprietor in the necessaries of life. It can enable him to subsist better, and to lodge and clothe himself better, than an ordinary workman. He can afford to indulge in the luxuries of life: and the preparation of these constitutes the employment of a very large population. It will be found very convenient to distinguish them by a particular name, even though we should not for

* See Appendix, Note A.   On the Rent of Land.

this purpose fix on the best appellation. We conceive that the fittest term by which to characterize
them, is one descriptive of a circumstance in which
their employment differs from that of the two first
classes. The two first classes are employed in the
preparation of articles which cannot be dispensed
with—the preparation of the first and second necessaries of life. The others are employed in the
preparation of articles which can be dispensed with.
A man can want luxuries—he cannot want necessaries. He might forego luxuries altogether; and
so dismiss from his service the whole of this third
class, who are employed in preparing them. Or,
he might commute one set of luxuries for another;
and so, without dismissing them from his service,
he might at least shift their employment in that
service. It is this liability of being transferred
from one employment to another, and this power,
on the part of their employers, of dispensing, if
they choose to make a surrender of their luxuries,
with their services altogether, which has led me
to affix to this class the title of the *disposable*.
They form the disposable population, in contradistinction to the agricultural and the secondary.

8. It is for the sake of defining, and not of stig-
matising; that we speak of luxuries. By this term
we would comprehend every thing prepared by
human labour, and which enters not into the average maintenance of labourers. The landed proprietor must at least have the food of other men—
but, in as far as, in style and in quality, it is above

that of common labourers, he indulges in luxuries;
and so there are cooks and confectionaries, and
many others employed in preparing delicacies for
the table, who should have their place assigned to
them among the disposable population.   He must
be lodged as well as other men ; but then, in as far
as his house exceeds in magnitude and elegance
that of an ordinary workman, for that excess, he
must have an additional service of masons, and
carpenters, and roofers, and smiths, who, in respect
of their contributing to this higher style, belong
not to the secondary but to the disposable population.   He must be provided also with furniture,
and clothing, up to a degree of comfort and tastefulness which prevail among the common people—
but, in as far as additional labourers are required,
for upholding a higher tastefulness, or a greater
abundance, there is a host of tradesmen, and artificers, tailors, and shoemakers, and upholsterers,
and cabinet-makers, who must be classified in thousands with the disposable population.   We shall
not attempt to enumerate the exceeding diversity
of employments, which the taste, and the humour,
and the artificial wants, and the wayward appetency
of the landed proprietors give rise to.   It is mainly
they who impress on the industry of the disposable
population, any direction which seemeth unto them
good; and who, by spending among them their
rents, or, in other words, by making over to them
the surplus produce of their estates, (or, which is
the same thing, by transferring to them the power

of purchasing that produce,) do, in return for their
varied services, effuse maintenance upon their
families. This disposable population must, like the
agricultural, have a train of secondaries attached
to them; and receive as much from their employers
as shall provide themselves with the first necessaries, and as shall suffice for the food of those who
provide them with the second necessaries of life.
It is not enough that the disposable population are
subsisted—this would only imply their being fed
by their employers. They must be *maintained*,
which, in addition to their being fed, implies their
being clothed, and lodged, and furnished, in all
those secondary accommodations that enter into the
average comfort of labourers. The price of their
services includes in it the power of purchasing food
for themselves, and food for all the secondary labourers who, either mediately, or immediately, are
employed by them.

9. This completes our view of the distribution
which takes place in society of the labouring classes.
The agricultural population are employed in providing all with the first necessaries of life. The secondary population, in providing all with the second
necessaries of life. And the disposable population,
in providing all who are elevated above the condition of labourers with the higher comforts of life,
its luxuries, its elegancies, which are not essential
to the maintenance of human beings, but minister
to the wealthy an endless diversity of gratifications,
and give rise to a like diversity of employments

among the people.   It is needless to explain here, how it is that the wages of labour, in all the three classes, are nearly equalised,—insomuch, that they who are toiling at the extreme margin of cultiva. tion, and there trying to force a return from soils which had never been attempted before, are equally remunerated for their services, with those who, in the walks of busy artizanship, are ministering to the most refined enjoyments of the wealthiest and the noblest in our land.   For this, and for many other doctrines which we pre-suppose, without any exhibition of their proof, we must satisfy ourselves with a reference to the general science of political economy.

10. Here, however, we cannot refrain from ob- serving the connection which obtains between the state of the soil and the state of human society. Had no ground yielded more in return for the la- bour expended on it, than the food of the cultiva- tors and their secondaries, the existence of one and all of the human race would have been spent in mere labour.   Every man would have been doomed to a life of unremitting toil for his bodily subsist- ence; and none could have been supported in a state of leisure, either for idleness, or for other employ- ments, than those of husbandry, and such coarser manufactures, as serve to provide society with the second necessaries of existence.   The species would have risen but a few degrees, whether physical or moral, above the condition of mere savages.   It is just because of a fertility in the earth, by which it yields

a surplus over and above the food of the direct and secondary labourers, that we can command the services of a disposable population, who, in return for their maintenance, minister to the proprietors of this surplus, all the higher comforts and elegancies of life. It is precisely to this surplus we owe it, that society is provided with more than a coarse and a bare supply for the necessities of animal nature. It is the original fund out of which are paid the expenses of art, and science, and civilization, and luxury, and law, and defence, and all, in short, that contributes either to strengthen or to adorn the commonwealth. Without this surplus, we should have had but an agrarian population—consisting of husbandmen, and those few homely and rustic artificers, who, scattered in hamlets over the land, would have given their secondary services to the whole population. It marks an interesting connection between the capabilities of the soil, and the condition of social life, that to this surplus we stand indispensably indebted, for our crowded cities, our thousand manufactories for the supply of comforts and refinements to society, our wide and diversified commerce, our armies of protection, our schools and colleges of education, our halls of legislation and justice, even our altars of piety and temple services. It has been remarked by geologists, as the evidence of a presiding design in nature, that the waste of the soil is so nicely balanced by the supply from the disintegration of the upland rocks, which are worn and pulverised at such a

rate, as to keep up a good vegetable mould on the
surface of the earth.   But each science teems with
the like evidences of a devising and intelligent God;
and when we view aright the many beneficent
functions, to which, through the instrumentality of
its surplus produce, the actual degree of the earth's
fertility is subservient, we cannot imagine a more
wondrous and beautiful adaptation between the
state of external nature and the mechanisn of human
society.

11. By this mechanism of human society, as far
as we have explained it, the exceeding diversity of
trades and employments may be accounted for.
Even were the barrenness of the land such, that it
only yielded food for an agricultural and a secondary population—this distribution would of itself
give rise to a considerable variety of distinct occupations ; and, under the system of a division in labour, we should have shoemakers, and tailors, and
weavers, and masons, and carpenters, and artificers
in hardware, and dealers, as well as fabricators in
sundry more articles,—making out on the whole
a pretty copious enumeration of separate callings,
with the separate interests belonging to them.
But when, in addition to the subsistence of an
agricultural and a secondary, there is fertility in
the land for the subsistence of a disposable population, the multiplication of trades and employments is thereby indefinitely extended—being as
numerous as the caprices of human fancy and taste,
or the varieties of human indulgence.   It is thus

that, in proportion as the mechanism of social life becomes more complex, it is also all the more bewildering ; and, amid the intricacy of its manifold combinations, we lose sight both of the springs and the limits of human maintenance. One very wide and prevalent delusion, more especially, and which has misguided both the charity of philanthropists and the policy of statesmen, is, that the employment in which men are engaged is the source of their maintenance,—whereas, it is only the channel through which they draw that maintenance from the hands of those who buy the products of their employment. This principle has in it all the simplicity of a truism—and yet it is wonderful with what perversity of apprehension, both the managers of a state and the managers of a parish miss the sight of it. Whether we look to acts of parliament, or to the actings of a parochial vestry— we shall find them proceeding on its being the grand specific for the relief of the poor, to find employment for them. Now, unless that employment be the raising of food, it does nothing to alleviate the disproportion between the numbers of the people and the means of their subsistence,— and if there be a limit, as we have already demonstrated, to the food, we may be very sure that this device of employment will not turn out a panacea for the distresses of an overburdened land.

12. But the fallacy to which we now advert, is not confined to the matters of practical administration. It may also be recognised in the theories of

those who have attempted to adjust the philosophy
of the subject.   In political economy it will often
be found, that the channel is confounded with the
source,—and hence a delusion, not in the business
of charity alone, but which has extended far and
wide among the lessons of the science.

13. And yet it is a delusion which, one might
think, should be dissipated by but one step of explanation.   A single truism puts it to flight.   Nothing appears more obvious, than that *any trade or
manufacture originates only its own products.*   All
that a stocking-maker contributes to society is
simply stockings. This, and nothing more, is what
comes forth of his establishment.   And the same
is true of all the other trades or employments which
can be specified.   They work off nothing, they
emanate nothing but their own peculiar articles.
Were this sure and simple axiom but clearly and
steadfastly kept in view, it would put to flight a
number of illusions in political science,—illusions
which have taken obstinate hold of our legislators,
and which to this moment keep firm possession in
the systems of many of our economists.   They
almost all, in a greater or less degree, accredit a
manufacture with something more than its own
products. The inclination is, to accredit it also
with the maintenance of its labourers.   In every
transaction of buying and selling, there are two
distinct elements,—the commodity, and the price
of the commodity; of which price, the maintenance of the labourers is generally far the largest

ingredient. Now, the thing to be constantly kept
in view is, that a manufacture should only be accredited with its own commodity, and not, over
and above this, with the price of its commodity.
These two stand, as it were, on different sides
of an exchange. To the manufacture is to be
ascribed all that we behold on the one side. It
furnishes the commodity for the market. But it
did not also create the wealth that supplies the
price of the commodity. It does not furnish society with both itself and its equivalent. The
latter comes from a distinct quarter; and we repeat, that by confounding, in imagination, two
things which are distinct in fact, a false direction
has been given, both to the policy of States, and
to the theories of philosophers.

14. This confusion of sentiment appears in a
variety of ways. When one sees a thriving and
industrious village, and that the employment of
the families secures for them their maintenance, it
is most natural to invest the former with a power
of command, tantamount to a power of creation
over the latter. The two go together; and because
when the employment ceases, the maintenance
ceases, it is conceived of the former, that in the order of causation it has the precedency. We affirm
of a shawl-making village, that all which it yields
to society is shawls. We accredit it with this, but
with nothing more. But it is accredited with a
great deal more, by those who talk in lofty style of
our manufacturing interest, and the dependence

thereupon of a nation's support and a nation's great-ness. We hold, that if, through the exhaustion of the raw material, or any other cause, there were to be an extinction of the employment, the country would only be deprived of its wonted supply of shawls ; but the prevalent imagination is, that the country would be deprived of its wonted support for so many hundred families. The whole amount of the mischief, in our estimation, would be the disappearance of shawls ; in theirs, it would be the disappearance of that which upheld an integral part of the country's population. It is forgotten, that though shawls may no longer be produced or brought to market, the price that wont to be paid for them is still in reserve, and ready to be ex-pended by the purchasers on some other article of accommodation or luxury. The circumstances which have brought the manufacture to ruin, do not affect the ability of those who consumed the products of the manufacture. The employment is put an end to ; but the maintenance comes from another quarter, and can be discharged in as great abundance as before, on as large a population. Their employment in making shawls was not the source of their maintenance ; it was only the chan-nel by which they drew it to their homes. The destruction or stoppage of the channel, does not in-fer a stoppage at the source, that will find for itself another channel, through which all that enters into the maintenance of our industrious families, might be effused upon them as liberally as before. We

dispute not the temporary evils of the transition.
We allow that a change of employment may bring
individual and temporary distress along with it.
But we contend, that the expenditure of those who
support our disposable population will not be
lessened, but only shifted by this new state of
things; and that, after the change is accomplished
in the direction of their industry, we should behold
as numerous a society as ever, upheld with the
same liberality in every thing (with the single exception of shawls, and the substitution of some
other luxury, in their place) that enters into the
comfort and convenience of families.

15. But we are further persuaded, that the confusion of sentiment which we are now attempting
to expose, has had a most misleading effect on the
views and the policy of statesmen: at one time,
inspiring a false hope on the promised extension of
trade and manufactures; and, at another time,
creating a false alarm on the appearance of their
decay. Our legislators do ascribe a higher function to trade and manufactures, than that of simply
furnishing society with the articles manufactured.
They conceive of them as the dispensers of a tran-
scendently greater benefit, than the mere use and
enjoyment of these articles. There are other and
nobler interests associated in their minds with the
trade and manufactures of the country, than the
mere gratification and convenience which individuals have in the use of their products. This will
at once be evident, if we resolve the manufactur-

ing interest into its several parts,—as the shawl-making interest, wherewith our senate would not for a moment concern themselves, if they thought that all which hinged upon it was the supply of shawls—nor the stocking-making interest, if in their opinion nothing else depended on it but the supply of stockings—nor the carpet-making interest, if it involved no other or higher consideration than the supply of carpets—nor the buckle-making interest, if they did not suppose that, beside owing to it the supply of buckles, we furthermore owed the maintenance and wealth of buckle-makers. And the remark may be extended from manufactures to commerce.* We should have had no grave deliberations on the China trade, or the Portuguese trade, or the West India trade, if something far loftier had not been associated with these respective processes, than that of serving the families of the land with tea, or wine, or oranges, or sugar, or coffee, or tobacco. These mighty commercial interests are conceived to be productive of something greatly more magnificent and national; and not only the income of all the capitalists, and the maintenance of all the labourers engaged in them, but the strength, and revenue, and political greatness of the State, are somehow associated with their

---

* In extending the observation from home to foreign trade, we presuppose, what we shall afterwards attempt to show more particularly, that the *terminus ad quem* of foreign trade, is the benefit, or enjoyment, administered by the commodities which it imports, to the inland consumers.

defence and preservation. It is forgotten, of each
trade and each manufacture, that it furnishes, and
can furnish, nothing but its own proper and peculiar articles ; and that, abstracting from the use and
enjoyment of these, every other associated benefit
is comprehended in the equivalent price which is
paid for them. All that the wine-trade of Portugal, for example, furnishes to our nation is wine—
and, in reference either to the public revenue
which arises from it, or to the private revenue
wherewith it both enriches the capitalists, and
supports the labourers employed in it, these are
yielded, not most assuredly by the wine, but by
the price given for the wine. The wine-trade is
but the channel through which these flow, and not
the source in which they originate. But, notwithstanding, there is yet a mystic power ascribed to
the wine-trade, as if part of the nation's glory and
the nation's strength were linked with the continuance of it. And hence a legislature tremulously
alive to the state of our relations with Portugal,
lest the wine-trade should be destroyed. Now
though, from the interruption of these relations, or
from any other cause, the wine-trade, on the one
side, were destroyed, the counterpart wealth, on
the other side, would not be destroyed. It would
remain with its owners, to be expended by them
on the purchase of some new luxury in place of the
wine ; by the natural price of which, the same return could be made to capitalists and labourers,
and by a tax on which, the same revenue might be
secured to government as before.

16. It must be obvious, that employment in agriculture is not an indefinite resource for an indefinite population—seeing that it must stop short at the land which refuses to yield the essential food of its direct and secondary labourers. And it should be equally obvious, that as little is employment in manufactures an indefinite resource—seeing that the definite quantity of food raised can only sustain a certain and definite number of labourers. The latter position seems, on the first announcement, to carry its own evidence along with it; yet there is a certain subtle imagination in its way, which we have attempted to dispose of. Our argument rests on the veriest truism—that a manufacture is creative of nothing beyond its own products. But truism though it is, it has been strangely overlooked, not only in the devices of the charitable, but both in the policy of statesmen, and in the doctrinal schemes of the economists. Yet we think a sufficient explanation can be given, both of the manner in which the perverse misconception at first arose, and of the obstinacy wherewith it still lingers and keeps its ground amongst us.

17. In opposition, then, to the principle, that employment is creative of nothing but its own products, it might be alleged, that the presentation of these products excites a desire for the acquisition of them, and so stimulates other employments in the fabrication of new products, to be given in exchange for the former ones. It was remarkably exemplified throughout the whole of Europe, at the

termination of the middle ages. Of this we have a masterly sketch by Dr. Adam Smith, in his Wealth of Nations;* when he traces the great economic change which took place, in virtue of a new taste and a new habit on the part of the land-holders. Historically, it was the presentation to their notice of those articles of splendour and lux-ury which manufactures had produced, and which commerce brought to their doors, that prompted the change. This was the moving force, which shifted their old expenditure, and gave another direction to it. They dismissed their idle retainers, and appropriated the surplus produce by which they had been fed, to the purchase of luxuries in dress, or of luxuries in equipage and furniture. They furnished subsistence to as many as before, but in a new capacity, and in return for a different service. The disposable population were differ-ently disposed of. Instead of so many idle ma-rauders, living, save at their seasons of warfare, in sloth and sordidness, on the domain of their feudal lord, they were transmuted into orderly, industrious citizens—as dependent, for the first necessaries of life, on the country as before, but yielding, in re-turn for these, not the homage of their personal attendance, but the tangible produce of their own handiwork. And along with this economic, there was effected a great moral change in the state of society. The contests of violence between adjoin-

* And by Dr. Robertson, in the Introduction to his History of Charles V.

ing proprietors, were exchanged for the more peaceful contests and rivalships of vanity. The hundreds, who in other days would have followed them to the field, on services of revenge or plunder, were now at peaceful occupation in their work-shops—congregated into villages, which grew into cities, and there placed under the protection of law and social order. Liberty, and justice, and civili-zation, and right government, all emerged from this altered condition of things ; and when we re-flect, that commerce was the prime mover in this great transition, by the new desires which it in-fused, and the change which it effected in the style of living and habit of our landlords—it must be allowed, that, historically, to commerce we owe benefits of a much high order, than the mere gra-tification of any of the physical or inferior appe-tencies of our nature.

18. But there is still another reason (beside the new direction given to the expenditure of land-lords) why commerce might be said to have been creative at that period of more than their own im-mediate products. When the landlords parted with their idle retainers, and they were compelled to be industrious for their livelihood—along with a new habit of indulgence among the proprietors, there sprung up a new habit of industry among the people. At one and the same time, the proprietors became more luxurious than before, and the people became more laborious than before. Even these latter par-ticipated to some degree in the taste of their supe-

riors, and were willing also to make their sacrifices, that they might be admitted to their own humble share in those recent gratifications which were beginning to be placed too within reach of the peasantry, and were every where raising the standard of enjoyment.   They accordingly made sacrifice of their indolence and love of ease, even as the grandees above them made sacrifice of their power and parade of attendance.   At the same time, the rights of all were beginning to be more recognised and respected; and, under the administration of more benign and equitable laws, the poor man felt a greater stimulus to labour than before, in the greater security which he now had for the possession and enjoyment of its fruits.   And then the severe and regular industry of manufactures, was followed by a more severe and regular industry than heretofore in agriculture.   The desire of each man to better his condition, now began to develop its energies in all the classes of society.   Landlords, with a larger and juster sense of their interests, disposed of their farms in the way that yielded the greatest revenue to themselves; and husbandmen, with the benefit of a now more industrious peasantry, so laboured the farms, as to work out the greatest remainder of produce for themselves. In addition to this, the business of the country participated, though never to such a degree, with the business of towns, in the benefits that result from the division of labour, and in the greater power given by mechanical invention to the implements of labour. Altogether, the limit of cultivation, under the operation of these various causes, has receded an immense way back within these three centuries. Millions of acres, that, under the old lazaroni system, had never been entered on, are now yielding subsistence to man ; and the increase of food has been surely and speedily followed up by an increase of population. The land of inferior soils, that formerly yielded nothing, is now productive ; and the land that formerly produced, is now, in virtue of deeper and more laborious culture, of tenfold greater fertility than before. Now, in Europe, all this may be in a great measure traced to the reaction of commerce upon agriculture. It was commerce which gave the impulse ; and, in addition to its own products, it, through the medium of the new system of society which it introduced, called forth products from the earth, that, but for it, might never have been extracted. In this instance at least, commerce seems to have been the creator, not of its own commodities alone, but of the equivalents for these commodities—a fountain-head, not merely for the products of its labour, but for the maintenance of its labourers.

19. It is not to be wondered at, then, that he who traced with so graphic and powerful a hand the reflex influence of commerce upon agriculture, should have sometimes forgotten the natural order of precedency betwixt them. He certainly did more than any of his predecessors in the science,

in restoring to agriculture the proper honours and
ascendancy which belong to her. Yet he does
give a power to the enterprise and the accumulation of merchants, which neither experience nor
the nature of things will justify. None was more
successful than he, in exposing the crude imaginations of those who thought to enrich the country
by means of a restricted commerce. But along
with this, he greatly overrated the effect of an
emancipated commerce, or of commerce set at
liberty from its fetters. He very clearly demonstrated the impolicy of those artificial checks,
which, in the shape of monopoly or prohibition,
had been laid upon trade. But he seems not to
have been fully aware of the natural check which
stands in the way of its indefinite extension—and
by which a gradual retardation, and ultimately an
immovable arrest, are laid on the progress of agriculture, and of population, and of capital, and so
of commerce. The truth does appear, throughout
the work of this great author, in occasional glimpses
—but not so explicitly, or with such application
and effect, as it would have done had the doctrine
of population been understood in his day. This
single element alone would have modified a number
of his conclusions; and more particularly, he would
not have held out to society the promise of an
endless advancement, as if every effort of parsimony, and every accumulation of capital, were infallibly to speed it forward. He seems to reason
as if the simple act of preparing commodities, and

placing them as it were on one side of an exchange, will, through the operation of stimulus, call forth into existence equivalent commodities on the other side of it.   This process, it is true, was conspicuously and memorably exemplified, at that period in history, which may be characterized as the period of transition from the middle to the modern ages of Europe.   But that was no sufficient cause, why it should have been regarded and reasoned upon as the universal process for all ages.

20. There is, in truth, a wide difference between the state of things at the commencement, and after the full establishment and continuance, of this new era.   Then the passion for war had just given place to the passion for wealth and luxury ; and this latter passion, when newly awoke, found a soil of boundless and yet unentered capabilities on which to expatiate.   The rude and infant husbandry of Europe had a mighty career before it, along which the increasing products of commerce met with their sure return in the increasing products of agriculture.   The spirit of mercantile adventure could safely indulge in every variety of caprice and speculation ; for the unsated appetite of the landlord found, in the before untouched resources of his land, the means of extended gratification.   Commerce appeared to anticipate agriculture, and might almost have ventured in reality to do so, yet not be disappointed ; for however it multiplied its wares and its whimsies, it found a ready admission for them in the growing wealth, and the now stimu-

lated fancy and taste of its country customers.   It
is really not to be wondered at, that men should
have been led to imagine, as if commerce had a
commencing and a creative virtue in this process ;
and that it had only to accumulate, and to employ,
and to produce, in order to carry forward the prosperity of the nation with uniform, or with accele-
rated progress.   Commerce, in fact, was the prime,
the executive agent in Europe, for unlocking the
capabilities of the soil ; and, at a period when these
were rapidly evolved, the articles which it fabricated and brought to market seldom failed to meet
with purchasers of sufficient wealth and sufficient
number ; and so also with a price which enveloped
in it the profit of all the capitalists, the comfortable
subsistence of all the labourers.   It was most natural, in these circumstances, to conceive of commerce as an *efficient cause,* not merely for the
commodities of its own workmanship, but for the
maintenance of its own workmen ; and, if agriculture was not just made of subordinate rank to commerce, commerce was regarded as of fully co-ordi-
nate rank with agriculture.   Nevertheless it will
be found, we think, on further consideration, that
however events may have fallen out historically in
the order of time, there is an order of nature, and
an order of influence, which must be attended to,
ere the essential relations of agriculture and commerce be rightly understood.   We hold the real
dependence of the latter upon the former, to be a
truth of capital importance in political economy ;

and that, if steadfastly kept in view, and carried forward to its legitimate applications, it would put to flight a number of those delusions and errors which, in the course of speculation, have gathered around the science.

21. One plain distinction, and a distinction not to be overlooked by the slight exceptions which can be alleged against it, is, that to agriculture mainly, we owe the necessaries of life ; whereas, many of its luxuries cannot be had without commerce and manufactures. This is a most momentous distinction, and a vast deal turns upon it. We not only see in it, that manufactures must necessarily, in point of extent, be limited by the produce of the soil ; but that the owners of the soil, in virtue of the property which belongs to them, have a natural superiority over all other classes of men, which by no device of politics or law can be taken away from them. The holder of what I cannot want, is the master of my services. He can impress upon them any direction which seemeth unto him good. He can transfer his demand from one luxury to another; and so, as far as his consumption goes, he can extend one manufacture at the expense of a proportional abridgment on another manufacture. Or, he can part with the use of some tangible commodity altogether, and, with the price which went to purchase it, may obtain for himself the use of a menial servant ; and, in so doing, he effects an absolute reduction in the manufactures of the country. Or, whether in the spirit

of a voluntary patriotism, or in submission to lawful authority, he may render to the State the price of many luxuries; and thus withdraw so many of the disposable population from the business of trade, to the business of our national establishments.   It is thus that any given change in the taste or habit of our landlords, would effect a corresponding change in the employment of the great mass of our disposable population.   They are virtually the holders of the maintenance of this class of labourers; and it is their collective will which fixes the direction of their labour.   Apart from the importation of food, there can be no more labourers in the country than the produce of their estates will subsist.   It is the quantity of this produce which fixes the amount of labour; and as far as the labour of the disposable population is concerned, it is the will of the holders of this produce which fixes the direction of it.   They are the natural masters of the country; and the ascendancy wherewith their property invests them, hinges on this clear and simple distinction—Men can want luxuries; they cannot want necessaries.

22. But more than this.   Every increase of food is followed up by an increase of population.   It is not so with any other manufactured goods, save in as far as that may work an increase of food, by pushing on the limit of cultivation in the way that we have already explained.   Such at all events is the difference between the two sorts of produce, that the market cannot permanently be overladen

with corn, even though its growers should persist
in keeping up and increasing the supply of it.
Unlike to all other articles of merchandise, an increased supply of food is surely and speedily followed up by an increased demand for it. It may
be a drug in the market for a year or two ; but
though it should continue to be sent in the same,
or in superior abundance, season after season, it
will not remain so. The reason is, that, unlike to
other commodities, it creates a market for itself.
Through the medium of the stimulus given to population, it does what no other articles of merchandise can do—it multiplies its own consumers. A
plenty of the first necessaries, is the only species
of plenty which surely and largely tells on the population. A plenty of luxuries has no such effect;
and not even a plenty of the second necessaries, as
shoes or stockings, or the materials of house-build-
ing. The proprietors of the first necessaries, are
on the only sure vantage-ground. They alone
have nothing to fear ultimately, from the indefinite
supply of their peculiar commodity. The produce
of agriculture may be made to increase, up to the
uttermost limit of its capabilities; for, whatever
the additional number may be which it can feed,
that number will rise to be fed by it.

23. We can therefore be at no loss to perceive,
how an indefinite supply of the products of agriculture, must be followed up by a like indefinite
supply of the products of manufactures, or commerce. The people whom it feeds, give, in their

handiwork, a return for their subsistence. But this does not hold true of the reverse proposition. The products of manufactures do not *indefinitely* call forth the products of agriculture. They did so historically, at that period when they effected a change in the taste and habit of landlords. They still do so gradually, when, in virtue of their greater supply by an improvement in the powers of labour, they reduce the numbers of the secondary class, and so push cultivation further among the inferior soils. But beyond this limit they have no power. An increase of agricultural produce will, through the medium of an increasing population, be followed up, *pari passu*, by an increase of manufactured commodities. But a mere increase of manufactured commodities, cannot force the existing barrier in the way of cultivation, or force an entrance upon that land, which is not able to feed its agricultural labourers and their secondaries. There is one way in which this barrier may be made to retire. Labourers may consent to be worse fed than before, or to put up with fewer of the secondary accommodations. If, with this reduction in the standard of enjoyment, they still work as hardly, or, if even with the same, and perhaps a higher standard, they are willing to put forth more than their wonted labour—this might widen the limits, and so multiply the products of agriculture. Still, after these modifications are admitted, there is a wide difference between agriculture and manufactures—the former influencing the latter, in a way that the latter cannot influence the former. Agriculture, with every permanent increase of its products, can, through the medium of an increasing population, command a like increase in the products of manufactures. Manufactures cannot by any increase of its products, while the standard of enjoyment, and the powers of personal and mechanical labour remain the same, force a like increase in the products of agriculture.

24. This distinction between agriculture and manufactures, would serve greatly to modify the reasonings of Dr. Smith, when, without reference to any such distinction, he tells of one species of commodities stimulating the production of another species of commodities. It follows not, because commerce had the power, by tempting landlords from an old to a new habit of expenditure, of extorting additional products from a soil whose capabilities had scarcely been entered on ; it therefore has this power, when agriculture, with its stationary or slowly receding limit, has either reached, or is so much nearer the uttermost length to which it can be carried. The stimulus might be as powerful as before. There might be as intense a desire for the increase of enjoyments, whether they be the enjoyments of pleasure, or those of pageantry. But this moving force is in contact now with an obstacle which stood then at a distance so remote, as to have permitted an advancing movement, and that a tolerably free one, for several centuries. We now begin to feel, and may indeed be said to

have long felt, the utter powerlessness of mere production in manufactures, to enlarge the wealth, or
speed forward the economic prosperity of a land.
What commerce did in an incipient, it cannot do
in an extreme state of agriculture ; and in the oldest and richest counties of Europe, the sanguine,
the splendid anticipations which the earlier experience awakened, checked and chastised as they
have been by the later experience, are now beginning to be abandoned.

25. But not only is there a visionary hope associated with this contemplation,—there is also an
alarm which, it is comfortable to think, is alike visionary.   They who so count on the reaction of a
stimulus, as to imagine, that every addition beyond
their present extent to our manufactures, will give
a proportional enlargement to our agriculture, might
also imagine, that every subtraction beneath their
present extent from our manufactures, will proportionally lessen and contract our agriculture also.
The two imaginations, in fact, are products of one
and the same fallacy.   He who thinks that it was
the creation of a manufacture which stimulated and
called forth an increase of agriculture, may well
be apprehensive lest the destruction of the manufacture should as much throw the agriculture back
again.   Now, it is not so.   Though a particular
manufacture should be brought to ruin, and the
employment in it should cease, the counterpart
maintenance will not cease ; and our security against
this effect is, that there would still remain a suffi-

ciency of objects, on which it were not only possible, but felt by the landlords to be desirable, that
they should still spend their incomes.   There is
not a luxury that can be named, the loss of which
would cause our agriculture to go back; even
though, historically, it may have been the first presentation of that luxury to their notice, which, by
its effect on the appetency of landlords, helped to
bring the agriculture forward.   Now that the revulsion has taken place from the habit of the middle ages, there is no danger of the surplus produce
of their estates lying idle in their hands.   They
will set their hearts on as large a revenue as before; and notwithstanding the ruin or disappearance of many separate trades, they will still find
use for it all.   In other words, amid the numerous
failures and fluctuations of employment, they in
the meanwhile will not let down the cultivation of
a single acre; so that there shall remain as large a
maintenance for the same population as before.
The expenditure of its holders would be changed,
but not lessened.   The destruction of one manufacture would be followed up by the creation or
the extension of another; or there would be a pro-
portionate addition to the retinue of our landlords.
At all events, we should behold as large a disposable class as well supported as ever.   It may be
Utopianism to expect, that beyond the limits of
our present agriculture, there lies before us a career of endless and ever-advancing prosperity; but
we might at least give up all our sensitive alarms,

lest by any revolution in the trading world, our prosperity shall ever be sensibly and permanently reduced beneath that limit. So long as we have law and liberty amongst us, our economic resources will be found as stable as the constitution of the seasons or of the soil. Unless we are struck from Heaven with the curse of barrenness, the present means of our subsistence will remain to us. We may have little to hope from a great enlargement of these means, yet have every thing to hope from a right distribution of them. There may be, there is, an impassable limit to the physical abundance of our products. There is no limit to the moral cultivation of our people. We may not be able greatly to increase our stores ; but with the stores we have, a mighty achievement remains to us. We may indefinitely increase the virtuous and prudential habits of the community ; and on these mainly, on these we should say exclusively, it depends, whether there shall or shall not be a high average of sufficiency and comfort among the families of the land.

26. It is now high time that the statesmen and philanthropists of the old world should take this direction. It is to a moral restraint on the numbers of mankind, and not to a physical enlargement of the means for their subsistence, that we shall be henceforth beholden for sufficiency or peace in our commonwealth. It is from the power of Christian education, and not from the devices of the economists, that our deliverance is to come. And yet

we abide almost as reckless of this truth, as if in
the morning of our history we had still the world
to begin, or had still in reserve a land of boundless
extent and fertility, on which, as in America, we
might expatiate unchecked by any barrier of physical necessity for many generations.   To employ
the language of the schoolmen, we are still looking
objectively to the enlargement of resources in the
outer world of matter, instead of looking subjec-
tively to the establishment of habit and principle
in the inner world of mind.   Yet thence, and
thence alone, will proceed our help and our emancipation from the miseries which beset and straiten
us; and nothing will more effectually demonstrate
the supremacy of the moral over the physical, in
the system of human affairs, than will the ameliorated condition coming in the train of ameliorated
character, after the tried impotency of all other
expedients.

27. Meanwhile, as the difficulties thicken, and
the pressure becomes more severe, the expedients
multiply.   This is a teeming age for all sorts of
crudities; and we have no doubt, that our very
nearness to the ultimate and immoveable barrier
of our resources, has made the necessity to be all
the more intensely felt, and so given additional
impulse to the speculations of philanthropists.
Among others, the favourite device of employment
has been acted on to a very great extent; though
its inefficacy as a resource, one might think, should
be abundantly obvious, on the simple axiom, that

employment is creative of nothing but its own products.   It was a far more rational and likely expedient centuries ago, in the earlier state of our
agriculture, than it is at present; nor need we
wonder, though in these days they should often
have experienced a most convenient absorption of
poverty and idleness in whole masses, simply by
providing and dealing out work.   There was room
then for such an absorption, when the increasing
products of the towns and villages could be met
by the increasing products of a land, whose capabilities were yet so far from being fully overtaken.
We accordingly meet with this expedient in the
innumerable parliamentary acts of other days, for
the suppression or the regulation of mendicity;
and it was long the favourite scheme, both of parochial counsellors, and of individual philanthropists.
The general rule of society is, that each man lives
by his business; and the first natural imagination
is, that this conjunction between work and maintenance is just, in every instance where poverty
and idleness are seen together, to be repeated over
again.   England is rife with this experiment
throughout her teeming parishes; and quarrying,
and road-making, and breaking stones, and digging
in gravel pits, and the manifold branches of in-door
labour in work-houses, have all been devised; that,
if possible, by the products of their industry, their
surplus people might earn for themselves their
subsistence, or a part of their subsistence.   The
conception is prevalent all over, and has been end-

lessly diversified into various ingenuities, alike amiable and abortive. The platting of straw, and picking of hemp, and various sorts of millinery and hand-manufactures, have all been tried and found wanting. The effect is a general depression in the price of the prepared article, whatever it may be; or if the article be altogether new, the purchasers who are allured to it, are withdrawn from the purchase of other articles. On either supposition, a whole body of regular labourers are impoverished by the weight of these additional products upon the general market; and so utterly fruitless indeed has it turned out as a permanent resource, that, in despair, the expedient has been abandoned in many parishes, and the extra population are suffered to lead a kind of lazaroni life in idleness, and in the mischief and crime which are attendant upon idleness. The truth is, that if home colonization fail, employment in manufactures is far more likely to fail. By the former, a certain portion at least of sustenance, is drawn from the earth in return for labour—though inadequate to the full maintenance of the labourers. By the other, something is produced too, but it is not sustenance; but a commodity to be offered in return for sustenance; and which cannot earn that sustenance for additional labourers, save at the expense of all previous labourers. The home colonist, at work among the inferior soils, may perhaps extract from them three-fourths of his maintenance, and leave the remaining fourth a burden upon society. The workman in a charity manufacture, burdens society with the whole of his subsistence.   The article he prepares becomes cheaper and more plentiful than before ; but he himself becomes the instrument of a general distress, by inducing a dearness and a scarcity on that which is most essential to families.*

* See Appendix, B.—On Machinery.

CHAPTER III.

ON THE INCREASE AND LIMIT OF CAPITAL.

1. WE use the term *capital*, in the sense which is assigned to it by the great majority of our economists; not as comprehending all material and monied wealth, but only that part of it which is employed in the business of production, and is generally so employed for the purpose of obtaining a profit. Stock is the generic term, of which capital forms only a part. Were a manufacturer to take account of his stock, he would put his dwelling-house, and his furniture, and his clothes into the inventory, along with all other things which belong to him; but his capital we should restrict to his machinery, and the houses which contain it, and his implements of labour, and the amount of money which he reserved either for the repairs of his trading establishment, or the payment of his labourers. They are these, and not his dwelling-house or furniture, which obtain for him the profit that constitutes his revenue. By laying up part of this profit, instead of spending the whole of it, he may add to his capital; and we hold it one of the most important inquiries in political economy, what the circumstances are which promote or limit

the augmentation of an element that enters so largely into the views and reasonings of the science.*

2. Capital behoved to make an early appearance in the history of human society. The rudest implement that was first used in preparing the ground for the reception of seed, possessed all the essential attributes of capital. If by the direct application of human hands to the soil, the requisite treatment of it could have been as easily effected, as with the intervention of tools and instruments, these latter would never have been employed. But the contrary of this was soon found; and when the branch of a tree was broken off, and rightly fashioned for scratching the surface of the earth, even at this rudimental stage do we behold the application of capital to agriculture. This primitive expedient for facilitating human labour, and making it more effective, exemplified the functions and the benefit of capital as distinctively, as do the spade or the plough that have superseded it, or as does all the various and complicated apparatus of modern husbandry.

3. Having, for the first time, introduced the element of profit to the notice of our readers, we

---

* Capital, as an instrument of production, is conceived to be bound up by means of agricultural improvement, with every piece of land, on the permanent amelioration of which, certain sums have been expended. And that part of the produce, which would have been yielded independently of this improvement, is ascribed, not to the capital which has been laid out upon the farm, but to the original powers of the soil.

think it right to premise this part of our argument, with two distinct notices regarding it.

4. The first is, that though profit enters as a distinct ingredient into the price of every article, yet that article may be supplied in far greater abundance, and, as it regards manufactured commodities, may be afforded far more cheaply to the consumer, than if there had been no capital applied to the production of it, and, consequently, no room for the imposition of such a charge. Even though it should require the constant labour of one man to make and to repair a plough, and the constant labour of another to use it, yet if, with one plough, as great an amount of work can be performed as with the mere handiwork of ten men, then, out of the maintenance of ten men, a liberal profit might well be afforded to the capitalist, and a large surplus produce, over and above, be afforded to the country. It is thus that capital, in the shape of farm-utensils of various sorts, by opening a descent to inferior soils, has inconceivably augmented the produce of the land, and so enabled it to maintain a vastly larger population. And furthermore, capital, by superadding mechanical to manual labour, has so augmented the amount of manufactured articles, that, notwithstanding the charge of profit to which it has given rise, both the luxuries and the second necessaries of life are furnished in much greater profusion, as well as greater cheapness, to society.

5. Our next notice in regard to profit is, that it

has the effect of attaching the services of the disposable population to other masters, beside the mere
landed proprietors.   We believe, that, in a country
constituted like ours, the latter will engross by far
the largest proportion of these services.   Yet every
man elevated above the condition of the working
classes has, more or less, the command of them.
Every man whose expenditure reaches higher than
the necessaries of life, has a certain amount of enjoyment ministered to him, by one or more of the
disposable population.   Their office is the preparation of luxuries ; and, when one looks to the style,
and the splendour, and the establishment of merchants and manufacturers, it is obvious that they
are admitted to a considerable share in the services
of this class, along with the proprietors of land.

6. With these preliminary remarks, we may now
inquire—What the real power of capital is for the
maintenance of a people ?   There is nothing more
constantly affirmed, in the writings of political
economists, than the connection between these two
elements :—" The power of a country to maintain
a population, is in proportion to its capital."   " Increase the capital, and you increase its power to
employ and to remunerate labour."   " Capital is
the fund, out of which the wages of labour are
paid, and labourers are supported."   These are so
many different expressions for an oft-repeated
aphorism in political science.   Now, capital is the
fruit of accumulation ; and one might be led to
imagine, from such representations, as if the fru-

gality of merchants were the primary fountain-head,
whence issued forth all the comfort and subsistence
of labourers. At this rate, indefinite parsimony
would be followed up by the indefinitely-augment-
ing power of maintaining labour ; and, through the
medium of personal economy, an unobstructed
highway would be opened to increasing and successive enlargements in the amount of the population, or in the general sufficiency of their circumstances. This is the unequivocal impression given
by the reasonings of Dr. Smith, on the subject of
capital, and the methods of its increase.* There
are checks to this progress, which he has either
altogether overlooked, or at least forborne to dwell
upon, and bring prominently forward. The rationale of a country's advancement in wealth and

* " Every prodigal appears to be a public enemy, and every
frugal man a public benefactor."—" Parsimony, and not industry, is the immediate cause of the increase of capital."—" Parsimony, by increasing the fund which is destined for the maintenance of productive hands, tends to increase the number of
these hands."—" By what a frugal man annually saves, he not
only affords maintenance to an additional number of productive
hands, for that of the ensuing year, but, like the founder of a
public work-house, he establishes, as it were, a perpetual fund,
for the maintenance of an equal number in all times to come."
—*Wealth of Nations.*

These, and similar passages, taken together, certainly give
the impression of an indefinite power, in indefinite parsimony,
to carry the capital of a country, and its power to maintain
labourers, beyond any limit which can be assigned. This has,
accordingly, been contended for by several of Smith's com-
mentators, in formal and express argument.

economic prosperity, has thus been misconceived. The limits, placed by nature and necessity in the way of this advancement, have not been sufficiently regarded; and more especially has it been thought, that there was a creative and an emanating power in capital, which could overleap these limits, and form a guarantee against all the evils that have been ascribed to redundant population.

7. And on this subject, too, we might learn a lesson at that place in the science, where so many other of its lessons are to be gathered—even at the margin of separation between the cultivated and the uncultivated land. We have already seen, that cultivation cannot be speeded forward beyond this margin, at a rate faster than the improvement in the powers of labour enables the land of next inferior quality to feed the agricultural labourers and their secondaries. If, by an undue increase of population, the cultivation is forced a greater way than this, then the land last entered on is not able to repay its cultivation, and distress is felt in the country because there are too many men. But as surely as there might be too many ploughmen, so there might be too many ploughs. If, in virtue of the excessive number of ploughmen, all cannot find employment, without forcing an entrance upon soils that would return inadequate wages for the labour, so, in virtue of the excessive number of ploughs, all cannot find employment, without a like return of inadequate profit for the capital. Nay, profit forms such a fraction in the price of

most articles, that a large fluctuation of price might not only diminish profit, but annihilate it, or even, by the conversion, as in algebra, of positive into negative, might transmute the profit into loss. It appears, from this instance, that just as agriculture might be overladen by an excess of labour, so might it be overladen by an excess of capital. And at the extreme boundary of cultivation, might there be distinctly seen the operation of that check which opposes the indefinite advancement of both. Diminish the wages of agricultural labour beneath a certain rate, and ploughmen will cease to be multiplied. Diminish the profit of agricultural capital beneath a certain rate, or, still more surely, annihilate profit, and ploughs will cease to be multiplied. Both the population and the capital are here brought alike to a stand; and, at the point now specified, both are alike impotent for the purpose of enlarging the wealth of the country. The boasted power of capital for the maintenance of labour is, in this instance at least, found to be an illusion. There is no virtue in the excess of ploughs to maintain the excess of ploughmen. Nothing but an adequate return from the soil can uphold either; and for want of this, each excess must at length disappear,—it being as true of the capital as of the population, that it is heavier than the land can bear.

8. Now, what is true of agricultural, is true also of manufacturing capital. If, as we have found already, there may be too many manufacturing

labourers, so may there be too many manufacturing implements of labour. On the former taking place, there is work done by human hands, without the return of an adequate human subsistence; and so a diminution of the population. On the latter taking place, there is work done by pieces of machinery, without the return of an adequate profit to their owners; and so a diminution of their capital. What is true of the living, is true of the inanimate instruments; both might be unduly multiplied. As there might be too many men, so might there be too many machines—too many power-looms, as well as too many weavers at hand-looms —too many cotton-mills, as well as too many cotton-spinners. There is a check to the one, in the lessening of wages; and in every way as sure a check to the other, in the lessening of profits. They have not looked far onward, who speak of the power which lies in capital to employ and to maintain labour. They have looked only to the first step in the process—that at which the capitalist enlists workmen into his service; and for one year, or one term, can pay them liberally and well. They have not looked to the second step—that at which the return is made by them who purchase and use the commodity that has been thus manufactured. If this return be not an adequate one, the capital is not replaced; and, after a single revolution of the economic cycle, it again starts in diminished magnitude, and with a proportionally diminished power for the maintenance of labour.

9. There has recently been proposed a just and felicitous distinction, between the work done by human hands, and that done by tools, or machinery of any sort. The one is called the product of immediate, the other the product of antecedent labour. Under this view or conception of the matter, it will perhaps be more readily seen, that there may be a redundancy of capital as well as of population. In respect of there being more of both, than there can be obtained any adequate return for, there is a complete identity between them. If there may be too much of immediate, so also may there be too much of antecedent labour, brought to bear both on agriculture and manufactures. Agriculture cannot be extended, unless the additional land that is taken in, be able not only to feed the ploughmen, but also the makers of the plough. A manufacture cannot be extended, unless the additional commodity produced, will more than exchange for the maintenance both of the workers of the machine, and the makers of the machine that is employed. In each case a return must be yielded, which shall both maintain the immediate labourers, and also remunerate the outlay that was expended, in maintaining the antecedent labourers. There is occasionally an excess of both : and the effect, in the one case, is the distress and diminution of workmen ; in the other, the distress of capitalists, and the diminution of capital.

10. The reasoning is just as applicable to monied

as to material capital. There is nothing in the
intervention of this new element to affect our
conclusion. Money, when consisting of the precious metals, is itself viewed as a commodity. It
may rather be regarded, as that which possesses
the property, or the power of lifting all commodities ; or, under the very general aspect, of being that which enables its possessor to lift by purchase, any commodities which may be presented,
or which may be had for sale,—the quantity thus
lifted, depending on the relative value which obtains between the money and the commodity in
question. It is of no consequence to any inference
of ours, whether gold or paper be the instrument
of exchange, or, in other words, what the *substratum* of money is ; of as little consequence truly, as
what the material is on which an order for payment
shall happen to be written. Enough that it is an
effectual order ; and, however interesting the other
questions may be, which relate to currency and its
fluctuations, it is sufficient, for the determination
of our particular question, that the existing currency, whether paper or metallic, possesses for the
time being, a certain power of lifting all such articles as are presented in a market, and so has the
substantial functions of a circulating medium.

11. Let us now imagine the sum received by
any merchant or manufacturer, at his great annual
sale, to be eleven thousand pounds; of which he allo-
cates one thousand to the expenses of his family, and
reserves ten thousand for the continuation of his

business. This latter sum he may be conceived to lay out in the repairs of his material capital, and in the maintenance of his workmen, who repeat the course of the by-gone year—that is, work up the same commodities for their employer; and which, if he again sell them for eleven thousand pounds, will enable him to start with the same advantage, and to enter on another rotation, in precisely the same circumstances as before.

12. The length of such rotations varies exceedingly in different trades, though they may all be generalized into one summary expression; and the world of trade may be conceived to revolve in what we shall call an economic cycle, which accomplishes one revolution, by business coming round again through its successive transactions, to the point from which it set out. Its commencement may be dated from the point at which the capitalist has obtained those returns, by which his capital is replaced to him: whence he proceeds anew, to engage his workmen; to distribute among them, in wages, their maintenance, or rather the power of lifting it; to obtain from them, in finished work, the articles in which he specially deals; to bring these articles to market, and there terminate the orbit of one set of movements, by effecting a sale, and receiving in its proceeds a return for the whole outlays of the period.

13. There is nothing in the intervention of money, which should disguise the real character of this operation. If landed proprietors be the chief

customers for the commodities in question, they do not just give, on the instant, the *ipsa corpora* of their wealth; but they give what is equivalent, a lifting power to a certain extent, or an order to a certain amount, for the produce of their land.　This passes from the hand of the capitalist to the hand of his workmen; and they, on presenting it at a shop or a market, just get in food, that chief article of maintenance, the proper and essential return for their labour.　It must be obvious then, that principally with the holders of this maintenance, is lodged the power of replacing the outlays of the capitalist. His power to uphold, and still more to extend production on the one side, is mainly dependent on their power of affording him equivalents for his products upon the other.　Economists have looked too exclusively to the accumulations of the merchant, as if these could indefinitely advance the wealth of a land.　They have not enough considered the nature or the limits of that replacing power, which lies in the hands of his customers. They have calculated too much on his ability to produce, without at the same time calculating on their ability to purchase.　It is thus that the check to the augmentation of capital, has not been sufficiently kept in view; and the most sanguine and splendid anticipations have been indulged, respecting the progress of society, without sufficient regard to those immovable barriers which nature and necessity have placed in its way.

14. In the first place, it is abundantly obvious,

that mere accumulation by merchants or manufacturers, can only go a certain way, and, without the
concurrence of other causes, must be speedily arrested.   The capitalist of ten thousand pounds,
who, upon its whole outlay, has eleven thousand
pounds returned to him annually, can afford to
spend a thousand pounds in the year, and to maintain, in a stationary condition, the principal which
belongs to him.   But it may happen, that the taste
for accumulation shall prevail over the taste for
splendour or comfort.   Let him reduce his yearly
expenditure from a thousand pounds to eight hundred, and he will be able to vest an additional two
hundred pounds in his business.   And he may
succeed by this, in realizing a proportional increase
of revenue, seeing that no individual parsimony of
his can sensibly affect the general rate of profit in
the country.   But suppose that the same passion
for accumulation should seize upon all the capitalists in the land.   Let the whole sum invested by
them in trade be ten millions; and their united
revenue, with a profit of ten per cent. will be one
million.   Should all this revenue be spent, both
the capital and the profit will remain stationary.
But if, in virtue of the change which we now imagine—a change in the average taste and will of
merchants—one-fifth of this revenue were saved,
and employed in giving additional extent to their
business; then, at the next revolution of the economic cycle, instead of ten millions, we should
behold ten millions and two hundred thousand

pounds vested in trade. The parsimony of one, or a few individuals, could have no noticeable effect; but such a general parsimony would tell most sensibly on the rate of profit. The truth is, that, *all other circumstances remaining the same*, the revenue of merchants would fall, and that to the very extent in which they had enlarged their capital. For the one saving of two hundred thousand pounds, they would just lose this sum yearly in all time coming. The producing power of manufactures would be extended by this accumulation of theirs, but the returning power of consumers may remain unaltered. There would be more goods brought to market than before, but the whole price given for them may not be greater than before. Anterior to the general saving that we now imagine, capitalists, for the prime cost of ten millions, receive, in the whole price of their commodities, eleven millions. But since that saving, they, for the prime cost of ten millions two hundred thousand pounds, receive the same sum of eleven millions. By the saving in question, they have become at once richer in capital, and poorer in revenue. For the two hundred thousand pounds which they have added to the one, they have sustained a greatly overpassing loss; for they have taken two hundred thousand, and that yearly, from the other. It might be safe and profitable for one capitalist, or a certain fractional number of them, to accumulate. But a general accumulation cannot take place, save at the expense of the general revenue of capitalists. It is true, that, so long as agriculture is in progress, there might be yearly additions to the returning or replacing power, by which as large, or a larger revenue, might be afforded to a still enlarging capital. But when the progress of agriculture becomes slow and difficult, or, most of all, when it touches upon the extreme limit, then the impotency of accumulation on the part of capitalists must be severely felt. Each new investiture, in fact, will then be followed up by an adverse re-action or recoil upon themselves. As they grow in capital, they will decline in revenue. There is no escaping from this consequence, after that the returning power has become stationary. Every addition to capital, causes just a permanent yearly abstraction of the same amount from revenue ; and the same return, on a larger prime cost, is all which the capitalists reap for their pains. Society obtains their enjoyments at a cheaper rate, when, by an overdone competition among capitalists, each strains at becoming richer than before. But if there be no increase in the wealth of customers, capitalists cannot persevere in such a walk of speculation, without impoverishment and ruin to many of themselves.

15. We may now see what the check is to an indefinite accumulation on the part of capitalists. If the returning power be represented by eleven millions, it is obvious that the capital vested in business cannot go beyond it. At ten millions, it would command a profit of one million to the ca-

pitalists; and, if they chose to accumulate to a
capital above this, they may successively advance it
up to ten millions one hundred thousand, ten millions two hundred thousand, ten millions three
hundred thousand, or ten millions four hundred
thousand pounds : in which case, they would as
surely reduce their collective income to nine, or
eight, or seven, or six hundred thousand pounds.
They might even, by the mere force of their own
accumulations, bring up the capital indefinitely
near to the eleven millions, but with the sure effect
of bringing down this revenue indefinitely near to
annihilation.   Could they afford to live on nothing,
they might push forward the capital to eleven
millions, and annihilate profits entirely.   Or if,
from some other source than their accumulations,
capital were still farther extended, and so as to
overpass the eleven millions, profit would be converted into loss, and there would take place the
absorption of a yearly excess.   At the termination
of the economic cycle, capital would constantly
revert to eleven millions.   Whatever the amount
of capital may be, which, at the commencement of
the economic cycle, merchants and manufacturers
are able to advance, its amount, in the end, must
of necessity be limited by what customers are able
to return.

16. This brings into view a most important element, which hitherto has scarcely been admitted
into the consideration of profit.   We are abundantly familiar with the idea, that the rate of wages

is dependent on the average standard of enjoyment among labourers. But we have not been
so accustomed to think of the rate of profit, as depending on the average standard of enjoyment
among capitalists. Nevertheless, it is actually so.
It is a question with every individual capitalist,
whether he shall spend the whole revenue of the
current year, or how much of it he shall reserve,
for the purpose of vesting it in trade, and so giving
additional extension to his business, or, finally,
whether he shall expend more than his revenue, and
so trench upon his capital? This question turns
precisely on the balance between two appetites of
his nature—between the appetite for eventual gain,
and the appetite for present comfort. Should the
latter prevail, *and prevail generally*, capital would
be kept down, and profit be sustained. Should
the latter prevail, and also prevail generally, capital
would be augmented, and profit be depressed. It
does not affect this conclusion, that the highway to
fortune, on the part of the individual merchant, is
to save as much, and spend as little of his revenue
as he can. It is true of every single capitalist, that
he is all the richer by saving than spending; and
that, under any given rate of profit, or with any
given general habit on the part of capitalists. But
it is not true that capitalists collectively, will become richer by saving than by spending; for, on
their general habit, the rate of profit immediately
and essentially depends. Could they effectuate a
combination amongst themselves, they might up-

hold, at their general and collective pleasure, the rate of profit and interest in the land. But they are not able to achieve so extensive a concert, nor would its members be individually faithful in their observation of it; and this is not the only instance, in which the good of society is secured by the impossibility of combinations. Meanwhile, nothing can be truer, than that just as the wages of labour depend on the collective taste and will of labourers, so the profits of stock depend on the collective taste and will of capitalists. With this view, profits are what capitalists in the aggregate choose to make them. And however little the rate of profit may have been associated in the minds of economists, with the standard of enjoyment in the middle classes of society—yet, ultimately and efficiently, this is precisely the element on which it turns.*

* Mr. Thomas Perronet Thomson has, with his accustomed shrewdness, noticed this connection, and thus felicitously remarks upon it:—

" And as opinions and habits determine the final or average proportion, which shall be maintained between the numbers of the labouring population and the funds for their support, or, in other words, determine the average rate of wages; so they also determine the average rate of profits of stock, which are only the wages of another description of labourers, consisting partly of the recompense of present labour exerted in the form of superintendence, and partly of the recompense of past labour exerted in the creation of their capital. Public opinion and custom require, for example, that a shopkeeper shall have a good coat—shall drink at all times malt liquor, and sometimes wine, and give them to his neighbours; that his wife and

17. But it will demonstrate still more forcibly and clearly the limit to accumulation, if we reflect

daughters, if he has any, shall wear clean linen, and moreover not wash it themselves; and that when they travel, it shall be by the stage-coach, and not by the waggon. Though he may do without some or other of these things, in a certain degree, when necessity presses, he cannot and will not do without them in the main. If, therefore, he is a man of foresight, he will at all events defer adding to the population of shopkeepers, till he sees a fair prospect of supporting a family in the way which public opinion pronounces to be respectable. But if he engages in it without foresight, he will keep down the population of shopkeepers in another way—for he will break. Bankruptcy is the check to the indefinite multiplication of traders, as the evils arising from diminished food are the check to the indefinite multiplication of the lower classes of labourers. In the same manner, if the higher order of traders would, or could, do without a certain rate of expenditure, they might remit something of their rate of profits. If a great brewer, for example, would drive his family to the two shilling gallery in one of his own drays; or a banker be content, as in India, to sit on a mud floor in the shop of his forefathers, and retire to swallow rice with the condiment of ghee,—there would be some chance of the thing being brought to pass. But the crowning city has determined, that her merchants shall be princes, and her traffickers the honourable of the earth; and they neither can, nor will resist the award. The opinion of society, therefore, is what, in the long run, determines and keeps up the rate of recompense in this class, as well as in the other; and though there may be individual exceptions, men in general will break, sooner than not live up to what is expected from them. The difficulty is not in finding men to live up to this mark; but in finding men who will live within their means. The profits of stock, like wages, may be momentarily elevated or depressed, by the fluctuations, in the proportion between the business to be done, and the men who are to do it. When

that the power of accumulating is not confined to capitalists; but that it may be, and often is, exemplified by their customers; and more especially by those who are the chief consumers of luxuries, and who have it therefore in their power to economise the use of them. We can imagine that part of our capital, which is connected with the industry of the disposable population, to amount to ten millions, being the prime cost of all the goods wrought up by this class of labourers, which enter into one revolution of the economic cycle. Should these be met by a returning power of eleven millions, the capital is fully replaced, and with a profit that enables the capitalists to live at a certain rate of

business is scarce, the competition may, to a certain degree, induce traders to do it at a cheaper rate; and the contrary. But if the scarcity of business is permanent, traders will begin to go out by the horn-gate of bankruptcy, and so the balance will be preserved."—*True Theory of Rent*, 7th Edit. pp. 16, 17.

Mr. Thomson does not, perhaps, advert distinctly enough to over-trading, as a far more copious source of bankruptcy than over-living. Under a system of universal parsimony, a permanent scarcity of business relatively to the capital would ensue, and the horn-gate might be far more crowded, than under a liberal system of expenditure on the part of merchants. It is true, that the same general recklessness which leads men to overspend, might lead them to overspeculate; but it is far more to the latter, than the former habit, that our bankruptcies are owing. On the other hand, the same caution which restrains a man from spending beyond his revenue, may restrain him from trading beyond his capital—as perhaps in Holland. It is from the latter exercise of caution, greatly more than from the former, that bankruptcies are so rare in that country.

luxury and comfort. But if, after the commencement of this revolution, the holders of the returning
power had been visited with the inclination to save
more and spend less,—if a general retrenchment had
taken place among them, so that instead of spending eleven millions, they had laid up five, and had
only assigned six millions to the purchase of those
articles which had been brought to market at the
expense of ten millions,—it is quite evident, that,
in this instance, the original capitalists of these
ten millions would find the market sadly overladen,
at least, with their commodities. They had enlisted into the service of their different establishments a disposable population, whose office it is to
work up luxuries for those who are enabled by
their revenues to purchase them. But should a
taste for luxury give place to a taste for accumulation, in the degree that we have now specified,
it is obvious, that the lessening of the effective demand from eleven to six millions, must just have the
effect of lessening, in this proportion, the price of
their commodities. And, so far from its being in
their power by parsimony, or in any other way, indefinitely to extend the capital in their hands; we
find that this is not only limited by the power of
their customers, but that, by a change in the will
or taste of these customers, this capital could be
wrested to any given extent away from them.

18. To intercept all evasions, it may be right to
trace the effect of this change a little farther. The
sum of five millions, that we conceive to have been

laid up by landed proprietors, is not therefore
hoarded.   Generally, it would be deposited in
hands which lay it out in quest of gain, or on production, for the sake of a profit.   We are aware of
its being equally spent in either way.   But, whereas
formerly it wont to be spent as revenue, and with
an immediate view to consumption ; now it is spent
as capital, and with an immediate view to production.   Let this conversion of revenue into capital
be supposed to have taken place at the commencement, or along the progress, of the one economic
revolution, which we suppose to have been signa-
lized by the change in question.   Then it had
been possible, that, prior to the result of a market
overstocked with luxuries, and the price of them
falling to the level of the reduced demand, this
sum of five millions might have been, imprudently
or unforeseeingly, vested in the manufacture of
luxuries—when, with fifteen millions expended on
their preparation, and a returning power of only
six millions to replace this outlay, the failure in
the speculation behoved to be all the more signal.
But, though this conversion of revenue into capital
had not taken place till the economic cycle had
fully revolved, still there would have been but a
return of six millions to a cost of ten millions ; and
a reduction to this extent behoved to have taken
place in the capital of the original manufacturers.
Or, allowing them, as before, a million a year for
their maintenance, they could only begin their
operations anew with a capital of five millions.   So

that this conversion of revenue into capital by consumers, has not increased the capital of the country.
It has only shifted it into other hands.   The sum
of five millions, that formerly wont to be spent, is
saved ; or, in other words, instead of going to replace capital in its old situation, it has gone to
create capital in a new situation.   The whole difference is, that, instead of being returned, it has
been retained; and for the original capitalists in
the possession of ten millions, we now behold their
capital reduced to five, and the remaining five in
the possession of so many customers, who, by their
savings, have enriched themselves, but only to the
extent in which the others have been impoverished.

19. We may pursue this hypothetical case a little
further.   The manufacturers of luxuries must now
reduce their establishments in the proportion of
the reduced demand.   Should only six millions'
worth of the commodities in which they deal continue to be bought, from year to year, they have
still capital enough left for this extent of business.
But, meanwhile, the sum of five millions, now in
the hands of their old customers, waits for a profitable occupation ; and, in seeking after it, they will
have been effectually warned, by the losses of their
predecessors, from the manufacture of luxuries.
Let us now, then, turn from this department of
business, that has just rejected the excess of capital,
wherewith it was overladen, and try to imagine a
settlement for the new-formed capital, in some
other branch of the national industry.   And there

is a great, and withal a distinct department of this
sort, where are prepared, not the luxuries of life
for the wealthy, but the second necessaries of life
for the general population.   This sum will be superadded to the capital already vested in that species of industry, which we may suppose to have
been previously of the amount of ten millions.   It
will thus be made to attain the magnitude of fifteen
millions.   By this change, the sum of five millions
is withdrawn from the support of industry in the
third class of labourers, and transferred to the support of industry in the second class.   The labourers, on the whole, will have the same money, but
not more distributed among them as formerly;
though a great change will be effected in the distribution of their industry—half the disposable population being taken off from the manufacture of
luxuries, and passing into the secondary population, whose employment is the manufacture of second necessaries.   At all events, the great customers for the second necessaries, the labourers, will
not be able to make larger offers of money in the
market for them than they wont ; that is, if, in the
purchase of second necessaries, they could only
afford to pay eleven millions previous to this change,
this is all the sum which they can afford still.   Formerly, they replaced the capital of ten millions, and
afforded an additional million in profit for the livelihood of the capitalists.   They would now fall
short of replacing the capital of fifteen millions,
embarked in the preparation of second necessaries,

by the sum of four millions. The capitalists who dealt in second necessaries, allowing them one million to live upon, would only be able to start, as before, with ten millions, and that notwithstanding the investiture of an additional five millions at the commencement of the last economic cycle in their business. Such a yearly investiture, in fact, all other circumstances remaining the same, would be followed up by a regular yearly extinction of the sum invested. There would of course, so long as it continued, be an unnatural cheapness of the second necessaries. Let the wealthy stint themselves to one-half of their usual luxuries, and then vest the produce of their economy in the manufacture of second necessaries, and this were tantamount to a gratuitous distribution, to that extent, of additional second necessaries among the general population. The additional investiture of five millions, calling forth no additional return from the purchasers, is, in effect, equivalent to a gift of five millions' worth shared among them. It is not necessary to strengthen our argument, by supposing the taste for accumulation to extend also among the common people. They would certainly be enabled to indulge this taste, by the cheapness of all the second necessaries, and might, if they so chose, spend less than their wonted sum on the purchase, and yet be as well clothed and lodged as formerly. This, as far as it went, would reduce their return for the fifteen millions, to a less sum than the eleven millions, and serve to enhance still more the proof of

an utter powerlessness on the part of indefinite
parsimony to create or to sustain an indefinitely
increasing capital.

20. As capital, then, would not continue to rush
into a business where the goods, from the excess
and superfluity of their production, sold for less
than prime cost, we may now, with all safety, conclude, that the five millions annually saved by the
landed proprietors, and which had been rejected
from the manufacture of luxuries, would be equally
rejected from the manufacture of second necessaries.   And should the saving continue to be made,
there only remains another great department on
which to try the investiture of this sum.   After
having sought in vain for the profitable occupation
of itself in the business of the disposable and secondary classes, we may now suppose, for a moment,
that it has found a landing-place in agriculture.
In this case, half the disposable population, withdrawn from their old employment, would be turned
to the new employment of cultivating the land—
spreading tillage over a greater extent than before
among soils which had been yet unbroken, and
carrying it to a greater depth and perfection than
before, in the soils that had previously been entered
on.   It should be recollected that, previous to this
accumulation and its investiture, the agriculture
had been already carried forward to that limit which
has so often met our notice ; and from the contemplation we may again draw an important lesson—
even that there is a like limit to the extension of

capital.   But, before adverting to this limit, we
would remark, in the first instance, that, if the
agricultural capital, previously to this new investiture, was ten millions, it now becomes fifteen millions.   And as there is nothing in this change which
can immediately, and at once, furnish the general
population with a greater returning power than
before, there would only, for one year at least, be
a return of ten millions for the now extended investiture of fifteen millions.   We believe, that, in this
department of business, the loss would be greatly
aggravated by the circumstance of the great increase that must at first take place in the food of
the country, without an instant corresponding increase of population.   This would cheapen the
article much beneath the rate at which luxuries or
second necessaries would be cheapened, from the
same cause of an excess in their production.   One
can indefinitely extend his use of luxuries, or his
use of second necessaries, but he cannot indefinitely
extend his use of the first necessaries of life.   One
can treat himself with double the amount of splendid furniture, or use double the amount of clothes,
but he cannot eat double the quantity of bread that
he wont.   It is thus that an excess of food causes
a much greater depression of its price than a like
excess of most other articles ; so that the return for
the fifteen millions of capital, now embarked in
agriculture, would, we are persuaded, be greatly
less than the eleven millions, formerly returned for
the ten millions that wont to be embarked in it.

This will always form a strong initial barrier in the way of vesting more capital in agriculture, than what the state of the country at the time admitted of. No distant anticipations could tempt capitalists very far in this walk of speculation, with such a grievous absorption to meet them at the outset, or could tempt men by their savings to become capitalists.

21. But although there were no fall of price from the extension of agriculture beyond its natural limit, there is a sufficient barrier to this extension in the unproductiveness of the land which lies beyond it. The agriculture stops where it does, just because the land of last quality is barely sufficient to repay the expenses of its husbandry; and, in the existing state of agricultural labour and machinery, no land beneath this could be attempted without loss to the cultivator. We might conceive of the next land beneath, that its produce fell short, by one-tenth, of the ability to feed its agricultural labourers and their secondaries; or, that it would require a hundred, made up from both these classes, to raise food for ninety labourers. This would obviously increase the whole means of subsistence in the country. By this single instance, there would be food for ninety labourers added to the whole previous amount of the national produce, although it did require the work of a hundred labourers to raise it. Were this instance multiplied into an extensive system of home colonization, there is no doubt that, in the first instance, there would be a sensible

increase of the chief necessaries of life, and a temporary cheapening thereof, to the sensible relief of
all the labouring classes in the land.   But the increase of population would speedily restore the old
price, when we should behold a larger, but not a
more comfortable peasantry than before ; and the
last land, now that the natural limit of cultivation
had been forced, only yielding the food of ninety
labourers in return for the work of a hundred.   It
may be asked, whence are the ten labourers obtained ?   The husbandry of these inferior soils, not
being able to repay itself, must be maintained,
either by the voluntary benevolence of individuals,
or by taxation.   In either way there is a sacrifice
of luxury on the part of the wealthier classes ; or,
in other words, so many labourers are withdrawn
by this operation from the disposable, and placed
in the agricultural or secondary classes.   The process by which food has been raised for an additional
hundred, has had the effect of at least withdrawing
ten from the disposable population.   It may be extended to land of the next inferior quality ; where,
for every additional hundred that can be fed by its
produce, twenty must be withdrawn from the disposable population.   This may be conceived to go
downward, till rent is annihilated, or the last man
is withdrawn from a disposable population, now
upheld by the landed proprietors.   So that home
colonization, the moment it passes beneath the
limit of that land which yields a profit to the cultivator, may be regarded as having entered on the

first step of a process that, if consummated, would give us a larger population certainly, but a population almost wholly made up of the secondary and agrarian classes; and, therefore, labouring for the supply of a now larger society in the mere necessaries of existence. Meanwhile, the disposable population must have waned toward its extinction. The community will have gained in numbers, but not in comfort, even to the general mass of families. And it will have lost the services which are rendered by the disposable class—a forfeiture this, not merely of the elegancies of life to the wealthier classes, but the far heavier forfeiture of all that can civilize the species, or subserve the purest and highest objects of patriotism.

22. But, without here pursuing this speculation so far, we may clearly see how, even at the outset of such a process, there is a limit to the profitable embarkation of additional capital on agriculture. The land which cannot even feed its direct and secondary labourers, will far less yield a remuneration to the capital which landlords may have saved from their revenue; and which, rejected from two of the great branches of national industry, is vainly endeavouring to find a profitable investment for itself in the greatest and most important of all—the agricultural department. The domain of cultivation is, no doubt, gradually widening with the improvements that are ever taking place

* See Appendix, C.—On Home Colonization.

in the methods of agricultural labour. But when capital makes a rash attempt beyond this boundary, it is sure to be absorbed. While landed property continues, and the owners have a free controul over their own movements, this cannot long be submitted to. The landlord will not continue to employ, on a land that brings no return, agricultural labourers, who might, for the sum he is yearly spending in the shape of unproductive capital, be serving him in the capacity of disposable labourers; and from whose hands he might obtain a substantial return of comfort for the same sum, when expended in the shape of revenue. Neither will the tenant persist in cultivating land which yields him no profit. There is no escaping from the conclusion. Accumulation, or the conversion of revenue into capital, has its limits in this as well as in every other division of the business of society. In other words, capital is hemmed on all sides by a slowly receding boundary, which it cannot overpass; and beyond which, if it attempt to enlarge itself, it is broken into surges at the barrier by which it is surrounded.*

* We may here remark, how extraordinary it is, that the doctrine of the impossibility of a general glut—or, which comes to the same thing, the doctrine, that capital might find indefinite room for its own profitable investiture—should have been strenuously advocated by the disciples of a school, which connects the rate of profit with the return that is yielded to the husbandman by the last cultivated land. It is sufficient, to establish our view of the question, that the land which can afford a rent is of finite quantity, and requires but a finite capi-

CHAPTER IV.

ON THE PARALLEL BETWEEN POPULATION AND CAPI-
TAL, BOTH IN RESPECT OF THEIR LIMITS AND
THEIR POWERS OF EXPANSION.

1. WE have now abundantly shown, how impossible it is to sustain or accumulate capital beyond what a country can bear in the existing state of its agriculture; though when the agriculture itself extends, every thing else extends along with it. The larger population, consequent on the increase of agricultural produce, demands a larger supply of the second necessaries, and the manufacture of these requires additional hands, and the investiture of new capital. The increase of rent, consequent

tal for the full occupation of it. Let the capital then exceed this, and flow over on soils of inferior fertility, and you will soon reach an agriculture, the produce of which cannot even feed the direct and secondary labourers. This affords a clear example of a return falling short of the outlay,—the food produced falling short of the food expended. Now, on the principle, and it is a just one, that the profit on all other business is commensurate with that on agriculture, we shall, in such a state of things, from the general exuberance of capital, have profit converted into loss, or what may be termed a negative profit, repressing this exuberance throughout all the departments of enterprise, and so keeping down the capital to what the country can bear.

on the descent among inferior soils, gives to landlords a larger command over the luxuries of life
than before; and hence, a greater disposable population, with room also for the employment of additional capital in this branch of the nations industry.   Only let the agriculture be such that the
population may be comfortably fed ; and there is
no fear of a right distribution for them,—falling in
as they will, among the agricultural, the secondary,
or the disposable classes, just according to circumstances.   And there is as little fear of the labourers,
in all the three, being rightly proportioned between
the immediate and the antecedent.*   Too many
labourers, on the whole, would argue an excess of
population ; and too large a proportion of antecedent labourers, would just as certainly argue an
excess of capital.   The one excess is limited by
the impossibility of labourers being subsisted beneath a certain rate of wages ; and the other excess, as effectually limited, by the impossibility of
capital being supported beneath a certain rate of
profit.   Historically, both undergo an increase—
but just as the increasing agriculture lets them.
Population wont force agriculture beyond a certain
limit; but agriculture will ever draw population
after it.   And the same may be as truly affirmed
of capital.   It wont force agriculture beyond a
certain limit,—and should it, in the moment of its
redundancy, seek to do so, it will be sunk or dissi-

* See Chap. III. Sect. 9.

pated, and so its excess lopped off. There is a prevalent mistake respecting the order of causation, or the order of antecedency in this matter. It is not an uncommon imagination, that let capital be only accumulated to any extent; and to that extent it will, without let or obstruction, speed on the agriculture. It were far more correct to say, that agriculture opens room for the occupancy of capital.

2. We are not blind to the circumstance, that population, through its excess, and the consequent lowering of wages, opens a way into inferior soils, which, under a higher wage, could not have been entered on—nor to the circumstance that capital, through its excess, and the consequent lowering of profits, causes a similar descent, and so an extension of the agriculture. Even such may be the redundancy of the former, that, in a general distress for provisions, land may be attempted, from which but a miserable subsistence can be wrested; and such may be the redundancy of the latter, that, in the general difficulty for a profitable investment, land may be attempted, which, instead of sustaining and extending, extinguishes the capital that is put upon it. In this view, both population and capital may be regarded as impellent causes, for hastening forward the progress of agriculture. Yet it is not the object of a wise policy, to stimulate, beyond the natural incitements to their progress, the increase of either. Grant but a state of security and social order—and the spontaneous

tendency, whether of population or of capital, is to increase with a rapidity far beyond the movement of that slowly receding barrier which, ever and anon, is checking the precipitation and repressing the increase of both. And better, we think, than that either should be urged forward against this barrier, by the inconvenience of a painful excess—better if the secret could be discovered, by which both might be taught to moderate their pace, and to walk in pacific and prosperous advancement, side by side with the natural enlargement of agriculture; that capital, as well as labour, might be saved from those visitations of distress, which are sure to come on both, when alike straitened and overborne, each by the weight of its own undue accumulation.

3. There is a parallel between population and capital, which, if more dwelt upon, would rectify the sanguine and extravagant imaginations, that are still afloat respecting the power and indefinite capabilities of the latter; seeing they are the very imaginations which at one time prevailed regarding the former. The days once were, when population was the great demand of patriots and political economists; and accordingly, it was held the wisest policy of a state, to encourage early marriages, and raise foundling hospitals, and artificially foster in every sort of way this one element of national greatness. The days still are, when capital is the great demand of politicians and philanthropists; and it is imagined, that by every effort of

parsimony, by retrenchment in all directions, whether public or private, by accumulation to the uttermost, we may build up to an indefinite extent,
this other element of national greatness.   The
limits of the first are now understood ; and also
its own spontaneous tendency to overpass these
limits, so as to supersaturate a country, and produce distress among families.   The limits of the
second are not understood ; neither is it seen, how,
instead of being the object of an anxious or watch-
ful solicitude on the part of statesmen, it may
safely be left to the operation of those natural
principles, in virtue of which it is ever tending to
its own redundancy, and working by its very excess the infliction of many a heavy misfortune on
the capitalists of the land.   In this respect, there
is no difference between immediate and antecedent
labour.   The one is liable to as great excess as the
other.   As too many human hands may be working *now*, and drawing in return an inadequate subsistence ; so too many human hands may have been
working *last year*, and the existent products of
their industry, whether in the shape of goods, or
instruments of future production, may be drawing
a return of gains that are wholly as inadequate.
What the action of low wages is upon population,
so the action of low profit is upon capital.   They
prevent the increase of both beyond a certain
amount.   Nay, support in the one case may decline into starvation ; and population be lessened
in consequence,—and profit, in the other case, may

be turned into loss, and capital be effectually lessened also.

4. But population and capital not only resemble
each other, in respect of the limit which opposes
their indefinite augmentation.   They are both subject to losses and deficiencies beneath this limit,
and they resemble each other in respect of the exceeding force and facility wherewith these deficiencies are repaired.   If, by the operation of
disease or war, any sudden and large blank have
been made in the population, it is now understood
how speedily this vacuum is filled again, by the
general translation of the families into better circumstances, and the stimulus given from this cause
to a number of marriages that would have otherwise been postponed.   And, accordingly, an unwonted number of deaths in one year is followed
up, as may be seen from the tables of political
arithmetic, by a like unwonted number of births,
throughout the short period of a few years there-
after.   But it is not adverted to, that the deficiencies of capital are repaired by a process still more
sudden.   Let the whole capital embarked in glass-
making, for example, be a million of money, which,
if replaced in one revolution of the economic cycle
by eleven hundred thousand pounds, would enable
the manufacturers to live, and to commence their
course anew in the same circumstances as before.
But we may conceive one of these manufacturers,
with the capital of a hundred thousand, to have
withdrawn it from business, and to have squandered

it in a fit of extravagance, so that, in a few months, there is not a vestige of his fortune remaining. The common imagination is, that the capital thus wasted by the dissipation of one capitalist, can only be repaired by a strenuous parsimony on the part of all the rest. But the truth is, it may be repaired, and that in the course of a single twelvemonth, from another cause. There is nothing, generally speaking, in the extravagance of this said glass-maker, that can affect the wealth or ability of his customers. It may lessen, for one year at least, the quantity prepared, but it lessens not the ability to purchase. If eleven hundred thousand pounds were in readiness last year, for buying up the glass that had been manufactured at the expense of a million, there is nothing, in the wasteful expenditure of one of the capitalists, that can prevent the same sum of eleven hundred thousand pounds, from being in readiness next year. The producing power is, for one season, impaired; but the returning power is as great as ever. And the effect is just a rise in the price of the article. When the effective demand is the same as before, the price, averagely speaking, is in the inverse proportion of the quantity brought to market. The price of eleven hundred thousand pounds, given last year, in return for the cost of a million, is given this year in return for the cost of nine hundred thousand. The capital is thus restored to its original magnitude; and that, without any effort or hard straining on the part of the remaining capitalists.

The truth is, that to them it has been a prosperous, a holiday season of high prices and flourishing markets. That extravagance which has ruined their brother capitalist, has enriched them. They, in a single year, have fallen both into his profits and his capital. So far from being more pains-taking, or penuriously economical than before, they might spend among them the ten thousand pounds which came to him in the shape of revenue, and still inherit the whole of his capital, or the hundred thousand pounds into the bargain. The glass-making capital is fully replaced, not with any sacrifice or self-denial on their part, but at the ex-pense of their customers—and with the temporary mischief to these, of a tenth less of the article of glass than they would otherwise have had, the capital starts again into as great extent and effi-ciency as before.*

5. It is thus that, in capital, there is a restorative virtue, which, as if by the instant force of elasticity, causes it, speedily and spontaneously, to recover the encroachments that have been made upon it.

* Or the capital may be repaired not at the expense of the customers, but at the expense of the manufacturing labourers, who, if they all keep by their wonted employment, must be satisfied for one year with a proportional reduction of their wages. In this way the usual quantity of glass may be supplied at the usual price, but with such a profit from the diminished outlay, as to make up the deficiency which had been created in the capital of glass-makers. This subject is treated at greater length in my work on the Christian and Civic Economy of Large Towns, Vol. III. p. 308, *et seq.*

Grant but a secure administration of justice, and a
well-regulated social economy, and as certainly as
the population of a country follows hard upon its
food, so certainly does the capital follow hard upon
all that business which,' in the existing state of
things, it is profitable or possible to carry on in it.
If in excess, then it over-produces; and, through
the medium of consequent low prices, the excess
is lopped off in one revolution of the economic
cycle.   If in defect, then it under-produces; and,
through the medium of consequent high prices, the
deficiency is repaired in one revolution of the economic cycle.   It is thus that, from year to year,
the capital may oscillate on each side of the returning power; but the latter is the place to which the
former is constantly, though tremulously tending;
nor will the vibrations ever go far, or for a great
length of time, in either way.   The capital, ever
adjusting itself to the likely returns, is just the
supply ever adjusting itself to the effective demand.
And whether that demand be for immediate labour,
or for the products of antecedent labour, it will,
according to its relative magnitude, act at one
time as a check, and at another as an encouragement, on population, or on capital, or on both.

6. The general effect of the reasoning in Dr.
Smith's Wealth of Nations, (and that notwithstanding his occasional recognitions of the truth,) is to
impress the idea, that by accumulation a country
makes unceasing advances, and without any let or
hindrance, *ab extra*, in wealth and economic pros-

perity. It is not mere hoarding that he recom-
mends, but the accumulation of productive capital,
or of capital turned to use, and going forth in repeated outlays on the business of production. But
to uphold the capital, these outlays must be replaced, which they can only be by the expenditure
of those who consume. Mr. Malthus, on this, institutes a question respecting the balance between
production and expenditure; arguing rightly, that
if it was to be no expenditure, the motive to production would cease, and if it was to be all expenditure, the materials and instruments of production
would be destroyed.* There must, then, be a line

---

* " Adam Smith has stated, that capitals are increased by
parsimony, that every frugal man is a public benefactor, and
that the increase of wealth depends on the balance of produce
above consumption. That these propositions are true to a
great extent is perfectly unquestionable. No considerable and
continued increase of wealth could possibly take place without
that degree of frugality which occasions, annually, the conversion of some revenue into capital, and creates a balance of produce above consumption; but it is quite obvious that they are
not true to an indefinite extent, and that the principle of saving, pushed to excess, would destroy the motive to production.
If every person were satisfied with the simplest food, the poorest clothing, and the meanest houses, it is certain that no other
sort of food, clothing, and lodging, would be in existence; and
as there would be no adequate motive to the proprietors of
land to cultivate well, not only the wealth derived from conve-
niences and luxuries would be quite at an end, but if the same
divisions of land continued, the production of food would be
prematurely checked, and population would come to a stand,
long before the soil had been well cultivated. If consumption
exceed production, the capital of the country must be dimi-

somewhere between production and expenditure,
which it were best, on the whole, for a country to
observe ; but whether it be possible verbally to describe that line or not, practically nature hath, as
in the case of population and food, provided both
checks and stimulants, in virtue of which the economic machine might, with all safety, be left to its
own movements.   There is, on the one hand, an
appetite for future wealth, and, on the other, an
appetite for present indulgence.   If either were to
take possession of the country, in the shape of a
universal mania, it might overturn the balance of
society.   But just in proportion as either of these
forces goes to excess, and so causes a deviation
from the line of optimism on one side, in that proportion is the other, or counteractive force, augmented, so as at length to recal the stray movement, and cause an oscillation towards the other
side.   Should accumulation go to excess, and so
the supply in markets overpass the demand, the
lowering of profits will check the farther tendency,
and the wealthy feel tempted to purchase present

nished, and its wealth must be gradually destroyed, from its
want of power to produce; if production be in a great excess
above consumption, the motive to accumulate and produce
must cease, from the want of will to consume. The two extremes are obvious; and it follows that there must be some intermediate point, though the resources of political economy
may not be able to ascertain it, where, taking into consideration both the power to produce, and the will to consume, the
encouragement to the increase of wealth is the greatest."—
Malthus' Political Economy, pages 8, 9.

enjoyment with the overflowings of their revenue, rather than throw them away on unproductive investments. Should expenditure go to excess, and so the demand in markets overpass the supply, the rise of prices will not only prove a check to farther expenditure, but will tempt the cupidity of capitalists to every possible accumulation, that they may multiply and spread out their investments to the uttermost, and so catch, each for himself, as large a share of the current prosperity as he may. It is thus that there are restraining forces in operation, which prevent the extremes either of accumulation or of expenditure from being predominant in the land. The capital never goes to such excess as to annihilate all profit, or that fraction of it—the interest of money. And the expenditure never goes to such excess, as to sweep off capital from any branch of industry where it can be safely or lucratively employed.

7. But instead of one universal mania on the side either of expenditure or accumulation, the former appetite may be in excess with a certain number of individuals in the community, and the latter appetite be in excess with a certain and distinct number of other individuals. This represents the actual state of society, and it may be right to consider for a moment the effect of it. It will be found that expenditure, though in great excess, and that too amongst a great number of people, may not, after all, operate to the extinction, or even to a stay on the proper increase of capital. The truth

is, that the love of indulgence in one quarter of
society, will ever be sufficiently met by the love
of acquisition in another quarter of society, to keep
up the capital of the country in an abundantly
effective state for producing all, which capitalists
find it their advantage and their interest to produce. We can imagine each appetite carried so
far, as that one set of men shall spend in extravagance more than their income, and another set of
men shall lay out in business more than their capital. Let us begin with the first supposition, and it
might make the effect more palpable, to make use
in illustration of large numbers, nor will it affect
the validity of our conclusion, though the numbers
should be greater than are ever realized. We shall
state the income of all our landed proprietors at
one hundred millions, and conceive that in virtue
of an extravagant habit amongst them, their whole
expenditure is one hundred and ten millions. It
matters not to the argument, whether they are enabled to spend this excess of ten millions, by means
of a credit directly afforded to them of the dealers
from whom they buy, or of a credit afforded to them
from men in whose written engagements the country has faith, and whose notes, therefore, have the
power which belongs to money, of lifting the commodities for which it is offered in exchange. In
either way, ten millions more have been offered,
and ten millions more have been received, for the
various articles of enjoyment and expense that
have been brought to market throughout the year,

than otherwise would have been, but for this wasteful extravagance on the part of the landlords. Had new purchasers to the amount of ten millions started up, this addition to the demand would just have raised the money price of all these articles; but not more than does this extended demand of old purchasers. The effect of extravagance, on the part of old customers, is just to raise prices as much, as if the additional purchases had all been made by new customers. There is no waste of productive capital incurred by this extravagance on the part of landlords. Capitalists may have been carrying on their operations, through one year of this extravagance, in the very same way; and of consequence brought the same quantity of finished goods to market, as if landlords had been spending their incomes only, and no more. And the whole effect of their spending more is just to raise the price of these goods. If they bring a pecuniary demand to the market, of ten millions more than they ought to have done; this raises prices, and accordingly profits, to the extent of ten millions more than they otherwise would have been. Extravagance does not immediately and of itself increase the quantity of goods brought to market. The individuals who are extravagant, engross a larger quantity of these goods for the year, than would else have come to their share. But they are indulging their love of pleasure at the expense of their own fortune, and also at the expense of the general enjoyment of all other consumers who may keep within their incomes, but have the disadvantage of greater prices, and, consequently, a less amount of enjoyment than they would have had, but for the wasteful expenditure of so many of their fellows. This extravagance for a year leaves the supply unaltered, but, by increasing the demand, raises for that year the price of all the articles on which so much of additional expenditure has been lavished. Landlords have been impoverished to the extent of ten millions by this extravagance; but to that very extent, through the augmentation of price or profit, have capitalists been enriched by them. As much as they have mortgaged their estates, and thereby reduced their own wealth, so much have they transferred of a lifting power that enables others to purchase land to the whole value of the mortgage. The extravagance of landlords does not have all the effect which is ascribed to it, in the way of reducing the property of the nation. Mainly, its effect is but to transfer the property of the nation. In as far as it keeps up prices and profit, it retards the progress of cultivation among new soils. And so long also as an estate is in the possession of a dissipated proprietor, this may be a temporary let in the way of its improvement. Yet, bating these exceptions, the extravagance of landlords does not produce a *reduction* in the property of the nation, but only a *rotation* of it.*

* By its effects on prices, this ultra expenditure of landlords lessens the share of the annual supply, which would otherwise have fallen to all other customers.

8. And the effect of overspending, on the part of consumers, to raise prices, is neutralized by the effect of overtrading on the part of capitalists, to lower prices. These two opposite vices may prevail to a great extent in society, and that too, from their counteraction of each other, without sensibly impairing the capital, or altering the rate of profit. As there may be an extravagant love of pleasure, leading one man to lay out on present indulgence more than his revenue; so there may be an excessive love of gain, leading another man to excessive speculation, or to lay out, on business, more than his capital. He is enabled to do this by the trust reposed in him, either on the part of those from whom he purchases the various materials of his speculation, or on the part of lenders, who accommodate him with money, or with written engagements, which have the virtue that belongs to money. At all events, if he purchase more than he ought, to that extent he raises the price of the things purchased, and so the cost of the articles which he manufactures, or of the articles in which he deals. But he furthermore pours a larger supply of these articles into market, and so far reduces their selling price. For every new adventurer, who enters any walk of commercial enterprise, or for every old capitalist, who has already entered it, and become more adventurous than before, the cost of the commodity is proportionally raised, and its price proportionally lowered. This soon meets with its corrective in bankruptcies and losing spe-

culations, by which some are driven from the trade altogether; and only those whose fortunes are reduced, but not annihilated, can keep possession of the field.*

9. In the matter of population, and consequently of wages, there may be a balance between the improvidence of many individuals on the one hand, who rush precipitately into marriage, and the licentious celibacy of many on the other hand, who, though entitled by the sufficiency of their circumstances to enter upon this state, prefer a life of dissipation. The one excess may so neutralise the other, as to produce betwixt them no aggregate

* The problem suggested by Mr. Malthus, in the passage which we have extracted at sect. 6. of this chapter, meets with its readiest solution, by connecting it with the influence which an increase of production on the one hand, or of consumption on the other, has on cultivation. The more that production prevails over consumption, as in peaceable, and industrious, and well regulated communities, the more do prices, and therefore profits fall, so as to carry down the cultivation among poorer soils, and by enlarging the agricultural produce, or the maintenance of labour, to make the country richer in all the products of labour. This will meet with its effectual check; when this superiority of production over consumption, with its effect on profit is carried so far, that the last returns, whether from agriculture or any other business, do not yield what has been called a living profit. On the other hand, in those countries where the consumption or expenditure bears a greater proportion to the production, as in demi-barbarous and unsettled, and oppressed communities, where profit and the interest of money are high, the cultivation is proportionally contracted; and wealth, as being mainly dependent on the amount of agricultural produce, is contracted along with it.

effect upon the population; but better, certainly, that neither excess obtained, and that the same result were brought about, by the avoidance alike of profligacy, and of premature marriages. So in the matter of capital, and consequently of profits, there may be a balance between the extravagance of many individuals on the one hand, and the reckless temerity of many commercial speculatists on the other. And the one excess may so neutralise the other, as to produce betwixt them no aggregate effect upon profit. But better too, in this instance, that neither the one excess nor the other did obtain; that no man spent beyond his income, and no man speculated beyond the fair and honest likelihoods of the business he was engaged with. It may cause no sensible difference to the two great public and economic interests of profit and wages; but there is involved in it a momentous difference to the worth of individual character, and the comfort of families. We feel no dread anticipation of national loss, either from profuse expenditure or from excessive speculation. But both habits are much to be deprecated, as being alike unfavourable to private virtue and happiness. And both these excesses may in fact be realised by the same individual—in whom the appetite for gain, and the appetite for indulgence, may meet together in hurtful and vicious combination. This we often find exemplified in the present age; when splendid extravagance is followed by splendid bankruptcy, out of the wrecks and ashes of which there sud-

denly ariseth a phœnix as splendid as before.   But
we deem that all the liberalities of such an age,
form no equivalent for those virtues of more severe
and unbending aspect, which flourished in other
days; when the good old temperament, of hard and
honest, sat more conspicuously than they do now
on the visage of plodding and painstaking, but
withal well-conditioned and well-principled citizens; and when, sturdy and well-built in all the
cardinal virtues, the grandfathers of our present
race, with their homely fare and their primitive
habits, were still uninfected by the vice and vanity
of modern times.   This we deem to have been
better and wholesomer far, than is a commerce of
proud and precarious adventure; and we do indeed hold the passions, and the profligacies, and
the gaming artifices of her now deeper play, to
be wretchedly atoned for, by all the gaudy efflorescence of her pageant style, and her mushroom
palaces.

10. We may with all safety conclude, then, that
under the protection of equitable law, capital is sure
to maintain itself fully up to the state at which it is
most beneficial; and even tends to go beyond this.
When reduced by any cause beneath this standard,
it evinces the same restorative force as that which
belongs to the element of population.   The increase of the one need be no more the subject of
demand or anxiety, than that of the other.   The
expenditure in excess of mere customers, as of
landed proprietors, does not lessen capital.   It but

raises money prices, and so the very extravagance which mortgages the land to the extent of ten millions, transfers the power of purchasing, to that extent, to some other quarter in society, and thus occasions a mere change or division in property, without a diminution of it. The expenditure of capitalists themselves may lessen capital, but the operation of a high profit almost instantly recovers it, just as when disease or war lessens population, the operation of a high wage is to act as a stimulus to marriage, and so bring in a little time the number of the people up to the means of their subsistence. There is no artificial fostering requisite for the upholding of either. Each may with all safety be left to itself, and the danger is as small, that we shall not have enough of antecedent, as that we shall not have enough of immediate labour. The less of population to the food, the more is there of plenty among labourers. The less of capital to the business, the more is there of profit among capitalists. But neither will the food remain long in excess, nor the profit in excess. With both there is a rapid tendency to excess the other way; that is, to an excess of population on the one hand, and an excess of capital on the other. It is not by the deficiency of these, but by the redundancy of these, that distress and inconvenience begin to be felt, first among the labourers, secondly among their employers. There is no need for exciting, beyond the operation of its own spontaneous forces, an increase of the supply of immediate labour; for, in truth, it is the over-supply of this, that, by the lowering of wages, spreads discomfort among the people. And there is just as little need for exciting, beyond the operation of its own spontaneous forces, an increase of the supply of antecedent labour; for it is the over-supply of this, which, by the lowering, or the destruction of profits, turns merchandise into a desperate game, and spreads disorder among capitalists.

11. We hear much from the economists of ruinous extravagance. Now individual landlords, and individual capitalists, will find it ruinous to themselves; but it is only because the extravagance of the former causes a rotation of wealth, by which it is moved away from them, and because the extravagance of the latter causes first a destruction, and then an almost instant replacement of wealth, which springs up in other hands. Meanwhile, and notwithstanding the play of these yearly oscillations, the property and capital of the nation abide in unimpaired magnitude. But the general fancy is, that if there have been a defalcation of capital, through the extravagance of some, it is repaired through the parsimony and painful accumulation of others. Instead of which it is repaired, and that almost *per saltum*, not by means of parsimony on the part of capitalists, but by means of high prices for a year, which is tantamount, we admit, to a privation for that time on the part of customers. Never are capitalists more exempted from the duties and the cares of frugality, than when

this restorative process is going on ; for to them it is a season of hey-day prosperity, wherein, without any change of habit, or rather, notwithstanding an increase, if they so choose, of expenditure and luxury, the capital, wasted or withdrawn from business by others, comes back, with almost instant reflux, upon themselves. They, without effort, fall into possession of the ground which the others had abandoned, and find it as full of capital, and as productive of revenue, as before. It is all an enlargement to them; and at no time was this more apparent, than when the borrowing system, by government, was in full activity : producing, therefore, a yearly extinction of capital, and yet closely followed up by its yearly regeneration. It was not regenerated, as Dr. Smith imagines, by parsimony, but by a rise of profits. The twenty millions, borrowed one year, and withdrawn from the business of production, just by the inverse action of supply upon prices, were replaced next year, to the great and sudden enrichment of all the monied and mercantile interests in the land. And the same loan to government, if repeated for ten years, would just be followed by the same effect; that is, a season of this duration distinguished by its high prices, and so by its high profits. The reality of this process stands palpably forth to observation in the price of stocks—which fall in war sometimes to half of their value in peace; and indicating, therefore, no less than a double rate of profit. This will suffice to account for the full maintenance of the capital of a nation, notwithstanding the repeated drafts on that capital by borrowing. The lenders withdraw their fortunes from business, and virtually become mortgagees upon the land; having their interest paid by a perpetual tax, that falls upon the country, and we think upon the landlords. The capitals which remain in trade, are then suddenly enlarged, by the impulse given to profits. The perfect sufficiency of this capital for the business of the nation, even under all the encroachments to which it is subjected by government loans, is abundantly obvious; and is ascribed, by Dr. Smith, to the compensation by the savings in one class of the community for the squanderings of another. But the true explanation is, that it arises from the high prices to which the community at large are subjected; it being, in truth, a season of privation to them, while a season of feverish prosperity to manufacturers and merchants. And, meanwhile, the expenditure does not diminish the property of the nation; it only transfers a part, and so divides it. The land is as good as partitioned between the landed-proprietors and the national creditors, who are the mortgagees. Should the debt overtake the wealth of our proprietors—should the mortgage equal the value of the land, and still justice be scrupulously adhered to, there would be no disappearance of property in consequence; there would only be the dispossession of existing proprietors. Landlords would have to do generally, in consequence of the extravagance of government, what

they have often to do severally, in consequence of
their own individual extravagance. They would
have to renounce their estates in favour of their
creditors; when, as we have already said, the ultimate effect of the expenditure would be found, not
in the main to have been a reduction of property,
but only a rotation of it.

12. Dr. Smith mourns over our national debt, as
if, by each successive act of its extension, the
country had been thrown permanently back in the
career of economic prosperity. It has been computed by some, how much more populous we should
have been, had the practice of innoculation been
discovered sooner; and, in like manner, he com-
putes how much richer we should have been, had
the different sums borrowed by government been
all retained as capital. But the truth is, that it
never could have stood as capital. The effect of
the debt, while under its process of formation, was
to subject the people to higher prices, and so to a
scantier supply of all the comforts of life. Had
there been no formation of a debt, and the people
been left to their wonted supply of these articles,
they would just have made all the larger use of
them; and if not, there would have been an excess
of capital beyond what the country could bear,
and so an absorption of this excess, in the losses
and the bankruptcies of over-trading. The whole
effect of the debt at the time of its contraction, is
to expose the people to those higher prices, which
have both to return the abiding, and to replace the

withdrawn capital. And the whole effect of the
debt afterwards, is to divide property, just as a
mortgage divides it between the creditor and the
landed-proprietor. We look to the wrong quarter
for its effect, when we look for a diminished capital. We are aware, that for a time it may keep
back the cultivation of the land, by the temporary
elevation which it imparts to profit; but even this
is speedily recovered, when the borrowing system
ceases, and profit falls again. The truth is, that
while this borrowing system lasted, capital was
upheld in full extent and sufficiency; and when
the borrowing system terminated, capital, unprovided with its wonted vent or absorbent, went to
dissipation, in the overflow of its own exuberance.
It was felt to be a paradox at the time; but we
think it admits of lucid explanation, that capitalists
flourished in war, and that in peace they suffered
the re-action of many adversities and losses.*

13. It is readily enough perceived, how soon the
population of a country recovers from the effects
of a desolating war; and how, with its agriculture
and its seasons unchanged, it witnesses, in a few
years, an equal number of equally thriving families.
But there is just as great vigour and indestructi-
bility in the element of capital; which, though
wrecked to the uttermost by victorious armies, will,
in the course of a few years, attain to all the magnitude, and all the efficiency, which it ever had. If,
by the multiplication of labourers, the country will

* See Appendix, D.—On the National Debt.

soon have enough of population ; then, simply by a
right distribution of them into the immediate and
antecedent, the country will almost as soon have
enough of capital. And this distribution may,
with all safety, be left to the guidance of individual
interest. The first effect of the lessened capital
would be a lessened production ; and in repairing
this, the chief and foremost effects would, of course,
be directed to those things that were of most urgent
necessity. Hence a greater than ordinary proportion of the people would be set to repair the deficiency of food, who, between their immediate and
antecedent labour, would speedily put the fields
into their wonted order, and give their wonted
completeness to the instruments of husbandry.
After this had been achieved, the great and extraordinary effort would then be transferred to the
manufacture of second necessaries ; for that would
now be the quarter of greatest demand, and at the
same time deficiency ; and where, therefore, under
the encouragement of highest price, capital would
be most readily allured, or rather, most quickly
forced up to its original magnitude. And so this
matter would proceed, till, in a very few years, the
recovery both of population and of capital would be
completed. By one revolution of the economic
cycle, what is termed the *circulating capital*, would
be nearly restored; and by a few revolutions more,
what is termed the *fixed capital*, would be fully restored ; and all this, not by the parsimony of successive generations, but by the privations of a very

few successive seasons. It has been a theme of
wonder to historians, that after the most sanguinary
and destructive wars, a country should so fast
emerge again into its wonted prosperity and
strength. Like the mysterious sanative principle
in the human body, it has had a mysterious appellation given to it, and been ascribed to an unknown
vis medicatrix in the body politic. But such a disguise for ignorance is altogether unneeded; for
there is no mystery whatever in the process. It is
all due to the action of forces perfectly understood,
however little applied to the explanation of the
phenomena in question. The effect of a high profit, on a deficient capital, may be just as lucidly
apprehended as the effect of a high wage, on a deficient population. They, in a very short time,
cease to be deficient. The facts of history upon
this subject are notoriously in accordance with the
principles of science; nor should we any longer
marvel, why Russia, and Prussia, and Austria, and
France, after having, to all appearance, exhausted
each other, should, in less than half a generation,
be able to renew their conflicts in as great force
and fulness as before.

14. It is in old and well-governed countries
where capital is most exposed to the discomfiture
of its attempts for its own enlargement. It is in
these where profit has sunk to the lowest state that
is consistent with the maintenance of capital; and
where, therefore, if capital were farther extended,
the profit might be annihilated, or even converted

into loss. A country, though well governed, yet
if new, may have its profits high, because of the
unbroken tracts which yet lie open for cultivation,
as in the United States of America; and on which
the exuberance of capital may overflow, and find
profitable investments for generations to come.
And a country, though old, yet if ill governed,
may also have its profits high. The insecurity to
which all property is exposed, from injustice and
violence, will prevent the wealthy, in such countries, from exposing their capital, without the promise of a considerable return. The high profit is
an indemnification for risk; and should be equal to
the ordinary profit in ordinary circumstances, with
a premium, over and above, for a very hazardous
insurance. In balancing the matter between the
value of a present indulgence, and that of a future
acquisition, the uncertainty attendant on the latter,
will tempt merchants to give a larger proportion of
their gains to expenditure; and this, by keeping
down their capital, upholds their profit. It is in
perfect accordance with this, that, in countries
under oppression, the cultivation should have made
so short a descent among the inferior soils. The
same consideration which operates in restraining
the application of mercantile, will also operate in
restraining the application of agricultural capital;
the latter of which requires, as much as the former,
the inducement of a large return in barbarous or
demi-barbarous countries. Hence the prodigious
capability of soils that lie without the margin of

cultivation, in far the greater number of countries in the world—in Asia Minor, in South America, in Hindostan, along the Northern shores of Africa, and, generally speaking, in all territories under the Mahometan yoke. This holds out the brilliant perspective of a great enlargement in the physical resources of the human family, as being the sure attendant of their growth in morality, and religion, and social order. Even the larger countries of civilized Europe have still this prospect in reserve for them ; as is evident from the higher interest of money in conjunction with the yet imperfect agriculture of such countries as Spain, and Austria, and Russia, and Poland. Perhaps there is no first-rate nation so near, in this respect, to its extreme limit as Britain, that has long been the seat of pure legislation, and of safe and prosperous industry. There, a low interest, a high-wrought agriculture, the distress both of a redundant population among the labourers, and of a redundant capital among the mercantile classes, go hand in hand. Ireland, with its higher interest of money, and its less perfect agriculture, has yet a career of greater advancement to describe than there is now room for in this country. One of the recipes often given for the medication of that interesting land, is to pour capital into it. But this is mistaking the consequence for the cause. The economic will follow spontaneously in the train of the moral improvement. With the progress of education, and law, and industry, capital will naturally be attracted

hither ; and, what is still better, a capital of home-
growth augmentation will speedily be formed.
Their slovenly agriculture, and unreclaimed wastes,
are to us the materials of a cheering anticipation;
for they tell how large are the still undeveloped
capabilities of Ireland. The redundancy of the
Irish population, is only, as compared not with the
potential, but with the actual amount and distribution of their produce, an amount which might be
doubled with a better system of husbandry ; and a
distribution which will become more thoroughly
internal than at present, when landlords begin to
feel, that on their own estates, and among their
own peasantry, they may taste the charm and tranquillity of home.   It is competent for moral causes,
and for these alone, to effect every desirable amelioration ; and, if man would but do his part, nature has in store for Ireland a liberal subsistence
for millions more of human beings than are now
famishing upon its territory.

15. If the disease in Ireland be a plethora of
population, the disease in this country is more like
to a plethora of capital. If there, the mendicity
be among the living instruments; here, if I may
be permitted such an image, the mendicity is
among the dead instruments of labour. If there,
immediate labour be wretchedly remunerated by a
low wage ; here, the low profit makes a wretched
remuneration for antecedent labour. The phenomena on this side of the water indicate as
surely that capital has its limits, as the pheno-

mena on the other side indicate that population has its limits. The annoyance one feels in the competition of porters for employment, is not more decisive of the one, than the annoyance he is exposed to from the competition of steam-boats or hackney-coaches is decisive of the other. The noisy clamour of beggars on the street, does not tell more significantly of an excess of population, than the signs of unoccupied houses, and the flaming advertisements of commodities at prime cost, and the incessant cheapening of articles to the bankruptcy and ruin of their owners, tell by another sort of clamour of the excess of capital. Between the two elements, in fact, there is a marvellous and multiplied accordancy. Both are subject to incessant checks from the want, each of its own proper aliment; the one from an insufficient wage, the other from an insufficient profit. And though both are greatly short, at present, of that magnitude which they may yet attain in the course of ages; both may press at all times on a slowly retiring limit—nor is there room in the world for the indefinite extension of either.

CHAPTER V.

ON THE POSSIBILITY OF OVER-PRODUCTION, OR OF A
GENERAL GLUT.

1. By our division of labourers into three classes, we are enabled to refute the modern paradox, of the impossibility of over-production, or the impossibility of a general glut. They who maintain this doctrine, represent what they term unproductive consumption, or unproductive expenditure, as an injury to the nation. They know, that though all wealth were turned into capital, there would just be as much expenditure as before; but it would be expenditure on the tools and materials, or on the maintenance of industry. Instead of spending my income of a thousand guineas in the year, it is certainly possible to stint myself to fifty pounds; and either directly, or through the medium of a loan, I may spend a thousand pounds annually in the employment of labourers, who shall work up a return for the maintenance bestowed on them. It is in virtue of this return, that the latter mode of spending a thousand pounds, has, in opposition to the former, been termed productive expenditure, when viewed as coming from the hands of the employer; or productive consumption, if viewed as going to the maintenance of so many workmen and

their families.   And their workmanship is the
product—a product that we should not have had,
if the owner of the sum, instead of giving it the
supposed destination, had spent it on his own personal or family indulgences.

2. The thing wanted, therefore, by these new
economists, is, that each man, laying out as much
as possible of his income on productive expenditure, should lay out as little as possible on his own
individual enjoyments.   And this can certainly be
done, till the man reduce himself to the necessaries
of life.   This is the extreme limit of the possibility
in regard to him ; and the extreme limit in regard
to the country at large, might be reached by all
men of wealth, higher than that of a labourer, doing the same thing ; that is, confining themselves
to the use of necessaries, and spending the surplus,
not in the purchase of existent products for their
own and their families further enjoyment, but in
the maintenance of workmen whom they put to
the formation of new products.   At this rate it is
obvious, that all luxuries would be proscribed.
These products would fall out of demand, and
cease to be fabricated.   The men now employed
in their fabrication would still continue to be supported, and by the same people too—only, instead
of being supported by them in the act of spending
their revenue on the old and customary products,
they would be supported by them in the act of
laying out that revenue, now turned into capital,
on the manufacture of new products.   And these

products, in virtue of this universal change that had taken place in expenditure, behoved to be either the first or second necessaries; seeing that, when society was brought to this state of alleged optimism, all men behoved to confine themselves to the use of necessaries, and devote the surplus of their incomes to that production, which it is impossible by this new doctrine to carry to excess. That this new production should be a production of luxuries, after the use of luxuries has been thus proscribed, and banished from the land, is surely out of the question. If production at all, it must be that of the first and second necessaries. In other words, by this change, the disposable population would be, not destroyed, but transferred. The class would be destroyed,—but the men who compose it would be supported, and as well supported as before, in other employments; or merged into the other two classes of agricultural and secondary labourers.

3. By tracing the effect of such a change in the habit of expenditure, (were it possible, which it is not, that such a change could be realized,) we shall find that it would be productive of no real benefit or blessing to society. We might perhaps satisfy ourselves with the certainty, that it is a thing not to be done,—but we hold it of importance furthermore to know, that it is a thing not to be desiderated. At all events it will be found, in the course of the investigation, that this new doctrine, of the impossibility of a general glut, is altogether a chi-

mera. And, like many other important lessons in
political economy, we think that this one too can
best be learned at the extremity of cultivation,—
at the limit of a country's food, beyond which it
is utterly impossible to carry any one economic interest, that is dependent either on the number of
human beings, or on the industry of human hands.

4. First, then, let us imagine that the farmer, in
any given state of the husbandry, lays out, and
persists in laying out, the uttermost he possibly
can, on the business of that production wherewith
he has to do. There can be no doubt, that the
less he spends upon himself, and the more he
spends upon his business, the faster will he carry
out upon his land the limit of cultivation. Even
when he has reached that soil, which can yield
no more than his profit, over and above the food
of its direct and secondary labourers, he may still
persevere in making a surrender of that profit;
and, instead of consuming it on his own enjoyments, may continue to put it out on the expenses
of a further cultivation. With this determined
sacrifice, year after year, of all the profits of his
husbandry, he will not only carry out the cultivation at a faster rate, but he will carry it further
than he could otherwise have done. He may be
obliged to stop at last, when he comes to a soil
which yields him no profit, and which can barely
feed the agricultural labourers and their secondaries; but yet he stops at a line ulterior to that
which would have bounded his progress, had he been

in the habit of spending the profits upon his family, instead of sinking them upon his farm. The land last entered on, would be further down in the gradation of qualities of soil, because it would have less to do; having only to yield the food of its direct and indirect labourers, instead of having both to yield that much, and a profit to the cultivator besides. This attempt then at production, on the part of the farmer, to the uttermost of his power—this surrender of his own profits to the cause, must give a certain stretch to cultivation, and be the means of reclaiming a belt that would have otherwise remained on the exterior of the domain of cultivation. There would have been room thus afforded for a larger, but not certainly on that account for a happier or a richer population. Their comfort, in fact, depending as it does, not on the absolute quantity of food, but on the relation which the quantity bears to their own number; and this again depending on their own standard of taste and of enjoyment,—all that the extreme parsimony of the farmer can work out for us, is a bulkier, but not a better-conditioned society than before; a greater number of families, but these not at all more thriving families than they were formerly. Let us state truly the effect of this straining after production, with all his might and all his means, on the part of the cultivator. He annihilates his own profit by it. He adds something to the magnitude of the commonwealth. He adds nothing to the prosperity or comfort of the individuals who compose it.

5. It seems needless to make a distinct argument, for it is essentially the same on the case of another species of capitalist; even him who heads, and who by his funds sustains, the manufacture of second necessaries. He too, like his brother agriculturist, may, in his zeal for production, choose to live as a labourer, and to embark all profit on the enlargement of his concern. The consequence would be a larger supply of second necessaries, and such a consequent cheapening of them, that profit should be annihilated. We have already demonstrated how this, too, would give a stretch to cultivation. It would, *pro tanto*, have the same effect, in this way, that we ascribed to the cheapening of second necessaries, by an improvement in the machinery employed to prepare them. It would not of itself lessen the number of secondary labourers requisite for this preparation. The last land would still have to feed the same number of these. But it would have no longer to feed the disposable population, that wont to be employed in the preparation of luxuries for the manufacturing capitalist. He, by the supposition, has given up this idle expenditure, and embarked all the proceeds of his retrenchment on the extension of his business. The effect of thus freeing the last land from the burden of subsisting so many as would have been otherwise required of it, is just to enable the cultivator to make a step down to worse land. By this change in the habit of the capitalist, a few of the disposable class would be transferred, as in the

former case, to the business of a now more extended agriculture; and, with the consequent increase of population, to the business of a then
proportionally extended manufacture of second
necessaries.   In both cases, there might be a temporary enlargement of comfort to labourers.   But
this, so long as the standard of enjoyment remained
the same, would soon be followed up, and therefore compensated, by an increase of population.
And so the result of this second effort at an indefinite production, would come, like the first, to a
very definite and limited result.   It would annihilate profit.   It would add something to the magnitude of the commonwealth.   It would ultimately,
or permanently, add nothing to the prosperity and
comfort of its individual families.

6. But the extension of agriculture that would
ensue from capitalists, whether agricultural or
manufacturing, giving up their profits, is as nothing to the extension that would ensue from
landed proprietors giving up their rents in the
cause.   We need not make a separate case of the
capitalists employed in the manufacture of luxuries,—for the most which they could surrender
to the object of increasing production, is the profits of their business.   But were their great customers, the landlords, to be enlisted in this warfare
against all unproductive expenditure, they could,
by giving up the use of whatever is superfluous,
turn, not merely the profit made on luxuries, but
the whole price of luxuries, to the purposes of

capital. The most that capitalists could do, by a
yearly sinking of their profits, would be to carry
down the cultivation to the soil that barely feeds
the labourers, directly and secondarily employed
on it. But landlords, by a yearly sinking of their
rents, could do a great deal more; could make, in
fact, the cultivation pass a very far way beyond
this line among the deficient soils.* With the exception of their own essential maintenance, which
they might reduce to that of labourers, they could
turn the whole of their immense revenues into
capital, for the object of production; though, from
the universal change which we now suppose in the
state of the demand, it behoved to be the production of first and second necessaries. Of course,
the present employments of the disposable population would be completely broken up, and we
should behold them spread in immense numbers
over the deficient soils of the territory,—where
they would be supported, partly by the scanty and
inadequate returns of their penurious husbandry;
but this made up by the successive outlays of that
revenue which landlords drew from their superior
soils. In effect, this scheme of production, to the
uttermost, would give rise to the very same distribution, and be attended by the same consequences,
with a scheme of home colonization carried to the
uttermost. The landlords would only be denuded

* We name those the deficient soils where produce is insufficient for the subsistence of their direct and secondary labourers.

of their revenues in a somewhat different capacity; not in that of philanthropists or leypayers, but in the capacity of over-traders. The ultimate effect of that system which the enemies of unproductive expenditure so strenuously recommend, supposing it carried to the uttermost, would be a regular yearly investiture of all the superfluous revenue of landlords; and that followed up, by as regular a yearly loss to them of the whole sums invested. There would not be the extinction of rent from the superior soils; but there would be the absorption of it on the deficient soils. There would be the extinction of a disposable population. There would be a considerable increase of the general population; but with this addition to the number, there would most assuredly be no addition to the comfort of families. With the surrender of luxuries on the part of the landlords, agriculture could be carried a great way beyond its natural limit; yet it is not illimitable. When the last luxury had been given up, and the last man been withdrawn from the disposable population, then would agriculture reach the farthest possible barrier which nature and necessity had laid in the way of its extension—as the beach, or the sandy desert, or the impracticable rock, or the climate of eternal frost, within which no esculent can be reared.

7. Our first remark on this process of indefinite parsimony, and of laying forth to the uttermost on production, is, that it never can be realized. We

have endeavoured to trace its effects ; but we are quite sure, all the while, that they never can be exemplified. Capitalists will not persist in stinting themselves to the bare necessaries of life, and laying out the whole surplus of their profits on the extension of their business, when they come to find, that, after all, these profits are at length annihilated. Landlords will not persist in foregoing such indulgences as might be spared, if they come to find, that any returns which might be made only go to make out the support of an increasing population, instead of coming back in the shape of additional wealth, and additional command over the enjoyments of life to themselves. No man would continue to superintend the operations of a capital, no man would continue to administer and manage the affairs of a landed property, if such were to be the result of it. The moving forces which actuate, and which lead either to the operations of merchandise, or to the arrangements of agriculture, would cease, on this system of production to the uttermost, and of no consumption save for the object of production. If such a system were once entered on, it would speedily be checked by its profitless, and, in many instances, by its positively losing and ruinous results. So that it is not in opposition to any apprehended practical evil, but in opposition to a theory, that we have been induced to frame, or at all to insist on our present argument.

8. But even though practicable, we should hold

it to be a process not at all desirable. That it would hasten the progress of agriculture, and so the growth of society in respect of population, is very certain. With a less amount of frugality in times past, we should have had, at this moment, a narrower domain of cultivation; and a domain so much the larger and more productive, had there been greater frugality, even though many owners and occupiers of land had starved or ruined themselves in the cause. There can be no doubt, that cultivation has often received a permanent stretch at the expense of an irrecoverable loss to the individual cultivator; and that, better than this, instances can be named, where, but for a large outlay on the part of owners, there are many extended improvements, at length yielding an ample, though distant return, which might have been postponed or never undertaken. Yet, with all these admissions, while we should deprecate the encroachments, by waste and extravagance, on agricultural capital; we should also deprecate the encroachments by parsimony, on the general habit of capitalists living in the enjoyment of their profits, and land-owners in the enjoyment of their rents. For ourselves, we have no fear whatever of the former encroachment, and would again advert to that beautiful compensation, by which the excessive love of present enjoyment on the part of spendthrifts, when carried to the length of abridging their capital, does, by its effect on supply and price, call forth a counteractive force in the opposite direction—by inviting others, in whom the love of gain predominates, the more to extend their operations, whether in trade or in husbandry. We have no alarm for the effect of economic theories on the habit of individuals; but even though they had the influence, which they have not, we should hold it a thing to be regretted, if they led our capitalists either to spend more, or to spare more, than they would spontaneously. We should rather confide the progress of agriculture to the improvement of its own machinery, and its own methods, than hasten that progress unnaturally by an extreme parsimony, whether among the owners or the occupiers of land. We have no demand for a forced increase either of food or population; neither do we look on that system as being at all friendly to our species, which, by an abridgment on the free control of every man over his own revenue, would either speed the advances of cultivation beyond the rate at which it might otherwise proceed, or carry it beyond the boundary at which it would otherwise stop. The final result of such a system, when consummated and brought to its perfection, were an agriculture carried not merely to the limit beyond which it could not produce so much as pay its own expenses, but to the limit beyond which it could not produce at all. Our preference is for an agriculture that stopped at the upper extremity of the deficient soils, rather than an agriculture that did not stop till it reached their lower extremity. In very proportion to the progress made among the deficient soils, are profits and rent encroached upon, and the disposable class dwindles away, by successive abridgments, till the last man is transferred to the agricultural or the secondary. We repeat, that we have no value for such a consummation; and, infinitely rather than this ultra agrarianism, would we have a more limited, because, along with this, we should also have the composition and the materials of a more secure and far happier society. We see not the good of an addition to the mere numbers of the commonwealth, if it can only be effected at the expense of the whole, and to the utter ruin of certain great interests which cannot otherwise be provided for than with a disposable population; implying, no doubt, the means of leisure and luxury to an opulent class, but implying also, beside a thousand bland and beneficent influences on the comfort and moral state of all classes, an ability on the part of the ruling power, to appropriate of these means for all the best and highest objects of an enlightened patriotism.

9. This is a great question; and something of far mightier import than the maintenance of a rank and a property for the upper classes is involved in the determination of it. We hold that, on the moment when agriculture overpasses its natural limit, and enters on the deficient soils, the condition of the general peasantry is put into a state of fearful precariousness. And it matters not whether this shall happen by a scheme of home colonization for the purposes of charity, or by the schemes

and speculations of over-trading, either for the sake
of a profit that wont be realized, or on the false
system, that all unproductive expenditure is ruinous.   If the first, or an undertaking of charity for
the good of others, we can prove, that though it
may land us in a greater, it will land us also in a
more wretched population.*   If the second, or an
undertaking of business for the good of ourselves,
it cannot long be persisted in under a continued
experience of the losses which are incurred by it;
and it is always to the distress of multitudes, when
any enterprise of industry, because of its unproductiveness, behoves to be abandoned.   We therefore deem it an alternative altogether big with
efficacy on the ultimate condition of our species,
whether they shall keep within the natural limit,
or, breaking through among the deficient soils,
push onward to the extreme limit of the agriculture.
Our preference is wholly, and that for the sake of
the prosperity of all classes, to the former term of
this alternative.   We should rather the liberal consumption of their rents, than the yearly absorption
of them in losing schemes of husbandry, on the
part of the landed-proprietors.   We should rather
a high rate of profit, upheld by a large expenditure
on the part of capitalists, than the utter degradation of this class by a parsimony that would annihilate profit, and sink their condition to that of the
general population; even although this larger expenditure and larger profit did somewhat retard

* Again see the Appendix, C.

the progress of agriculture.   And we should infi-
.nitely rather, on the part of labourers, behold them
keeping within the superior soils, in more limited
number, but in larger sufficiency, than flowing
over on the deficient soils, and there bringing down,
by the very weight of their redundancy, the state
and circumstances of the whole order to which
they belong.   We are sensible that, at this rate,
we should have a more contracted agriculture, and
therefore a less populous world ; but our preference
is for a higher wage and higher profit too with a
narrower, rather than a lower wage and profit with
a wider cultivation.   It is at the natural limit of
cultivation that we should feel disposed to take
our most resolute stand—assured as we are, that if
the attempt to pass beyond it be, from whatever
cause, largely and systematically prosecuted, a
general want and wretchedness among labourers
or capitalists or both, would follow in its train.

10. But it is now time for addressing ourselves
to the argument of our more recent economists,
for the impossibility of a general glut, in the terms
which they themselves have employed when pro-
pounding it.   Their reason for their being no such
thing as over-production, or for a general glut being
impossible, is, that any partial over-stockings of the
market which may accrue, arise, not from an excess of commodities upon the whole, but from the
excess of certain commodities, and so a wrong or
mistaken distribution of them.   They ground their
proposition on the indefiniteness of human wants,

or rather of human desires, in virtue of which, they affirm, there can be no excess in the supply, if known only what the desires specially are. The mal-adjustment in the market, according to them, has arisen, not from the desires of men being over-satiated with too many objects, but from these desires not being met by the right objects. If, for example, there be an excessive quantity of cotton goods in the market, they become immoderately cheap, and purchase less than they otherwise would, of all other commodities, which of course are in reference to this one commodity immoderately dear. This must proceed, it is argued, from an excess of labour employed in the preparation of cotton goods, and a corresponding deficiency of labour in the preparation of the other articles which come into exchange with them. Had a certain portion of labour, then, been transferred from that quarter, where it has been in excess, to those quarters in which it has been deficient—the equilibrium would have been restored, and the cotton goods been exchanged, with all others, at a fair relative value. At this rate, there would have been no glut of any one commodity; and yet the quantity of commodities, on the whole, would have been as large as ever. On these grounds it is contended, that there can be no glut arising from over-production in the general, but only from a miscalculation as to the real state of the demand; and so a disproportionately large supply of certain articles of merchandise, with a corresponding defect and diminution in the supply of others.

11. Now, in the first place, it must be obvious, that so long as the food of a country is ahead of its population, there is no danger of such a general glut extending to all commodities, as shall produce general distress among labourers; and less danger than otherwise, of such a partial glut in some of them, as shall bring distress to certain classes of labourers. The holders of this food, are the holders of that which is the chief ingredient in the maintenance of families; and, holding it in excess, there can be no doubt, on the average, of an ample remuneration for the products of manufacturing industry. Even should the first holders, the landed proprietors, confine themselves exclusively to the use of certain favourite commodities, and neglect the others; by their more intense demand for the former, they raise their price, and transfer to the venders of certain articles the whole of that surplus food, which might have otherwise been distributed among the venders of all articles. But after this food, or which is the same thing, the power of lifting it, has been placed in the hands of the second holders, the fortunate calculators on the taste of the original ones, there will still be a surplus to them, the whole food being in excess to the population, which rather than left to moulder in their own idle possession, will find its way either to such articles as can be found, or to the purchase of labour for the preparation of other articles. It is thus that, in the state now supposed, the products of industry will seldom miss being exchanged

with a liberal maintenance to workmen; or, at all events, workmen will seldom miss of a liberal maintenance.   Capitalists may suffer a diminution in their gains, or even a positive loss, by miscalculation.   But in a general excess of food, this will not affect the general comfort of labourers; as exemplified now in America, and as perhaps exemplified in various stages, in the enlargement of European agriculture since the termination of the middle ages.

12. But periods of general comfort are periods of frequent and early marriages; and so of more frequent, as well as larger families.   An increasing population follows in the train of increasing food, and at length overtakes and presses on it.   That the pressure be felt, even long before the agriculture has come to its uttermost perfection, it is enough if the rate of increase in the population exceed the rate of increase in the means of subsistence.   The nearer the agriculture is to its extreme limit, the pressure will be the more felt; and it will be greatest of all, when, instead of a slowly receding barrier, the food of the country has reached its maximum, and the barrier has become stationary.   Hence the straitness that is felt in the old countries of Europe, as marked by the tide of emigration, compared with America; where vast tracts of yet unbroken land await the enterprise of adventurers, and afford additional harbourage for additional millions of families.   It is in the former countries, where those gluts, which create a re-action of poverty and distress amongst the working classes, are of most fre-

quent occurrence.   It is there that miscalculation occurs most readily, and it is also followed up by the severest consequences.   It is in countries of saturated population, where the workmen who had been engaged in the preparation of a neglected commodity, experience the most fearful distress, when dismissed in thousands by their employers, because unable, from the want of returns, to up-hold their establishments.   Had this taken place in a country where there was a sufficiency of food for all, the discarded labourers might still have met with their subsistence in return for some new service to those who were the holders of it.   But there is no such resource, when the food is already engrossed by those more fortunate of their class, who have been engaged in the preparation of the more favoured commodities.   It is thus that, in every country so situated, when there is any disproportion among the manufactured articles which are brought to market, there must fall a weight of suffering on certain classes of the industrious ; even the makers of the articles which are in excess.   But it is a mis-take to imagine, that by simply rectifying this dis-proportion, the suffering will be done away.   It would only be more divided than before.   There might be no increase of severe distress in any one quarter ; but in exchange for this, there would be a straitness and certain feeling of penury amongst all the operatives in the land.   Still there would be a glut ; though not proceeding from excess in cer-tain *manufactured* articles, with a corresponding de-

ficiency in others. After the adjustment of the best
relative proportion had been established between
them, there would remain a glut of these commodities upon the whole ; and that proceeding from
an anterior glut, not to be rectified by any skill in
the transference or new distribution of capital; even
a glut of human beings, which nothing can prevent,
but the reign of prudence and principle amongst
families; and nothing can correct, but the famine,
and disease, and war, which are so many chastise-
ments inflicted by the hand of nature, on human
guilt and human improvidence.

13. It is vain to say that, in these circumstances,
a transference of labour should be made from
manufactures to agriculture.   We have already
seen, that there is not room for an indefinite employment of labourers in the one department more
than in the other.   The population who are now
working on the land last entered, or on the land
that is placed along the extreme margin of cultivation, only obtain from it a produce which feeds
the agricultural labourers and their secondaries,
and which remunerates the capitalists.   An additional population, if it anticipate and exceed the
natural progress of agriculture, as already explained, behoved to enter upon land of inferior
quality to this; which land could only continue to
be cultivated with loss to the capitalists, or by
means of an under-fed or inferiorly-maintained
population.   It is thus, that there can be demonstrated to exist a limit all round to the employment

of labourers. And for the right direction of philanthropy, for the purpose of giving effect to her devices and her doings, to save the wasteful or the pernicious expenditure of her powers, it is well that all the false lights should be extinguished, which may have heretofore bewildered her, and that she should be no longer misled by a delusive confidence in impotent or fruitless expedients.

14. There is nothing more fitted to inspire this delusive confidence, than the doctrine which we now endeavour to expose. It suggests the idea of an indefinite harbourage for the people,—let them multiply and increase to whatever extent they may. It gives a virtue unlimited to credit and commerce, and the enterprise of merchants ; and removes from contemplation that barrier to the extension of agriculture, which must ever prove a barrier, alike firm and impracticable to the extension of trade. It overlooks the obvious truth, that there may be too much production, just because there may be too many producers. It is this which may give rise to a general glut, at least of all but the first necessaries of life. It is but a poor evasion, that because there is a deficiency in these, the glut is not universal ; so that if all sorts of products were included, the doctrine has still a foundation to rest upon. It needs but one qualification to meet this. *Generally*, and with one single exception, even that of food, there may be an excess of products ; and *universally*, or inclusive of food and of all things else, there may be an excess of productive

effort.   We shall at length come to a limit, beyond which the expense incurred in the fabrication must exceed the expense of the thing fabricated.   At, or rather beyond, the natural margin of cultivation, we see this truth in all its nakedness; stripped of those accompaniments which, in the shape of marketing, and money, and exchanging processes, but obscure the character of the proceeding without essentially changing it.   Then it becomes quite palpable,—for then the food which has been consumed by workmen, during the process of their labour, exceeds in quantity the food which they raise. There is no mere distribution which can avert this calamity; a calamity that, wherever it occurs, is felt throughout the whole community of labourers. And a scanty return for the labour bestowed on the production of the one commodity of food, is very generally associated with a glut of all other commodities.   Commensurate to a smallness of produce in the department of agriculture, is there a smallness of price in the department of commerce and manufactures.   When immediately, and without exchange, there is a scanty return for the last agricultural labour expended on our overwrought fields, then mediately, and with exchange, is there a like scanty return for all manufacturing labour, and that because of our overstocked markets.   It is thus that starvation, or more severe distress, may be realised from the want of first necessaries; in the midst of general abundance, both as to the second necessaries and luxuries of life.   This, if there be not a virtuous and well-educated commonalty, is the ultimate state of every industrious nation; a state from which it can only be saved, not by the multiplication of its products, but by a wholesome and moral restraint on the multiplication of its people.

15. This, then, is the substantial refutation of the new doctrine—that there can be no glut, if capitalists, in their speculations, would but speculate soundly—or, that they cannot overload the market, if they would but select and offer the right commodities for sale. The reasoning in behalf of this doctrine we hold to be wrong, even though we should admit the supposition whereon it rests— which is, that the object proposed, in every presentation of commodities for sale, is to obtain other commodities in exchange for them. Although this were true, still there is one sense in which, notwithstanding the nicest possible adjustment, in the way of proportioning the respective articles to the respective demand for them, there yet would be a glut. There might be an over-population of the country, and so a glut of men—who, with the best possible accommodation of their industry to the taste and the wants of those who hold the materials of human sustenance in their hands, may still find the products of their industry to be too abundant, and therefore too cheap for their obtaining an adequate maintenance in return for them. The escape from this conclusion is, that still the glut is resolvable into a mistake in point of proportion, food

being in defect, and all other commodities in excess ; and that so a rectification would be brought
about, were a portion of the capital transferred
from the preparation of the latter to that of the
former—or, speaking generally, from manufactures
to agriculture. But this goes on the presumption
that food can be raised by turning capital to this
object, just as indefinitely as houses, or ships, or
steam engines, can be multiplied in the same way.
The state of matters at the extreme margin of cultivation is not adverted to. It is forgotten why,
in the present circumstances of the country, that
is the margin ; and why it cannot, without loss,
be carried further onward or downward than it
actually has been. The ulterior land would not,
in the present state of agricultural science, feed
both the primary and secondary population who
should be employed on it. At least, it would not
do this, and also remunerate the capitalist for his
outlay. Nay, there is the utmost hazard, or rather
certainty, in such a state, of lighting upon soils so
ungrateful, as to convert profit into loss, and so
diminish the capital. It were well if this check to
indefinite enlargement could be fully kept in view;
for a recklessness to limits, and necessary laws on
the part of the *savans* in political economy, might
induce a corresponding recklessness on the policy
of statesmen, and even on the general habits of society. There are certain recent doctrines in the
science, which, beside being unfounded in themselves, have precisely this effect. In particular,

the position that there is no limit whatever to the means of productive and profitable employment, is really tantamount to the position, that there is no necessary limit on the numbers of the species. If work can thus be augmented indefinitely, then might workmen be augmented indefinitely.   It is under the influence of some such maxim as this, that a delusive confidence is encouraged, and relief for a straitened and over-burdened community is always sought for in the wrong quarter—in the enlargement of work, rather than the limitation of workmen—in the increase of produce, when nothing will effectually or permanently keep the country at ease, but a check on the increase of population.

16. We feel unwilling to protract an argument already too much lengthened out ; else, instead of viewing the outlay of capital for the sake of production in the form of a material, we might proceed to view it in the form of a monied investiture. Under this distinct aspect, the reasoning might be so managed as not only to demonstrate a fallacy in the conclusion of our adversaries, but to detect a fallacy in the assumption on which their argument rests.   And a further advantage would be, that without adverting to the limit of agriculture at all, the possibility of a universal glut might be established, in whatever state or at whatever stage society might be,—whether bordering on the extremity of its resources, as in some countries of Europe ; or in the rapid progression of infancy and

youth, as in America. Let any country be imagined, whose monied capital for the year amounts to a hundred millions, which by one revolution is replaced with a profit of ten millions, to be expended by the capitalists in the shape of revenue. Matters might be conceived to go on easily and prosperously at this rate, with a fair wage to the workmen, and a fair profit to their employers. And yet even here, without supposing any glut of men, there might be produced a glut of commodities; and that simply, from an increased desire, beyond a certain limit, on the part of the wealthy to become wealthier still. Under the influence of this desire, consumers might, at one and the same time, be led to save, and capitalists to speculate. Landed proprietors, for example, might by dint of economy abridge their expenditure by twenty millions in the year; and, instead of laying it out on those ulterior soils that would not repay, might lay it up in banks, and with the prospect of an interest for the sum deposited. This sum, on the other hand, lent out to capitalists, will increase their facilities of speculation; and extend the monied capital embarked in production, from one hundred to a hundred and twenty millions.* In this

* Here it may be said, that the capitalists will still have to start anew with only a hundred millions, because the twenty millions which they have borrowed, only come in place of the twenty millions that were withdrawn from expenditure the year before, and by which sum their capital fell short of being replaced in the last revolution of the economic cycle. This is only saying, that the glut takes place a year earlier than we think necessary to insist upon for the purposes of our argument

ratio then, will the monied cost of the country's products be increased; but what is the result when they are brought to market? Instead of being met by a proportional monied price, they will be met by a returning power, just as much reduced as the producing power has been increased. The twenty millions that have passed from one side to the other will overturn, for one year at least, the balance between production and consumption; and that year there is an over-production or glut, to the annihilation of all profit, and the positive loss of thirty millions over and above—or even of forty millions, if the capitalists spend as much in the shape of revenue as before. At all events, the capital of a hundred and twenty millions, laid out on commodities, would be met by ninety millions only on the part of purchasers.

17. It cannot surely be said, in this instance, that still the producers had erred in working up more of certain commodities than were wanted. Their error simply lay in over-production; and this was an error, from the consequences of which no imaginable shifting of the production to other commodities could have saved them. What new accommodation to the taste of their customers who had only ninety millions to spend, could have enabled them to dispose with a profit, the hundred and twenty millions worth of goods which they had brought to market? The consumers did not want other commodities in lieu of those which were presented. They simply wanted to be richer than

before ; and that, not by possessing themselves in greater abundance than before of certain special commodities, but by possessing themselves of a greater general power than before to purchase all commodities. It is the oversight of this distinction, we think, which has led to this new doctrine on the subject of gluts. When a consumer refuses certain commodities, it is not always, as has been assumed, because he wants to purchase others in preference—but he wants to reserve entire the general power of purchasing. And when a merchant brings commodities to market, it is not generally in quest of other commodities to be given in return for them ; so that were these other commodities in defect, then had a portion of the capital expended on the first been transferred to the second, the balance would have been restored ; and neither set of commodities being either too cheap or too dear, there would have been a glut of neither. This is not the way of it. The proper object of the merchant is not to obtain, in return for the articles wherein he deals, any one species of commodities more than another ; but it is to extend his general power of purchasing all commodities. It makes no valid evasion, that money is a commodity. This may complicate the question, but does not affect its essential character. The truth is, that the real metallic money for which a merchant has any use, does not amount to more than a small fraction of his capital, even of his monied capital ; all of which, though estimated in money, can be made, on the strength of written contracts, to describe its orbit, and be effective for all its purposes, with the aid no doubt of coin, but of coin amounting to an insignificant proportion of the whole. The great object of the monied capitalist, in fact, is to add to the *nominal* amount of his fortune. It is that, if expressed pecuniarily this year by twenty thousand pounds for example, it should be expressed pecuniarily next year by twenty-four thousand pounds. To advance his capital, *as estimated in money*, is the only way in which he can advance his interest as a merchant. The importance of this object to him is not affected by fluctuations in the currency, or by a change in the real value of money. It is possible that he may succeed in advancing his fortune, by the business of one year, from twenty to twenty-four thousand pounds; and yet, from a decline in the value of money, he may not have increased thereby his command over the comforts and conveniencies of life. Still it was as much his interest to have engaged in the business, as if money had not so fallen; for else, his monied fortune would have remained stationary, and his real wealth would have declined in the proportion of 24 to 20. Better than lose this ground, is it for him to have laboured as he did, even though he should only succeed in keeping himself even with what he was at the outset. So that the great aim of every trading capitalist is, to increase his fortune as estimated in money. Commodities are not his terminating object, save in the spending

of his revenue, and when he purchases for the sake
of consumption. In the outlay of his capital, and
when he purchases for the sake of production,
money is his terminating object. If he start at
present with a certain sum expressed in pounds
shillings and pence, the great end of his exertion
or enterprise is, that after the current speculation is
completed, he might start anew on another speculation, with a larger sum, expressed as before in
pounds shillings and pence; whether these have
meanwhile increased or decreased in their value.
Had this consideration been kept in view, we feel
persuaded that the doctrine of the impossibility of a
universal glut would never have been framed.

18. There is nothing in the operations of credit
to affect, but rather to confirm this reasoning.
Generally speaking, when men trade upon credit,
the only difference which it makes is, that they
trade not with their own capital, but with that of
other people; and there is nought surely in this,
which should lead us to modify any of our conclusions on the subject of capital. Very often too,
when trading upon credit, it is not strictly with
the capital of others; and yet it may be a credit
which has a substantial basis to rest upon. A
landed proprietor may bind himself to a future
payment, on a written deed or instrument which he
makes over to a trader; and in this way a species
of wealth, that is not fitted in itself to perform the
functions of monied capital, is made available for
this end. The truth is, that his written engage-

ments, just like the notes issued by a bank whose credit is unexceptionable, because grounded on the immense landed wealth of its proprietors, have in them all the virtue of money. It is curious to trace the effect of such an operation. We can imagine an additional ten millions created in this way; and that at a time when the trade of the country was moving evenly and surely, with the annual outlay of capital to the extent of a hundred millions, and the return of a hundred and ten. If the additional ten millions that we now suppose, are created for the purposes of speculation, this has just the effect of advancing the cost of all the means and materials of manufacture; and so, causing an outlay of a hundred and ten with the old return of a hundred and ten, profit would be annihilated. If the additional ten millions be created for the purposes of extravagance, this has just the effect of advancing the price of all the finished articles in trade and manufactures; and so, causing a return of a hundred and twenty to the old outlay of a hundred, profit would be advanced from ten to twenty millions. In either way there would be effected, not the reduction of wealth, but the rotation of it. Should landed proprietors over-speculate to the extent of ten millions, to that extent do they mortgage their estates; and their creditors may be traced to the holders of the means and materials in manufacture, who, by a commensurate rise in the price of these, have become as much richer as the speculatists have become poorer. Or, should landed proprietors overspend to the extent of ten millions, to that extent also do they mortgage their estates; and their creditors may be traced to the holders of all sorts of finished articles for sale, who, by a commensurate rise in the price of these, have become as much richer as the spendthrifts have become poorer. In the latter case, the error lies in turning to revenue that which should have been suffered to remain unalienated and undisturbed in the bosom of their property. In the former case, the error (and in spite of all the demand which there is by economists for capital to the uttermost, and production to the uttermost, the one is just as great an error as the other) lies in turning to capital that which should have been suffered to remain alike undisturbed and unalienated.

19. However interesting to pursue credit into all its issues and final consequences, we must not detain ourselves among the varieties and numerous modifications of which it is susceptible. We shall only instance the case when credit is entirely fictitious, but in virtue of a delusive confidence obtains currency to its notes or instruments for a time—as to the bills which are drawn and accepted by men of no capital, and the issue of engagements by a bank beyond its power of liquidation, should they have been turned to the prosecution of rash and ruinous undertakings. These, while their credit lasts, have the same power of effecting exchanges as money itself has; and one can imagine, that in this way there may be sent afloat into the world of

enterprise an additional sum of ten millions, while
the whole pecuniary returns for the outlay of monied capital were the same as before.   There behoved, in consequence, to be a diminution of profit
to the extent of ten millions.   Amid the general
losses which ensue by this overtrading, the adventurers, it is possible, may come in for a fractional
share of the returns along with the previous traders
amongst whom they have thrust themselves.   But
in as far as fictitious credit in the hands of some
has thus made good its encroachments, it will be
found to have been by the shifting of a solid capital that was before in the hand of others, now el-
bowed out by the more fortunate gamblers who
have succeeded them.   One melancholy effect
often is, that labourers, thrown adrift and defrauded
of their wages, have to live many days in penury.
But for this excessive and unwarrantable speculation they may have continued in their wonted fulness ; so that in this instance, too, capital may be
said to have been forced, though by anticipation,
out of that which should have been left to its proper
destination; and which, instead of being speculated
with by merchants in the shape of capital, ought
to have been spent by workmen in the shape of
revenue.

20. At all events, the phenomena of credit, though
we can afford to dwell upon them no longer, lend
the most ample and satisfactory confirmation to our
views on the subject of capital.   In a season of
great commercial distress, occasioned by many

failures, we often hear the calamity ascribed to so
many people trading upon credit, instead of trading
with capitals of their own.   But this very circumstance proves, that capital cannot be carried beyond
a certain limit in any country.   Grant that the sum
embarked this year on mercantile transactions was
raised by credit from a hundred to a hundred and
ten millions, there need have been no failure, had
the return for this sum, in the price of the goods
prepared and brought by it to market, been a hundred and ten millions, with a sufficient profit beside
to all who were engaged.   But if, instead of this,
the return is but a hundred and ten millions without
any profit, then, on the supposition that capitalists
have lived as usual, there must be failures to the
amount of ten millions.   It is not, however, the
mere circumstance of these commodities being
manufactured partly by capital and partly by credit
that has produced this result.   It is simply the
excess of commodities over the effective demand
for them ; an excess that would have been the same
although wrought up altogether on capital, instead
of partly on capital and partly on credit.   If, after
that a hundred millions were embarked on the
yearly business of the country, there was no room
for adventurers trading in addition on a credit of
ten millions, there would have been just as little
room for them trading to this amount with capitals
of their own.   The same loss would have ensued,
with this only difference, that capitalists to the
amount of ten millions would have lost their own,

instead of adventurers losing the same sum to other people. In the one case, the rash adventurers, and they who trusted them, would have received their chastisement. In the other case, the excess of capital would have been lopped off. Whether it be an excess of production from rash adventure or redundant capital, the result is altogether similar. And thus it is, that just as population, when pressing on the food of a country, limited in its power of subsisting labourers, receives a check by poverty and disease; so capital, when pressing on the business of a country, limited in its power of returning the outlays with a profit, receives as effectual a check by the losses of real, and the bankruptcies of fictitious capitalists.

21. In conclusion, we would only observe, though at the hazard of some reiteration, that the number of human beings in a country, is very nearly on a level with the amount of human subsistence, and tends to go beyond it. Labour is the return given by the general population, to those who uphold them in the necessaries of life; and the products of this labour, may be either turned by their owners into self-consumption, or laid up by them for the purpose of future production. But just as labourers cannot be multiplied beyond the possibility of a wage to sustain them, so neither will the products of antecedent labour, be multiplied and employed as capital, beyond the limit at which profits are diminished, so as to be on a level with the least possible maintenance of the

capitalists. When a country is improved to the uttermost, and is, therefore, pressing on its ultimate resources, the necessaries of life have become stationary in their amount; and then nothing can raise wages but a diminished population, and nothing can raise profit but a diminished capital. An increase in the necessaries of life, would afford room for the enlargement of both. So long as there is fresh land to be entered upon, there is scope for the investiture of more agricultural capital; and in the larger demand of an increasing population for second necessaries, as well as the larger demand of the new, and now wealthier proprietors for luxuries, there is scope for the investiture of more manufacturing capital also. While this is in progress, profit is upheld from sinking so rapidly as it would; and so the interest of money, which is proportional to profit, is higher in America, than in the old, and, at the same time, well-governed countries of Europe. But though, for a long period, agriculture may thus draw capital after it, it follows not that capital can, beyond a certain limit, force agriculture. In proportion as that limit is approached, profit falls; and capital, ever tending to an overflow, feels itself beset within the confines of a field too narrow for the advantageous occupation of it. The days have been, when the great prescription of political empiricisn, for the distresses of a weak or wretched country, was an increase of population; but this has now gone by. The next remedy, at one time embodied in the acts of government, and still proceeded on in the schemes of provincial or parish philanthropy, was the increase of employment ; but this too, in ways innumerable, has proved itself to be a resource that is not indefinite. There is still an unbroken faith in the increase of capital, as a specific for the distempers of a land that labours, and is oppressed under the multitude of its suffering families. But this device too, is impotent like the rest ; and we must look to some other quarter still, ere we can find the secret principle of a nation's secure and permanent well-being.*

* In the following extracts from Say's Political Economy, the reader will observe his assertion of the doctrine which we have attempted throughout this chapter to expose as erroneous :—

" Neither individuals, nor communities, can extend or fertilize their territory, beyond what the nature of things permits ; but they have unlimited power of enlarging their capital, and, consequently, of setting at work a larger body of industry, and thus of multiplying their products ; in other words, their wealth."—Book I. Chap. v.

" Moreover, it may be remarked, that the powers of man, resulting from the faculty of amassing capital, are absolutely indefinable ; because, there is no assignable limit to the capital he may accumulate, with the aid of time, industry, and frugality."—Book I. Chap. xi.

In the following extract, he seems to overlook what the real distinction is, between an old and a new country, in respect of the slow accumulation of capital in the former, and its rapid accumulation in the latter ; and, in overlooking this distinction, he of course must miss altogether the perception of any absolute limit, beyond which capital cannot be extended :—

" In point of fact, capital is of much more rapid accumula-

CHAPTER VI.

ON THE LIMITS OF A COUNTRY'S FOREIGN TRADE,
AND ITS SUPPOSED POWER TO FURNISH A PEOPLE
WITH EMPLOYMENT AND MAINTENANCE.

I. *The case of a country whose population is
limited by its agricultural produce.*

1. The next resource which dazzles the imagination of philanthropists and statesmen, is foreign

tion in new countries, than in countries long civilized. It
would seem as if the colonists, in abandoning their native
country, leave behind them part of their vicious propensities;
they certainly carry with them little of that fondness for show,
that costs so dear in Europe, and brings so poor a return. No
qualities, but those of utility, are in estimation in the country
they are going to; and consumption is limited to objects of
rational desire, which is sooner satisfied than artificial wants.
The towns are few and small; the life of agriculturists, which
they must necessarily adopt, is, of all others, the most economical; finally, their industry is proportionally more productive, and requires a smaller capital to work upon.
" The character of the colonial government usually accords
with that of individuals; it is active in the execution of its
duties, sparing of expense, and careful to avoid quarrels; thus
there are few taxes, sometimes none at all; and, since the
government takes little or nothing from the revenues of the
subject, his ability to multiply his savings, and, consequently,
to enlarge his productive capital, is very great. With very
little capital to begin upon, the annual produce of the colony

trade. This is held to be a fountain-head of wealth and of employment; which, in the eyes of many, are altogether indefinite. Such is the virtue, indeed, associated with the very names of capital and commerce, that many wonder how, in a country where these have attained an unexampled magnitude, there should be any distress, and far more, aught like general distress among its families. One might understand how a people, confined within the limits of their own home trade, should be in a straitened condition. But open the

very soon exceeds its consumption. Hence the astonishingly rapid progress in its wealth and population; for human labour becomes dear in proportion to the accumulation of capital; and it is a well known maxim, that population always increases according to the demand."—Book I. Chap. xix.

It is pretty evident from this passage, that, in order to keep up as fast a rate of accumulation in an old as in a new country, all which Mr. Say holds to be necessary, is, that the individuals, and government of the former, should equal those of the latter, in frugality and good conduct.

We conclude this list of extracts, with a passage which depones to the fact, of the speedy restoration of a spent, or diminished capital, to its original magnitude; but indicates the prevalent misconception which obtains, as to the principle or reason of the fact.

" It would seem that there exists in the politic, to a stronger degree than even in the natural body, a principle of vitality and elasticity, which cannot be extinguished without the most violent pressure. One cannot look into the pages of history, without being struck with the rapidity with which this principle has operated. It has nowhere been more strikingly exemplified, than in the frequent vicissitudes that our own France has experienced, since the commencement of the Revolution."—Book III. Chap. vi.—See Appendix E. on Profit.

world to them, and the conception is, that all
straitness and limitation are necessarily put an end
to. With access to all the markets of the globe,
it is felt, as if every clime, and every nation, were
made to contribute to our abundance ; and that a
horn, filled with treasure from the various regions
of the earth, were thereby poured over the towns
and villages of our land. The imagination is
greatly confirmed, when we see the largest towns
of the empire, in special connection with foreign
countries, and, to all appearance, upheld by the
demands and the payments of customers there.
The very existence of these large and flourishing
establishments, and the maintenance of their thousands, and tens of thousands of industrious families,
are ascribed to a foreign trade ; the annihilation of
which, would involve the annihilation, not merely
of their work, but of their livelihood, and the extension of which, it is thought, would carry along
with it a proportional extension of support for an
unprovided, or a yet unborn population.

2. And this popular imagination receives great
countenance from the representations and the views
of our most distinguished economists. Home
trade consists in the exchange of one set of home
products for another. But over and above these,
there might be commodities produced at home,
for which there is no demand within the country ;
and for which, therefore, no equivalents can be
obtained among ourselves. These Dr. Smith terms
the surplus produce of the nation, the exchange

of which, for equivalents from abroad, gives rise to foreign trade. Now, he so represents it as to give the impression, that without these equivalents there would have been no surplus produce—that the former, in fact, have stimulated the production of the latter—and that, therefore, without a foreign trade, we should have wanted not merely the exportation of a surplus, but the very existence of one. He clearly accredits foreign trade with a gain to the nation, equal to the value of this surplus, which, but for the excitement of what is given in return for it, would not, he intimates, have been called into being. Had there been nothing to import, there would, according to him, have been nothing to export; and this gives currency to the notion, that neither would our present exports, nor *aught else in place of them*, have been produced. At this rate the foreign trade is a superinducement on the home, which tells in the way of a distinct addition to the wealth and resources of the country. If a million of our people be employed in the manufacture of export commodities, there is a very general imagination, and certainly an imagination which the views of our distinguished economist do not serve to correct, but to confirm, that they are employed in a business which foreign trade has called into existence; and, as their employment is the vehicle of their support, that to this foreign trade we are indebted for the support of a large proportion of our families.

3. Let us now attend, for a moment, to the real

character and effect of these interchanges in foreign trade. Let us put, for an example, the two
countries of Britain and Portugal: the hardware
of the one country being exported, and the wine
of the other being imported; a million-worth of
hardware, and a million-worth of wine. The
manufacturers of hardware in Britain, become the
creditors of Portugal to the extent of a million—
and to the same extent do the wine-growers of
Portugal become the creditors of Britain. And
there is a set of debtors, as well as a set of creditors in
each of the countries: the Portuguese debtors being the receivers of the hardware, and the British
debtors being the receivers of the wine. The ex-
porters in each country look to the consumers of
the other as their customers; yet, in fact, neither
receive payment, by a direct pecuniary remittance,
from those to whom they have sold their respective
commodities. The matter is adjusted in this way;
and the description applies generally to the interchanges of foreign trade. The importers of hardware into Portugal pay their debt, not to the ex-
porters of the hardware in this country; but they
pay it to the exporters of wine in Portugal, and
receive in return for their payment an order on
the importers of wine in Britain. This order they
remit to the exporters of hardware in Britain,
who, on presenting it to the importers of wine,
there receive payment. Generally speaking then,
the adjustment takes place by bills of exchange,
which have the effect of making over the debtors

in Portugal, not to their creditors in Britain, but to the creditors in Portugal; and the debtors in Britain, not to their creditors in Portugal, but to their creditors in Britain. The parties thus brought into relation, may be alike unknowing and unknown to each other; transacting, as they do, through the medium of the bill-broker, who alone comes into contact with both. Still, virtually and in effect, the export manufacturers of our hardware, receive their payment from the importers of our wine. They hold themselves to be labouring in the service, and to be maintained by the wealth of customers abroad; but, in point of fact, they are labouring in the service, and are maintained by the wealth of customers at home.

4. It is practically felt by commercial men, and clearly demonstrated by economical writers, that the power of exporting with advantage, is limited or measured by the power of importing with advantage; and that when the one stops, the other must stop also. The export trade ceases to be beneficial, on the moment that the returns which come back in the exchange between ourselves and all other countries cease to be disposable. The deficiency of imports from one foreign country may be made up, by an excess of imports from another; and a circuitous adjustment is then made by round-about bills of exchange. But a general deficiency of imports will lay an arrest on a farther increase of exports. In other words, we are enabled to send British commodities abroad, just be-

cause there is a demand for foreign commodities
at home.   The manufacturer of export articles is
just as much indebted for his maintenance to our
inland consumers, as the manufacturer of articles
for home consumption.   The only difference is,
that whereas the latter works up a commodity
which is immediately purchased by home consumers, the former works up a commodity which goes
to the purchase of that which is immediately purchased by them.   In as far as he prefers hardware
to wine, he gives a price for it to the manufacturer,
who in this instance works for the supply of the
home market.   In as far as he prefers the wine to
the hardware, he gives a price for it to the wine
importer, who is enabled thereby to meet the bills
of the export manufacturer who has been working
for the supply of the foreign market.   It is thus
that the export manufacturer works, though not
directly and ostensibly, yet virtually and really, in
the service of the inland consumer.   If not employed in the fabrication of that for which the inland consumer has demand, he is at least employed
in the fabrication of that which goes in exchange
for such things as the inland consumer has a value
and demand for.   He works up, not that which
the consumers at home want, but that which will
purchase what the consumers at home want.   He
is the instrument of obtaining for them their gratification, although that gratification comes to their
door in the shape of a foreign luxury.   In effect,
he labours for their enjoyment, and, in effect, by
them he is paid.

5. We are now able to appreciate the doctrine, that foreign trade not only provides a vent for our surplus produce; but that foreign trade called it into being. The million-worth of hardware exported to Portugal, may be denominated surplus produce; seeing that there is no effective demand for it at home. But neither would there have been effective demand for it in Portugal, had Portugal not had the power to purchase it; and what gives this power to her million-worth of wine, is just, that for that quantity of wine there is an effective demand, and, of course, a power to purchase it in this country. But for the million-worth of maintenance in the hands of our inland consumers, and discharged by them through the medium of the wine-merchant, or the export manufacturers of hardware, to that extent would our imports have been lessened, and to that extent would our exports have been lessened also. Virtually, it is an antecedent ability on the part of inland consumers, which called this surplus produce into being. In the order of dependence, or in the order of cause and effect, the primary rank is due to the inland consumers, and the secondary or derivative, to the export manufacturers. And the plain reason is, that the manufacturers cannot do without the maintenance, but the consumers can do without the wine. Should their maintenance be destroyed by a permanent blight that would reduce the fertility of our fields, their manufacture would cease; but should their manufacture be destroyed

by some barrier of interception that stopped both
the exportation of hardware and the importation
of wine, their maintenance would not, on that account, cease to be produced as liberally as before.
The effect of the first catastrophe would be a permanent loss to the country, both of a certain population, and of the fruits of their industry. The
whole effect of the second would be, a change of
one enjoyment for another to our inland consumers; and, not a loss of people, but merely a change
in the direction of their industry. We deny not the
temporary inconvenience of this transition from
one employment to another; but, after the transition had been effected, we should behold the same
spectacle of as great and industrious a population
as well employed and as well maintained as before.

6. On this subject, the history of wealth has given
rise to an erroneous philosophy of wealth. We
are aware that they are facts which form the materials of sound philosophy; yet a false philosophy
may be constructed of facts misinterpreted and
misapplied. And this we hold to have been strikingly exemplified in the case before us. It is quite
true, that at the termination of the middle ages, it
was mainly the presentation of luxuries from abroad,
which impressed a new habit upon our landlords,
and gave a new direction to their expenditure.
It is quite true that their insatiable appetite for
personal enjoyment, when once excited, proved a
far more powerful spur to the cultivation of their
farms, than a mere desire to support or to extend

the coarse and feudal hospitality of the olden times.
The love of finery and of sensual indulgence, greatly
more inclined them to make the most of their
estates, and to draw forth of them the uttermost
of their produce, than did the love of a crowded
attendance upon their persons, or of a crowded assembly in their halls. It is thus that commerce was
a moving force, which speeded their transition from
one habit of expenditure to another; and that it
was a transition which led to a far more strenuous
agriculture than heretofore. There can be no
doubt that the carpets, and the looking-glasses, and
the wines of other lands, gave an impulse to husbandry all over Europe; and that historically, at
that time of day, the produce of foreign parts had
in it a force of allurement, which not only attracted
to itself a pre-existent, but gave birth to a new
produce in the various countries of Christendom.
But now that the transition has been made, and
the modern habit of our landed proprietors has
been fully established; are we to imagine, that the
withdrawment of any one, or even of all foreign
luxuries put together, would cause the agriculture
to narrow itself within its ancient limits, or put so
much as one field or furrow of land out of cultivation? Whatever the wine of Portugal may have
done *then* in adding to cultivation, has it so much
as a particle of influence *now* in keeping up that
cultivation? Although port should, in all time
coming, disappear from our markets; is there a
landlord in Britain, who, on that account, would

let down the cultivation of a single acre of his property? Would he forego the hundred a year that
he wont to expend on this luxury, because the
luxury was no longer to be had? Would he bid
his tenants remit of their wonted activity, because
he had now remitted so much of their wonted rental—having no use for it, in consequence of this
stoppage which had taken place in one of the out-
goings of his previous expenditure? Though
debarred from one of its accustomed channels,
would he not find, and that most readily, new channels of expenditure, through which to impress on
industry some other direction, and to discharge the
same maintenance on an equal number of people
in some other employment? Would he refuse an
income so large as before, because, in the absence of
some luxury furnished by a single branch of foreign
trade, or because, in the absence of all the luxuries
which foreign trade had placed within his reach,
he was now at a loss for objects on which to lavish
as great an expenditure as before? And besides,
is there not a charm in the enlargement of income,
apart from all thought of the enlargement of expenditure? Wealth, no doubt, is an abstraction, when
separated from the comforts and enjoyments which
it purchases. But abstraction as it is, does it not
tell on human conduct with all the power of a living and substantial reality? When the offer is
made of an advanced rent for land, must the proprietor calculate on the additional wine, and dress,
and equipage, it will afford, ere he becomes alive

to the happiness of the offer, and is led to close with it? But do we stand in any need of this argument, in the exhaustless variety of nature's gratifications, and the infinitude of resources or openings for expenditure? Amid all the failures and fluctuations which take place, whether in home or foreign trade, will not the desire of a larger revenue, and with it of a larger command over the services of others, remain an indestructible principle in his bosom? Is any conceivable obstruction in the intercourse with other countries, so to change the nature of humanity in this country, that we should no longer behold the men of it in the same attitude as before, as keen in the feeling of their interests, as insatiable in their longings and aspirations, and each on the full stretch of endeavour for bettering his own condition and his own circumstances? Landlords would just be as eager to receive a rent, and tenants as busy in their callings to pay the rent, and appropriate the largest possible surplus to themselves. In other words, many a particular trade may be destroyed; but the great and primary aliment of all trade would not be destroyed. There might be a shifting of human labour; but there would be no lessening in the amount of it. And, in the act of shifting, there might be partial and temporary distress; yet, conceding this, we should surely and speedily behold as much well-paid industry as before—and that yielded by the hands of as large a population.

7. We may thus perceive what the whole effect

would be, were our trade with Portugal suspended, or even brought to permanent extinction. Our inland proprietors would lose their wine, and our export manufacturers would lose one of their markets. But though, on the one hand, the wine should be lost, the ability to purchase it is not therefore lost. It remains entire in the hand of its old possessors, and is ready to be discharged on the purchase of some other gratification. And, on the other hand, though the market should be lost, the maintenance of those who wont to prepare commodities for the market is not therefore lost. There is on the one side the spare maintenance, and on the other the unemployed population. We may be very sure that things will not continue in this state,—that, in the first place, the maintenance will not be suffered to lie waste; and, in the second place, that the population will not be suffered to lie unemployed. There will, to the proprietor, be the substitution of one enjoyment for another. There will, to the labourers, be the substitution of one employment for another. In as far as the revenue that wont to be expended on the wines of Portugal goes to the purchase of foreign articles, there is just the loss of one branch of foreign trade replaced by the extension of other branches. In as far as this revenue goes to the purchase of home articles, there is just a diminution of the foreign trade, compensated by a proportional enlargement of the home trade. Ultimately, there is no one interest affected by the change, but the interest of the consumers, who are now obliged to put up with an article which they like not so well as the one they have been forced to abandon. The very fact of their preference for Portuguese wine when they could get it, is a proof that there has been a sacrifice of taste in passing from the old luxury to the new; and so, a descent of enjoyment. This difference of enjoyment to them, is really the whole amount of the calamity which such a change can inflict upon the nation. Every other interest is comprehended in the price paid by the consumer, and which goes full fraught with all its powers and its blessings into the new direction that has now been opened up for it. It comprises as large a maintenance to the workmen. It comprises as large a profit to capitalists. And if the former luxury was taxed, and so made the vehicle of a revenue to government; this, too, enters as a constituent into the price, and the same price may still be made to comprise as large a public revenue as before.

8. We see, then, that the *terminus ad quem* of foreign trade, is consumption at home. The maintenance of all those engaged in it—the wages of the labourers—the profits of the capitalist—the tax laid on foreign articles,—these emanate not from the trade, but from the antecedent ability of consumers, who may be regarded as the real supports and fountain-heads of the trade. What is true of home, is true also of foreign trade. It should be

accredited with no more than with the commodities which it brings to the door of our inland
purchasers. This it does, but it does no more than
this. There is mysticism in the assertion, that a
stocking-maker does aught more for the nation
than simply contribute stockings; and there is just
as delusive a mysticism in the assertion, that the
wine trade of Portugal confers any other benefit
on the nation than simply the benefit of wine, or
the West India trade than sugar and coffee, or the
China trade than tea. We are aware of other and
far more magnificent interests being associated
therewith—as the sustenance of a great population;
and along with it, power, and public revenue, and
national greatness. It is imagined, that by the
excision of a given branch of foreign trade, there
would be an excision from the land of the means
and the maintenance of all who are engaged in it;
whereas, there would simply be an exchange to
the consumers of one article of enjoyment for another; and to the people, the exchange of one kind
of employment for another, but with as ample
means and maintenance as before. The East and
the West Indies are regarded as the two hands of
the empire; and the imagination is, that were our
connection with these destroyed, Britain would suffer as much as from the lopping off of two hands, or,
in other words, would be shorn of its strength and
its capacity for action, in virtue of this sore mutilation. It would positively be shorn of nothing but

its sugar and tea.* Were our intercourse with the
East and the West conclusively broken up, we

* I argue on the supposition of these being their only, as
they form their main commodities. When, to vindicate the
importance of foreign trade, the superior worth and usefulness
of its import articles are insisted on, as of timber from Norway,
or nitre from the East Indies, which are important in a national view, the reasoning proceeds on a principle to which we
render all homage; its subserviency to the benefit of consumers
at home, being the only principle, in fact, on which we concede
any value whatever to foreign trade. But this is not the only,
not even the chief principle, on which our mercantile economists would rate the importance of foreign trade. They look
to the interest of the sellers and not of the buyers; although
in the price paid by the buyers, every interest of the sellers is
comprehended.

And when once the real worth of foreign trade is placed on
its essential and only proper foundation, there is much that
can truly and without exaggeration be alleged in its behalf.
Even its very luxuries may fulfil, to a certain extent, the part
of necessaries in disguise. The tea, and sugar, and wine, which
come to us from abroad, supersede a very great consumption
in the shape of milk, or malt liquor, or spirits, which, though
not absolutely essential to subsistence, would still have been
indulged in, and so have trenched on the amount of that home
produce which now goes purely and nakedly to the purposes of
food. Even the food itself is often imported from abroad in
large quantities; but this forms a distinct case, and in our next
chapter it will form the subject of a distinct consideration.

Nay, it may so happen that, in virtue of its foreign trade, the
agriculture of our land may descend farther into the inferior
soils than had otherwise been possible. If any of the second
necessaries of life can be obtained, through its imports, with
less labour; or if any of our farm implements can, by the same
means, be either had cheaper, or made more effective; these
would obviously tell at the extreme limit of our agriculture,

should lose the services, first of our tea-grower, and then of our tea-sweetener—for so might these

and have the effect of somewhat pushing it onward to land of greater sterility.

And in those cases where we could have had a home substitute for some foreign luxury, without trenching on the food of our population; yet, if the actual preference is for the foreign luxury, it is because we have the enjoyment we like best at a less price, or, which is tantamount to this, a greater amount of that enjoyment for the same price. But this, too, is altogether an interest wherewith the consumers, and not the producers have to do. The producers will be equally well maintained by the consumers, in any way that the latter may choose to employ them. But it is the wisdom, and for the benefit of consumers, that they should encourage, by their demand, the foreign rather than the home trade; when, as the result of their so doing, they obtain either a better quality, or a greater quantity of enjoyment.

Still, with all these qualifications, had our estimate of foreign trade been reduced, and rectified, and set on its proper basis; governments would have as little thought of going to war for the purpose of giving laws to commerce, as of going to war for the purpose of giving laws to taste. They would have felt the matters of trade to be as much beyond their province, as the matters of fashion; and as little legislated in order to secure for us a market in other lands, as in order to arrange the dishes and wines of our entertainments, or the dresses of our ball-rooms.

The following extract from Say, is pertinent to the subject of this note :—

" Although all products are necessary to the social existence of man, the necessity of food being, of all others, most urgent and unceasing, and of most frequent recurrence, objects of aliment are justly placed first in the catalogue of the means of human existence. They are not all, however, the produce of the national territorial surface; but are procurable by com-

regions be denominated. It is thus that we would reduce the importance of foreign trade to its humbler but juster dimensions; and then assert the independence of Britain thereupon. The noble flotillas which periodically leave our shores, and return laden with the spoils of every climate, form altogether an imposing spectacle; and by which commerce has had a most bewildering glare thrown over it. But this commerce is really not a superinducement from abroad; it is the efflorescence of an inherent vigour and vitality at home. Foreign trade is not the creator of any economic interest; it is but the officiating minister of our enjoyments. Should we consent to forego these enjoyments, then, at the bidding of our will, the whole strength at present embarked in the service of procuring them, would be transferred to other services,—to the extension of home trade—to the enlargement of our national establishments—to the service of defence, or conquest, or scientific research, or Christian philanthropy. The only change would be a change of object and of end to consumers; and a change

merce, as well as by internal agriculture; and many countries contain a greater number of inhabitants than could subsist upon the produce of their land. Nay, the importation of another commodity may be equivalent to an importation of an article of food. The export of wines and brandies to the North of Europe, is almost equivalent to an export of bread; for wine and brandy, in great measure, supply the place of beer and spirits distilled from grain, and thus allow the grain, which would otherwise be employed in the preparation of beer or spirits, to be reserved for that of bread."

of employment, but not a lessening of their maintenance, to those who are now labouring in the various departments and stages of foreign trade for
our gratification. It would greatly subserve the
cause of peace and of enlightened policy, were this
juster estimate on the subject of all trade, and more
especially of foreign trade, adopted by statesmen.
The great majority of wars are mercantile wars,
which never might have been, but for the illusion
of those great names and imaginary interests that
are associated with commerce. We feel persuaded,
that the fearful conflicts of other days would not
now be repeated, could the nation but clearly see
that the only interest for which it was called upon
to fight, was a somewhat more luxurious break-
fast, or a richer dye to the vestments which covered
them, or an easier access to certain wines, or a
more liberal importation of shawls and silks, and
figs and oranges. It was never the menaced loss
of one or all of these which formed the jealousy
or the provocative that led to war. It was the apprehension of a far more serious disaster,—the loss
of revenue to some large class of our merchants,
of support to some large class of our industrious
population. Had foreign trade been seen in its
true character and effect, we cannot imagine that,
for the preservation of a monopoly or a sugar
island, so many a struggle would have been entered on. A sense of national honour may still
have excited the spirit of discord among the king-
doms of the earth—but not a sense of national interest.

9. But it would appear as if no experience could unschool our politicians and patriots out of their obstinate imaginations upon this subject. In the loss of our American colonies did many a statesman anticipate the downfal of the British nation. And in spite of the utter vanity of this anticipation, do they cling with as fond tenacity to our remaining colonies as before, and would still brave in their defence the expenditure of countless millions. It is not seen, how, with the unabated fertility of our own fields, and those resources, far beyond the reach of any distant influence, which lie within the circle of our own shores, we would be in possession of as ample means as before for calling forth and rewarding the services of all our population. Could this only be apprehended, statesmen would not be so tremblingly alive to the interests of any particular trade, nor would they think the prosperity of our island grounded on aught so precarious as the brittle foundation of commerce and of the seas. They would leave commerce to its own spontaneous courses; and instead of undertaking, with anxious heart and uncertain hand, as their predecessors did before them, the guidance or guardianship of its concerns, they would sleep secure in the midst of all its fluctuations. But this never has been, nor is it yet the policy of statesmen. The doctrine of its natural insignificance is not understood by them; and both in the sigh of Napoleon's heart for ships, and colonies, and commerce, and the splendid vision of Canning, who

thought he had conjured up the resources of a new world, by which, through the conveyances of trade, to multiply without limit and without end the riches of our nation, do we recognise that subtle delusion which has misled the legislators of all ages.

10. The agriculture of China is represented as now pressing on its extreme limit, yet, over and above this, Dr. Smith tells us how much richer that country would have been by the accession of foreign trade. The only effect, we imagine, of foreign trade to a country circumstanced as China is said to be, were the withdrawment of a population from the direct service of ministering to the enjoyment of their maintainers by the preparation of home articles, to the indirect service of working up export articles for the purchase of commodities in foreign lands. There would be an accession to the enjoyment of the inland consumers, seeing they preferred the product of the foreign, to that of the home manufacture. But to the people, there would only be the transference of so many hands from one employment to another, without any accession either to their numbers or to their maintenance. To whatever extent a foreign trade was superinduced, to that extent the home trade would be diminished. And, in like manner, when a new market is opened up, the imagination is, that all the business created by it is a clear accession to the country. And hence the gratulations that we hear, both in and out of parliament, when the market of South America, or the free market of the East In-

dies, or any other ample and accessible field, is
presented to us for the egress of British commodities. But the truth is, that an egress can only be
sustained by means of an ingress ; nor will exports
continue to be carried out with advantage any
longer than the imports which come back in return
for them can be purchased at home. The only
advantage of a new market is, that the wares which
it offers may chance to be more agreeable to the
taste and the fancy of certain of our inland consumers, than those of any other markets which previously lay open to them. In which case, there
will be a transference of expenditure from old to
new articles of demand—the formation of a new
foreign trade, we admit, but at the expense either
of the home trade, or of another foreign trade that
had been formerly in existence. The extent of
our foreign trade is, in fact, limited by the means,
or by the extent, of human maintenance in the
hands of our inland consumers. The opening of
a new market can do no more for the general
wealth of our country, than the setting up of a new
stall can add to the wealth of customers at a fair.
It may present new commodities more agreeable to
the taste of purchasers, or even old commodities at
a cheaper rate than before. Either of these is an
undoubted advantage to customers. But it cannot
add to the amount of the purchase money ; so that
if the new stall be at all resorted to, it must be by
a partial forsaking of the old ones. The same is
true of the world at large, where each new country

that is opened for commercial enterprise may add
to the number and variety of our nation's markets,
yet not add to the general amount of its marketing.   There is thus a natural, and, for the time,
an insuperable barrier in the way of the extension
of foreign trade.   It is necessarily limited by the
wealth of the consumers at home.   And hence the
mockery of those splendid anticipations which
dazzle the fond eye of speculators, when, either by
political changes, or by the abolition of monopoly,
a new country is laid open to their enterprises.
The dream is speedily broken up ; and in the spectacle of glutted markets, both at home and abroad,
may we learn that there is a limit to the extension
of foreign trade, which no country can overpass.*

11. The truth of the principles which we have
laboured to expound, was put historically to the
test, when, on the one hand, Bonaparte, in utter
ignorance of them, thought he was levelling a
death-blow at Britain, by the exclusion of our
commodities from all the markets of the continent ;
and, on the other hand, our alarmists at home, in
equal ignorance of them, trembled for the result.
Neither of the parties understood, wherein lay the
secret of our country's strength and resources ;
that is, in the ability of our inland consumers to
turn the manufacturers of our prohibited exports
into any other direction, and in that direction to
support them equally well as before.   The truth
is, that the extinction of foreign trade in one

* See Appendix, F.—On Free Trade.

quarter, was almost immediately followed up, either by the extension of it in another quarter, or by the extension of the home trade. The stoppage of all intercourse with France, if it should hinder the exportation of our British cloths, would equally hinder the importation of their French wines; and, the price of these, paid by the in-land consumers, as it supported the manufac-turers engaged in the old line of commerce, would equally support them in some new line, most cer-tain to be struck out, on the former being aban-doned. Even had every outlet abroad been ob-structed, then, instead of a transference from one foreign market to another, there would just be a universal reflux towards a home market, that would be extended in precise proportion, with every suc-cessive abridgment which took place in our exter-nal commerce. We never deny the consequent change that would thus take place on the enjoy-ment of consumers; but, along with that, we again repeat, that after this revolution in our affairs, there would survive as large a maintenance to our labourers; as large a profit to our capitalists; and the means, with perhaps some new modifica-tion of taxes, of as large a revenue to government as before. The great apprehension, indeed, con-nected with the non-intercourse acts of other coun-tries, was, lest the public revenue should irreparably suffer from them; and an astonishment was felt, when, on comparing successive years and quarters of the national income, it was found that there had been no diminution. It is in beautiful accordance with these views, that a lessening in the produce of the customs was generally followed up by an enlargement in the produce of the excise, marking the re-action of the foreign on the home expenditure; and verifying, what we might with all confidence have expected beforehand, the certainty of a full compensation, if not in respect of luxury or physical enjoyment, at least in respect of every substantial economic interest; or of all in short which either patriot or philanthropist needs to care for.

12. It is not our province minutely to explain the variations of what has been called, the rate of exchange between two countries, or the causes on which they are dependent. But it is a truth, theoretically understood by economists, and experimentally felt by practical men, that the mutual imports and exports which pass and repass, cannot exceed a certain disproportion; that they must so reciprocate as to be nearly of equal value, the one to the other; or, at least, that there is a certain difference or excess of the one over the other, which neither of them can pass. The possible amount of exports is limited by the possible amount of imports, and conversely; and this is distinctly and numerically indicated by the state of the exchange. If there be a certain point at which the import trade ceases to be profitable, that determines the point at which the export trade ceases to be profitable. When there is a

deficiency of imports, this produces a state of the exchange unfavourable to the export merchant, and which goes in deduction from his profit; so that should he enlarge his exports any farther, the profit might cease to be a remunerating one. In other words, his power to export is limited by the power to import; and this latter power is evidently limited by the ability to purchase on the part of our inland consumers. It is therefore in vain to talk of the indefinite demand for our commodities on the part of other nations. This will avail us nothing for the extension of our trade, unless it be followed by an indefinite power on the part of our inland consumers, to purchase the commodities which come back to us in return. It is conceivable, that there might be a demand in a foreign country, and, but for the obstacle we now insist upon, effective demand too, for British exports; the preparation of which would require the industry of a million of people, over and above the numbers already subsisted by the agricultural produce of the island. And, could the agriculture be so enlarged as to afford this additional subsistence, there would be no difficulty in meeting this demand from abroad. For the larger imports necessary to meet the now larger exports, could then all be absorbed. Let the maintenance be stretched out to the support of an additional million of human beings, and the wealth of the holders of this maintenance is thereby stretched out to a capacity for purchasing, either

the immediate products of their industry, or the
equivalents given in exchange for these products.
The additional maintenance given in return for
the new imports, goes to the support of the people
who labour in preparing the new or additional
exports.   It is thus that, with every stretch in the
agriculture of a country, there is room for a corresponding stretch in its foreign trade.   But
should the population of that country have access
to no other agricultural produce than that which
is raised within its own territory, then, with the
difficulty or the impossibility of extending the
agriculture, will there be found a like difficulty or
impossibility of extending its foreign trade.   It
is by an exchange adverse to him that the export
merchant is brought to the test and the feeling of
this difficulty.   It is when imports cannot find a
sale, because there is not wealth in the country to
purchase them, that foreign trade meets with ob-
structions to its increase.   It is then that the tendency to an excess is counteracted by the heavy
diminution which profit suffers, from an unfavourable exchange.   The limit, in fact, of our agriculture, is also the limit of our commerce ; and so
again, do we find the margin of cultivation to
be a place in the science of political economy,
whence another of its important lessons may be
drawn.

13. This subject admits of some weighty and
important applications.   First, there is a fortunate coincidence between the tendency to excess

of Britain's export manufacturers, and the tendency of British gentlemen to reside and travel in foreign parts. It will be seen, on consideration, how the expenses of our landed gentlemen abroad give an impulse, because they give a real advantage to the business of our export manufacturers at home. They tell favourably for that business on the rate of exchange. Had the non-residents of Britain spent their incomes at home, it must have been chiefly in the purchase of home, and but fractionally in the purchase of foreign commodities. Only a small proportion of their revenue would have been appropriated to the purchase of returns from abroad, and, with this limitation on the imports, there behoved to be a corresponding limitation on the exports also. But when, instead of this, they take up their residence, or are much personally in foreign countries, their whole, or at least the far greater part of their expenditure, must be given to foreign produce ; and this, in as far as the effect on exchange is concerned, is precisely tantamount to a larger importation of produce into Britain. The export merchants of this country have the same benefit from the residence of British landlords abroad, that they would have had from the importation of all which they consume abroad. The growth of a taste for foreign travelling, or foreign sojourning, has the same favourable effect on their interest, as the growth of a taste for foreign articles of expense among the gentry who never go from home.

It matters not whether the *British consumption* of foreign produce takes place within our country or out of it. In either case, the price is paid by Britons, and is equally set over and against the price paid by foreigners for our export articles. The sum paid by Britons for articles raised abroad, is, in truth, the great fund out of which those merchants and manufacturers are paid, who carry abroad the articles which are raised at home. If this sum be any how enlarged, then, proportionally to it, will the amount or the profit of our export trade be enlarged. The only difference is, that our export manufacturers, instead of working in the service of British consumers at home, work in the service of British consumers, who have chosen to transport their persons and their ex-penditures abroad. In the one case, they are paid by bills on our merchant importers. In the other case, they are paid by bills on the agents of our absentee proprietors; and an abundance of bills on either of these classes is alike favourable to the business of exportation. If British landlords, to the extent of a million of rental, have chosen to take up their residence in France, and a million worth of British goods be annually exported there, the adjustment can take place as effectually by bills, as if our landlords had staid at home, and there had been the importation of a million worth of French goods into Britain. The British ex-porters are paid by bills on the rent collectors of the British absentees. Or, the British landlords have their rents remitted to them by bills on the receivers of British exports in France. There may have been no agricultural produce exported from Britain for the payment of this rent. The full value of it may have been exported in British manufactures; in which case, both the capitalists and the workmen of this country are as effectually maintained by the ability of our non-resident landlords, as if these had been living on their own estates, and spending their revenues within the country. This non-residence may not have lessened the amount of British industry. It might only affect the direction of that industry. Instead of working in the service of landlords at home, by preparing articles which partly would have been bought by them, and partly been exchanged for imports to be bought by them; there are so many of our population employed in the service of these same landlords abroad, by preparing articles to the full value of their rent, and making an entire exportation of them. The receivers of these articles in France pay the price of them to the British residents there, and thus these obtain their rents. The preparers of these articles can, by means of orders from the British absentees on their agents, or tenantry, draw from the rent which they owe; and thus these obtain their remuneration. In the whole of this process, there need not be the transportation of any food from Britain to France, even though they are the proprietors of Britain's food who are there spending their incomes. The whole

of that food may go to the support of British industry notwithstanding; and, in spite of denounced
and deprecated absenteeism, may there be a population in the midst of us, fully commensurate to
the maintenance that we raise, and maintained too
in as great fulness as if the great and wealthy of
our land never strayed beyond its borders.

14. There is much that we cannot demonstrate at
full length, which, nevertheless, we might venture,
with all safety and confidence, to affirm. The superiority of our exports to our imports is connected
with peculiar facilities, and tends also to cheapen
both the travels and the residence of our countrymen
in foreign parts.   A gentleman of England, in any
foreign country, will find it possible to negotiate
his orders on home, both with greater ease and
economy, than one having the same territorial
wealth in Poland.   Wherever he goes, he meets
with the debtors of his own nation, who would
prefer a bill from him, for the settlement of their
accounts, to the expense and hazard of a pecuniary
remittance.   It is thus that he may get a premium
for his bill, when the traveller of another kingdom
would need to offer such a premium, ere he could
obtain the conversion of his order into money.
The exports of England may be regarded as the
instruments by which she can obtain accommodation and service for her sons in any quarter of the
world whither she might send them.   The deficiency of return imports to England, is made up
by the demand and the wants of Englishmen on

the spot. What they purchase there, comes in lieu of imports. And so long as their expenditure abroad does not exceed in value the superiority of our *manufactured exports* over our imports, we hold that the non-residence of proprietors may be carried to any extent, without the infliction of any *economic* evil upon the nation.

15. But when a country, instead of exporting manufactures, exports agricultural produce, the economical effect of absenteeism ought to be stated differently. The non-resident landlords of England have their rents sent after them; not in the produce of their estates, but in the workmanship of a people who remain at home, and are fed by that produce. But the absentees of Ireland are paid, not in the work of Irish labourers, but in the food of labourers. The effect of their non-residence is to carry off, not the ultimate products of industry, but its maintenance—not the food transmuted into the handiwork of those who are sustained by it, but the food itself,—to the positive lessening therefore of the means by which a population are supported. Should the absentees of England be recalled, it might add nothing to the maintenance, but only affect the direction of labour. But should the absentees of Ireland be recalled, the maintenance of thousands, now sent off in annual shipments, would be retained within its territory. This is another resource in prospect and reserve for that interesting country, when, in the further development of moral causes, it shall have

become the congenial home of its own proprietors. This single change in their habit, would as effectually augment the produce applicable to the subsistence of Irishmen, as a better cultivation would; another proof, that however overpeopled in reference to its present condition, the physical and economic capabilities of the land are adequate to the liberal subsistence of a much larger population.

16. But there is another application still more interesting. Connected with the facilities which belong to England, for the manufacture of valuable exports, she has not only the power, beyond other countries, of commanding personal services abroad to Englishmen individually, but she has also the same superiority of power, for commanding public and political services to the state nationally. Food, speaking generally, is far more bulky and uncarriageable than workmanship; and, when we come to certain of the finer and lighter fabrics, we shall find, that within the limits of one vessel, a hundred-fold greater value may be comprised in the products of human industry, than in the articles which serve for the maintenance of human industry. It would require, for example, an enormously greater expense to transport into the heart of France, a given value of agricultural produce from Poland, than to find way into Austria for the same value of muslins, or of precious hardware from Britain. It is thus that we are enabled, by the mere conveyance of our manufactures, to obtain a claim or right of command, over the pro-

perty and services of a country in some distant part of the world. Instead of taking back in imports the value that we have exported, we may transfer it by loan to the government of the country; we may agree to subsidize its sovereign, and make good our contract by granting him bills on the receivers of our exports there, who are his own subjects; we may, by the same expedient, command the maintenance of our own armies in foreign parts, or we may pay for the services of mercenary troops. It is thus that, in fact, we have intermeddled with all sorts of distant politics, and have the means of doing so influentially. Even though Russia had equal wealth with Britain, so that the whole products of the one nation, if brought to the same market, would fully exchange with the whole products of the other, yet the wealth of the former is not so transportable as that of the latter. Russia and Britain have both great ascendancy in Europe, but the forces by which they can assert it, are put forth in a different way. The former country, though not so densely peopled, yet, in virtue of its prodigious extent, may be said to abound in men, and in the sustenance of men. She can collect an overwhelming host from her provinces; and either send along with her armies the materials of their maintenance, or find, by plunder, these materials in the countries through which they pass. It is thus that her ascendancy is made good by a ponderous locomotion; whereas that of Britain may be upheld in the midst of peaceful and civic pursuits, and without the departure of a single soldier from her shores. Instead of sending soldiers abroad, she can hire and employ them in foreign parts, by the labour of her artizans at home. With the products of that labour, she can purchase the aid of foreign troops, or the co-operation of foreign governments in her schemes. It is this which has given her a mastery in the negotiations of European policy; and she has made ample use of the powerful and peculiar weapon that her carriageable exports have put into her hands; carriageable, both from her position in the waters of the sea, and from the nature of the exports themselves. It is interesting thus to connect the politics with the economics of Britain, and trace her influence in other lands to the simple circumstance, of her being able, by manufactures, to comprise much value in little room, of her dealing in such light and transportable wares. Dr. Smith, and others, had long remarked the impulse which a foreign war gave to our exports. It is because our expenses abroad, just serve the very purpose of importation from abroad. Government pays our export merchants, by purchasing their bills on their foreign correspondents; and, in making over these bills to commissioners, or subsidized governments abroad, they put their schemes of warfare into action. The demand for these bills gives a mighty benefit and enlargement to the business of exportation; so that, connected with our great public expenditure on foreign objects, there is a glowing industry in our manufacturing districts and great commercial out-ports.

17. And here we feel tempted to remark on the egregious delusion of that most mercantile of all our politicians, who founded every calculation of Britain's strength and Britain's glory on the prosperity of her trade; and verified the maxim of ignorance being the mother of devotion, in the idolatry which he rendered to commerce, whilst all unintelligent and unknowing of its internal mechanism—we mean the late Mr. Pitt. Year after year did he lull the British parliament into mischievous security, by the oft-repeated tale of the superiority of British exports. It never once occurred, that a foreign subsidy, or loan, would of itself create that superiority. If we contract for twenty millions to Austria, it is only by the difference between our exports and imports that the contract can be made good. Had there been no loan, there would have been no such excess to boast of; as the whole payment for what had been sent abroad, would then have been made to us in the return of commodities sent back again. But there were no such returns, just because the whole of this vaunted superiority in our exports had been absorbed in our foreign expenses. The phenomenon of a perpetual superiority in our exports, is explained by the perpetual yearly expense of our foreign establishments, as at Gibraltar, and the Greek Islands, and South Africa, and New Holland, and the other colonial dependencies of Britain in various parts of the world.

And the phenomenon of that prodigious superiority in our exports, which ministered such complacency and triumph to the mind of Mr. Pitt, was just the enormous addition which he made to this expense by his foreign subsidies and wars. We cannot imagine a more complete specimen of inverted mental vision, than was given on these occasions—when the country was bidden to rejoice during the heavy additions that were making to the mortgage of the state; and to read, in the necessary effects of this expenditure on the balance of trade, the symptoms of our national prosperity and greatness.

18. And whatever it is that we want done in any foreign region, the exportation of British goods to that region, or to its vicinity, facilitates or furnishes a mean for the doing of it. This holds true, let the business be what it may that we wish to have executed—whether the business of war, or the business of Christian philanthropy. The very circumstances which have invested Britain with such effectiveness in the political contests of far distant territories, mark her out as pre-eminently qualified, among the nations, for the glorious contest with human infidelity and vice all the world over. We have only to look intelligently at the process, and it will disarm the vulgar complaint, that by supporting missionaries abroad we send money out of the country, and so impoverish our own people. If I indulge in the use of foreign luxuries, when they are brought to the country they behove to be paid for; and they are paid by our exports. Sup-

pose me to abandon this gratification altogether, and that I transfer the expense of it to the support of a missionary enterprise. To myself there is a change—the substitution of an exalted moral, in place of a physical enjoyment. To the country there is no change, at least no such economic change as ought to be deprecated. The people who prepared the exports, that wont to pay the foreign luxuries which I used at home, may still prepare the same amount of exports to pay the expenses of the missionary whom I support abroad. It is thus that the agents of our apostolical benevolence and zeal may depart in thousands from our shores, and be upheld by us in the whole cost of their expedition and their doings, and yet may we retain a population as great as the agriculture of the island can subsist, and keep them in the same comfort and well-paid industry as before. The peculiar advantages of Britain enable her to do this without the transportation of any food; and simply by the transportation of her manufactures, through the medium of which, she can, without sustaining any economic injury whatever, send remittances, to an inconceivable amount, for the support and equipment of her missionaries. Instead of impairing, it would, in certain directions, give an impulse and extension to our trade; while to ourselves, the contributors, there would be but the exchange of a sensible for a spiritual gratification—the giving up, it may be, of foreign luxuries, for the higher luxury of foreign benevolence. We

as effectually support our export manufacturers in
the one way as in the other; and though still, the
expense of her missionaries forms too insignificant
a proportion of British wealth to be admitted into
the reasonings of economic science, yet the time
may come, when our nation shall exchange her
glory in politics and war, for a nobler and more
enduring glory, and be the prime instrument of
that splendid prediction, that many shall run to
and fro upon the earth, and knowledge shall be
increased.

19. On the whole, then, it is obvious that foreign trade will always, or very nearly, maintain itself up to that point which is desirable in the given
circumstances of a country; and this without the
anxious or artificial fostering of any national policy.
Foreign, like home trade, is only to be accredited
with the service of furnishing to consumers its own
articles of enjoyment; and not with the maintenance of those who are engaged in it.   When two
countries enter into mutual trade, the common idea
is, that each stands indebted to its customers in the
other, for the maintenance of its foreign-trade
population, just as a shopkeeper is maintained by
his customers; and the enjoyment which each has
in the use of the other's commodities, is regarded
but as a subordinate advantage, as being a thing
more of individual gratification, than of national
importance.   Now the real state of the matter is,
that each stands indebted to the other, only for the
enjoyment which it has in the use of the other's

commodities; but that, save where there is a transportation of agricultural produce, each maintains
its own foreign-trade as effectually as it does its
own home-trade population. This view would
reduce the natural importance of foreign trade,
and so reduce the alarm that is felt in the prospect of its fluctuations or its failures. The simple consideration, that they are the consumers
at home, who maintain the manufacturers of the
articles sent abroad, should keep us easy under
all the casualties to which foreign trade is liable. The threatened loss of their subsistence to
hundreds of thousands of families might well make
us fearful ; but the threatened loss of oranges,
or dye-stuffs, or tobacco, or even of sugar, wine,
rum, tea, tamarinds, nutmegs, mahogany and coffee,
ought not to make us fearful. We might feel an-
noyed by the loss, or rather the change of our personal enjoyments. But there are many things which
annoy that should not alarm; and when such magnificent objects as political greatness, and national
security, and the sustenance of many thousands of
industrious workmen in the cities and manufacturing districts of our land, and the revenues of the
state, and the consequent support of our establishments, whether civil or military—we may rest assured of a delusive imagination, when these come
to be associated with that trade, which but supplies
us with foreign luxuries and does no more. The
destruction of our intercourse with any foreign land,
between which and ourselves a prosperous and satis-

factory trade may now be going on, will but stop an outlet for our commodities, and an inlet for theirs; but will not destroy the maintenance which, through a process already explained, now passes from the consumers of our imports to the manufacturers of our exports. It will influence the direction of our industry, but not the amount of it; and leave to the industrious as good a wage and as liberal a maintenance as before.

20. But like every other economic interest, by which it is vainly attempted to provide indefinitely for an indefinitely augmenting population, foreign trade, too, has its impassable limit, beyond which it cannot be carried. In most countries, it may be said to repose wholly on an agricultural basis; and in no country of any great extent, can it be made far to overlap the limits of the maintenance raised at home. The imports and the exports mutually limit and determine each other; and, generally speaking, whatever foreign trade a country can support, it is not in virtue of an originating force from without, but in virtue of an inherent ability that resides and has its origin within the territory. If export manufacturers do prosper in any country, it, in the vast majority of cases, is owing to the power of maintaining them in the hands of inland consumers. Wanting this, to uphold a foreign trade, there would behove to be a process of exportation without a counterpart importation; a process which economists can demonstrate by reasoning, and which merchants feel in experience to be

impracticable.   And the simple reason why foreign
trade generally stops at the point, when, if extended
further, there would need a larger manufacturing
population than the agricultural produce of the
country can subsist, is, that agricultural produce is
of such expensive transportation.   But the further
development of this peculiarity we postpone to
our next chapter.

CHAPTER VII.

ON THE LIMITS OF A COUNTRY'S FOREIGN TRADE,
AND ITS SUPPOSED POWER TO FURNISH A PEOPLE
WITH EMPLOYMENT AND MAINTENANCE.

II. *The case of a country which imports agricultural produce.*

1. IT must be at once obvious, how much more carriageble the products of manufacturing industry generally are, than the agricultural produce is, which forms the chief maintenance of that industry. This, of itself, causes a great saving; when instead of sending forth the food which maintains the workmen, or the raw materials which form the substratum of any manufacture, we can, in return for our imports, send the finished and wrought commodity itself. There can sometimes a hundred-fold greater value be compressed within the same space, in a finer article of manufacture, than would be occupied by the food which went to the subsistence of the labourers employed in it. Unless the food, then, be relatively in greater abundance, or the country labours under some peculiar disadvantage for manufactures, it is for its profit to send forth the workmanship of human hands, rather than the subsistence of workmen;

seeing that one cargo of the former is often of greater value than twenty of the latter. It is thus that the same value can be transported at less expense, or, which is tantamount to this, a greater value of commodities at the same expense can be landed in a foreign market, in the former shape, than in the latter; and can there command a greater return of commodities to be sent back as imports. The export merchant finds that he can bring goods cheaper to a foreign market in the one way than in the other; or, with the same cost to himself, can there dispose of articles which bring him larger equivalents; and the country also finds, that, in this way, it obtains a larger return in foreign articles of use or luxury, and so at the same expense can command a larger amount of enjoyments.

2. But more than this; there may be such facilities for manufacture, as to put a country in the condition of having to import its agricultural produce. It may so abound in the best materials; or it may possess such a quantity of coal, that great impellent of machinery; or it may be the seat of so many mechanical inventions, each, so long as it is undivulged, conferring a monopoly on the possessor of the secret; or it may be so distinguished by the industrious habits of its people; or, lastly, it may have such superiority over other nations in respect of geographical position, and also in respect to the extent of its sea coast, and so its easy and convenient access to distant places; that, with the benefit of these various facilities, it may be

enabled to work up many a goodly fabrication, and many a desirable commodity, far cheaper than can be done in any other region on the face of the earth. It is thus that the products of its industry may become the objects of a very general demand throughout the world. In these circumstances, the export manufactures which are carried abroad, may soon be equal in value to the imports which are used at home. They will even tend to exceed this value; in which case, should there be any barrier, whether natural or artificial, against the importation of agricultural produce, the superiority of exports over imports will tell unfavourably on the state of exchanges for any further exportation, which will thus be limited by the difficulty of finding disposable returns.

3. Now this is the very state in which, on the non-existence, or the removal of such a barrier, agricultural produce will flow into a country from abroad; seeing that its importation, notwithstanding the heavy expense attending it, may, to a certain extent, be profitable, and therefore practicable. If, by its advantages for manufacturing, a country can work off commodities cheaper than its neighbours, it may be so much cheaper as to countervail the expense attendant on the importation of food. To meet the general demand for our better and cheaper manufactures, may require the services of a population over and above what our own agricultural produce can maintain. For the maintenance of this extra population an extra produce

must be fetched from abroad, subject of course to
the charges of its conveyance. But as there cannot be two prices for an article of the same quality,
the home and the foreign grain, if equally good,
will be disposed of in the market upon equal terms.
The same necessity which caused the importation,
must have raised the nominal value of our own
agricultural produce. The necessaries of life will
have become dearer than they would have been in
other circumstances; but connected, as this is, with
an additional demand for workmen, labourers will
not on that account let down their standard of enjoyment; and so manufacturers will have to lift up
the money price of labour. It is thus that the
peculiar advantages of a country for export manufactures, are met by a counteractive disadvantage,
which will at length limit the amount of exportation. But so long as the cheapness of our manufactured goods, arising from the greater productiveness of British labour, compensates, or more
than compensates for their dearness, arising from
the more expensive maintenance of British labourers; the extra demand for our commodities will be
upheld or extended; and along with it, the importation of food from distant lands. A population
will be formed in our territory over and above
what the territory itself can maintain. For the
sake of distinction, we shall estimate the *natural
population* of our island by the number of human
beings within it, actually subsisted on the produce
of its soil; and whatever the excess of our whole

population beyond this may be, we should term the *excrescent*, or the superinduced population.

4. Those export manufactures then, the labourers in which belong to the natural population, are exchanged for foreign manufactures or foreign luxuries.* Those export manufactures, which are wrought up by the excrescent population, are exchanged for the agricultural produce of foreign countries; on which countries, then, we so far depend for the first necessaries of life, the means and the materials of human subsistence.

5. This excrescent population will not accumulate in a country beyond a certain limit. In the first place, along with every extension of it there must be an increased importation of food, which will therefore have to be fetched from greater, or more impracticable distances than before. The sea-coasts, or river-sides of an exporting country, will only supply a given demand for corn;† and should the demand exceed this, the additional supplies must be drawn from the interior, and the heavy expense of land-carriage added to the expenses of navigation. It is thus that, with every accession to our excrescent population, there must

* Foreign manufactures are not always foreign luxuries.— See Note, Chap. vi. Sect. 8.

† See Jacob's Report to the House of Lords on the Corn Trade. A land-carriage of twenty-four miles adds the expense of $13\frac{1}{2}$ per cent. to the original price of the grain; from which it may be seen how soon, by having to fetch it from greater distances, the process of deriving supplies from abroad behoved to be terminated.

be an accession to the price of grain, and so to the money-price of labour—a process which must stop, whenever the disadvantage to which a manufacturer is liable in the high wages of his workmen, exceeds the advantage which he has in the facilities of his British situation; for at that point will he begin to be undersold, and so shut out from any further enlargement of his business by the competition of foreigners. But secondly, with every addition to the excrescent population, there must be an enlarged exportation of British goods, which will become cheaper in foreign markets in proportion to their supply. These two causes act together in powerful co-operation; so that between the increasing dearness of their maintenance at home, and the increasing cheapness of their manufactures abroad, an arrest must at length be laid on the increase of an excrescent population. Add to this the constant approaches to equalization, between different countries in industry and the arts of life. Britain cannot for ever perpetuate the monopoly which is grounded on the secrets of her superior skill, or on the superior habits of her population. Other countries must at length come nearer to us, both in respect of their machinery and of their men, so as to supply themselves, and likewise their neighbours, with many of our commodities cheaper than we can. It is because the workmanship of human hands is so much more transportable than the sustenance of human bodies, that the interchanges of commerce lie far more in manufactured

goods than in agricultural produce.   The bulkiness
of food forms one of those forces in the economic
machine, which tends to equalize the population of
every land with the products of its own agriculture.
It does not restrain disproportion and excess in all
cases; but in every large state it will be found,
that wherever an excess obtains, it forms but a
very small fraction of the whole population.

6. It is all important, then, in our reasonings
upon this subject, that we advert to the distinction
between the two sorts of foreign trade—that for
which the returns are made in the manufactures or
luxuries of foreign nations, and that for which the
returns are made in agricultural produce.   Each
trade must have an agricultural basis to rest upon;
for in every process of industry, the first and greatest necessity is that the workmen shall be fed.
But it makes the utmost practical difference between these two, that the former rests on the basis
of a home, and the latter on the basis of a foreign
agriculture.   In most cases, and more particularly
where it is a nation of extensive territory, the whole
of their foreign trade is of the first description—
the home population engaged in it subsisting exclusively on home produce.   When, over and
above this, there is an excess of population that
requires foreign produce for its subsistence, it will
be found, in larger states more especially, that it
forms but a small fractional part of the whole.   In
other words, generally speaking, the excrescent
bears a very minute proportion to the natural po-

pulation of a country; and almost no where does
the commerce of a nation overlap, but by a very
little way, the basis of its own agriculture.

7. By keeping this distinction in view, we shall
better estimate the precise character and effect of
that calamity, which either the suspension or the
loss of foreign trade inflicts upon a nation. In as
far as foreign trade rests on the basis of a home
agriculture, the trade may be destroyed—yet, on
that basis all the people employed in it will continue to be upholden. The export manufacturers
will be discarded, no doubt, from their present occupations; yet, supported as they were formerly by
a maintenance in the hands of our inland consumers, by that maintenance they will be supported
still, only in return for a new service. As we have
often said already, there will ultimately be no loss
to them, and but the loss of some enjoyment to
their virtual maintainers; or rather, the loss of
any difference, if there be a difference of superiority, which the old enjoyment had over the new
one. It would greatly mitigate our fears of a calamity, and at least take away all sense of its national importance, could we but perceive of foreign
trade, that its destruction involved in it no other
suffering than this—that is, a certain disappointment to the taste or fancy of consumers; but leaving withal, the same amount of well-paid industry
in the land, as sufficient a maintenance as before
for as large a population. It is different when the
foreign trade rests, either in whole or in part, on

the basis of a foreign agriculture. There is no
disruption between the people and their maintenance, by the extinction of the one trade—there is,
by the extinction of the other. Let an end be
put to the first, and our export workmen will still
find footing, in some new capacity, on the soil that
sustains them—where, in the midst of home resources, they will be sure of a harbour and a landing-place. If an end be put to the second, it will
be tantamount to a sentence of decimation on the
families of the land—a sentence which exile or
famine will carry into effect. The destruction of
foreign trade, in a country which subsists itself, may
abridge the enjoyments of the community ; but it
will neither abridge the population, nor the industry of the population, though it changes the direction and the products of that industry. The destruction of foreign trade in a country which has to
import agricultural produce, would cancel from the
land an integral part of its population and its industry. To depend in part on other countries for enjoyment, is but a slight matter, when compared with
depending on other countries for our existence.
The effect of a disruption, in the one case, is not to
be compared, in point of vast and fearful importance, with the effect of a disruption in the other.
Yet from want of a right discrimination, the two are
blended and confounded into one. Politicians look
with misplaced and exaggerated alarm to the loss
of foreign trade in the general—to the loss of all
or any foreign trade. The bugbear and the reality

are both viewed with one common feeling; and an event which involves but the disappointment of families in respect of luxurious indulgence, is regarded with the same apprehension, as if it endangered the stability or very being of the nation.

8. When the excrescent bears a great proportion to the natural population, as it sometimes does in smaller states, and more especially in independent cities—then, when their commerce abandons them, their all, or nearly their all, abandons them. They sustain a mutilation by every abridgment of their foreign trade, seeing that the returns are chiefly made in the first necessaries of life; and that with the disappearance, therefore, of such a commerce, so much of their population and their industry must disappear along with it. In ordinary cases, the discarded population are thrown back on the agricultural basis, which upheld them before, and which is broad enough, and solid enough, to uphold them still. But in this case, a population, dissevered from their maintenance, are thrown adrift on the wide world; and, with their dispersion, there is a corresponding decline of national strength and national greatness. There is all the difference in the world between that commerce, the annihilation of which would but involve the loss, or rather the change, of luxuries, and that commerce, the annihilation of which would involve the loss of the first necessaries of existence. In the latter circumstances of a country, we are not to wonder at the commercial jealousies which have

actuated its governments. To be undersold by neighbours, were to them a death-warrant, involving, as it does, their exclusion from those markets whence they fetch the very aliment of their being. This accounts well for the fragility and the precarious existence of all such states—of Tyre, and Carthage, and Venice, and the Hanseatic towns of Germany, which pass before us in splendid, but ephemeral succession, as we contemplate the history of past ages. When deserted by their trade, the very foundation on which they rested gave way under them; they having no such foundation in any territory of their own. They, in fact, became as helpless as any inland town of home shops or manufactures, when deserted by its country customers. This is enough to account for the speed and splendour of many a mushroom elevation—for the speed of many a helpless and irrecoverable fall—for the decay of commerce in smaller states—and the utter destruction of its isolated cities. Hence the desolation of Tyre, and hence the departed glory from the north of Italy.

9. Now they are such histories as these, which have inspired many of our compatriots with the same feeling of insecurity for Britain. We have a splendid commerce, which somewhat overlaps the basis of our agriculture, and, of consequence, a certain amount of excrescent population, and that probably would be enlarged, in some degree, were the present restrictions on the corn trade wholly done away. Yet it is consolatory to un-

derstand, that, in our years of greatest scarcity, when all our ports were thrown open, and the utmost encouragement was given to the trade, the importation scarcely exceeded one-tenth of the annual importation of the island; and that the average importation of ordinary years would not serve our population for eleven days.* We should not imagine our present excrescent population to be so much as a thirtieth part of the whole; nor do we believe that, on the removal of all fetters from our trade, we should permanently superinduce upon the country an addition of one-tenth to that population who are subsisted by the produce of our own agriculture. The circumstance of having any excrescent population at all, exposes us certainly to an inconvenience on the interruption of our commerce, which should not otherwise be felt. Yet, whatever that inconvenience might be, it is our confident persuasion that Britain would weather it. That a deficiency, by one-tenth of the usual supply in the first necessaries of life, would be seriously felt is very certain; and the price would be enhanced much beyond the proportion of this defi-

* Colonel Torrens, in his able Essay on the External Corn Trade, urges this argument with great effect against the alarmists. He quotes the authority of Mr. Jacob for the importation during the years of greatest scarcity being considerably less than it is stated in the text—namely, that—if the one be correct in his calculation, and the other in his quotation—the importations of 1800 and 1801, taken together, did not amount to five weeks' consumption, or to little more than two weeks' consumption for each year.

ciency. Yet we believe that the country would experience a speedy, an almost elastic recovery from the evils of such a visitation. The very dearness of an article impels to a thousand shifts and expedients for economizing it. The people would, for a season, put up with fewer of the second necessaries; and this, of itself, would have the effect of at once extending the husbandry to poorer soils, and transferring so many of the secondary into the agricultural population. There behoved to be an increase of food, from the additional stretch thus given to the cultivation; and there might be a greater increase still, from the lessened consumption both of animal food and spirits, and from the stoppage of distilleries by an act of the legislature. With these compensations in our power, we have little to fear, even though the violent improbability, " *Britannos toto cœlo divisos*," were to be realized. We should remain as independent, as stable, and as great a nation notwithstanding. Let commercial failures and commercial fluctuations be what they may, they can never liken our history to that of the Venetian States, or the Hanseatic cities. The maxim, " *Carthago est delenda*," is not applicable to us; and, though lifted in menace by a whole continent, would fall powerless upon our shores. Our commerce, after all, is mainly but the efflorescence of our agriculture; and though lopped off by the hand of violence, it would leave untouched the strength and stamina of the nation. Could we only brook the loss of our foreign luxuries, we might have a means and a maintenance at home for all our population, whom we could employ in the preparation of other luxuries; or with whom, enlisted in the service of patriotism, we might raise a wall of fire around our island, and brave the hostility of the world.

10. This distinction between the natural and the excrescent trade of Britain, when it comes to be understood, will hush the inquietude of our present alarmists. The one is based on a maintenance produced at home, the other on a maintenance imported from abroad. The export manufacturers belonging to the former are a disposable population, labouring in the service, and subsisted by the wealth, of inland consumers. The export manufacturers belonging to the latter, both labour in the service, and are subsisted by the wealth, of foreign customers. They are a disposable population too, but at the disposal of landlords at a distance, instead of landlords at home; of men who, in changing the direction of their expenditure, would desert them altogether, instead of men whose change of expenditure would but transfer them to a new service. That is altogether a false analogy, by which Britain is likened to those states of ephemeral glory, whose greatness and power but lasted with their commerce. Our excrescent population and trade bear no such proportion to our natural, as theirs did. Should a disruption take place between ourselves and foreign countries, the excrescent, with us, would speedily be absorbed in the natural. When

Venice was separated from her customers, the foundation, on which she mainly rested, gave way under her. Our foundation is our own territory. Though separated from our customers, we are not therefore separated from the maintenance of our population.   The one would be a change undoubt- edly—a change of pursuits to the working, and of enjoyments to the wealthier classes of our commu- nity.   But, with this exception, it would be as great and flourishing a community as before—as competent to all the purposes of defence and na- tional independence; and, though shorn of her commerce and colonies, though bereft of these showy appendages, as available, and we think more so, for all the dearest objects of patriotism.

11. This view, we think, should serve to mo- derate our commercial ambition, and to quiet one of our great commercial jealousies. So long as Britain can pay cheaper for her imports, by the ex- portation of manufactured commodities, which are in effective demand abroad, she will never need to export agricultural produce ; and so, to alienate from her shores the materials of human subsistence, wherewith to purchase foreign articles of any kind for her consumers at home.   Her peculiar facili- ties for manufacture, will always secure for her this independence ; and her only danger is, lest her overpassing facilities shall make her indepen- dence a precarious one, by landing her in an ex- crescent population.   In which case, the only ef- fect of being undersold by her neighbours, is the

abridgment of this excrescent population. What a mockery does this lay on the fears of our mercantile statesmen, and on the whole system of their policy. Their great dread is that of being undersold by foreigners; while yet the chief effect of the commercial superiority they are so anxious to preserve, is just to enlarge the sale of British exports beyond the possibility of their being paid for, either by the luxuries, or the other goods not agricultural, that come in return for them from other lands. In which case, there is a surplus of exports that must be paid for in agricultural produce. The population is thereby enlarged, beyond the power of the country to feed them from her own stores; or, which is the same thing, the trade is enlarged beyond the limits of her own agricultural basis. There are additions made by this to the weight or dimensions of the superstructure; but without addition either to the strength or amplitude of the foundation. The only effect is to foster an excrescence, which, if not mortal to us as to other commercial states, is just because, with the uttermost of our false and foolish ambition, we cannot overstretch the foreign trade so far as they did, beyond the limits of the home agriculture. By thus seeking to enlarge our pedestal, we make it greatly more tottering and precarious than before; for, like the feet of Nebuchadnezzar's image, it is composed of different materials, partly of clay and partly of iron. The fabric bulges, as it were, into greater dimensions than before; but while its na-

tive and original foundation is of rock, the project-
ing parts are propped upon quicksand; for the
sake of lodging a few additional inmates in which,
we would lay the pain of a felt insecurity, if not an
actual hazard, upon all the family. We rejoice in the
luxuriance of a rank and unwholesome overgrowth;
and, mistaking bulk for solidity, do we congratu-
late ourselves on the formation of an excrescence,
which should rather be viewed as the blotch and
distemper of our nation.

12. But more than this, we are not to imagine of
the excrescent, that it either indicates or creates
the same addition to the resources of the country
as an equal number of the natural population.
Suppose that the excrescent should amount to a
thirtieth part of the whole, we would estimate the
matter wrong by conceiving that a thirtieth part
had been added thereby to the whole previous
wealth and ability of the nation. Let us compare
ten thousand of the disposable class taken from
the natural population, with ten thousand of an
excrescent population. The former give the products of their industry, or, if engaged in export
manufactures, exchange them for other products,
by which they obtain their equivalent maintenance
from proprietors at home. The latter give the products of their industry in exchange for a maintenance which they draw from proprietors abroad.
For each ten thousand of the natural population,
we can put to the account of the country's wealth
the work of ten thousand and the maintenance of

ten thousand. For each ten thousand of the excrescent population, we can only put to that account the work of ten thousand, for their maintenance cometh from abroad, and becomes only ours by parting with the commodities which are given in exchange for it. In estimating the wealth that is indicated by the existence of the former, we must take into account both the produce of the land which maintains them, and of the labour which they give in return for their maintenance. In estimating the wealth that is indicated by the existence of the latter, we can only take the produce of the labour into account, without the produce of land. In the one case, we can reckon as the property of the nation, both the work and the ultimate equivalents of the work. In the other case, we can reckon but the work—for the ultimate equivalents are produced elsewhere, and form an integral part of the wealth of some other land. Dr. Smith defines the wealth of a country to consist in the annual produce of its land and labour. An industrious member of the natural population, adds the produce of his labour to his country, and by means of it he fetches a counterpart produce from the land, which is also to be added to the country's wealth. An equally industrious member of the excrescent population, also adds the produce of his labour to his country's wealth—but the counterpart produce of land which he purchases therewith, must be reckoned to the wealth of another country. If the former do not create, he at least represents a double wealth in the country, beyond what the other does. So that a given excrescent population betokens only half the wealth which an equal natural population does. If the excrescent population amount to a thirtieth of the whole, the wealth associated with their presence will amount to a sixtieth of the whole. The commerce that is pushed beyond the agricultural basis, to the extent of employing an excrescent ten thousand men, does not effectuate the same addition to a country's resources, as if the agricultural basis were itself extended by means of reclaimed land, or of an improved husbandry, so as to afford the additional subsistence of ten thousand men. In the one case, we have the additional work of ten thousand; but we must accredit the wealth of another country, and not our own, with their maintenance. In the other case, we have the additional maintenance of ten thousand; and, followed up as this must be, with an increase of population, we should soon have the additional work of ten thousand to the bargain.

13. But it will still more strikingly exhibit the insignificance, in a national point of view, of the excrescent, when compared with the natural population; if we attend to the relation in which they each stand to the revenue or service of the state. The excrescent population is made up exclusively of labourers and capitalists; and every tax, whether on their income or on the commodities they use, lessens their remuneration, so as to make a

higher price necessary for the commodities prepared by them, in order to keep up that rate of
wages and rate of profit, without which their manufacture or business could not possibly go on.   But
in this way the price may rise so high as to cut
them out of foreign markets altogether; the advantage of their British situation, in virtue of which
they might have been enabled to undersell the
traders of other countries, being so much countervailed by British taxation, as that they at length
come to be undersold.   It is thus that every such
tax lessens the amount of our excrescent population; and, if carried to a certain extent, would
cause it wholly to disappear from our borders.   At
the most, then, the excrescent population can only
be made to yield a small fraction, and that a very
precarious one, of their wealth to the exigencies
of the public service.   But let us compare with
ten thousand of their number, any ten thousand of
the natural disposable population.   In the first
place, as to those of them who are engaged in
home manufactures, however high their wages may
be raised by taxation, the inland proprietors, for
whose enjoyment they labour, cannot escape from
the consequent high prices of those commodities,
in the preparation of which they are employed.
In the second place, as to those of them who are
engaged in export manufactures, their wages admit of being raised by taxation, till the inland consumers shall find that they can obtain the return
articles from abroad, at a cheaper rate, by the ex-

portation of agricultural produce. In either way, it will be found that, compatibly with their existence and full extent, the natural population could bear to be much more highly taxed than the excrescent population could. But what is more, the landlords at home, who maintain ten thousand of the natural population, can be reached by a direct tax; so as not merely to transfer a certain fraction, but any fraction whatever, nay, even the whole of this natural population, to the service of government. If a landlord abroad still continue to purchase the manufactures of our excrescent population, though they come to him at a price enhanced by taxation a tenth part more than they would otherwise have cost him; then, for every ten of our people whom he maintains in his own service, he may be regarded as maintaining also one in the service of the state. It is thus that for each ten thousand of our excrescent population, government may raise as much by taxation, as might enable it to command the services of a thousand men. But it could, by means of that higher taxation, which would abridge or annihilate the excrescent population altogether, command a much larger proportion of the services of our natural population; and, by means of a direct tax upon landlords, could obtain a command over the services of the whole ten thousand. An excrescent population indicates but half the wealth of an equal portion of the natural population, whatever direction that wealth may be left to take. But the proportion is far more insignificant, when we compute the respective amounts of wealth from each, that might be made available to the public revenue, or to the general good and service of the nation.

14. Yet insignificant in point of national advantage, nay, hazardous in point of national security as we hold this excrescent population to be, we would not recommend a corn law to prevent the formation of it.* But still less would we recommend any of the expedients of a mercantile policy, to foster it into being, or force it into greater magnitude than that at which it would naturally settle. More especially, in the circumstance of being undersold by our neighbours in any of the branches of commerce, we can read no symptom whatever of disaster to the country, but would rather hail it with satisfaction, as that which tends somewhat to limit or to abridge the excrescent population. This points to a policy more generous far, than the narrow and heart-burning system of prohibitions, alike dissatisfying to the people abroad and the people at home. We would not, on the one hand, restrain the freest importation of food ; but neither, on the other, would we restrain the freest exportation of British skill, whether in the shape of British artificers or British machines, our living or our dead implements of labour. All that we gain by the opposite proceeding, is the very questionable good of an excrescent population,

* See Appendix, G.—On Corn Laws.

who expose us to danger, and yield us no counter-
vailing benefit in return for the room they stand
upon.   We have enough of natural superiority in
our situation and products, to secure us at all times,
against any large or permanent exportation of food ;
or, in other words, to secure for us a population
commensurate to our agriculture.   The advantage
of having a population beyond this, is far too pro-
blematical to be worthy of the contention and the
keenness, by which the rivalry of merchants is
characterized.   We can afford to participate freely
with our neighbours in all the advantages which
belong to us as a manufacturing people ; and, so
far from regarding with any sentiment of jealousy
the exportation of British capital or intelligence to
other shores, we should conceive, that in this instance too, the magnanimous policy would be found
the best for the true interest and safety of the nation.

15. On the whole, however, we believe, that in
a perfectly free state of things, there might be a
considerably larger importation than now of foreign
grain into Britain, and of course a larger excrescent population.   The causes however already
specified, the increasing dearness of imported corn,
the increasing cheapness in foreign markets of
British commodities, and lastly, the constant tendency to equalization, in point of skill and other
advantages between our own and other nations,
would all conspire to limit the amount of this importation ; and our hope is, that both the foreign

and the excrescent might ultimately settle down
into a very small and manageable fraction, first of
the natural produce, and second of the natural
population of our island.   Still to this quarter we
may look for a certain stretch or enlargement of
external resources, whereby room and sustenance
would be afforded for a greater number of families
than we can now accommodate.   Yet, after all,
like every other augmentation in the outward
means of support, it would but afford a temporary
relief to the pressure under which we are at present labouring.   As is usual with every increase,
from whatever quarter, of the means of subsistence,
it would be speedily followed up by a multiplication of our numbers, and so land us in a larger,
but not on that account, a better-conditioned community than before.   They who are sanguine of
this and other resources, as if a permanent sufficiency for all our families were to be the result of
them, would do well to consider the vast enlargement that must have taken place within the last
half century, in the produce of our home agriculture; and yet, the actual straitness that is felt in
spite of it.   The phenomenon admits of an easy
explanation, palpable as plainest arithmetic to the
understandings of any, who will but compare the
censuses of different periods, and reflect on the
rapid increase of our British population.   And on
what principle can we expect, that an enlargement
of resources from any other quarter, will not be
followed up by as full a proportional increase of

population as heretofore; and, of consequence, that we shall still find ourselves overhung by the same pressure, and in the midst of the very same difficulties as those which now encompass us. That the pressure may be somewhat lightened, for a moment, by the abolition of corn laws, and by several other abolitions and changes also, we cannot deny. But the same important remark is applicable to all of them. It is not by means of economic enlargements, but of moral principles and restraints, that the problem of our difficulties is at length to be fully and satisfactorily resolved. No possible enlargement from without will ever suffice for the increasing wants of a recklessly increasing population. We look for our coming deliverance in a moral change, and not in any, or in all, of those economic changes put together, which form the great panacea of so many of our statesmen. Without the prudence, and the virtue, and the intelligence of our common people, we shall only have a bulkier, but withal as wretched and distempered a community as ever; and we repeat, that a thorough education, in both the common and Christian sense of the term, forms the only solid basis, on which either the political or economic well-being of the nation can be laid.

CHAPTER VIII.

ON THE SUPPOSED EFFECT OF TAXES IN AGGRAVATING
THE CONDITION OF THE LABOURING CLASSES, WITH
THE CONVERSE EFFECT WHICH THE REMISSION OF
TAXES IS CONCEIVED TO HAVE ON THEIR RELIEF,
AND THE ENLARGEMENT OF THEIR COMFORTS.

I. *Effect of a tax on the net rent of land.*

1. THERE is not a more popular topic of declamation than the oppressiveness of taxes, and, more especially, their injurious effect on the condition of the working classes in society. The imagination is, that, when laid on the necessaries of life, they trench directly on the comfort and sufficiency of the labourer; and that, when laid on profit, or laid on commodities in general, they trench upon capital, and so upon that power which exists in the country for the remuneration of labour. It is thus that the distresses of the poor, and the straitened condition of the lower orders generally, stand associated in many a mind with the exactions of government. The effect of this opinion is, not only a rancorous politics on the part of the turbulent, but, even among calm philanthropic men, there is the pretty frequent persuasion, that each retrenchment in the expenditure of the state is so much clear gain to the com-

mon people; and that, by pressing an indefinite
economy upon our rulers, they are on the right way
for an indefinite augmentation of personal comfort,
not to particular classes only, but to society at large.
It is therefore of importance to investigate the
matter; for, if this abridgment of taxes be really
not the specific, which is to charm away all want
and wretchedness from our land, the attention of
the patriot may, in the meanwhile, be diverted from
the best expedient for the relief and amelioration
of its families.

2. Now, there is one species of tax which, by
the consent of all economists, stands exempted from
the charge of infringing on the comfort of the working classes.   We mean a tax on the net rent of
land.   The incidence of such a tax is altogether
upon the landlord.   He is made poorer by it; but
no other individual or order of the community needs
to be at all affected.   A portion of the power which
he had to purchase commodities, or to maintain
labour, is doubtless taken out of his hands.   But it
is not annihilated.   It is only transferred.   After
the imposition of the tax, the united expenditure
of government and the landlords equals precisely
the whole expenditure of the landlords previous to
the tax.   In the new state of things, there might
be just as large a profit to capitalists as before, and
just as large a maintenance to workmen as before.
By every such tax, the power of government to
uphold or reward industry is just as much enlarged
as the power of the landlords is lessened.   A cer-

tain part of the disposable population, employed in
preparing luxuries for the proprietors of land, are
placed by the operation of the tax at the disposal
of government. To them it needs be no other
change than a change of masters—a change of employment. From the hands of their new employers, they may obtain as large and liberal a support
as they did from their old ones. They may have the
same support as before, but for a different service.
They exchange the service of working up luxuries
to private consumers for the service of the state.
They are withdrawn from the business, either of
home or export manufactures, by which they ministered to the enjoyment of landed proprietors, to the
business of manufacturing government stores ; or of
fabricating the whole material of government service, such as ships, and fortifications, and barracks,
and churches, and colleges, and prison-houses ; or
finally, to the direct business of war, or justice, or
public instruction. Artizans may, in thousands,
be transferred thereby into soldiers, or into artizans
of another species. Master manufacturers may,
in tens, or hundreds, be transferred thereby into
officers, or judges, or clergymen. And the latter
may be upheld in as great splendour, and the former in as great sufficiency as before. The wealth
thus transferred into the coffers of government,
can be discharged with as great liberality and effect on the various servants of government, as it
formerly could when discharged by the landed
proprietors themselves, through the countless chan-

nels of trade and manufacturing industry in the
land.   After this change, we may still behold the
spectacle of as large a population, in every way as
liberally upholden, with the only difference of being differently employed.   There is no effect produced on the reward of industry, but solely on the
distribution of it.   They who are paid by the tax
may live as well as before.   They who pay the tax
are the only sufferers.   They lose so many of their
luxuries—or rather, they exchange them for the
objects of the public expenditure; perhaps, through
the medium of fleets and armies, for national independence ; perhaps, through the medium of schools,
and churches, and colleges of justice, for the protection of society from crime and violence, and for
the increase of national virtue.   Even to them, the
tax-payers, it may not be a dead loss, but the substitution of one benefit for another—possibly the
substitution of a greater for a lesser benefit.

3. Yet it may be observed, even of this least obnoxious mode of taxation, that it may be conducted
in such a way, as to lay an arrest, or even to impress a retrograde movement, on the wealth of the
country, and essentially to injure it in all its economic interests.   Under a government of capricious
despotism, and unmeasured rapacity, even though
it confined, which it would not, its exactions to the
net rent, and left untouched all the profits of agricultural capital, as well as the capital itself—the
cultivation of estates would languish or decay, from
the want of consent and of active countenance on

the part of the landlords. The proprietor would lose every inducement to patronize an improving tenantry, if he were sure that all the additional rent, which accrued to himself, was to be absorbed in taxes. Even if he were not sure—if in a state of insecurity whether he was to get any of the additional rent that is yielded by land on its better cultivation, or of ignorance how much he would be permitted to share of it—there behoved to be, on his part, the feeling of a slackened interest, and so a far less careful and vigilant administration of the property. It is thus that the taxations of a government, which wanted steadfastness of principle and good faith, would relax and retard the agriculture of a country, even though these taxations were restricted to the share which accrued to the landlord, in the produce of the soil. But the case is very different when it is a taxation of principle; justified by the urgencies of the occasion; levied alike upon all in like circumstances; not liable to fluctuate, as in Turkey, with the cupidity of the rulers, though liable to be extended with the necessities of the state, of which necessities the landlords themselves, through the organ of a free and representative government, are the effectual arbiters. In these circumstances, there is scarcely any centage of taxation, however great, that would discourage cultivation. Nay, we believe that, in many instances, it has led to the extension of husbandry; and that to the income tax of England, while it lasted, we have to ascribe the breaking up of many a lawn, and pushing forward agriculture to many outfields which had not been entered. The tax, in these cases, stimulated the cultivation. The landlords sought, by a more strenuous agriculture to compensate for the deprivations which the tax laid on them. They drew upon the land for an additional produce, wherewith to meet the impositions to which they were subjected; and though this cannot be done indefinitely, yet done it was in many instances, when, from negligence or pleasure, an estate had not even the average cultivation bestowed upon it. We are aware that, under an oppressive and arbitrary system, the tax would not operate in this way. In a country where the government could seize on individual property, no man would try to indemnify himself for one imposition, by means of an additional produce that might just bring on another imposition. The case is altogether different, when the tax, though severe, is equitable, that is, laid in like proportion over the whole country. Each proprietor, feeling that he is safe from any wanton or unlooked for exaction in future, seeks from the capabilities of his soil, after all the reimbursement which it can afford, for the exactions that already lie upon him. In these circumstances, we really cannot specify to what extent the taxation on net rent may not be carried, because of the discouragement it would give to cultivation. For this purpose, the taxation would need to be not only excessive; but discretionary, partial, at the mercy of a wayward and

unprincipled government, and altogether such as
left no reasonable security for the enjoyment of
any remainder by the landlord. The effect is to-
tally dissimilar, when the landlords are not only
the payers; but through the predominance of their
will in parliament, the establishers of the tax. And
then, when the question is put, how far might this
taxation on themselves be carried, without injury
to the economic interests of the nation; it is obvious that it might be carried indefinitely near to
that point, at which having surrendered all their
luxuries, they satisfied themselves for a season with
the necessaries of life. This may be regarded as
the extreme limit of the taxation on net rent; and
by the actual distance of our landlords from this
limit, by the degree in which they still can command and enjoy the luxuries of life, do we estimate
the power which remains with them, of adding to
the revenue of the state. They could, on some
high call of patriotism, transfer to the service of
government, all the disposable population whom
they employ. They could transform a million of
manufacturers into soldiers. They could, if the
emergency called for it, assemble round the standard of the nations independence, a host many times
greater than has yet been exemplified in British
warfare ; and, so far from touching on the *ne plus
ultra* of our public resources, we, on the test of
that command which still remains with our landlords over the luxuries of life, do confidently aver,
that never was our nation in greater sufficiency for

such sacrifices as might conduce to some high object of patriotism or the public weal.

4. We admit, that by a tax upon net rent, the
power of the landlord to improve his estate is
abridged; and yet, we hold, that the progress of
this improvement does not, now-a-days, materially depend, either on his capital or on his enterprise. It is not at this time of day, that we have
to complain of the want of capital for any operation, capable of yielding a return, or of replacing
the outlay with a profit. We must recollect the
opulence of our tenantry, and their ability to enter
on improving leases, in all parts of the country
where improvement is hopeful. Or, if the proprietor behoves to be the improver, we must recollect the perfect facility, wherewith he can now
borrow to any extent, on the security of his lands.
When capital is at a loss all round, for a profitable
investure of itself; and, labouring under the weight
of its own plethoric magnitude, is ever and anon
getting the relief which it needs in the bankruptcies attendant on all wild and precarious speculations—we may be very sure, that nothing is wanted,
but the prospect of a safe though moderate return
for drawing capital to agriculture. In other words,
capital will never be wanting to agriculture, so
long as agriculture is able to yield a profit to capital. The truth is, that capital has, in every business, a constant tendency to overshoot itself, by
the application of it in larger quantities than the
business can replace with a profit. And this is

just as much the case in agriculture, as in any thing else. So that though every landlord were to spend to the uttermost of his power, whether on his own private gratifications, or in the support of government, we have nothing to fear for the progress of cultivation. There is perfect security that, on the one hand, a more productive agriculture will bring on a larger population; and that, on the other, an increasing population will so uphold the demand for food, as to encourage and speed onward the progress of agriculture. Meanwhile, the landlord, though sitting merely as a recipient, if he but give his consent and countenance to the requisite administration, will reap the benefits of a process in which he takes no active share. His rents flow in upon him without exertion on his part. He will be glad to receive the whole—but should government interpose with its taxations, he will not reject the part which remains to him. The man of a thousand a year will be glad of an additional hundred—but not more so, than a man of five hundred a year is of an additional fifty. A tax then of fifty per cent. on the net income of landlords, would still leave them in possession of as zealous an interest as heretofore, in the improvement of their property. And should government but leave the profits of capital and the wages of labour untouched by their exactions, we are not able to say when it is that the share which government appropriates of the net rent becomes so large, as, by its adverse influence on the mind of the proprietor, to arrest or even to retard the progress of cultivation.*

5. Anterior then to all consideration of what might be yielded, if indeed any thing is yielded by profit and wages to the service of the state, there is at least one source of public revenue that might well stand exempted from the obloquy of indignant patriotism. A tax on the net rent of land needs not to trench on the income of capitalists; for the united expenditure of government and the landlords can afford them as large an income after the tax, as did the unbroken expenditure of the landlords before it.† It trenches not on the comfort of labourers; for all the power of maintenance that has been withdrawn from individual proprie-

* "Both ground rents, and the ordinary rent of land, are a species of revenue which the owner, in many cases, enjoys without any care or attention of his own. Though a part of this revenue should be taken from him in order to defray the expenses of the state, no discouragement will thereby be given to any sort of industry. The annual produce of the land and labour of the society, the real wealth and revenue of the great body of the people, might be the same after such a tax as before. Ground rents, and the ordinary rent of land, are therefore, perhaps, the species of revenue which can best bear to have a peculiar tax imposed upon them."—*Smith's Wealth of Nations*, Book V. Chap. ii.

† We employ the term income, rather than profit; because the expenditure from the hands of government being more directed to the support of what economists term unproductive labour, may be more in the shape of annual payments, and less in the shape of prices for commodities, than when that expenditure came from the hands of the landlords.

tors, may still be discharged as liberally as ever
from the coffers of the treasury. It changes only
the direction of industry, and not the remuneration of it. As many of the disposable population
as the produce of the tax can maintain, were employed in the manufacture of luxuries; or, while this
produce was suffered to remain in the hands of the
landlords, they laboured in the service of the landlords. When this produce was taken out of their
hands, the maintenance of that population was
transferred into the hands of government, and
themselves were transferred to the service of government. There might be an abridgment of
trade and manufactures by this process; for, instead of preparing tangible luxuries, the greater
part of those whose employments shall have thus
been shifted, might be engaged, in what many economists call the unproductive service of naval or
military defenders. This new distribution of our
people would have the effect of lessening the trade
of the nation; and to those who idolize trade, as if
it possessed some mystic virtue in itself, over and
above the power of ministering through the medium of its own articles to the enjoyment of customers, this might appear a great national evil.
But, in truth, the gratification which consumers
have in the use of its commodities, is the great,
the only service which trade renders to the commonwealth. This we admit is destroyed by the
tax. This is given away in exchange for whatever
benefit the tax may be laid out in purchasing.

Landlords have lost their luxuries. But there is no other loss. Every other benefit which has helped to associate in the minds of men the idea of prosperity, with the idea of trade, is fully and perfectly retained. Whatever power lay in the produce of the tax, when in the hands of its original owner, abides with it still, when in the hands of government. And with the single exception of landlords being shorn somewhat of their household, or stinted somewhat in their personal enjoyments, do we behold the spectacle of as large a population, in circumstances of as great comfort and sufficiency as before.

6. Having this view, we cannot sympathise with the despondency of those who represent our nation, as in a state of extremity and exhaustion. And neither do we comprehend how it is, that taxation cannot be further extended, without bearing oppressively on the maintenance and industry of the people. We hold that there is a world of delusion in the invectives upon this subject, whether of demagogues out of parliament, or of the champions of reform and retrenchment within its walls. There is at least one direction, in which taxation may be carried further, without even the semblance, and certainly without the reality of any encroachment on the means of the general population. A territorial impost, any where short of the net land-rent of the kingdom, would but trench on the luxury of landlords, without at all trenching on the livelihood of the other classes. And to speak of our

yet touching on the limit of our resources, or even being within sight of it—when the equipage, and the splendour, and the thousand effeminacies of luxurious expenditure, are so paraded before our eyes! We are aware that the national debt falls with the weight of a mortgage on every estate in the island; a weight, too, that has of late become more oppressive, by the change which has taken place in the value of money. But, looking comprehensively at the matter, these mortgagees should be regarded in the light of landed proprietors. By the national debt, there has virtually been a division between them and the land-owners of the territory of the empire. Regarding, then, both the land and the stock-holders, as in fact proprietors of the soil, and as sharing between them the net rent which accrues from it; who will deny, that between these two classes, there is at this moment a greater fund for taxation and for the exigencies of the state, than there ever was in any former period of the British history? We have only to survey the distance at which, in habit and expenditure, they stand from the necessaries of life; and, looking on this as the intermediate ground, on which government might proceed indefinitely to appropriate for its own uses the price of their luxurious indulgences, we venture to affirm, that never was there a greater capability than now, for enlarging the number and allowances of the public functionaries, or for imparting efficiency and extent to all the departments of the public

service.   A levy of ten per cent. both upon land
and fund holders, would at this moment invest
government, if not with a larger nominal revenue,
at least with a real power of command over the
services of a larger disposable population, than the
same levy would have done at any former period
in the history of our affairs.   The funds for such
an enlargement of the national revenue do exist
in the country; and, without the injury of one
economic interest, these funds may be drawn upon,
with no encroachment whatever on the sufficiency
of the common people, and no other loss to the
classes above them, than the loss of a splendour
and a luxury unknown to their forefathers.

7. By disentangling and keeping distinctly apart
from each other, the sources out of which a public
revenue might be drawn, we are enabled to perceive, in spite of the very prevalent notion to the
contrary, how far we yet are from the extremity
of our national resources.   Even at the time, when
an additional revenue seems hopeless, from any,
or all the branches of trade put together; there
might still be a fund, convertible by taxation to
the purposes of government, and of greater amplitude than at any former period of our history.   It
follows not, because wages are sinking in every
department of industry, or profits are brought to
that minimum condition, beneath which the capital
of a nation must decay—it follows not, on these
accounts, that government has arrived at the *ne
plus ultra* of her possible income or possible expen-

diture. This would be true, if the only way in which a public revenue can be raised, is by extracting out of the existent trade of a country some fraction of its gains. Whereas, instead of this, let there be a tax on the net rent of land, and then a certain portion of the trade would of necessity be destroyed; when, instead of drawing by an impost upon commodities, but a part of its value, the whole gross value of the destroyed trade may in fact be transferred to the coffers of the treasury. The capitalists and workmen disengaged in consequence, may be as liberally supported as before in the service of the nation; while the capitalists and workmen who remain may have still the same remuneration in the trade which survives. This then is a species of tax to which the common-place declamations, of an overburdened commerce, or an overburdened and oppressed industry, are wholly inapplicable. Both may be overburdened by the weight of their own redundancy, when capital and population are alike in excess; but taxation, when confined to the proper revenue of landlords, is innocent of it all. And the proper test for the capability or the possible extent of this taxation, is just the power of land and fund holders, to maintain a disposable population, who prepare for them the superfluities of existence; and never, may we venture to affirm, was there a greater length and breadth of this capability than at the present moment. Never had government less excuse for foregoing any of the high objects of patriotism,

because of inability fully and liberally to provide
for them all. We repeat, that it is not the necessity
of the lower, but the luxury of the higher classes,
which at all stands in the way of our great public
interests; and that every one of them might be
most generously supported, with but an abridgment
to the luxuries of the one class, and with no aggravation whatever to the necessities of the other.
It is only because things are looked to with dis-
torted vision, that the retrenchments, which are
now made at the altar of popularity, are hailed as
so many acts of relief to the general population;
when, if beheld in their true character, they would
be regretted, by every sound patriot, as a sacrifice
of the public good to the splendour and effeminacy
of the upper orders in society.

8. The notion is very prevalent, both among
economists and statesmen, that commerce and
manufactures are the fountain-heads of the public
revenue; and that if, by any chance, these are
obstructed or dried up, the great source whence a
government obtains its supplies is dried up along
with them. The tax on a commodity forms a fraction of its price; so that when the commodity ceases
to be produced or sold, when no price is given for
it, the tax, in its present form, necessarily disap-
pears: and it would therefore seem as if, with the
cessation of the trade, government were to lose part
of its income. It requires, we should think, no
great stretch of vision to perceive, that the manufacture is not the originator of a revenue to govern-

ment, but only the occasion, or the channel, through which government reaches the purchaser of the manufactured commodity; and that though the manufacture were destroyed, the wonted ability of the purchaser is not therefore destroyed. The truth is, that, by means of a direct impost, government could draw from him the whole price of the article in question, instead of a fraction of that price by means of a tax on the article. It is neither the sugar, nor the tea, nor the wine trade, which produces a revenue to government. These produce nothing but sugar, tea, and wine; and did the nation consent to the sacrifice of these luxuries, government might receive the whole price now given for them, instead of a proportional part in the shape of duty. What else, but an undue sense of the virtue which resides in trade and manufactures, could have led Dr. Smith to assert,* that a commercial country, like ours, could afford no more than a hundredth part of its population for the business of war; else its commerce, deemed by him the very source of those finances by which war is supported, would go into languishment and decay— whereas, though the whole of that immense com-

---

* He at least states what the common estimate is, without qualifying or contradicting it. " Among the civilized nations of modern Europe, it is commonly computed, that not more than one hundredth part of the inhabitants of any country can be employed as soldiers, without ruin to the country which pays the expense of their service."—*Wealth of Nations*, Book V. chap. I.

merce, which is busied in providing the superfluities of life, were this instant to be annihilated, it
would still leave in the hands of the consumers the
maintenance of the whole disposable population,
out of whom a ten-fold greater military strength
might be made to arise, than our illustrious economist dared to contemplate.   And how else can we
explain the egregious error of Mr. Pitt, who confidently foretold the overthrow of France, because,
in the ruin of her trade, he conceived that her
means of defence and of warfare were utterly exterminated ?   The truth is, that it was the wreck of her
commerce which created her armies.   Her disposable population, disbanded from their former pacific
employments, flocked in myriads to the standard
of independence, and at length of aggression and
conquest over all her enemies.   Their old employments failed them, but their maintenance did not
fail them.   It remained in the hands of those who
wont to be their customers; and, when surrendered
by them, at the call of patriotism, or the bidding
of an energetic government for the necessities of
the state, it was made available for the support of
the same population, now transferred from the
business of trade to the business of war.   This destruction of their trade, on which Pitt founded his
calculations of their downfal, was the very thing
which made them the scourge and the terror of all
Europe.   It transformed millions of artizans into
soldiers; and in very proportion to their decay as
a manufacturing, was their extension and their

growth as a military nation. Their fancied weakness turned out to be their real and formidable
strength; and in that mighty re-action, which took
place on the breaking up of the old system of their
affairs, have the principles which we now try to
expound received, from the finger of history, their
most signal and conclusive demonstration.

9. We gather, from this argument, that there
might be a misplaced antipathy to taxation. We
could understand the sentiment, and would also
share in it, should it be made to appear of any tax,
that it dries up the springs of our economic prosperity, or trenches, in the slightest degree, on the
comforts of the poor man and the labourer. But
if, on unravelling the mechanism of human society,
it becomes evident, that there is but the semblance
of this effect without the reality, it ought to mitigate our indignation, and in certain cases, perhaps,
to transfer our generous and patriotic sensibilities
to the opposite side. A tax on the net rent of land
is clearly of this description; abridging nothing,
by its operation, but the luxuries of the wealthier
classes; and appropriated, as its produce may be,
to the extension of the best interests of the commonwealth. The popular representation of the
matter is, that, in virtue of our enormous taxes,
the minions of government are allowed to fatten
on the spoils of the nation, to the further hardship
and oppression of its starving multitudes. We
believe the juster representation to be, that, in virtue of a sweeping and blindfold retrenchment, the

affluent proprietor is enabled to live in greater splendour and delicacy; and that by a farther reduction on the hard-worn earnings of those who are the public's most useful and laborious servants. The monarchy is shorn of its splendour; the great offices of the state are stripped of their graceful and becoming dignity; the system of public instruction is stinted of its needful allowances; the requisite agency for the business of government is crippled in all its departments; our gallant warriors pine in sordid destitution; science, in the Gothic barbarity of our times, is unfostered and unrewarded; in a word, the glory and substantial interests of the nation are sacrificed,—and all with no other effect, than so to ease the landed and the funded aristocracy, that they may be more delicately regaled, or more magnificently attired and attended. The tax, we repeat, does not trench on the livelihood of the poor, but on the luxuries of the rich; and statesmen, misled by a false political economy, or looking only at the surface of things, have made surrender, to a very phantom, of the highest objects of patriotism.

10. We confess that, on this subject, we have no sympathy with what has been called the spirit of the age. The very worst effects are to be dreaded from it. Every thing now is made a question of finance; and science, with all which can grace or dignify a nation, is vulgarized and brought down to a common standard; the standard of the market and of the counting-house. It does look menac-

ing, to take one example out of the thousand which may be specified, that it hinged on one solitary vote,* whether the trigonometrical survey of our island should be permitted to go on—a work which, like the doomsday-book of England, might after the lapse of a millennium still survive, as a great national index for the guidance of our most distant posterity. It makes one tremble for some fearful resurrection of the old Gothic spirit amongst us—when one thinks that we were within a hairbreadth of this noble enterprise being quashed. And this is the spirit of the age!—an age of unsparing retrenchment; a regime of hard and hunger-bitten economy, before whose remorseless pruning hook, lie withering and dissevered from their stem, the noblest interests of the commonwealth; a vehement outrageous parsimony which, under the guise of patriotism, so reigns and ravens over the whole length and breadth of the land, and cares not though both religion and philosophy should expire, if but some wretched item of shred and of candle-end should be gained by the sacrifice; this, though now the ascendant policy of our nation, elevated into power by the decisions of the legislature, and blown into popularity by the hosannahs of the multitude, will be looked back upon by posterity as an inglorious feature of the worst

* It is but fair to say, however, that the majority of one for the continuance of the survey, was in the vote of a committee, which, though it had been adverse, would still have been subject to correction in the House of Commons.

and most inglorious period in the annals of Britain; the befitting policy for an age of little measures and little men.

11. We are aware of the sacrifices which are now being made at the shrine of popularity. A loud call for economy, in all the branches of the public service, has been met to the extent of a most hurtful reduction, both in the number of our national functionaries, and in their allowances; without, we venture to affirm, one particle of addition to the comforts of the general population. In as far as the taxation falls upon landlords, then, it but transfers the services of the people to other masters, without effecting necessarily a diminution of their wages; and the remission of such taxation will but commit them back again to their old employers, and without the increase of their wages. We therefore hold, that those politicians and philanthropists are altogether on a wrong track, who act as if this were the expedient by which aught like permanent relief is to be obtained for the working classes of society. Let capital continue to press on the business of the country as before, which it will do, so long as the appetency for wealth preponderates over a taste either for the luxuries which wealth can purchase, or the generosities which wealth enables us to exercise; and let population continue to press on the food of the country, which it also will do, so long as the love of animal enjoyment predominates over a taste for the comforts and decencies which even humble

life might attain to; and nothing within the compass of human wisdom can be devised by which to save either the distempers of our commerce or the destitution of our peasantry. Government will have the mortification to find, that, after having dismantled its various establishments, to the great damage of great national interests, it will have still the same encounter to maintain, (and that, too, in midst of the weakness and helplessness to which itself has involuntarily descended,) with as wretched, as dissatisfied a population as before.

12. But we have only reasoned, hitherto, on the effect, not of all taxation, but of a special taxation, even that on the net rent of land. But the great majority of our actual taxes appear to fall on profit and wages; and on the incidence and effect of these we reserve ourselves for the following chapter.

CHAPTER IX.

ON THE SUPPOSED EFFECT OF TAXES IN AGGRAVATING
THE CONDITION OF THE LABOURING CLASSES, WITH
THE CONVERSE EFFECT WHICH THE REMISSION OF
TAXES IS CONCEIVED TO HAVE ON THEIR RELIEF,
AND THE ENLARGEMENT OF THEIR COMFORTS.

II. *On the taxes which seem to affect profit and wages.*

1. WHEN a tax is laid upon net rent, the landed proprietor can obtain no indemnification for it, from the other classes of society. There is not a sounder principle in political economy, than that it is not the rent of land which causes the high price of agricultural produce—but that the high price of agricultural produce, brought on by other influences, is the cause of rent. The landed proprietor cannot indemnify himself for the tax, by putting, at his own pleasure, a higher pecuniary value on the products of the soil. It is not the will of the landlord which determines their price. The price of corn fluctuates, like that of every other commodity, with the proportion which the quantity of it brought to market bears to the demand. If, on the one hand, the population choose to multiply, though with the surrender of a part of their wonted comforts; this, by adding to the number and com-

petition of the buyers, will raise the price of corn,
without any will or exertion on the part of the
landlords. Or if, on the other hand, it be the collective will of the population, to forego the pleasure of early marriages, for other and higher pleasures—this may so slacken the demand for corn,
that its price, relative to labour, may become lower
than before. It is not the landlord, who either
raises the price of grain in the one case, or lets it
down on the other. He is the mere recipient of
a surplus, the amount of which is determined, by
causes extrinsic to himself and independent of
himself. He cannot augment this surplus at his
pleasure, so as to indemnify himself for the share
which government chooses to assume of it. They
take from him the maintenance of a certain part of
the disposable population; and, along with this,
they take from him the services of that population.
But this change does not affect, either the number
of the disposable population, or their power of purchasing. These remain unaltered; and so the
price of agricultural produce remains the same as
before. Landlords, therefore, have no way of
making their escape from the impositions of government; or, of shifting the burden from themselves to any other class of society. And, if it can
be proved, that, in this respect, they stand distinguished both from capitalists and labourers; if
these find relief from the taxes which are laid upon
them, in the higher prices of what they sell, or in
the higher wages of what they work; then, all

taxes, however ostensibly laid, in the first instance, will be found, ultimately, to land on the proprietors of the soil.

2. Many are the instances in which it is quite palpable, that the first incidence, and the ultimate effect of a tax, lie on different persons. Perhaps the most frequent and familiar example of this is, when a tax on commodities falls at first upon the manufacturer or the dealer ; but he indemnifies himself by raising the price, and so transfers the burden of it to the purchaser. He shifts the imposition away from himself to another ; and the question is, whether there are not whole classes of men, who, though they do pay taxes ostensibly, do not, in fact, substantially and really, pay them at all. If a merchant, in particular, can escape from the tax laid on the commodity in which he deals, can he not equally escape from all attempts to reach him by taxation in some other way ? If, by raising the price of his article, he can indemnify himself for a tax upon commodities, has he not the same resource against a tax upon profits, or a tax on any of the objects of his expenditure ?* Certain enough it is, that a tax on

* Mr. T. Perronet Thomson, in commenting on the opinions of an economist, who distinguishes between certain taxes which do fall upon purchasers, and certain which do not, shrewdly, and, in my opinion, soundly observes,—" It would be curious to know how he convinces himself, that this is true, when the tax is demanded from the producer, under the title of a tax on his commodities, and would not have been true, if the same sum had been demanded from him, under the title of a tax on his profits."

profits cannot be carried to the annihilation of all
profit, or a tax on the expenses of living to the
annihilation of the livelihood of capitalists, else
trade and manufactures would altogether cease.
On the first blush of the matter, then, there do
appear to be certain compensatory processes, by
which we are sure that some taxes are made up for
to the capitalists; and which, perhaps, have enough
of power and efficacy in them, to make up for all
their taxes whatever. In like manner, it seems
conceded, that no tax, either upon the person of
the labourer, or upon his maintenance, can trench
so far upon his means, as to leave him without the
power of supporting himself and family, in such a
way as shall at least keep up the population of the
land. In this department of society too, then, it
would appear, that there is a compensatory process,
by which the taxes that bear on the subsistence
and comforts of the labourer, are either partially
or entirely made up for; and must therefore be
transferred to some other class who bear the burden of them. If it can be proved, that all taxes,
affecting the status of the capitalists, are made up
for to them by higher prices; and that all taxes,
affecting the status of the labourers, are made up
for to them by higher wages—this would seem to
conduct us to the old doctrine of the French economists, though by a different process from theirs,
that all taxes fall ultimately on the net rent of
land. The common imagination is, that this is a
doctrine which has been long exploded. The

reasoning may be exploded, but yet the doctrine may be true notwithstanding, and may be established on the foundation of other reasoning.

3. There is one argument connected with this doctrine which has been occasionally touched upon by economical writers ; and did we not hold ourselves in possession of another argument on the same side, still more clear and conclusive, we should have expatiated on it at greater length. Let us briefly advert to it before we proceed to the main reason, on which we ground our general affirmation, that taxes are not paid either by capitalists or labourers ; or, to state the principle in more unexceptionable language, that they receive full compensation for the taxes which they do pay; the one in higher profits, and the other in higher wages, than without the taxes they would have received.

4. This argument which, in point of strength and obviousness, holds, in our estimation, but a collateral or subsidiary rank, when compared with the one on which we should feel inclined to rest the cause, is still worthy of being noticed, because it helps to explain the speed, wherewith a compensation arises to the capitalist and labourer, for those taxes which ostensibly fall upon them. The principle of the argument is, that whatever causes a more rapid, or rather a more copious circulation of money, without at the same time increasing the supply of commodities, raises the money price of them. We can thus conceive one way in which a capi-

talist might obtain, at least in as far as circulating capital is concerned, an almost immediate compensation for a tax on profits. If, previous to such a tax, there be an hundred millions annually laid out, in bringing goods to market, which are there sold for a hundred and ten millions, this capital is replaced with a profit of ten millions to its owners. But should a tax of ten per cent. be laid upon these profits, this, in the first instance, affects not the ability of those who purchased to the extent of a hundred and ten millions, seeing that the tax is laid upon the capitalists and not upon their customers; and, in the second instance, it enriches government to the extent of one million. Suppose this million to be expended by government in the purchase of commodities, then would the hundred millions of capital, after the tax of one million upon the owners, be replaced by a hundred and eleven, instead of a hundred and ten millions; or, in other words, the tax which they pay to government would reciprocate back upon themselves, in a consequent rise of the money price of the commodities wherein they deal.

5. And the same is still more palpably true of a tax on the wages of labour. Should a hundred millions be given annually in wages, and government lay an impost of ten per cent. upon the labourers, the ability of the original hirers to make offer of a hundred millions next year for service, is not at all affected by such a tax. But then the effect of it is, that it enables government to com-

pete with them effectually in the labour market, to
the extent of an additional ten millions; or, in
other words, a hundred and ten millions may now
be brought annually forward for the purchase of
labour, instead of a hundred millions as before.
But as there is no additional supply of labour by
this process, the money price of labour would just
rise to the full amount of the tax which has been
laid upon it. The labourers would obtain a full
indemnity for the tax, by the produce of it coming
almost immediately back upon themselves. Insomuch, that were a poll-tax of five pounds a year
laid upon each labourer, we hold, that an almost
instant compensation would take place, by a rise
to the same extent in the money price of labour.
He bears it ostensibly, but not actually. In point
of semblance, it is a tax upon him; but, in point
of real incidence and effect, it is wholly upon his
employers.

6. Before we take leave of this argument, let us
state it in terms of greater generality. Let, on the
one hand, the quantity of capital and labour in
the country remain unchanged, and, on the other,
the power of replacing the capital, and remunerating the labour also remain unchanged—and, however the latter power shall be broken down or
divided, profits will remain the same, and wages
the same. The effect of a tax on profit, or of a
tax upon wages, would just be to bring an additional quantity of money, to the extent of the
tax, into the market for goods, or the market for

labour; and, to that extent, raise the money price
of both. The effect, again, of a tax upon net
rent, would be, to diminish the purchasing power
of the landlords; to the extent only, however, that
the purchasing power of the government was increased; and, without any increase of money-
price, profits and wages would continue in name,
as well as in substance, what they were before.
The operation of a tax on profits and wages would
be nominally to raise the income both of capitalists
and labourers; though, substantially, they would
continue what they were. If the tax were laid
upon net rent, it would diminish the income of
landlords, without raising money-prices; and, therefore, without raising the income of the other two
classes, either nominally or substantially. After
the imposition of such a tax, the united expenditure
of the landlords and government would be equal to
the entire expenditure of the landlords before; and,
under the new system of an expenditure undimi-
nished in its amount, and only changed in its distribution, we should behold both capitalists and
labourers in possession of the same money, as well
as the same real income as formerly.

7. The same reasoning applies to every tax on
those commodities which enter into the maintenance, either of capitalists or labourers; so as to
show, that they can make as effectual escapes from
the indirect as from the direct taxes which are laid
upon them. We are sensible, at the same time, of
the many evasions which might be practised, to ob-

scure, if not to frustrate this argument; and of the
many adjustments which it were necessary to make,
ere we could fully meet all the difficulties that might
be cast in its way.   But we feel how superfluous it
were to take the more laborious, when there is a
shorter and easier path by which to arrive at our
conclusion.   We think that the argument employed
hitherto, serves well to account for the very instant
compensation which accrues to capitalists and
labourers, when taxes are laid, either on their expenditure or their income.   But whether this argument shall be sustained or not, there is still another, which proves irresistibly to our minds, that,
in point of ultimate and permanent effect, taxes do
not fall on either of these classes; a position, which
will be all the more convincing, if we but attend
to the fundamental and efficient principles, by
which both the rate of profit, and the wages of
labour are determined.

8. We shall, in the first instance, keep out of
sight the effect which taxation may have in contracting the agriculture of a country ; and that, for
the purpose of bringing out singly, and therefore
more clearly, the main reason why, ultimately, the
income of neither capitalists nor labourers can be
trenched upon by taxation.   We shall, after establishing this, take the agriculture into account, in
order to complete our whole view of this subject.

9. If we but adverted to the dependence which
profit and wages have on a mental or moral cause,
we should at once perceive, of both these elements,

how little either of them can be affected by taxation. Of the first of them, profit, we know that, *other circumstances remaining the same*, it falls with every increase of capital, and rises with every diminution of it. This circumstance will at once let us see, that its rate depends on the taste and choice of the capitalists themselves; that is, on the proportion which their inclination to save bears to their inclination to spend. If the whole amount of revenue arising from profit, be ten millions in the year, and it be the collective will of the capitalists to spend that sum annually; then profit undergoes no variation. If they spend less than this, capital increases and profits fall. If they spend more, capital decreases and profits rise. With this element brought into the computation, it will be perceived, how a tax might be laid, in the first instance, upon profit, and yet in effect not be paid by the receivers of profit. They have only to persevere in their wonted habits of expenditure and indulgence, and they can throw the whole burden of the tax upon their customers. Let it but be their collective will, to spend on their own gratification ten millions in the year, and the imposition upon them of a tax to the extent of one million, need not trench on their ability to maintain this expenditure. If their capital of a hundred millions was, previous to the tax, replaced by a hundred and ten; then, if after the tax they should continue to spend the ten millions and to pay the one, this would reduce their capital to ninety-nine millions; when, in the consequent higher prices of next year, they might have a full compensation for the tax. Let the replacing power, notwithstanding the tax, continue as before, at a hundred and ten millions; this sum, given in return for the ninety and nine, would raise the profit from ten to eleven millions, and so meet the whole imposition that had been made on this branch of the national revenue. The burden would thus be effectually thrown off from the capitalists, and laid on those who purchase their commodities.

10. And the same would be the result of a tax upon wages. *Other circumstances still being equal,* they fall with the increase, and rise with the decrease of the population. The rate of wages, therefore, has a close dependence on the proportion which the inclination of the people for marriage, bears to their inclination for the comforts and the decencies of life. In other words, it is ultimately decided by a mental or a moral cause. Give the people a high standard of enjoyment, and, rather than sink beneath it, they will postpone matrimony for a season; or, in other words,, we should have later marriages and smaller families. Through the medium of popular intelligence and virtue, this result will be permanently arrived at—and through no other medium. The rate of wages is fixed by the collective will of the people themselves. They are the arbiters of their own condition; having absolute control over that element on which there hinges the amount of their remuneration for labour;

and, if they choose not to exert that control, there
is positively no other expedient by which a commonwealth can be saved from the oppression of an
underpaid and degraded peasantry.   But if, on the
one hand, no devices of philanthropy can save a
population of sordid and grovelling habits, from that
most over-mastering of all oppressions, the oppression of their own numbers—on the other hand, no
weight of imposts can permanently depress a moral
and educated people beneath that elevated position
which themselves have fixed upon, and which themselves are abundantly able to maintain.   This alliance between a people's character and a people's
comfort, is far the most valuable lesson in political
science, and is convertible to the most precious applications which can be made of it.   We do not
think that even the immediate effect, or at least the
effect beyond one year, of a tax on wages, is to
lessen the remuneration of the labourer ; but even
if it had, it could have no such effect permanently.
It could not reduce the economic state or condition
of men, who have an absolute dictation over the
proportion between the demand for labour and the
supply of it.   They can countervail the operation
of such a tax by their habits ; and, having unlimited
command over the supply of labour, they can, by
a moral economic check on the magnitude of this
supply, sustain, in the midst of all adverse elements,
whether physical or political, the attitude of an
erect and well-conditioned peasantry.

11. A tax on profit leaves the capitalists at free-

dom to embark less of capital on business than before; and, failing an immediate rise on the price of their commodities, if, on the average, they choose to keep up their wonted personal and household expenditure, and the tax compel them, for this purpose, to trench upon their capital, they have, at length, a full compensation in the increased profits of trade. A tax on wages leaves the labourers at liberty to marry later than before; and, failing an immediate rise on the money-price of work, if, on the average, they choose to postpone marriage, till they are enabled to enter upon it without any compromise of their wonted enjoyments, they may at length, from a lessened population, have an equally full compensation in the consequent rise of the value of labour. A certain average style of expenditure, resolutely adhered to by manufacturers and merchants, could, through the medium of a diminished capital, act upon profit, so as to yield them an indemnification for their tax; and the same principle, a certain average style of expenditure, resolutely adhered to by labourers, could, through the medium of a diminished population, act upon wages, so as to yield them the same indemnification. Both classes, ultimately speaking, are alike exonerated from the weight of taxation; and in the increased price, whether of commodities or labour, the whole burden of it is tranferred to the proprietors of the soil.

12. These principles serve to demonstrate, that a tax on commodities falls as little upon capi-

talists and labourers, as either a tax on profits does
upon the one, or as a tax on wages does upon the
other. It matters not, whether the attempt to reduce their standard of enjoyment, be made by a
direct assessment on their income, or by an impost on the articles which they use. Both attempts can be alike resisted, by a resolute adherence
on their parts to their respective standards of enjoyment, and their resistance can by each be carried into
effect; that of the former class, through the medium
of a retardation, or even a diminution, effected
on the capital, by means of an expenditure which
they will not consent to reduce; and that of the
latter class, through the medium of a retardation,
or even a diminution, effected on the population,
by means of the moral preventive check, whose
effect is to sustain that style and habit of enjoyment among labourers, which they will not
consent to let down. It is thus that their collective will can maintain for them the level, whether
it be a high or a low one, in which they choose
to acquiesce; and that this level, it is in their
power to uphold, in opposition to all taxes, whether on profits, on wages, or on commodities. They
hold in their hands, in fact, the two instruments of
capital and population, which they might regulate
at pleasure; and thus it is, that every tax, which,
without such command, would depress their condition, may be effectually countervailed.

13. The general conception is, that dealers can
ensure their own escape from a tax upon their com-

modities, by laying it through means of a higher
price upon their customers; when that tax is a partial one, or does not reach to all commodities. And
the way, it is imagined, in which they do make
their escape, is by withdrawing a portion of capital
from the trade which is taxed, to that which is not
taxed; in which case, the price rises in the former
trade, and so transfers the burden of the taxation
which has been laid upon it, from the dealer to the
consumer. But if this be the only way in which
capitalists can escape from taxation, every new tax
on commodities, however partial, would be attended by a general fall of profits. The transference of capital from a taxed to an untaxed trade,
will of course raise prices in the former, but will
depress them in the latter; so as, after an equilibrium is established, to depress somewhat the
general rate of profit. If the general rate of profit
be ten per cent. and a tax of ten per cent. be laid
upon sugar; this would drive off so much capital
from the sugar-trade, and so raise its price to the
consumer. But if there be no other outlet for the
withdrawn capital than other trades, then its investiture in these will bring down their profits,
till an equilibrium be established among all the
trades; when, after this transference, the general
profit on all commodities might be imagined to fall
down to nine per cent. But at this rate, profit
would be subject to successive deductions, with
every new tax laid upon commodities, till at length
we might imagine a general impost of ten per cent.

carried round the whole circle of commerce; when, if there be truth in the representation frequently given, all profit would be annihilated, and so all trade come to a stand from the want of inducement to continue it. But this is so manifestly absurd, that there must be some other outlet for the capital withdrawn from the trade that is taxed, than that of vesting it as capital in other employments. Now it can, and often does, find such an outlet, by being turned to the purpose of a revenue, and thus absorbed in the expenditure of capitalists. This is the way, then, in which they have a control over profits, and a refuge from the effects of taxation. They can not only withdraw capital from one business to another, but they can withdraw it in part from all business; and, by thus limiting the extent of its application, they can counteract the whole operation of a tax on their commodities, by such a rise in their price, as will shift the burden of it entirely to the consumers. It will be allowed on all hands, that if taxes can be made in any way to fall upon profit, capital will not *accumulate* so fast as it would otherwise have done; and so *future* prices will be higher than they would otherwise have been. And it is just as obvious, that if, in virtue of taxes, capital is not at this moment *applied* so plentifully as it would otherwise have been, *present* prices must be higher than they would otherwise have been. All we need, then, for the establishment of our position, is the *postulatum,* that taxation, which restrains the future accumulation of capital, will also, if the holders of capital so choose, restrain the present application of it. In virtue of the future increase of capital being restrained, prices will not be so low at some future time as they otherwise would have been. In virtue of its present application being restrained, prices are not so low at the present time as they otherwise would have been. In other words, as without the tax prices would have been so much lower, with the tax they are as much higher; and in these higher prices, the capitalist gets his full indemnification. And the labourer can find his way at length to the same immunity. Both have that state of things within their reach, in which they can alike make head, or stand their ground, against the imposts of government.

14. But though the principle we have now attempted to unfold, is competent to achieve a full immunity for these two classes from the burden of taxation, the effect may be suspended for a time, in consequence of the influence which certain sorts of taxation have upon agriculture. The most interesting conclusions may be gathered from this part of the subject. We have often said of the extreme limit of cultivation, that it, of all others, is the place where the greatest lessons in economical science are to be learned. It will serve to modify some of our former positions, and lead to the establishment of new ones, if we attend to the effect which the different species of taxation produce upon this limit.

15. First, then, a tax on net rent would not re-strain cultivation. It might somewhat retard the progress of it; but, certainly, there is nothing in such a tax, to prevent the agriculture from being carried as far down among the inferior soils, as if the landlords had been subjected to no such bur-den. We are quite aware of a retardation that might be caused by a slower accumulation of capi-tal among the proprietors. But capital will arise, and has arisen, in other quarters of society ; so that, in fact, its tendency is to overflow beyond the possibility of its profitable investiture, whether in the business of husbandry, or in any other business whatever. In these circumstances, the cultivation will soon be carried as far with a tax upon net rent as without one. The land that is last entered on, if it pay no rent, is subject to no burden from the tax. The land immediately above it in the scale, does pay rent; and this rent is subject to a frac-tional deduction in consequence of the tax. But the recipient, the landlord, will not now refuse to let out this land, because he only gets half a crown instead of five shillings from the acre of it. Pre-vious to the tax, he does not stop the letting of his land at the point, when it only yielded him half a crown the acre—and neither will he still. The truth is, that in giving over a farm to cultivation, he commits the whole soil of it, with all its varieties, to the management of the tenant, who will culti-vate every acre of it that can yield him a profit; whether or not, over and above this, it yields an

excess, which goes in the shape of rent to the landlord.   Let this excess be shared as it may between
his landlord and the government, it affects not his
operations; and that, because it affects not the
capability of the land last entered upon, to give
him the return of an adequate profit for the expenses of its cultivation.   What this profit shall be
depends upon himself, or rather upon the collective will of all the capitalists in the land; who,
either by their accumulations can reduce the profit,
or by their expenditure can uphold, nay, augment
it at their pleasure.

16. Again, a tax upon luxuries, in as far as they
are used only by the landlord, would just, in point
of economic effect, be tantamount to a tax on the
net rent.   It would not lie as a burden on the cultivation at all.   The domain of agriculture would
remain as widely extended as before.   All the
land lying fully within this domain, would still
yield a rent to the landlord; while that placed
along the margin, or the land last entered on,
would retain its capabilities for yielding a satisfactory profit to the tenant, however the rent of the
proprietor might be encroached upon by the demands of the government.

17. But, thirdly, a tax on profit, or even on the
luxuries used by those whose revenue lies in profit,
has a limiting effect on cultivation.   We have already proved how it is, that capitalists can find
their compensation, either for a tax upon income,
or upon the commodities on which that income is

expended. Should they choose to maintain their
wonted establishment, and pay all their taxes to the
bargain; this latter payment, by encroaching on
the capital, keeps up the profit; and the tax is
paid, not out of their income, but out of the higher
prices now laid on the commodities in which they
deal. This, in the first instance, will operate a
contraction on the agriculture, by adding to the
price of the second necessaries of life, and so adding to the expenses of farm management. And
besides, like all other capitalists, farmers will refuse to embark more of capital on their business,
than what they can obtain a satisfying return for;
or, in other words, they will refuse to enter on the
cultivation of land which returns not a certain net
profit to themselves; or which enlarges not that
profit when its power is trenched upon, of commanding for them their wonted enjoyments, by the
imposition of a tax on the articles which they use.
This, then, is the effect of a tax which goes to limit
the income of capitalists, or to limit the amount of
their enjoyment in the expenditure of that income.
Farmers will not carry their agriculture so far down
as otherwise they would have done. They will
stop short at that better soil, out of whose returns
they can both pay the tax with the augmented expenses, and remunerate themselves. The agriculture is contracted; or, the effect of such taxes is a
lessening of the country's subsistence, a lessening
of the country's population.

18. And, lastly, the same is still more palpably
and largely the effect of a tax, either on wages, or

on any of those commodities which enter into the maintenance of labourers. The land last entered on must at least yield a produce, which can feed the agricultural labourers employed on it, and their secondaries. But by a tax, either on the wages of labour, or on any of those commodities which enter into the maintenance of labour, more than this is exacted from the last cultivated land. It must not only be able to feed the agricultural labourers and their secondaries; but it must at least be able to feed as many more as can be subsisted by the produce of the tax. If a portion of such land require the labour of five agricultural workmen, and they again require the labour of five others to uphold them in the second necessaries of life; that land must at least be able to feed the families of ten workmen. But should the taxes, whether on wages or necessaries, be equal to a fifth part of the labourers' income; then no land can be entered upon without loss by these five direct labourers, which is not able to feed at least twelve labouring families. All such taxes, therefore, operate to the contraction of the agriculture; and so, eventually, to the diminution of the numbers of the people. And conversely, the remission of these taxes would, as if by the removal of an obstruction, let out the agriculture to poorer soils than have ever yet been attempted. It would be followed by an increase of the means of subsistence; and, eventually, by an increase of the population.

19. A tax then on profit, a tax on wages, or a tax on any of the commodities which are used by

capitalists or labourers, will tell on the limit of
cultivation. The imposition of these taxes has
the effect of drawing in, and the removal of them
the effect of letting out, the agriculture. The immediate effect then of the former measure, were
a fall of wages, because of a reduction in the
quantity of food, without a corresponding reduction all at once in the numbers of the people;
and also a fall of profit from the reduction that
would take place, not only in the agriculture of
the country, but in all the business of providing
for the necessaries and luxuries of a society, whose
extent was commensurate to the agriculture; and
so a reduction in the business of the country,
without a corresponding reduction all at once in
its capital. Yet, though the first effect of these
taxes is to depress both profit and wages, the
ultimate effect in which it settles down, is to depress the revenue of the landlords. The capital
will gradually recover its rate of profit, in the
process of its own declension; and the population
will gradually recover their rate of wages, in the
process (we admit a melancholy one) of their own
decay. After these processes are consummated,
we see the whole of these taxes virtually transferred to the proprietors of the soil. They have,
in the first instance, to pay a higher price for the
commodities which they use, and the labour which
they employ. They, in the second instance, pay,
by its being withheld from their rents, the whole
addition which taxation lays on the expenses of

husbandry. *These two together,* if there be truth in our argument, *should make up the whole revenue which accrues to government.** But beside mak-

* The position, that all the revenue drawn by the State from the *natural population,* is, in effect, taken from the landlords; is so much the more startling, when one compares the accounts commonly given of the landed rental of Great Britain, with the actual amount of the public income. The rental is frequently estimated at beneath 60 millions annually, whereas the public revenue has at times exceeded that sum; and it is a most natural question, How the doctrine of our text can be made to harmonize with the arithmetical and experimental truth in this matter?

The following statements may serve to explain this difficulty, and to elucidate various of the positions which we have had occasion to make in our reasonings upon the subject.

Let us assume 60 millions as the landed rental of the kingdom, and that the public revenue is even as large as 60 millions also. The question is, How, in these circumstances, can it be made out, that the proprietors of the soil would not be losers, if a commutation were made of all our present taxes, and the whole amount were laid on the net rent of land? How is it possible that this rent can bear the burden of a transference, that would seem, *prima facie,* to annihilate the whole wealth of the landlords?

Though our reply to this be on hypothetical data, it will be quite enough to prove what the elements are which serve for an explanation of the difficulty. Let us therefore, still proceeding on assumptions, take the interest of the national debt at 30 millions; and, considering the fund holders as mortgagees, or as co-proprietors of the land, the whole taxable wealth may, in this view, be regarded as 90 millions.

Let us further imagine the expense of living on the part of the affluent, to have been doubled by the actual system of taxation; or, in other words, that were there no imposts on commodities and other objects, these proprietors of 90 millions income, could have commanded the same amount of comfort and enjoyment with an expenditure of 45 millions. Then it

ing up for the tax in this way, they have to undergo a distinct and additional loss, in the limita-

is quite palpable that they would not suffer, though all our present taxes were abolished, and replaced by an income tax of 50 per cent. on land and fund holders.

But such a tax would only yield 45 millions to government, and there remain 15 millions to be accounted for. According to Mr. Colquhoun, whose estimate is understood to be a moderate one, the number of cultivated acres in England and Wales alone, amounts to upwards of 30 millions. We have already seen how, by taxes on commodities, the expenses of husbandry are raised. Let us imagine them to be so raised ten shillings an acre. This makes a deduction from the rent of 15 millions on the whole; a sum therefore paid to government by the landlords, because effecting a diminution to that extent in their incomes. This completes the proof, that after taxation has had its full effect on profit and wages, or when these recover their ultimate compensation, they are the land and fund holders; or, generalizing the expression, by regarding the mortgagees as joint owners of the territory, they are the proprietors of the soil who pay all taxes.

When asked then, How the landed proprietors, with only 60 millions a year of net rent, can be said to bear the whole expenses of the State, even though these should amount to 60 millions in the year? our brief reply is—First, that in the additional expense which they incur by taxation as at present constituted, they pay annually .... 30 millions. That their mortgagees, the national creditors, do
    also, in the same way, pay .... 15 millions.
And lastly, the landlords sustain a reduction of rent,
    from the additional expenses which taxation
    brings on husbandry, to the extent of .... 15 millions.
Making out of these items the whole revenue of
    government, or .... 60 millions.

Suppose all present taxes abolished, this would be followed up by a rise of rent to the landlords, to the amount of 15 millions;

tion of the agriculture. The rent of those soils, which taxation may have compelled the farmers to

making their whole revenue 75 millions, which, added to the revenue of the national creditors, would afford 105 millions for the whole taxable income of the country. A tax of about 57 per cent. upon this sum, would furnish an income to government as large as before. There would, by this change, be a hardship to the fund-holders, in that they had to pay 57 per cent. on their income, in exchange for the relief of only 50 per cent. in the expenses of their living. There would be a proportional benefit to the landlords, who, in the increased rent of their lands, would receive an addition of 25 per cent. to their income ; and, along with it, only an addition of 7 per cent. to the exactions of government. This advantage over the fund-holders, may, of itself, supersede the necessity of any such adjustment, as we have suggested in Appendix G. between these two classes, on the event of an abolition of the corn laws.

But the advantage to the landlords does not terminate here. They would receive a greater addition to their rent than ten shillings an acre, or 15 millions from the whole of that land which is already in cultivation. The rise of ten shillings an acre, would be afforded from the land *as at present* cultivated. But the same relief from taxes, which permits an additional rent of ten shillings an acre from this land, would also let out the cultivation to inferior land, and allow a more strenuous cultivation over the whole of the cultivated territory. Over and above the 15 millions, which make up all the expenses that taxation lays on the present husbandry, landlords would receive something in the shape of rent from an extended husbandry ; that is, both from a new agriculture, which would reclaim a belt of inferior land, and from a more intense agriculture, which may be said to reclaim a stratum of the whole. We might imagine additional dozes of capital, furnishing in succession, nine shillings, and eight shillings, and seven shillings, down to one shilling an acre, in rental to the landlord, as the product of that more intense culture, which, before the remission of our present taxes, abandon, forms but a small part of this loss. For they are further compelled by it, to abandon

would have been unprofitable. The arithmetical mean of these numbers, or five shillings an acre,'would furnish no less than $7\frac{1}{2}$ millions of additional rent to the landowners. And if the belt of inferior land should furnish only half a million, then eight millions of rent from the extended agriculture, must be added to the 15 millions of additional rent from the relieved agriculture, making an addition in the whole of 23 millions to the rent of land, as the fruit of that commutation of the taxes, the very cautious, but at length total adoption of which, we feel inclined to recommend.*

Let us conclude with a short recapitulation, to place in one view before the reader, the benefits which the landed interest would receive from this great change in the financial system of the country.

We have supposed the present income of landlords to be 60 millions, and that the public income is of the same amount. Of this the fundholders, though they should pay only 50 instead of 57 per cent. would contribute .... 15 millions. And the landowners paying 50 per cent. also, or a rental of 83 millions, ... $41\frac{1}{2}$ millions.

Making an income to government (only $3\frac{1}{2}$ millions inferior to what it was,) of .... $56\frac{1}{2}$ millions.

Even though this sum of $3\frac{1}{2}$ millions, instead of being taken from the fundholders, were taken by an additional territorial impost from the landlords, they would still have 38 millions to expend, after the charges of living had been reduced one-half; which is tantamount to 76 millions in the present state of things. In other words, they would have as much benefit by the proposed change, as if, with the continuance of the present prices, they were to receive an addition of 16 millions, or of more than 25 per cent. to their present incomes.

The following extract from Mr. Perronet Thomson's Essay,

* See Appendix H. On the gradual reform of our Financial System.

those extreme degrees of cultivation, extending to
the whole land that is under the plough, which,
before the tax, may have been profitable, but
which, after the tax, have ceased to be so.   They
are thus forced to relinquish the difference be-

on the True Theory of Rent, may still further illustrate our
argument.

It is said by a writer of name in economical science, that,
" the fact that tithes, and other taxes on raw produce, do not
form a deduction from rent, but go to increase the price of produce, is obvious from this circumstance, that the tithe of expensive crops, and which require a great expenditure in their
cultivation, frequently amounts to *four* or *five* times the rent of
the land.   The Rev. Mr. Harlett, by far the ablest advocate of
tithes, and whose authority cannot therefore be questioned, in-
forms us, that the tithe of an acre of hops, raised on land worth
forty or fifty shillings an acre, is, after deduction of drying and
duty, generally worth from three to four pounds; and he further
states, that he had known seven or eight pounds paid for the tithe
of an acre of carrot-seed, where the land was not worth twenty
shillings !   In such cases, it is plainly as great an absurdity to
affirm, that tithes fall exclusively on the rent of the landlord,
as it would be to affirm, that a *part* is greater than a *whole*."

To which Mr. Thomson makes this distinct and decisive reply :

" The whole of this is a confusion of ideas, arising from the
two meanings of the word *rent*.

" When a tax or tithe is said to form a deduction from rent,
this manifestly *means, from the rent as it would be without the deduction of the tax*, and not as *it is after the deduction*.

" Nobody ever said, that the eight pounds, which is the tithe
of an acre of carrot-seed, is taken out of the twenty shillings,
which is left for the landlord afterwards ; but that it is taken
out of the nine pounds, which is the residuum, after paying the
expenses and necessary profits of cultivation, and that it is because eight pounds is taken for tithe, that only twenty shillings
is left for the landlord."

tween the products of the more and the less
strenuous cultivation. By drawing in the agriculture, they have not merely to give up a *belt* of
inferior land, lying, as it were, without the limit
of the cultivated domain ; but they have to give up
a *stratum* of deeper cultivation within the limit,
and co-extensive with the whole length and breadth
of the territory. So enormously do the landlords
suffer from taxes, which, though ostensibly laid
upon others, fall really, and with accumulated
pressure, upon themselves. So great would be the
advantage, though few or none of them perceive
it, if they would but commute all the taxes upon
commodities into a territorial impost upon net
rent.   Capitalists and labourers are the temporary, but landlords are the principal and the permanent sufferers, by the taxes in question. They
lose, in fact, a great deal more than the government receives. They at length have not only to
pay, in advanced prices and the additional expenses of husbandry together, the full amount of
the taxes ; but, in virtue of the straitened cultivation which has taken place in consequence of
them, they have to meet the charge with a proportionally less income than they would otherwise have had. Immediately, and ostensibly, these
taxes bear hard upon the other classes ; but they
are truly the landlords, on whom the whole weight
of them ultimately falls—and that, not merely with
a permanent, but with an aggravated pressure.

20. What disguises the truth upon this subject,

is, that in the immediate or the apparent, we
lose sight of ultimate and abiding consequences.
The tax upon wages, or upon aught that enters
into the maintenance of the receivers of wages,
will be felt, (irrespective of its effect in limiting
the agriculture of a country,) and is indeed a real
hardship on the payer of the tax for the first year
of its imposition. A part of what he has got, or
would have gotten that year, has been fairly taken
from him; and that, before any compensation
could have arisen from the larger demand of the
government for labour, or the larger ability on
their part to support it. But in a single year, we
believe, a compensation arising from this source
would be made good; when the tax would only
be paid by him in appearance, while in reality,
and through the medium of his advanced wages,
it would be paid by his employer. Still the semblance has the same exasperating effect upon his
feelings, as if it had been the reality. And it is
most natural for him to conceive of government as
his natural enemy, and standing in the way of his
comfort; and more especially, when the remission
of the tax would operate as substantial a relief to
him *for one year*, as he suffered of substantial hardship for one year at the first imposition of it. This
remission would prove a real boon to him for one
year, and an enlargement beside for a brief season
longer, by letting out in some degree the agriculture; when, first, by a fall in the money-price of
labour, and then by an increase of the population,

he would soon find, in spite of all that he promised to himself from the abolition, that he was in circumstances of as great straitness and penury as before.

21. And the same holds true of the profit on circulating capital, where the investiture can be contracted immediately, and in one year a full compensation can be had for any tax which may have been laid upon it. But a remission here too would be felt as a boon at the first; and, in as far as it tended to let forth the agriculture, would enlarge somewhat, and for a season, the operations of trade. We are not to wonder, then, if the appetency for immediate relief, and an enlargement however short, since not seen to be so, should create as intense a desire, on the part of merchants and manufacturers, for the abolition of the taxes which bear ostensibly upon them, as if this were to translate them into a condition of sufficiency and ease which was to abide for ever. It is no less the truth, however, that should this remission take place, a larger application of capital at first, and a rapid accumulation of it afterwards, would speedily bring on as limited returns, after the abolition of these taxes, as are experienced at present. It is not the capitalists, but their customers, who pay all such taxes; and, in the long run, they are only the customers who would feel the relief of their being done away.

22. But if the truth lie concealed in the case of wages and profit on circulating capital, it lies under deeper concealment still in the case of fixed capital. When a tax is laid on the profits of the

latter, its investiture cannot be contracted so suddenly, and therefore, the effects of the tax cannot be recovered so suddenly, as in the other instances. The cotton manufacturers cannot let down the number of their cotton-mills with the same facility, that certain other manufacturers, who operate with a circulating, rather than a fixed capital, could abstain from hiring the wonted number of workmen. The tax, therefore, is not so speedily countervailed in the case of a fixed, as in that of a circulating capital. The compensation is reached at length, and in a course of years—not by this capital being withdrawn, but by its being suffered to decay to a certain extent without being replaced. It may thus require some years before the proprietors of fixed capital can be reinstated in their wonted gains, when at length the whole burden, both of their taxes and of all others, falls upon the rent of land; whether that rent be given for the original powers of the soil, or for those powers aided and extended by the successive applications of a capital so fixed as now to be immoveable, and which has realized an amelioration on the land that has been the growth of centuries, and will never pass away.

23.* Had the taxes at present under considera-

* It is surely unnecessary to dwell on the obvious effect of such a commutation as we recommend, in augmenting the value of all fixed money-incomes; and so far, in laying a burden without any equivalent compensation upon the landlords. If the pecuniary allowances to all public servants should remain the same, it were tantamount to an augmentation of their pay, and an augmentation, therefore, of the burden upon the tax-payers.

tion, had no effect in contracting the agriculture, we hold, that sooner or later their whole effect on the clear income of capitalists and workmen, would have been countervailed by a rise in the money-price of commodities and the money-price of labour. But they do contract the agriculture; and the effect of this is, that both these classes take a longer time of reaching their compensation; and that, by a gradual and intermediate process of decay. We should at length be landed in a smaller society, and a smaller capital for the conducting of its business. But, with the same standard of enjoyment as before, among our merchants and our peasantry, we should behold as well paid labour, though now a reduced population; and as well remunerated, though now a reduced capital, as before.

24. We are not insensible to what has been alleged as the likely effect of such a process. It very possibly might give a shock to the standard of enjoyment in both classes; and permanently, or for the space of some generations, degrade it. The taxes in question, by the limitation which they impose on agriculture, do operate, just as a large encroachment of the sea would, or as a blight on the quality of the soil. This bereavement of territory, or this curse of barrenness, would, by a lessening of the country's food, lead, through a midway passage of penury and distress, to a lessening both of the capital and population. But the apprehension is, that the people, thus fami-

liarized to privation, would lose the ideas of comfort, the respectable taste and habits of the better state from which they had fallen. They would undergo, it is feared, a moral change, so that the moral check might, in efficacy and vigour, fall beneath the exigencies of the occasion. There is a certain recklessness, a desperation of character, that might ensue from the more desperate condition in which they shall have been placed ; and, while it is admitted, that any enlargement in their means may yield but a temporary augmentation to the comfort of families ; the reverse process of an encroachment on their means, may, by an operation purely mental, permanently and irrecoverably degrade them beneath the higher ground which they now occupy.

25. But, practically, we are not called upon to stop at this contemplation. The more cheering alternative is within our reach. In the reform of our financial system, the readiest and most convenient changes are all in the opposite direction. Every commutation of a tax from commodities in general use, to the rent of land, lets forth the agriculture, instead of contracting it. The people are translated into better circumstances ; and they may be taught, in the season of intermediate abundance, to have a permanently higher demand for the enjoyments of life than before. They may be raised to a higher status; and of that status they may be enabled to keep the permanent occupation, in virtue of their higher standard of enjoyment. Were

the economic only followed by the moral enlargement, then, instead of a brief evanescent holiday for
the people of our land, the whole platform of humble life may be elevated, and made to sustain an
erect, and independent, and prosperous commonalty, to the most distant ages.

26. But we have failed altogether in our general
argument, if we have not made good the position,
that the economic without the moral, will, in the
long run, achieve nothing for our families ; affording us only a larger society, but, along with this,
a proportionally larger mass of want and wretchedness than before. The successive stretches which
are made in respect of room and of abundance will
soon be overtaken; whether these proceed from
a gradual relaxation of the corn laws, or a gradual
remission of the taxes which bear on the mercantile and industrious classes. The full effect of
these two measures, even were they perfected,
would not secure a greater addition to the food of
the country, than we have received during the
last twenty years from the natural progress of our
agriculture. And who will affirm, that, with our
larger population to our larger means of subsistence, we are not in circumstances of as great
difficulty, and as closely beset all round with the
feeling of straitness and limitation as we ever
were ? There is no other specific, we repeat, for
the economic well-being of our land, than that of
moral and Christian education. One vain expedient after another may become the object of the

popular cry, and the popular confidence : and they
may yield, too, a momentary ease. But on the
great scale of national policy, and with the view
to an abidirig and comprehensive benefit which
shall be felt throughout in society, and last for
generations, it will be found, that, without intelligence and virtue among the people themselves,
they, one and all of them, are but specious and
delusive mockeries.

27. Yet it ought never to be forgotten, that,
powerless and insignificant as all merely economic
objects are, when there is a reckless and degraded
population, they nevertheless form the great moving
forces by which the changes that take place in the
progress of society are determined. It matters not
to the men of the existing generation, whether future generations will have a benefit or not, from
the measures they are so clamorously and intensely
set upon. The great prevailing appetency with
them, is for the present relief, the present enlargement. Though a free corn trade should only ease
the commerce and population of the country for a
very few years; this is enough to enlist all the
energies, both of the multitude and of the mercantile world in its favour. Though the remission of
the taxes which bear upon the maintenance or employment of the industrious, be but the momentary
loosening of a bondage, immediately followed up
by a growth, which will cause the pressure to be
sensibly and really as great as before ; this does
not make the complaint less impetuous, or the

demand for relief less urgent or less influential.
Though it be true, that on the removal of every
artificial limit, there will be but the felt enlargement of a very few years, and then as close and
besetting a confinement from the natural limit as
was ever before experienced ; still the impatience
under the existing restraints is as loudly expressed
by the country, and will at length place government under as strong a necessity for yielding to it.
They are not the evils of posterity, nor yet the evils
which, in a few little years, will come upon themselves, that practically affect men. They are decided by the feelings of the present, and not the
anticipations of the future. They, in fact, have
no clear nor correct anticipations upon the subject.
The sure and present relief by which all will be
eased for a season, and many of them will individually be enriched, is truly all that they care for ;
and so the cry for emancipation, whether from
taxes or prohibitions or monopolies, is as loud and
general, as if an everlasting prosperity were to be
the result, or a millennium of abundance to all the
classes of society.

28. There is a world of delusion in these anticipations. Yet it is quite the wisdom of our statesmen, in this particular instance, to proceed in the
current of the general feeling. We are far from
the opinion, that *vox populi*, is *vox Dei ;* yet, on
the present question, it so happens, that the demand of the many, runs in the direction which is
best suited, both to their own interests and the in-

terests of all. Never was there a more fortunate
conjunction of a popular with a sound policy, than
in the example before us. Government have it in
their power, by a series of commutations from taxes
on commodities to taxes on income, at once to in-
gratiate themselves with the community at large,
and to augment that territorial wealth which forms
the source and the sustenance of all other wealth in
the country. Doubtless the hopes, the extravagant hopes of the manufacturing and commercial
classes would be signally frustrated; but so also
would the extravagant fears of the landed and agricultural classes. The proprietors of the soil would
be the only class who should *individually* feel richer
in consequence of the change. The subsequent
enlargement of wealth amongst the trading classes,
would soon be so overtaken by the increasing capital
and population, that, *individually*, there would be as
great straitness amongst them as before. But then,
they could no longer charge their distresses upon
government. It would be palpable, that the over-
speculation of capitalists, or the over-population of
the community at large, were the real causes of
every economic calamity that came upon the land.
The heart-burnings of political rancour and disaffection, would no longer come to be associated
with the depression or the vicissitudes of trade.
Government would be relieved from the burden of
all that odium which so endangers the cause of order and authority in the commonwealth; and thus
nothing, we are persuaded, would contribute more

than the reign of a sound political economy, to sweeten and harmonize the politics of Britain.

29. And it were no small advantage if landlords were made to bear the whole burdens of the state ostensibly, as they do really ; that the importance, the paramount importance, of landed wealth and of the landed interest, would stand forth, nakedly and without disguise, to the recognition of all men. So that it were well for them, if compelled, even though against their will, to pay all taxes. The men who hold in their hand the necessaries of life, have the obvious superiority over the men who but minister the superfluities or the comforts. They have the natural ascendancy ; and we think it wholesome and befitting, that they should have the political ascendancy also. We hold it the most exceptionable feature in the modern scheme of representation, as being a violation of the rightful and natural order, that the agricultural interest is not sufficiently represented in parliament. We think, that, in partitioning the matter between the landed and the commercial, the supreme importance of the one, and the merely subordinate or subservient character of the other, have not been enough adverted to. But, perhaps, the very violence thus done to the natural propriety of things, may speed the manifestation of the truth upon this subject. The proprietors of the soil have been a vast deal too tardy in learning the lessons which relate both to their own and their country's well-being. It is better that the repeal of the corn

laws, and a reformed system of finance, should
both be forced upon them.   They will maintain
their ground notwithstanding.   They may be overborne for a season ; but their indestructible wealth
will at length appear manifest to all men, as being
that which constitutes the main strength and support of the nation.   It will even make head against
the inequalities of our representative system, and
secure for them, in opposition to every device and
every provision in the framework of our constitu-
ency, the ascendancy in parliament—an ascendancy
which will the more readily be deferred to, when
it becomes clear as day, that they indeed bear all
the burdens of the commonwealth.   The lords of
the soil, we repeat, are, naturally and properly, the
lords of the ascendant.*

    * In Sir Henry Parnell's interesting work on Financial Re-
form, we meet with much that we approve, but with much also
that we should feel inclined to modify.
    In the first place, we cannot sympathize with his zeal for
retrenchment, believing as we do, that if taxes were rightly
laid, and the produce of them rightly expended, they admit of
being most beneficially increased for the best interests of the
nation ; and with no other sacrifice, than a sacrifice of luxury
and splendour on the part of the landed proprietors.
    Again : we agree in the desire, that the taxation should be
lightened which falls upon manufactured goods, whether at the
earlier stage of their preparation, on the raw materials, or at
the later and ultimate stage, on the finished articles.   But it
depends on what the species of commodity is, whether we shall
think the tax to be productive of economic injury to the nation.   Let the commodity in question be one of the higher
luxuries ; and, for the sake of greater distinctness to our argu-

CHAPTER X.

ON TITHES.

1. Among the questions which now engage us, there is a most important distinction to be observed, between the ultimate and the immediate effect of any given change in the circumstances of a society.

ment, let us conceive that it is consumed only by landlords, who expend a million on the purchase of it. A tax of half a million upon this commodity, whether drawn from the raw or the wrought material, would just have the effect of limiting the enjoyment of the customers to one half of what it was; and, without lessening the means or maintenance of the population at all, would only distribute them differently from before,—one half of those employed in this manufacture being transferred, but as well supported in the service of the state. And conversely, relief from such a tax would doubtless extend the manufacture; yet in no way extend the comfort of labourers, to whom the only change would be, a change of employment back again from the service of government to that of individuals. In the whole reasoning of the work upon this subject, we may observe no obscure traces of the prevalent, the almost universal conception, that a manufacture yields something more than its own products; and that it not only employs, but supports the people who are engaged in it.

The only taxes productive of economic injury to the nation, are those which make the maintenance, whether of labourers or capitalists, dearer than before. This, in the way we have often explained already, must limit the agriculture; and will proportionally limit the population, and the amount of industry

We have affirmed, that the remission of taxes on wages, or profits, or the commodities used by capitalists and labourers, would let out the agriculture among poorer soils than had yet been entered on; and thus, the first effect would be, a plenty and cheapness of the necessaries of life; and an increase of business, not merely in agriculture, but in trade and manufactures, from the larger supplies that would then be required for the various wants of an increased population. There would be an intermediate season of abundance and prosperity to the poorer classes; and we are not to wonder, if

in the land. On this principle, we hold that the taxes on tea and sugar, which enter largely into the maintenance of all classes, do more to lessen the amount of British industry, than any tax would on the raw material of the silk manufacture, which would do little or nothing to abridge the employment of labourers on the whole, however much it might abridge the particular employment of silk-weavers.

Further: though we cannot agree with the author of this important work, in his views, either as to the additional capital that would have been in the country, but for the national debt; or as to the need of an extreme economy in peace, that we might be enabled to meet the expenses of a war: yet we hail with cordial satisfaction, all his proposals and views on the subject of an income tax, into which, in fact, all other taxes might be beneficially commuted, and which might, in every case of great and expensive emergency, be carried to such an extent as to supersede loans. It were well if a beginning could be made now, though it were by an imposition so small as of one or two per cent.; that, in the first place, all pretext for discontent on the part of the labouring classes might be done away; and, in the second, an end be put to our present system of ultra and unsparing economy.

the taxes which obstruct the commencement of such a season, should be regarded as a burden upon the labourers. But without an elevation in the standard of enjoyment, this season would be temporary. An increasing capital would soon fill up the new fields which had been opened for its profitable investiture, after which the gains of the merchant might become just as limited and precarious as before. An increasing population would soon bear as hard as at present, on the augmented food of the country; and thus the wages and comforts of the peasantry be just as stinted as they are at this moment. Every thing, in fact, short of a moral economic check on the multiplication of the species, and that through the medium of the people's education and improved habits, will turn out but an ephemeral expedient for enlarging their means of enjoyment, and raising their status in the commonwealth. Without this, we shall behold, after an interval of brief prosperity, the very straitening in their circumstances, and hear the very outcries of complaint, that we are now exposed to. There will, in virtue of the change, be a larger, but not necessarily a happier society,— more of absolute produce, both of land and labour, we allow, but a produce shared among a number so much greater, that we shall at least have the same proportion of individual distress, as we have at this moment. Capitalists will have to complain of as low and precarious profits as formerly,—labourers, of as overstocked markets, and miserable wages, and frequent visitations of commercial depression and distress, as formerly. Society would undergo a speedy expansion, and a sort of hey-day prosperity be felt during the progress of it. Yet after the transition, and that a very quick one,* had been accomplished, might there in every way be as great a mass of wretchedness, or rather one of larger and more unmanageable dimensions than before. We cannot, in these circumstances, regard taxes so much in the light of a burden upon the people, or the remission of taxes so much in the light of a deliverance to the people. That it would be followed up by a temporary enlargement in their circumstances, we most willingly allow; but the only class who would reap a permanent benefit, and a benefit placed beyond the reach of chance and fluctuation, are the landlords. They would have the whole advantage of the cheapness, induced both on the articles of private expenditure, and on the operations of husbandry, by the abolition of the present taxes; insomuch, that they would lose nothing, though government should levy the whole amount of the taxes from themselves. And besides, they would have a clear and

* The quickness of the transition would arise from the rapidity wherewith the population advances, upon any augmentation that takes place in the means of subsistence. Suppose that a given reform, whether in tithes or taxes, opened the way for subsistence to an additional million of population, the extreme shortness of the time wherein this can be overtaken, may be inferred from the fact, that from 1803 to 1812, upwards of a million was added to the population.

uncumbered gain from all the enlargement which had taken place in husbandry. They would derive a new rent from soils formerly beyond the pale of cultivation; and, what were of vastly more consequence, they would derive an augmented rent from all their old soils, in virtue of the now more strenuous cultivation, which, with the lessening of farm expenses, could be profitably expended on them. The change that we venture to recommend, would spread an augmented richness and value over the whole of their property. It were for their incalculable benefit, could they only be made to perceive it, that all taxes were commuted into a territorial impost. They would then appear ostensibly what they are really—the alone contributors to the public revenue; the only class in the community out of whose wealth the expenditure of government was defrayed. Every pretext, on the score of taxation at least, for the discontent of the other classes in society would be swept away. The chief inflammatory topics, by which it is that demagogues keep alive the fermentation of prejudices and political antipathies in our land, would be wholly done away; and the lords of the soil would henceforth hold that undisputed sway in the commonwealth, wherewith, by the very nature of their property, they are so rightfully invested. They would prodigiously augment their wealth by the commutation that we now recommend; and they would augment tenfold both their security and their influence.

2. But they are the urgencies of the present, and
not the anticipations of the future, which are the
great moving forces that operate in society.   If the
remission of taxes yield but an immediate relief,
though only for a short period, to the existing
generation, this is enough to create an intense
appetency and clamour for the removal of taxes.
It explains, and perhaps justifies, the popular outcry against them.   But it is a weighty consideration
for the legislature, that though, by unsparing retrenchment, they may silence for a little hour the
discontents of the nation, there is a gathering
pressure that will surely and speedily recur, when
the country will be again involved in the same
difficulties, and the government, stripped of its
efficiency and its means, will be less able than ever
to withstand it.   The champions of economy are
not aware, we think, of the very short-lived deliverance which all their efforts will ever effectuate for
the people of the land.   It is right that government
should be relieved from the odium of being their
extortioners or their tyrants ; but this might be as
well done by a commutation of our existing taxes,
as by a simple abolition of them.   With every reduction of a tax upon commodities, were there the
substitution of a centage on the net rent of landlords, this, without any injury to them, would at
once conciliate the affections of the people, and
preserve a requisite agency for the service of government in all its departments.   It is the way to
reconcile the necessary support of government with

the utmost demands of liberalism; and, in these days of fearful conflict between the two elements of order and liberty, we believe that nothing would more effectually harmonize them than this discharge of the general community from all the burdens of the state, along with the distinct and total imposition of them on the proprietors of the soil. We want the whole weight of our taxation to lie upon them visibly, even as we think that it lies upon them virtually and substantially. They would be indemnified by the cheapening of all commodities, consequent on the removal of the present duties; and, more than indemnified, they would be rewarded by the new rents yielded to them from the enlargement of the agriculture.

3. Meanwhile, and under the continuance of the present delusion, great public objects might be sacrificed; and that, too, under the guise of patriotism—and not with the semblance only, but under the real impulse of a generous philanthropy towards the poorer orders. And certain it is, that the remission of taxes would yield an immediate, although a briefly ephemeral relief to them; while the ultimate and permanent effect would be to augment the luxuries of the higher classes. The question, Shall we impair, or let down, the needful establishments of the country, that we may ensure the blessings of well-paid industry to the families of the land? is altogether different from the question, Shall we let down these establishments, that proprietors may live in greater splendour, or be more

deliciously regaled than heretofore? Now, the former is only a question for a moment; and the benefit which it contemplates for manufacturers and workmen, will speedily be snatched from them in the progress of capital and population. The latter is the real state of the question; and it is from it, and not from the other, that we would characterize the policy, and estimate the effect, of that economical mania, which is now so prevalent, both throughout the community, and in the councils of our nation. It is certainly in its abiding, and not in its temporary consequences, that we should be disposed to read the character of any measure which might be proposed to us; and on this principle we hold, that, speaking with a view to the permanent fruit of it, we cannot but regard this work of retrenchment as carrying in it a substantial boon only to the landlords; while, to the working classes of society, it may turn out but the phantom and the mockery of a blessing. We hold it unfortunate, that, on this question, all the seeming, and all the sentiment, should be on the side of unsparing retrenchment; when, in substance and in very truth, there is nothing accomplished by it, but the sacrifice of the most noble, or the most essential of public objects, at the shrine of vanity—the permanent result of it being, not that the poor shall live in greater comfort, but that the wealthy shall luxuriate in greater splendour and effeminacy than before. This will be the final upshot of our present economical reforms; and this the conclusion to the lying

promises of our reformers—the promises, we think,
however, not of deceivers, but of deceived. We
object not to their immediate demand, but rather
desiderate, with them, a reduction, or a removal, of
our present taxes—only, however, if followed up
by the substitution, in their place, of a tax on the
net rent of land. Were it rightly perceived, between what two things it was that the real opposition
lay, we should feel as if the cause of taxation might
be advocated with a more assured countenance,
and a more intrepid voice ; for then it would become palpable, that the support of public objects
might be called for, in the spirit of purest benevolence and of loftiest patriotism ; not in opposition
to, or with any encroachment on, the comforts of
the poor, but in opposition to, and only with partial
encroachment on, the superfluities of the wealthy.

4. Tithes, as at present levied, are in the very
predicament of those taxes which restrain the progress of agriculture. Like them, they oppose a
barrier to the entrance of the cultivator on poorer
soils than the last which has been occupied ; and
like them, too, they prevent the superior soils from
having so deep and thorough a cultivation as they
otherwise should have had. Under this system
cultivation is not so extensive, because prevented
from going forth on so poor an out-field as it might ;
and neither is it so intensive, because prevented
from doing its uttermost on the land already under
process of husbandry. Without the burden of
tithes, fresh land might be taken in, so long as it is

able to feed its agricultural labourers and their secondaries, and yield to the tenant a remunerating
profit.   But, with this burden, the land is required
to do all this, not from its whole produce, but from
only nine-tenths of its produce.   And so the cultivation is sooner arrested, having now to make an
earlier stop, at land from which more is exacted,
and therefore at better land.   Cultivation makes its
last effort at the point where it ceases to be profitable ; and this will be all the sooner, when required
to do, with nine-tenths of its produce, that which,
in a natural state of things, it would have been left
to do with its whole produce.   At this rate, the
cultivation will stop short at land at least a tenth
better than that to which it might otherwise have
stretched itself.   We can offer no computation as
to the extent of intermediate soil, between the natural and the artificial limits, which is thus left uncultivated ; but certain it is, that, in virtue of tithes,
the operations of husbandry must be confined within
narrower boundaries.*   We are aware that the system is not fully acted on.   As far, however, as it
is carried, it is an incubus upon our agriculture.
And so the immediate effect of its abolition would

* The amount of the contraction suffered by agriculture in
consequence of tithes, is much greater than is often estimated.
There are calculators who reason on the supposition that we
only lost a belt, that is, the out-field and inferior land, which,
but for tithes, might have been brought under tillage.   Now,
in addition to the belt, we lose a stratum; or that additional
produce which would be raised over the whole territory from
its more strenuous cultivation.

be to enlarge the domain of cultivation; and, by an increase of food, to diffuse for a time a greater plenty over the land.

5. Still the ultimate effect would be the same from the abolition of tithes, as from the abolition of taxes on the necessaries of life. It would lead to an enlargement of the wealth of the landowners; while to the population, if their standard of enjoyment be not raised, it would lead to no other enlargement than an enlargement of their numbers. We should have a more numerous, but not a better-conditioned peasantry than before. Still it would yield a sensible and immediate, though but a temporary, relief to the working classes. And it is this, perhaps, which forms one of the most imminent dangers of the Church of England. Economists tell us, and in these days of extremity and pressure, that tithes are a burden on the consumer, and add to the price of the necessaries of life; and certain it is, that their doctrine would have the appearance of being experimentally verified, *in the first instance*, by the speedy reduction of price that would ensue on the abolition of tithes. This is quite enough to give the men of the present generation a pressing and a practical interest in the removal of tithes. Nor would it cool their appetency after this reform, though told, that, in a very few years, we should behold a population in as great straits and difficulties as before; and should find, that, in point of ultimate effect, the measure had operated exclusively and permanently to the enrichment of the

landlords. They, in the long-run, would monopolize the whole benefit of the proposed change. It is the immediate, however, and not the distant effect, which tells on the feelings and wishes of the public; and, certainly, the English church is placed in the awkward and unfortunate predicament, that it stands in the way of an immediate, though but a temporary, enlargement to all the classes of society. This is enough to arouse a mortal hostility against it; and accordingly we find, among all the other adverse influences, the strong expectation of a great economic good in the downfal of that venerable hierarchy; helping still more to exasperate and alienate the minds of a people, not only loosened of all attachment to the church of their forefathers, but bent, we fear, upon its overthrow.

6. And here we cannot but signify our regret, that the doctrine of the economists, upon this question, should be framed in the terms of the immediate and temporary effect that would take place on the abolition of tithes, and not in the terms of the ultimate and abiding effect that would ensue from it. We doubt the philosophy of such a procedure, and we are quite sure of its mischievous tendency. It is true, that if tithes were abolished, then, on the instant, grain would become lower; and also, that at this instant of time, grain is higher than it would have been, had tithes been abolished a year ago. But the actual price of grain is not higher than it would have been, had there never been tithes in the country, or had they been abo-

lished a century, or even but ten years ago. We should have had a larger, but not a wealthier peasantry than now; the land yielding a greater produce, but the land peopled up to that produce; and its labouring families, therefore, in the very condition, whether of penury or of comfort, in which we now behold them. The abolition of tithes would just do for England, what the recess, to a certain extent, of the sea from its shores would do for it, on supposition that the new land were shared in proportional quantities among the existing proprietors. The population would flow over on this newly-formed territory, till the whole margin that had been superadded to the island was taken into occupation. Capital would find a fresh field for its investiture; and a season of intermediate cheapness and plenty would encourage, for a time, the multiplication of families. But who does not see that profit and wages would speedily subside again to their wonted level; and that, after a bright interval of prosperity, we should behold only a richer aristocracy, but a commonalty as stinted in their means and maintenance as before? We think it all important to the question of the real incidence of tithes, that the removal of them would but temporarily ensure a higher wage to the labourers; whereas, it would permanently ensure a higher rent to the landlords. It is this which inclines us to represent them, not as a burden on the people, but as a burden on the proprietors of the soil. We dispute not the force of the temptation,

on the part even of the general community, to be
rid of them; seeing, that to them also, a brilliant
though brief season of prosperity would ensue from
it.   Yet, ultimately and everlastingly, the gain
would not be the people's but the landlord's; and
we therefore cannot but lament, that science
should, in this instance, have lent itself to a popular delusion.   That it has practised any unworthy
reticence, is not to be imagined; but certain it is,
that the whole truth has not been told by it.   The
consequence has been, the semblance of an unnatural coalition between the principles of philosophy
and the worst passions of the multitude; and, if
not a louder, at least a more formidable and effective outcry than ever, against the greatest and the
best of our national institutes.

7. The error of the Ricardo system of political
economy on the subject of rent, has been well
characterized by Mr. T. Perronet Thomson, as the
fallacy of inversion.   It confounds the effect with
the cause.   It is not because of the existence of
inferior soils, that the superior pay a rent; but it
is because the superior pay a rent, that the inferior
are taken into occupation.   There does not occur
to us any logical term, by which to denominate the
fallacy that is now under consideration.   But it is
not less a fallacy notwithstanding.   It confounds
the temporary with the permanent; or rather,
gives that virtue and distinction to the former,
which belong only to the latter.   In assigning the
incidence of tithes and taxes, the disciples of this

school would represent them as a burden on that class, who can only suffer from them for less than half a generation; instead of being a burden on that class, who, after the lapse of this ephemeral period, would have to bear their whole weight, and that during the whole currency of their existence. And conversely, it is certain, that if these impositions were done away, the relief would be felt, in the first instance, and for a few fleeting years, by the labourers; but the old pressure would gather upon them speedily, when the relief would, wholly and for ever, be felt only by the landlords. Science has, in this instance, made a most unworthy descent, from that high ground which she ought never to abandon. She has forsaken the proper objects of her contemplation, which are permanent results, and not brief or fugitive accompaniments; nor does it extenuate, but rather gives a tenfold aggravation to the charge, that, in so doing, she has ministered new strength to the prejudices of the blindly or wilfully disaffected; and exasperated still more that fierce and frenzied clamour, which nothing will appease, but the subversion of all authority and order in the commonwealth.

8. It will be the subject of infinite regret to every enlightened patriot, if, for the sake of what at best will yield but temporary relief, and ease them of public clamour and discontent for a moment, our legislature shall barter away the best securities for a nation's safety and perpetual well-being. It will be particularly grievous, if, to lighten a pressure

on the community, that is sure in a few years to recur with all the strength which orginally belonged to it, the best instrument for putting into operation the only sound expedient for the amelioration of the people's circumstances, even that of Christian education, shall be stripped of its efficacy, or done away altogether. All other expedients will be found to terminate in mockery. They at best but enlarge the bulk of society, without any reduction, save for a short-lived moment, of the individual or the family distress which abounds in it. They may cause the limit to recede, and to widen somewhat; but they restrain not the pressure within that limit, which is the real cause of a general penury among the poorer orders of the commonwealth. A vessel might be made more capacious than before; but this will not alleviate the distension upon its sides, if there have been no abatement of the elasticity from within. Now the whole effect of the common expedients is, not to ease the distension of the vessel, but only to make it more capacious. Home colonization, for example, will yield no indefinite harbourage; and yield no enduring relief to labourers. Neither will the devices, however multiplied and ingenious, for finding them employment. Neither will any possible accumulation on the part of capitalists—nor any conversion, we may add, of revenue into capital, as when government lavishes its millions upon public works, for the occupation of the people. Neither will all the openings of foreign trade, though pushed to the uttermost of its practicable extension. Neither will the remission of taxes— and, lastly, neither will the abolition of tithes. But what the abolition of tithes cannot do, that great institute, which is now supported by tithes, may do. The one expedient but widens the field of occupancy; and that to be speedily filled again, with the same pressure of inconvenience as before. The other does not widen the field of occupancy, but it may do better; for, by the efficacy of its moral lessons, it may lay wholesome restraint on the amount of occupation. And this, not with tyrannic force, but by a mild and grateful influence, on the hearts and habits of the occupiers. Through the medium of Christian instruction, a rightly organized church will do more for the economic comfort of the families of the land, than all the other schemes of philanthropy and patriotism put together.* It will indeed be the egregious blunder of men, looking to the wrong quarter for the permanent emancipation and enlargement of our people, if, in grasping for a short respite from their ills, the hold shall be irrecoverably lost of the only instrument by which their comfort and their indepen-

* We are sensible that we here assume the superior efficacy of an *established church*, for the religious education of the people. For a fuller exposition of our views upon this subject, and of the reasonings by which we endeavour to support them, we refer to two former works, the one entitled, " The Christian and Civic Economy of Large Towns," the other, " On the Use and Abuse of Literary and Ecclesiastical Endowments."

dence can be ultimately secured.   At a time when
churches and schools would need to be multiplied,
when what may be termed the educational apparatus of our land would need to be greatly extended,
instead of being mutilated and curtailed, it bodes
peculiarly ill for the future destinies of the nation,
that the authority of a reigning school has lent
itself to that menacing outcry, which, if carried
into effect, would annihilate an order of men, with
whose efforts in the cause of popular instruction
stand associated the best hopes and interests of
England.   The difference between the one set of
expedients and the other, is this : The object of
the former, is to make room for a pressure which
yet no expansion can alleviate ; the object of the
latter, is to restrain and regulate the pressure itself.
Under the operation of the one, the people may
still be pressing on the limit of the means of subsistence.   Under the operation of the other, the
people, in obedience to their own taste and sense
of dignity, will keep themselves a little way, and
therefore comfortably, within this limit.   The
former alone will never achieve the result of a
well-conditioned peasantry, let the physical abundance be what it may.   The latter can make good
the spectacle of thriving families, even in the midst
of scantiest natural resources.   It is thus that we
behold, in rugged and intractable Norway, a flourishing population, while China, in spite of boundless
fertility, labours under the want and wretchedness
of its teeming millions.   It is thus also that Eng-

land, though enlarged in the culture of its territory, if withal stinted in the moral culture of its inhabitants, may grow in population and penury
together; while, whether her soil be liberated from
the bondage of tithes or not, she, in virtue of an
efficient system of instruction, might realize the
blessings of abundance in all her parishes.

9. But we would do both. That is, we would
both maintain the church, and relieve the agriculture; and so at once enlarge the room, and, through
the medium of religious instruction, keep up that
wholesome influence on the habits of the peasantry,
which best serves to mitigate the pressure arising
from the recklessness and brutality of a neglected
population. The clergy, in particular, should rejoice in the church being exonerated from the
odium that now lies upon it—should be the first to
hail and to help forward the consummation of a
measure, by which the hierarchy of England might
be extricated from a position so obnoxious, as that
of even appearing to stand in the way of the nation's
wealth, or the comfort of its families. The reformation of the present system were an incalculable blessing to the church of England; and that,
not merely because it would disarm the hostility
of statesmen and economists, but because it would
do away the topic of a thousand heart-burnings in
every parish of the kingdom. And, in like manner,
as we have pled, not for the abolition, but the commutation of taxes; so would we plead, not for the
abolition, but the commutation of tithes. The

support of the clergyman would no longer operate
as a bar to agriculture, if given either in land, or
in right proportion, not to the produce, but to
the net rent of landlords. At this rate, the existence of an established and endowed priesthood,
would no more obstruct the progress of cultivation,
than would the existence of landowners, as a distinct order in society. They would, in fact, be
joint proprietors along with them ; and, whether
restricted to their own separate estates, or sharing
in the rent of their parishes at large, they would
stand completely innocent of all cumbrance upon
the soil. It were a relief to agriculture, but a far
greater relief to the church. It is only the extension of the one that is limited by the present
system, but the very existence of the other is
threatened by it.

10. But it ought not to be overlooked, how much
the wealth and interest of the landlord would be
augmented by the proceeding, even though not
only a fair, but liberal commutation were granted
to the clergyman. He can well afford to negotiate
the matter equitably, for to him the enlargement
would be incalculable. By the consequent descent
of the agriculture among inferior soils, and, commensurate with this, a more intense cultivation of
all the superior ones, he would extract a greater
rent than heretofore, from every acre of his property ; and thus, (after a full equivalent had been
rendered to the church for its tithes,) there would,
over and above, accrue much clear gain to himself.

It were hard, indeed, if the alleged prejudice of the church to the other classes of society, were the cause of its overthrow; when, by a simple modification of its revenues, the general community would receive all the enlargement which it can possibly look for, and the proprietors of land be greatly enriched to the bargain. But should the latter look and long for more than this, they are seeking their own aggrandizement by means of an unprincipled spoliation. We have heard much of the rapacity of a sanctimonious priesthood. But there is danger, and that to the best interests of the state, from another species of hypocrisy; lest the country should be rifled of its moral and literary provision, and that too under the guise of patriotism—a specious covering for the dishonest selfishness of men, who, in the most emphatic sense of the term, would be the pests and plunderers of the commonwealth.

11. In point of principle and effect the analogy is perfect, between the commutation of the tithes and the commutation of those taxes, which, bearing either on the operations of husbandry, or on the maintenance of those who are engaged in it, add to the expenses of farm management. By the abolition of all such taxes, there is a fully tantamount addition made to the rent; so that the landlord could, without loss, bear the substitution, in their place, of an income tax upon himself. By the abolition of tithes, there is a corresponding similar addition made to the rent; and so that the landlord could, also without loss, minister, in a direct way,

as liberal support to the clergymen as before. In both cases, then, an equivalent compensation is thus made out to him. But in neither case does the re-action in favour of the landlord stop here. The removal, whether of the taxes or of the tithes, gives scope both to a more extensive and a more intensive agriculture; to a surplus produce, both from a belt and from a stratum, neither of which had been entered upon before. The landlord obtains not merely an equivalent, but an overplus: first, in the new rent which accrues to him from the reclaimed—and, secondly, in the additional rent which accrues to him from the more improved, territory.

12. In the commutation of tithes, we behold a still more beneficial adjustment to the peculiar circumstances of Britain, than in the commutation of taxes on the second necessaries of life. The latter commutation lowers, and that permanently, the money-price of labour; and so would make us still more an exporting country, and land us in a still larger excrescent population than before. It is true, that it would also extend the home agriculture, so that there might not be a larger proportion of the excrescent population to the natural, after this commutation than before it. But the like advantage which there is in the commutation of tithes, is not subject to this deduction. There is nothing in this commutation that should permanently reduce the money-price of labour; so that from this quarter we are not exposed to any increase

of the excrescent population. We should derive from it, however, a large increase of agricultural produce, and so a large increase of the natural population; which will therefore lessen the proportion of the excrescent to the natural. By the abolition of tithes, there will both be a larger expenditure on the part of landlords than before; and a larger agricultural population, whose second necessaries, consisting, in many things, of imports from abroad, as tea and sugar, will require a larger exportation from this country to pay for them. And so, many of those exports which wont to be met by agricultural produce in return for them, may, after this change, be met by luxuries and goods of another description. It is thus, that, with every extension of our agriculture, there may be an increase of British exports, without any increase of our dependence on other lands for the first necessaries of life. We may have a greater number of export manufacturers, and yet, in virtue of our extended agriculture, they may be subsisted on home-produce, and so fall into the natural population. The cause of our having an excrescent population is, that, ere our foreign markets are saturated with British exports, the ability of our inland consumers to purchase the goods and the luxuries which come in return for them, has been fully overtaken. When the exports go beyond this point, no other return-import can be beneficially disposed of, but agricultural produce which goes to form and to subsist an excrescent population. Now, every stretch given to

our agriculture does increase the ability of our inland consumers—whether they be the landed proprietors, who, in consequence, have a larger revenue to spend; or a larger agricultural and secondary
population, who, though furnished by an enlarged
agriculture with the first necessaries, will derive
many of their second necessaries from abroad.   In
this way, the return of commodities for commodities
is longer kept up, without coming to the necessity
of importing food from other countries, in exchange
for the manufactures of our own.   In virtue of the
larger exportation that may now be carried on
without the return of agricultural produce, it is
possible that foreign markets may be saturated with
our goods, ere they need to be paid for in that
produce.   The enlarged agriculture may enable us
to raise a sufficient quantity for ourselves.   It is
thus that the removal of every let or hindrance, in
the way of our agriculture, lessens our dependence
for food upon other lands; and that the abolition
of tithes, in particular, may suffice to absorb our
excrescent, either partially or altogether, into a
natural population.

13. In virtue of our proposed commutation, the
church may be upheld without injury to any economic interest; and it is therefore all the more
unfair, that economists have lent the authority of
their speculations, to inflame still more the popular
hostility against it.   Never was there a more unjust
or misdirected indignation.   The support of a
priesthood has been set in opposition to the general

comfort of families. Its only opposition is to the greater wealth and luxury of landlords. The men who do something are eyed with jealousy, because in possession of an interest and a property, which, if not theirs, would but serve to enlarge the affluence and useless splendour of the men who do nothing. Never were the feelings of generous and high-minded patriotism more egregiously misplaced, or the public good more in danger of being sacrificed to the mere semblance of a principle. We often hear of the omnipotence of truth; and that the prejudice of many ages, the deep-laid institutions of many centuries, must at length give way before it. If the ecclesiastical establishments of our land shall be of the number which are destined to fall, and that because the temporalities which belong to them have been pronounced, by the oracles of our day, as an oppression and a burden on the general population, then, instead of truth being their judge or their executioner, they shall have fallen at the hand of cunning and deceitful witnesses, they shall have perished in the midst of strong delusion, at the mandate, and by the authority, of a lie.

14. When power gets into the hands of the multitude, the danger is, that it may be exercised, not for guidance, but for destruction. They generally act by impulse, and not by discernment; and, if only possessed with the idea, or rather with the watch-word, that the church is an incubus on the prosperity of the nation; no voice of wisdom

will arrest the determination of sweeping it utterly away. We hold that a church establishment is the most effective of all machines for the moral in‑ struction of the people; and that, if once taken down, there is no other instrumentality by which it can be adequately replaced. We are aware that it may be feebly and even corruptly administered; but the way to rectify this, is, not to demolish the apparatus, but to direct its movements. We should hail the ascendancy of the popular will, if it pro‑ ceeded on this distinction; and, instead of depre‑ cating, should rejoice in the liberalism of the pre‑ sent day, did it but know how to modify so as not to extinguish. It is because democracy, instead of a regulating power, is a sweeping whirlwind, that we dread its encroachments. It is hers, not with skilful fingers to frame and adapt the ma‑ chinery of our institutions; but, with the force of an uplifted arm, to inflict upon them the blow of extermination. We are abundantly sensible, that the re‑action of this tremendous energy, is never called forth, but when provoked by the doings of a corrupt and careless government; and that, had our national churches been virtuously patronized, and vigorously and well administered in all former days, they had had nothing to fear at this moment from the hostile or vindictive feelings of an alien‑ ated people. And yet it were surely their more excellent way, if, instead of passing sentence of annihilation on the church, or rifling it of its es‑ sential support, they were simply, by the authority of their opinion and will, to influence the patronage. Never had public sentiment a greater controul over the proceedings of government, than at this moment. And it may well make us despair of any good to society from its merely political ameliorations, if, at the very time when the collective mind of the nation could, in virtue of its rising strength, impress the most beneficial direction on the most beneficial and best of our national institutes—the first use it made of the acquisition, was not wisely to regulate, but wantonly to destroy.

15. We cannot afford to expatiate on the superior efficacy of a church establishment—a lesson which we have abundantly urged and expounded elsewhere.* But never, without the peculiar facilities and resources of such an institution, will there be a full supply of Christian instruction in the land. A practical heathenism will spread itself over the rural provinces; and will deepen and accumulate more and more in our cities. When the people are thus left to themselves, and, in great majority, have forgot and forsaken the decencies of a Christian land, all economic or external resources will be of no effect on the comfort of families, given up, by this time, to profligacy and utter recklessness. It is vain to look for a well-conditioned peasantry, when, brutalized into a state of moral and religious

* In a work, more especially, entitled, " On the Use and Abuse of Church and College Endowments;" beside a few chapters in the " Christian and Civic Economy of Large Towns "

indifference, they are wholly bent on animal indulgence, and, in reference to all the higher sensibilities of our nature, are in a state of hopeless and
immoveable apathy.   The expense of a well-orga-
nized and purely-administered church, otherwise
lavished, in unproductive consumption, on the
luxuries of the affluent and the idle, would be repaid many times over, if we, in consequence, beheld among the people a higher standard of character, which never fails to be accompanied by a
higher standard of comfort in society.   But when
once the moral interest is sacrificed, there is no
enlargement of the economic interests or capabilities which can possibly make up for it.   A church
may be so conducted, as to secure and perpetuate
the one; and it may be so provided for, as not to
trench, by the slightest iota, upon the other.   In
these circumstances, its overthrow were a most
grievous perversion—an act of national madness,
having its rightful consummation, first, in the anarchy of the state, and then, in the growing vice and
wretchedness of the people.

16. Whatever the coming changes in the state
of our society may be, there is none that would
more fatally speed the disorganization and downfal
of this great kingdom, than if a hand of violence
were put forth on the rights and revenues of the
church of England.   Even with the present distribution of her wealth, it will be found, that the
income of her higher, as well as humbler clergy,
has been vastly overrated ; and nothing, we believe,

would contribute more to soften the prejudices of
the nation against this venerable hierarchy, than a
full exposure of all her temporalities, grounded on
the strictest and most minute inquiry. And certain it is, that, with the best possible distribution of
this wealth, it will be found hardly commensurate
to the moral and spiritual wants of the now greatly
increased population. If all pluralities were abolished, and the enormous overgrown towns and
cities of the land were adequately provided with
churches, it would be found, that the whole of the
existing revenues would hardly suffice for a requisite number even of merely working ecclesiastics. We cannot imagine a policy more ruinous,
than that which would impair the maintenance of
a church that has long been illustrious for its learning, and that promises now to be the dispenser of
greater blessings to the people, than at any former
period of its history, by the undoubted increase of
its public virtue and its piety.

CHAPTER XI.

ON THE DISTINCTION MADE BY ECONOMISTS BETWEEN PRODUCTIVE AND UNPRODUCTIVE LABOUR.

1. Such is the influence of language upon thought, that, to the practical effect of mere epithets, may be traced some of the most mischievous delusions, by which the views and sentiments of men have ever been perverted. We hold the definition, by economists, of productive and unproductive labour, to be an example of this; and that it is not only unsound, when looked at in strict relation to their own science, but pernicious, because of the opposition which it has suggested between the moral and the economic good of society. It has laid discouragement on certain employments most conducive to the well-being, because, according to the established nomenclature, not conducive, but, on the contrary, prejudicial to the wealth of the nation. And as wealth is a term which stands associated, in almost every imagination, with the power, and greatness, and security of the state, as well as with the family and individual comfort of its members, we are not to wonder, if, in respect to such high interests, it has been recommended, as the best policy of a government, to abridge and economize to the uttermost, in the maintenance of

unproductive labourers. To this class have been referred, the ministers of religion ; and whose support, accordingly, has been represented as a burden and a bane to the prosperity of the commonwealth ; because a deduction from those funds, which, instead of being lavished on unproductive, might have been expended on the maintenance of productive industry. We hold it, therefore, a proper appendix to our argument on the operation and effect of tithes, that we should bestow some thought upon a definition, which has laid disparagement, not on ecclesiastics alone, but on many other orders of men, whose services are indispensable, either to the public interests of the state, or to the private and personal comfort of families.

2. The wealth of a country has been defined to consist in the produce, by which is meant, the *material* produce, of its land and labour ; and they only are regarded as productive labourers, who add to the amount of that produce. He only is a productive labourer, by this definition, who adds by his work, to the value of some tangible, and therefore, some vendible commodity ; a commodity which might be laid up in a store-house, or exposed for sale in a market. A clergyman is clearly excluded by this definition, unless in so far as he shares in the manufacture of that tangible commodity, a volume of sermons, from the class of productive labourers; and so also is the school-master, and the physician, and the lawyer, and the judge, and the soldier, and the statesman. We

may guess from this enumeration, what those interests of the commonwealth are, at which many of our economists are disposed to look suspiciously and hardly. But their proscription extends further than this; for menial servants, and musicians, and players, and all in fact whose industry has not impressed some marks of its operation, more or less durable, on some marketable commodity, are ranked by them among the unproductive labourers in society. Some of these are certainly not the most useful and respectable of functionaries; and, associated as they are with the former by the common epithet of unproductive, we are not to wonder, if certain of the professions have been viewed with a degree of jealousy by our economic patriots, as creating an obstacle in the way of some great and prosperous enlargement, or as being a heavy deduction from that maximum of good which the country might else have realized.

3. And yet, to expose the utter futility of this distinction, let us think for a moment how much it amounts to. One man's labour ministers to my enjoyment, through the medium of a tangible commodity ; another man's labour, ministers to my enjoyment without this intermedium. The confectioner, whose delicious morsel I swallow, is a productive labourer : the musician, whose delicious tune I listen to, is an unproductive labourer. And yet, what economic injury is sustained, though I should pay the one as much for his performance, as I pay the other for his preparation ? The grati-

fication to me is equal, or rather greater in the
music than in the eatable, seeing that I preferred
it. The maintenance to him who administers the
enjoyment is the same, whether I have chosen to
spend my custom on the productive, or the unproductive labourer. And thus it makes no difference
to the wealth of the country, whether the consumers incline more to those gratifications, which
come through the vehicle of a tangible commodity,
or to those which, without such intervention, yield
the same, and perhaps a superior enjoyment. The
labourers who are supported by the wealth, are
equally well supported on either supposition; and
the proprietor who spends the wealth, by being
left to purchase that which he likes best, is only
permitted the exercise of a liberty, without which,
wealth would lose part of its value, and cease to
be so desirable.

4. The end of all production is consumption.
The *terminus ad quem* of all labour, is the enjoyment of those who buy its products; whether these
shall be material or immaterial. This last difference is surely, to all purposes of any worth or consideration, a futile one; and it will be found, that
there is an equal futility in any other difference
which can be alleged betwixt them. For example,
it has been said of unproductive labour, that its
effect is momentary, and that all the good of it
expires with the performance; whereas, the tangible thing that issues from the other, can be laid up
in a shop or store-room, and be there appealed to

as a solid addition to the annual wealth of the country, or recorded among the items of a national inventory. Now it is very true, that when a tune is ended, there remains no equivalent for its price. But the same is true of the coat after it has been worn, or of any vendible and substantial commodity, after the consumption of it is terminated. In process of time, there remains no vestige, either of the productive or the unproductive labour; and, to balance the consideration, that the effect of the one is shorter-lived than the other, it should be remembered that this might be made up by the perpetuity, or frequency of the service. A suit of clothes may last with me a year; and, during the whole of that time, I have a use and an enjoyment in the wearing of them. But, with their price, I may hire for a year, the attendance of a menial servant; and so experience, for the same length of time, the daily benefit and convenience of his labour. And besides, in point of endurance, there is often a vast superiority in the effects of the unproductive, over those of the productive labourer. To the physician, I may owe the continued health of a life-time—to the lawyer, the preservation of my family estate, along a line of successive generations—to the soldier, the independence of my nation for centuries—to the clergyman, the virtue of the people, and the imperishable good of their eternity. So that the effect of the one species of labour, may be as lasting as that of the other; and there is really nothing in this particular characteristic which at all justifies the distinction that has been made of them.

5. In the case of productive labour, there is often a long interval of time between the exertion, and the fulfilment of the object for which the exertion was made. The cloth may have been manufactured many months before it is worn—when, meanwhile, it occupies a place among the goods of a warehouse, and might, during that period, be registered as one of the constituent parts in the actual wealth of our nation. But surely there is nothing in this delay, which intervenes, between the performance of the industry, and the whole purpose for which the industry was set agoing, that can at all attach a preference to the labour which ministers enjoyment through the medium of commodities, over that labour which, without such a medium, still ministers enjoyment. The gratification arising from music, comes immediately on the back of its execution—the gratification that lies in the use and consumption of a manufactured article, might not commence for a great many weeks after the completion of it. If there be any difference here, it should be in favour of that process, where there is the least delay between the aim and the accomplishment, or where the labour, and the thing laboured for, come the nearest together. When a process of busy action is entered upon, which is to terminate in the attainment of some object of desire, it is surely better that we should have to wait a short rather than a long time for it. The power

of realizing any fulfilment that our heart is set upon, is all the more valuable, the more speedily that we are able to realize it. So that, on this particular ground, there seems no superiority in productive labour, according to the economic sense of the term, over that which is unproductive.

6. It would be impossible to maintain this distinction against the many examples which might be alleged in opposition to it. A manufacturer of fire-arms, by the definition in question, is a productive labourer. The soldier who uses the fire-arms, and but for whose use of them they would never have been fabricated, is an unproductive one. The cook within doors is unproductive. The confectioner out of doors, though the very same work is done by him, would be recognized and honoured as a productive labourer. Yet both impress additional value on a tangible commodity—only, in the former instance, we want the shop ; and, so in the hands of the cook, it is not, as in the hands of the confectioner, a vendible commodity. A singer, or even a performer on a musical instrument, is unproductive. But the maker of the instrument is a productive labourer—and should it be an instrument that can perform of itself, such as a musical automaton, then we should have a clear addition to the wealth of the country, without the alloy or the deduction of any unproductive labourer having at all to do with it. It is thus we should imagine, that a thousand manufacturers of Æolian harps, must be regarded with all complacency by

our economists, as undoubted contributors to the material produce, which, by their definition, is tantamount to the wealth of the nation. But should the demand be changed from inanimate to living music, and the thousand artificers be trans-formed, of consequence, into so many vocal per-formers—we must suppose, that, at this transition, a reduction of wealth has taken place, although all the labourers are as well maintained, and all the employers are better pleased than before. We have already stated, that a preacher of oral sermons is unproductive—but that should he publish a vo-lume of written sermons, he forthwith stands out in the capacity of a productive labourer. In short, without regard to that which is nevertheless the real *terminus ad quem* of all trade and manufac-tures, even the enjoyment of consumers; and, without regard to the reward or maintenance of those who are engaged in them, for the mainten-ance is in every way as liberal whether they are employed in the capacity of productive or unpro-ductive labourers—this definition proceeds on some mysterious virtue which is figured as residing in the mere vehicle of the enjoyment. Unless that vehicle be a piece of matter, wealth, and all the blessings of which the term is comprehensive, are conceived to be somehow impaired by it. In a word, they cannot conceive how wealth should be in any thing, unless it be a something which the hand can handle. Without this all is unsubstantial in their eyes. And though, by one mode of expenditure, health, and security, and virtue, and education, and justice, and science, are purchased for the community, at the hands of so many un-productive labourers, yet if, by another mode of expenditure, other blessings, however inferior, but unlike to these, laid up in packages or bales of merchandize, are purchased from the hands of pro-ductive labourers—economists there are, both in and out of parliament, whose whole philosophy would enjoin them a contempt for the airy nothings, and a longing appetency for the bales.

7. The principle, against which we contend, as-sumes a different form, in the argument at least, if not in the convictions of those who admit the value of a work, even though done by unproductive la-bourers; but who desiderate more of that work for the same money, or, in other words, that the work shall be done more cheaply. With the principle of this demand we have no quarrel. It applies equally to both kinds of labour. It is just as desirable that the machine of a literary or ecclesi-astical establishment should become more effective, as that a stocking-machine should become so; and if, in virtue of this, either enough of literary and religious instruction can be rendered, or enough of stockings can be made for less money, than is now expended on these objects, the community would just have the more to expend on other objects, and the enjoyments of human life be multiplied of con-sequence. We do not fear to bring either our church, or our schools and colleges, under the ex-

amination of a tribunal, that shall adopt this principle, and shall honestly proceed on it. We believe
the conclusion would be, that the educational apparatus of our island, whether in respect of Christian or literary tuition, was defective both in extent
and provision; and we should hail it as a subject
of patriotic congratulation, if, at the expense of an
inroad on that wealth which is now lavished on
material objects of expenditure, more ample allowances were given for the support of religion and
learning, even though it should lead to the multiplication of the unproductive labourers in our land.

8. In this preference of the productive over the
unproductive labourer, there lies a subtle delusion,
by which the political economy, both of many a
student and of many a statesman, is pervaded.
One distinction between the two species of industry
is, that the products of the former cannot, from
their very nature, be tangibly laid hold of, and in
this shape be made the subjects of any commercial
transaction. Whereas the products of the latter
have generally an intermediate stage to pass, between the labourer and the consumer, during which
they are exposed to sale in a shop, or have to undergo, in some form or other, a process of marketing. Now they are the shop and the market,
which, in the eye of many a politician, are the
great symbols of national prosperity. A work done
by a cook within doors, is not so gratifying to their
patriotism, as that done by a dealer in pastry without; because it deprives them of the agreeable

spectacle of so much trade.   There would not be
the same amount of ostensible buying and selling
under the one arrangement as the other.   It matters not their being told, that the consumer may
be better served at the hands of the unproductive,
than at the hands of the productive, or, at least,
served in the way he himself likes better ; and that
the labourers, under either system, are equally well
remunerated for their industry.   In addition to
these two interests, which appear to be the only
essential interests in the transaction, there is another, which we should like our mercantile economist distinctly to define, but which, we are sure,
he will find to be impossible—because really it has
no existence, save in his own shadowy imagination.
He cannot state any rational difference to our national wealth, between what is contributed by the
well-paid manufacturer of a musical instrument,
and the equally well-paid performer on that instrument ; or even though, without an instrument, he
should only perform with his own voice.   Under
either economy, the labourers are equally well paid;
and, under the actual economy, the employer is
better pleased.   It is a most unmeaning preference,
that, under the one, there is an apparatus of coun-
ters and customers, which is wanting in the other.
There is a deep-laid imposition here, and by which
the gravest of our legislators have often been bewildered—when idolising trade, as if it were the
fountain-head of a wealth, to which it owes its own
dependent and subordinate existence ; and which,

apart from its own commodities, or rather, from the gratification which consumers have in the use of these commodities, has not one earthly interest belonging to it, that either patriot or philanthropist ought to care for.

9. But more than this. The distinction, that we are endeavouring to expose, stands associated with certain notions on the subject of capital. Material products are conceived to have this advantage over immaterial, that they alone can be laid up as capital, and in that capacity be made to subserve the object of future production. This is not exactly true. The immaterial products of security wrought out for us by our warriors, or of health by our physicians, or of the people's equity and sobriety by our clergymen, subserve industry and the enjoyment of its fruits, just as any of those commodities do, which may have been accumulated for the support of future labour. And besides, there is no advantage in the laying out of capital, if that capital is not to be replaced, which it only is by the expenditure of consumers. The outlay incurred in production by the one party, is ever regarded as wasteful and undesirable, unless it be met by an adequate return made in the expenditure of the other party. Now it so happens, that this expenditure may as effectually replace capital, in the case of unproductive as in that of productive labour. A master tailor may not have more capital, than the master of an orchestra who heads a party of musicians. The capital by which the one is enabled to pay his journeymen,

and to uphold his very scanty implements of labour, is often not so great, as the capital by which the other is enabled to pay his performers and to uphold the apparatus of an opera. So that the expenditure by attendance on a place of entertainment may, in fact, subserve the maintenance of a larger capital than the expenditure incurred by the purchase of clothes. But the short way of disposing of this consideration is, that it serves no earthly interest or end, to accumulate capital beyond the power or possibility, of its being advantageously invested. Up to that point, there is no fear of capital being maintained. This is a matter which regulates itself. To give a preference for productive over unproductive labour, that the products of the former may be laid up in store for future production, is a process which must soon run itself aground; and, altogether, the interest in question is of vastly too secure and independent a character, to require that we shall proceed on any arbitrary definition whatever, for the purpose of upholding it.*

10. Altogether, then, the distinction seems to be nugatory in principle; and withal, mischievous in application. The agricultural class, or those who are employed in raising the first necessaries of life, are all of them, in the sense of the definition, productive labourers. The secondary are chiefly, though not exclusively so; there being a demand,

* The reader will perceive that the error involved in this definition, is connected with the error that capital admits of indefinite accumulation.

even among our general population, for education, both in Christian and in common scholarship; and which they frequently pay out of their own wages. And who can deny, that, by this part of their expenditure, even though it goes to the support of unproductive labourers, they secure a blessing to the land, which nothing could compensate, if their revenue were wholly laid out on tangible commodities? And then, as to the disposable population, it positively signifies not to any economic interest which is worth the caring for, according to what proportion they shall be divided, into productive and unproductive labourers. It altogether resolves itself into the taste and inclination of their employers; and to this, it should be altogether left. It were a deduction to them, from the value of their wealth, if not at liberty to spend it in the way they like best. In as far as they have a preference for commodities prepared by our own countrymen, their demand will go to sustain home manufacturers; and we shall behold so many of the disposable population engaged in this species of industry. In as far as their preference is for the luxuries of other climes, we shall behold so many more of the disposable population engaged in the business of shipping, or of export manufactures, wherewith to purchase commodities from abroad. And, in as far, again, as their preference is for a retinue of servants, or for theatrical amusements, or for the education of their families, or for enjoyments of any sort, yielded directly and without the

intervention of material products; in so far will
the disposable population consist of those who are
termed unproductive labourers. What the proportion shall be is a matter of no signification whatever, to any one interest which should enter into
the computation of national prosperity or national
greatness. It will not affect the extent of the disposable population. It will not affect the amount
of comfort or abundance diffused throughout the
members of it. It will neither affect the revenue
of government, nor its power to enlist what proportion it may, of the disposable population, into
the service of its own establishments. It will neither affect the prosperity nor the numbers—it will
only affect the employments of the population.
And in whatever way the expenditure of consumers is apportioned, between productive and
unproductive labourers, while to them a maximum
of gratification is secured by their being suffered
to spend their wealth as they will; we shall behold,
under all the possible varieties of their taste and
demand, the state equally powerful and flourishing,
and comprising within its limits as great a number
of thriving families.

11. We have entered at so much length into this
argument, because we think the political economy
of our day bears a hard and hostile aspect towards
an ecclesiastical establishment; and we have no
doubt, that to this, the hurtful definition of Smith
has largely, though perhaps insensibly, contributed.
The services of a church are mainly performed by

unproductive labourers; and, from this single circumstance, we can imagine, on the part of a de-
luded patriotism, many a secret wish and aspira-
tion for its overthrow. It is therefore of all the
more importance, to expose the futility of the distinction, that has been made upon this subject;
and, setting aside, as a frivolous and unmeaning
accessary, the presence or the want of a tangible
intermedium, by which the good of any service is
conveyed to us; we would found the question between one distribution of employment and another,
wholly and exclusively, on the nature and magnitude of the good itself. We should not be afraid
to rest upon this issue the cause of a religious establishment, even though the spoils, to be gathered
from its overthrow, were capable of being diffused,
in the form of a secure and permanent increase,
to the physical comforts of the population at large.
But we hold ourselves to have a far mightier argument on our side, in that the result of such a
catastrophe were but the enrichment of our landed
proprietors, and that no appropriation of the wealth
of the church can prevent this from being the ultimate destination of it. Even though allotted in
the first instance to the necessities of the state, and
followed up by the remission of taxes, this, after
affording scope for a season to the increase of population and capital, would but pour the wealth or
our ecclesiastics into the bosom of the landed aristocracy at the last. We have already explained
how that scope might be afforded, and yet the

church be upholden in all her temporalities; and
after this, on weighing the only real terms of the
alternative, a moral good to the community against
a large accession to the splendour and luxury of
our landlords, we cannot hesitate for a moment on
the question, whether the exchange of the one for
the other would prove a bane or a blessing to our
nation.*

12. After all then, the property of the church
has created but a division of wealth, and not a
diminution of it. The landed proprietor may still
complain of its existence, but with no more reason,
than the owner of a thousand acres, has to complain of the contiguous but separate estate of a
hundred acres lying beside him, and which he
should have liked to be in his own possession, rather than in that of another man. The clergyman
stands in the same relation to the landlord, that

* We gladly observe in the pages of M. Say, a recognition
of immaterial products, as forming an addition to the wealth of
a country. The revenue of our landlords, in as far as it is
spent by themselves, is absorbed in unproductive consumption.
The taxes and the tithes which they pay go to the support of
public functionaries, or are consumed productively; and, if on
the one hand, the former be paid to a well-administered government, and on the other hand, the latter be commuted and
paid to a well-administered church; then taxes and tithes, (the
very reverse of what has been ascribed to them,) go to enrich
and not to impoverish a nation. The civil, and military, and
ecclesiastical labourers, give a return in their services for a
revenue that would otherwise have been expended without a
return, and the value of these services forms a clear addition to
the amount of national wealth.

the small proprietor does to his neighbouring large one; but, with this mighty difference to the public good, that his property involves in it an obligation of duty, whereas the other is in a state of simple ownership. There are some who hold that the property of the island is not enough divided, and complain of the large estates that are vested in single individuals or families. The institution of a church, even apart from the service which it renders to society, is, at least, a mitigation of this alleged evil. But its main vindication is its usefulness. The clergyman is bound to do something for his share in the soil. The proprietor to nothing. The public would be gainers, if still more of the country's wealth were placed in the condition, of having a duty and a service attached to the possession of it; or, in other words, in opposition to the popular and prevailing cry, we hold, that too little of the produce of the land goes to the support of functionaries; and that, of course, the mere proprietors, the ' *nati fruges consumere,*' are allowed to reserve too much of it.

13. The united expenditure of the clergy and the landlords, gives as great an impulse to trade, and as large a support to labourers, as would the entire expenditure of the landlords, had there been no clergy, and our ecclesiastics been so many small proprietors. That then is an interest clearly not affected by the institution of an established church. Apart from such a provision, its revenues would have yielded so much enjoyment to possessors of

land; but, in their present state, they yield as much
enjoyment to the holders of our ecclesiastical bene-
fices ; so that, looking to the subject under this
view likewise, there is no loss incurred by the system for which we are contending.   But again,
landlords are under no positive or prescribed obligation, of rendering any service to the community
for their share in the produce of the soil.   Clergymen are ; and though they should fall short of dis-
charging their whole obligation, yet, should they
discharge it in part, and so as that some positive
balance of good to society is done by them on the
whole, to that extent is society benefitted by the
church, and to that extent would society be a
loser should the church be overthrown.   Theirs is
not, to use the language of some of our economists,
unproductive consumption.   That of the landlords is.   Let immaterial products be included
along with material, as Say and others would, in
the enumeration of a country's wealth ; and the
institution of a church may serve, not to impoverish, but to enrich a community.   It is the means
of turning so much unproductive into productive
consumption.   Without a church, the whole of
our ecclesiastical wealth would have been in the
hands of those who give no return for it.   With a
church, we have the returns of all its usefulness—
its theological learning—the protection which it
affords against a desolating infidelity—the service
which it renders to the morality of the commonwealth—and, above all, to the eternal well-being

of the individual members who compose it. These are not the less substantial, that they enter not into the common definition of wealth, as consisting in the tangible produce of land and labour. Let tithes and taxes be but commuted as they ought; and, in the hands of a purer church and a purer government, it will become quite obvious, that they do indeed augment the national wealth, in the best sense which can be annexed to the term—turning that produce, which would otherwise have been idly or unproductively consumed, into an instrument of the highest benefits and blessings to society.

CHAPTER XII.

ON THE LAW OF PRIMOGENITURE.

1. ANOTHER of the vague imaginations for the relief of the country, and for the diffusion of a greater comfort and abundance through all its classes, is the more equal diffusion of property. The expenditure of the landlords seems by many to be regarded in the light of an abstraction from the maintenance of the other orders of society— as if this very expenditure did not consist in a transference to the industrious of sustenance and support for their services. In spite of this obvious consideration, there does obtain the expectation of a great enlargement, to ensue from the abolition of the law of primogeniture. And, certain it is, that, in the politics of our day, there is a growing and gathering strength of opposition to the system, which guarantees our landed aristocracy in the possession of their ample and unbroken domains from one generation to another. We have already said, that the advocates of a more equal partition of the land, should, on this ground at least, befriend an established church, by which, at all events, one species of partition is carried into effect. This, however, is in no way our argument for such an institution—it being of far less importance in our

view, that property should be more equalized, than that property should, if possible, be placed to a greater extent than now in the state of having a public service and obligation attached to it; and that, consequently, less of it should be left in the state of simple and unconditional ownership. We happen not to think, that a more equal division of the land is in itself desirable ; and far less, that the indefinite subdivision of it would prove a blessing to the country. Let us shortly contemplate the effects of such a process, in the train of which, if once entered on, there would follow both political and economical effects of the utmost magnitude. It is not only, however, because of these that we invite attention, but because we hold it to involve a question of professional importance, as bearing on the subject of the incomes allowed to ecclesiastics, as well as to all the other public functionaries of our land.

2. The effect, then, of an indefinite subdivision of the land, would be to lessen indefinitely, not the population on the whole, but that class of them which goes by the name of the disposable.*

* We must not, however, ascribe to the largeness and integrity of its landed estates alone, the very great proportion which the disposable bears to the other two classes of labourers in Britain. Both its more perfect system of leases, and the superiority of its methods and machinery, whether in farmwork or in manufactures, contribute to the same result. They cause that, by means of a much smaller agricultural and secondary population, the same amount of food is raised in Britain than perhaps in any country of Europe; leaving a greater sur-

3. The landed proprietor, in expending that surplus produce of his estate, which goes under the
name of rent, must himself be upheld in the first
and second necessaries of life ; and so far must he
draw on the services both of the agricultural and
the secondary population. But whatever he is
able to expend over and above, he, by our definition, expends upon luxuries; and in so far he upholds a disposable population, who, by our definition also, are employed in preparing them. Let
us imagine him able to expend the maintenance of
four such ; but that, in the next generation, his
estate is divided into two parts, each having a
separate proprietor. The surplus produce has now

plus of hands for the service of the affluent in the preparation
of luxuries, or for the services of the state. This is the real
secret of a power and political greatness so much beyond the
absolute population of our island. It is not by its absolute, but
by its disposable population, that the strength of a nation is to
be estimated. We are much behind France in respect of the
former, but not of the latter comparison.

And as we have adverted to the varieties of land-letting, we
would only remark, that there is surely nothing in these which
can at all obscure a truth that so announces its own evidence,
as the utter incapacity of land, which but feeds its agricultural
and secondary labourers, for yielding a rent in any shape. If,
over and above this, its cultivators can render personal services,
or pay taxes, or afford part of the produce to their superiors;
these are not the same in kind as the money rents of Britain;
but still they are varieties of rent, and proceeding too from
the same cause, from a surplus produce, or a superior fertility
in the soil, over that which could but remunerate the expenses
of its husbandry.

to maintain two proprietors in the first and second necessaries of life, instead of one. It was formerly divided between the essential maintenance of one proprietor, and four labourers of the disposable class—it will now be divided between the essential maintenance of two proprietors, and three labourers of the disposable class. At this point one of the disposable population has been withdrawn, and a proprietor has come in his room. At the next descent, should the same rate of subdivision hold, we shall have four proprietors on the land which originally belonged to one; and, instead of four of a disposable population, attached by service to the property, there will only remain one of that description. At the next descent, the whole of the disposable population, formerly attached to the owner of the property in question, behoved to disappear. The surplus produce would not, in fact, be equal to their maintenance in the first and second necessaries, or to what may be called their essential maintenance—and their owners behoved to help out their support by entering on that part of the gross produce which is detained for the expenses of the husbandry; which they could only do, by sinking, partly into the agricultural, or partly into the secondary class of labourers themselves. The tendency of such a system, then, is to extinguish the disposable population, in as far as their services are attached to the proprietors of land, and to substitute a merely agrarian population in their room; each perhaps labouring at the husbandry of his own scanty portion, and it to be frittered into still smaller shreds and pendicles with the rising up of the next generation. The disposable population would not be annihilated, even with the farthest consummation of such a process. There still behoved to be so many attached to the service of capitalists, who, in expending their profits, would be enabled, as at present, to purchase the luxuries of life for themselves and for their families. Mainly, however, our landed aristocracy would disappear; and, whether as it respects the state of society, or the direction and distribution of employment among the people, we know not how a greater revolution could be effected, on the internal economy of our nation, than by the abolition of the law of primogeniture, and the enactment, in its place, of a law of equal inheritance among the children of a family.

4. Now, assuming, what we surely need not prove, that the agricultural produce of a country, in this comminuted state, is not, and cannot be greater, than when the land is parcelled out into sizeable and well-stocked farms; it will be obvious that there is no security whatever for the better economic condition of an agrarian, than of a disposable population. The moral preventive check might operate with equal efficacy in both; and, if this check be wanting, the distress of both is equally unavoidable. The want or the well-being of a nation, resolves itself exclusively into this; and, apart from this, there is no expedient which

can be devised, that will ultimately and permanently serve to elevate the comfort of the poorer orders.   We have indeed many experimental symptoms within our reach, of the misery incidental to a mere agrarian population.   In Ireland, the degradation of the peasantry has been ascribed to an indefinite subdivision in the occupancy of the soil ; and the very same result may be looked for, in the indefinite subdivision of its ownership. In those country hamlets, the erection of which has been encouraged by the attachment of a slip of land to each of the tenements, what an amount of want and of wretchedness is often realized ! A headlong deterioration in the circumstances of the people, is just as possible and likely under this agrarian system, as any other.   Nothing, in fact, will save the community at large, from the miseries of an oppressed and straitened condition, but an elevation of the popular character and mind ; and more especially of this expedient of family equalization may it be said, that while, ultimately, it cannot restrain the people from descending to as low a grade as they would have done under any other economy, it, at the same time, weakens to an incalculable extent the general interest of the state ; besides preventing the formation, or the increase, of certain other and subordinate interests, which best serve to grace and to dignify a nation.

5. What we mean by the general interest of the state, is the interest which lies in the amount of its public revenue, and its consequent command

over the services of the population. It is quite
evident, that all those enlisted in the direct service
of government, provided that their whole time
is given to it, must belong to the disposable class;
as, with a given population in the country, and a
given standard of enjoyment among them, neither
the agricultural nor the secondary classes can possibly be trenched upon. It is out of the disposable population, then, that a government draws its
soldiers, and sailors, and civil servants, and all the
agency of its various establishments, on the supposition of this public service being, not their occasional, but their perpetual occupation. Even
then, before we have entered upon any financial
consideration, it must be obvious, that whatever
limits the disposable population, lessens the power
of a state to extend its permanent establishments.
It may command the temporary service of all its
citizens. It may compel each man to be a soldier;
and thus enact a composition of professions between the civil and the military. But it cannot,
consistently with the full benefit that lies in the
separation of the professions, or in the division of
employment, it cannot have such numbers at its
disposal; when, by any cause, an abridgment has
taken place on the disposable population. The
landed property, which has four disposable labourers attached to it, can be so taxed, as to place a
greater quantity of labour under the control of
government, than when, by its first division, the
number of such labourers is reduced to three, and

still more, than when, by its second division, the
number is reduced to one. Or, to exhibit the
same thing in money, if an estate be worth two
hundred pounds a year to its one proprietor, and
fifty be allowed for his essential maintenance;
then, the sum of a hundred and fifty pounds may
be regarded as the taxable fund that is yielded by
the property. But, after it comes into the hand
of two proprietors, there must be the deduction of
a hundred pounds for their essential maintenance,
and the taxable fund is thereby reduced from a
hundred and fifty to a hundred. It is thus, that,
by every step in the process of subdivision, a reduction takes place in the amount of that produce
which government can reach by its taxations. A
territorial impost could not raise so much from a
country divided into small as into large properties,
without a far greater sense of depression and discomfort on the part of its owners. And these may
at length be so multiplied, that, reduced to the
necessaries of life, they could pay no such imposts
at all. It is thus, we think, that the law of primogeniture stands essentially connected with the
strength and power of a nation; and that every
government is sure to wax feeble, under a system
by which the land crumbles into fragments. At
every new subdivision, the disposable population
is lessened; and just because the surplus maintenance, which went to uphold them is lessened—there
being always a greater and a greater proportion of
it absorbed by those agrarians, who are left to

multiply without limit, on a soil that will soon be unable to sustain them. The people, individually, are not more comfortable; while, collectively, their strength and greatness must decline. France, under her present system, and in spite of the convulsive efforts made by her in seasons of great public excitement, has entered, we believe, on a sure process of decay; and, without a more comfortable peasantry than before, will she sink in the long run, beneath the pre-eminence once held by her among the nations.

6. We are aware that, generally, it is not by an income tax, that the public revenues, in the different states of Europe, are raised. Still the argument holds, in as far as they are raised by a tax on the luxuries of our landed proprietors. This is a source of income to government, that is perpetually lessening, under the system of territorial division. And its tendency is to land the nation in that state, when nothing will remain for taxation, but the profits of capital, and the wages of labour, and such commodities as enter into the consumption of capitalists and labourers. We have already explained, how the effect of such taxation, is to limit the agriculture, by causing it to stop all the sooner, in its progress downward among the inferior soils; the last soil entered on, behoving to be of such capability, as will not merely yield a satisfying remuneration to the capitalists and labourers, but yield, over and above, the payment of all the taxes to which the capitalists and labour-

ers are exposed.*   One great recommendation that
we insisted on of a tax upon net rent, is, that it
lays no such impediment on the progress of cultivation ; insomuch, that if the whole of our national
revenue were drawn from the landlords, they would
not only have a full compensation in the cheapness
of the commodities used by them ; but, in addition,
they would have an enlargement of their income,
by the agriculture being relieved of its present ob-
structions, and let out to the uttermost limit of
which, apart from taxation, it is capable.   There
is thus a double infliction attendant on an indefinite subdivision of the land.   It necessarily confines the taxes to such objects, that they oppose
the extension of the husbandry, and thus limit
the natural produce of the country ; while it lessens that proportion of it which can be made
available to public or national objects.   In counterpart to this, there is a double benefit in that

* So much do we hold this to be the truth, that, if there is
soundness in our principle, it is still the land which yields all
the taxes, even after it may have been so subdivided, as that
all which bears the semblance of rent shall be annihilated.
The mere capitalist finds a refuge from taxation in higher profits, and the mere labourer in higher wages.   It is the residuum
of farm produce, over and above that which defrays the natural expenses of farm management, that pays all the public
revenue; and it is conceivable, that, in that payment, it may be
so wholly absorbed as to be lost sight of altogether.   That land
should be able to sustain this burden, it must be of a superior
quality to that which forms the natural limit of the agriculture;
or, in other words, the agriculture must stop at a higher point
of fertility than it otherwise would do.

system of larger properties, which would admit of the revenue of government being wholly territorial. It would both enlarge the national wealth, and enlarge that proportion of it, which might be devoted, through the means of taxation, to any of the objects of patriotism. The nation might become both individually richer, and collectively stronger than before.

7. This double benefit speaks strongly in favour of the law of primogeniture. Under this law, and with the system of larger properties to which it gives rise, there is room for a higher territorial impost, insomuch that the whole public revenue might be raised by a tax upon net rent. And were the method resorted to, of making the centage of imposition higher as the income was higher; a much greater amount could be levied for the public service, with less of individual hardship to those on whom the taxes had been laid. The proprietor of ten thousand a year could not only part with a larger sum annually, but with a larger proportional sum, than the proprietor of a thousand a year. But this is not the only advantage of the system for which we are contending. Government can not only obtain, in consequence of it, a greater fraction of the country's wealth, but the wealth itself becomes absolutely greater. Every other tax but one on net rent, more especially if laid on articles of general consumption, contracts the agriculture of the country; and, along with it, the dependent and subordinate interests of the population,

and the trade and the manufactures. With the commutation of all general taxes into one on net rent, every artificial limit to the extent of cultivation is done away, and the wealth of the country is carried forward to the uttermost of its capabilities. Government is not only enabled, first, to raise a larger proportion; but, secondly, to raise that larger proportion from a larger subject. This is the way by which to draw the maximum of public revenue, for the benefit of all public interests; and that, by an imposition on landlords alone, without even so much as the semblance of hardship on the community at large; a way, by which taxation may be carried, if necessary, beyond all former example, and without hurt or heart-burning to the general population.

8. The topics of popular invective often cross each other. The loudest against the burden of taxation, are also the loudest against the law of primogeniture. Little do they know, that this law might be the instrument of a great and general immunity to the people; that, by the help of it, taxation, though levied and expended for the benefit of the whole, might be transferred in full to the landlords—these objects of their fierce jealousy —who yet would not be injured by the commutation, but would only become ostensibly, what they are really, the sole tributaries of the commonwealth.

9. We have before said, that, had no land yielded more, in return for the labour bestowed on it, than enough to feed the agricultural workmen and their

secondaries, the whole species behoved to be engrossed with the cares of providing for a subsistence. There could have been no leisure for
higher and more dignified occupations. It is interesting, thus to connect the fertility of the soil
with a disposable population, and with all which
that population renders for the pleasures of human
life, and the embellishment of human society. It
is the overplus produce of land, after that the agricultural labourers and their secondaries have been
fed—it is out of this, in fact, that law, and protection, and philosophy, and the ministry of religion,
and art, and all that goes to decorate and to dignify
human life, are upholden. It is because this overplus is possessed in quantities large enough, not
only for the essential maintenance of its owners,
but for enabling them, by the maintenance of
others, to purchase a thousand gratifications both
for the mind and the person—it is because of this,
that the luxuries, whether of a more sensual or
refined character, so abound in society. We feel
quite assured, that a system which would fritter
down this overplus into indefinitely minute portions, must tend to vulgarise a community, by
absorbing, in the mere subsistence of an ever-increasing multitude of owners, what is now divided
in subsistence for those who yield, in return for it,
a thousand elegancies and enjoyments, that would
have been otherwise unknown. It is no adequate
reply to this, that these enjoyments and elegancies
are monopolized by a few ; for, by the controlling

power of the state, the fund, out of which they are purchased, can be drawn upon indefinitely, not for the support of political interests alone, but for the support of Christian education and a national literature, and other benefits, of a high order, that are diffused among the many. Such a system of landed property, is not only the best fitted to enrich and enable a government for the support of liberal institutions and the effective patronage of genius; but the system is, in itself, a guarantee for the maintenance of enough of leisure, among a class sufficiently numerous to form an extensive reading public, and call forth the exhaustless varieties of an authorship, that is ever keeping the mind of society in vigorous play, and adorning it with the graces of taste and cultivation. So that, altogether, with the size and integrity of our landed estates, would we associate a greater amount of mental power and cultivation—both the benefits and the beauties of a more intellectual and polished commonwealth.

10. When it is alleged that, under the existing system, the luxuries wrought up by the disposable population, are monopolized by the few, the imagination is, that were the system broken down, by the abolition of the law of primogeniture, the same amount of luxury would be diffused throughout a vastly greater multitude. But the truth is, that, in virtue of the process which would ensue, the disposable population would constantly be lessening, and the luxuries they rendered would every

year be diminished in their amount.   The tendency
is to an ultimate state, where, instead of luxuries
or elegancies being divided among many landed
proprietors, these proprietors would be unable to
afford any luxuries or elegancies at all.   Even for
their own comfort, it would have been as well that
they had been labouring in the ranks of the disposable population—as labouring, each in sordidness and straitness, on some little acre, from which
the subsistence of a family could hardly be ex-
torted.   The drudgery of an artizan, in the manufacture of luxuries, is not worse than the ignoble
drudgery of an over-crowded agrarian population.
Under the system in question, the manufacture of
second necessaries might be kept up in its original
extent ; but the manufacture of luxuries would be
indefinitely diminished.   There would thus be very
few, if any, of the landed proprietors that could
command any of the higher enjoyments of life.
There would also be fewer or smaller capitalists in
the land ; and, instead of our present beautiful
gradation, we should behold a general levelling of
all conditions, and nearly the whole of human society reduced to one common state of penury and
toil.

11. And it is not true, that, in virtue of elegance,
and luxury, and leisure, being the inheritance of a
few, there is not a blessing in the present system of
things to the whole mass of society.   Under the
opposite system, there would be nearly one unbroken level, the whole of which behoved, in time,

to be as sunk and degraded, as is the state of our
present labourers.   Now, it is a level, rising into
frequent eminencies, of greater or less height, and
of radiance, more or less conspicuous.   And what
we affirm is, that, from this higher galaxy of rank
and fortune, there are the droppings, as it were, of
a bland and benignant influence on the general
platform of humanity.   There is one very palpable
evidence of this in the moral effect of a residing
gentry ; and we might also allege the consequent
economic good of such a distribution, seeing that
the moral and the economic in society are so intimately blended.   The truth is, that the very elevation of mind and manners, caught as if by infection from the higher, forms our best security against
an extreme wretchedness in the lower orders.   If
the people were once innoculated with a higher
taste for the comforts and decencies of life, the
else difficult, or rather, unresolvable problem, of
a secure and permanent sufficiency for all their
wants, would receive its most effectual accomplishment.   And we appeal to general observation, if
the symptoms of such a taste are not greatly more
frequent and conspicuous around the habitations of
our rural aristocracy.   And, independently of its
virtue in raising and refining the general tone of
the people, it is surely, reasoning on the capability
of things, a vast accession to a community, when
there is in it a quantity of mind disengaged for
general speculation, and therefore, if under patriotic and enlightened direction, in a state for de-

vising the best institutions and the best economy
of things for the well-being of a nation. Law, and
education, and charity, and all the collective interests of a state, are more likely to be put on their
best footing—not, we admit, where arbitrary and
despotic power stands associated with great property, but where regulated freedom and respectable
property are blended. We feel quite assured, of
every land of law and liberty, that, with an order
of men possessing large and independent affluence,
there is better security for the general comfort and
virtue of the whole, than when society presents an
aspect of almost unalleviated plebeianism. And
it is of the utmost importance to the argument,
that the breaking down of this affluence would
ultimately do nothing for the enlarged sufficiency
of the lower orders. Whatever beneficent effects,
then, can with justice be ascribed to the existence
and secure establishment of such an affluence—
these we have all to the bargain. They form so
much clear gain to the commonwealth; and though,
at first sight, the whole good of it may appear to
be absorbed by the children of fortune, there is,
beside this absorption by them, a reflection on the
commonwealth at large—a secondary influence,
that is felt throughout the extent of society, and
which goes down to the very humblest of its members.

12. For the best construction of a social edifice,
in every large country like ours, we would have a
king upon the throne—not rising like a giant among

the pigmies, or as an unsupported may-pole in
the midst of a level population ; but borne up by
a splendid aristocracy, and a gradation of ranks
shelving downwards to the basement of society.
We doubt if the other monarchy could stand ; or if
France, with its citizen king, amid a mighty and
ever-increasing swarm of smaller and smaller agrarians, can maintain its present economy for a single
generation. We think of our own political fabric,
that it not only affords a vastly greater number
of noble and graceful spectacles, in the minarets
and the blazing pinnacles which crowd its elevation ; but that, abstracting from the degradation
which has been caused by its accursed law of pauperism, it would have had a more elevated basement in its well-conditioned peasantry, than any
other country or kingdom of the civilized world.
It is not for the sake of its ornaments and its chivalry alone—it is not for the sake of these chiefly,
that we want the high rank and fortune of our aristocracy to be upholden. It is because we think
there is a soul in chivalry, which, though nursed
in the bosom of affluence, does not cloister there ;
but passes abroad from mind to mind, and lights
up a certain glow of inspiration throughout the
mass of a community. Let it only be a land of
intelligence and freedom—and, we think, that
where there are nobles, the common people are not
so ignoble; and that, while the property of the rich,
though scattered, as by the law of France, into innumerable fragments, would not add by a single iota

to the average comfort of our plebeian families ; yet the presence of the rich infuses a spirit that, by dignifying their characters, enables them, through the medium of their own habits and exertions, to dignify their condition also. It is thus, we hold, that there are materials in Britain, for the composition, altogether, of a finer, and higher, and happier society, than there are in America; and that, without one taint of the pusillanimous in the spirit of our people, there might be a deference to rank, and withal a truer greatness of soul and sentiment, than republicanism, with all its coarse and boastful independence, can ever realize. We would therefore, on the whole, leave the existing framework of our own community undisturbed ; and, instead of letting down the peerage of our realms to the external condition of our peasantry, we should rather go forth among the peasantry, and do all that lies within the compass of education, both to elevate their standard of comfort, and to pour such a moral lustre over them, as might equalize them, either to peers or to princes in all the loftiest attributes of humanity.

13. We again recur to the absenteeism of Ireland, in support of our argument. The crying evil of that land, is not that the wealth of its proprietors is withdrawn from its shores. Even though detained and spent amongst them, yet, did the people continue as reckless, and of as degraded habits as now ; then, through intervention of the sure principle of population, we should only behold a

larger, but in every respect as wretched a community. The benefit of a residing gentry lies, not
in the money which they spend, but in the moral
and humanizing effect of their presence. The
peasantry, under this influence, would soon cease
to be so degraded; and, through the medium, not
of external aid, but of their own internal principles
and tastes, would attain to a more secure and respectable sufficiency. The popular cry, and on
sound economic grounds too, is for a residing
gentry; yet, with marvellous dissonance thereto,
there is another cry for the spoliation of the church,
that would, in fact, annihilate the best supplement
for a residing gentry, which Ireland at present enjoys; we mean a clergy bound, in a vast majority
of instances, to dwell and to officiate among the
people. There is also a well-founded cry against
the absence of proprietors. But they are little
aware, that the cry for a system of pauperism, is a
cry for that which will rivet this calamity, and
make it irrecoverable. We do not say, that a compulsory provision for indigence will banish its large
landed proprietors from Ireland, but it will annihilate the order altogether. For the non-residence
of the gentry, it will bring on what is far more
hopeless—the non-existence of a gentry; when
the population, the victims of the most insensate
experiment, that, in opposition to all the lights
both of observation and argument, was ever attempted by statesmen, will remain in as great destitution, and withal in greater helplessness than ever.

14. We know that there is a mighty force of sentiment and natural affection arrayed against the law of primogeniture. But here is the way in which we would appease these feelings, and make compensation for the violence done to them. We would make no inroad on the integrity of estates; or, for the sake of a second brother, take off a portion, to the extent of a thousand a year, from that domain of ten thousand a year, which devolved by succession on the eldest son of the family. We should think it vastly better, if by means of a liberal provision in all the branches of the public service, a place of a thousand a year lay open to the younger son, whether in the law, or in the church, or in colleges, or in the army, or in any other well-appointed establishment, kept up for the good and interest of the nation. We would still have the state to support the younger branches; yet that not by the violation of its integrity, but by a more severe taxation than our politicians of the present day have the courage to impose. Under the one system, the second brother would have his thousand a year, but give no return for it in any kind of service. Under the other system, he would also have his thousand a year, and the public have the benefit of a duty and a service from him to the bargain. Instead of a rustic idler, we should behold him a public functionary; and, under this arrangement, therefore, we should combine, with a provision for the younger branches of families, a greater efficiency and amount of public

service; a remedy against the destitution of younger children, and withal, a better served nation.   The one system only proposes a single object—a provision for younger children ; and this object, in the course of that indefinite comminution which must take place upon the territory, would at length be completely unattainable after a lapse of generations. The other system proposes a double object—a provision for younger children, along with a fully equipped and full-paid agency in all the departments of national usefulness.   And this object could be permanently upholden.   The integrity of estates is not necessarily violated by a large taxation on the owners of them.   Through the organ of government, each estate may be looked upon as loaded with jointures for the sake of the younger members of families; who, at the same time, instead of simple receivers, have to labour, in some vocation or other, for the benefit of the community.   And, believing as we do, that the real incidence of the taxes is upon land, we would enlist all the forces of natural sentiment and affection on the side of a larger revenue to government, and a larger allowance to public functionaries of all orders.   We would infinitely prefer, that these feelings, generous and natural as they are, took a direction towards the increase of taxes, than towards the abolition of the law of primogeniture.   But it were well, in the present delusion, if these taxes were laid directly and ostensibly upon land.   The whole work of retrenchment, that is now the favourite cry of pa, triots, both in and out of parliament, proceeds, we think, on a short-sighted view, or rather, a total misunderstanding of the real interests involved in the question.   A large taxation is just a right corollary to the law of primogeniture.   And the nibbling economy of those who would cut and curtail in all directions, is most perversely at variance with the consistent and comprehensive policy of every country where that law is in operation.

15. It will not for a moment be imagined, that, while we would apportion a much larger amount of the nation's wealth to the objects of public service, we contend for any hereditary or family right to that portion, on the part of the younger brothers of our aristocracy.   It should lie open to the competition of all the worth and talent which may exist in any quarter of society.   In the exercise of a virtuous patronage, it should always be disposed of to those who can give the largest return for it, in the value of their services.   It is because of the greater ascendancy which the public mind has over the counsels and the doings of government, than at any former periods, that we feel both the safety and the advantage of a more largely-provided and better-paid agency in all the departments of the state, and of far more generous allowances to public and professional men.   Now that the public mind has become more influential, we should like that the part it took were to direct the machinery of our national institutes, rather than to impair or to destroy it.   This machinery the public will not

grudge to see extended, after that, under a reformed
system of finance, it shall have become patent to
general observation—that, with the law of primogeniture, the whole expense of supporting it is
really drawn from the eldest sons of our landed
families.   And we contend for no more, in behalf
of the younger sons, than that they should be admitted on equal terms to the competitions of this
then larger and wealthier preferment, along with
men of the requisite intelligence and accomplishment from all other classes of the community.*

16. It may be asked, if there is such a benefit in
the size of estates, how far ought that principle to
be carried; and would it really be desirable that
the territory of our island were shared among a few
large proprietors, each having a domain equal to a
princedom, and so with the entire annihilation of
such a gentry as compose the actual landed aristocracy of Britain?   We admit, though the subject
be, from its nature, not very definable, that there
is an extreme in that direction too, against which,
however, we have a sufficient practical security, in
the existing order of things.   But with the law of
equal division in families, there is no security
against the rapid descent of the nation into the
opposite extreme.   The land would speedily be
frittered into shreds; and, under the load of an

* It is thus that taxation accomplishes what ought to be the
popular object, of placing within the reach of general society,
a portion of that wealth which would otherwise be restricted
to hereditary proprietors.

agrarian population, ever augmenting and accumulating, the best interests of the community would
most certainly be overborne. Having these views,
it is with us a theme of gratulation, that there
should be a law of primogeniture; but we would
earnestly contend, that this law, and a liberal provision for all public functionaries, should go hand
in hand. This is the way of reconciling the highest
interests of the public with the rights of families;
and that without injury to any of those economic
objects, against which all taxation, however imposed, has been so unfairly set in opposition. We
rejoice, more particularly, to think, that a church
may be upheld in all its endowments, without being,
in any right sense of the word, an incubus upon
the nation—while it serves to mitigate the hardship
which has been imputed to the law of primogeniture. We are aware that this is not the precise
and proper argument for a religious establishment;
yet, convinced, upon other grounds, of the vast
utility of such an institution, we cannot but regard
it as one beneficent consequence of the law in
question, that it enlists on the side of a church the
warmest affections of nature, the sympathies and
feelings of domestic tenderness. We are aware of
the reckless and unprincipled patronage to which
this has given rise; and that a provision for younger
sons has been viewed as the great, if not the only
good of a church, by many who hold the dispensation of its offices. It is this which has alienated
from the establishment so large a portion of the

community ; and, if the abuse of an institute were a sufficient argument for its destruction, perhaps the church of England will be found to have sealed its own doom, and to have brought upon itself the sentence of its own overthrow.   But we still hope the impetuous spirit of the times may be tempered with discrimination, and that it will be judged better to direct the machinery than to destroy it.   An apparatus, in its own nature beneficial, may have been perverted to evil ; yet the way is not to demo- lish or cast it aside, but to regulate its movements.

CHAPTER XIII.

ON EMIGRATION.

1. THE felt necessity of emigration from a country is, in itself, a practical evidence, that its resources are not illimitable. We may be assured, that if other remedies for the destitution of the people were at hand, they would have the preference over this. Could home colonization, or the invention of new employments, or the increase of capital, or the openings of foreign trade, have furnished ready and withal indefinite resources for our population, we should never have witnessed to any great extent among them, a disposition to renounce the scenes of their infancy, with all the charms and associations of home, for the chances or the perils of distant and unknown lands. We have already endeavoured to prove how it is, that the commutation of taxes and tithes must make room for a larger population; though that room would soon be occupied to the full; and after a brief season of general prosperity among all the classes of society, there would ensue the same straitness and difficulty as before. Proving, that, in every direction, and on all sides, there are limits at home, which throw back, as it were, the tide of our increasing numbers on the general community,

and produce a feeling of pressure and discomfort
there ; against which, relief is sought by an efflux
of population from a land that is too narrow for
them. We have now only to estimate the strength
and the efficacy of this expedient, after which we
shall enter, though briefly at this time, on the
question of public charity; the last of all the expedients, which, if tried and found wanting, would
seem to land us in the conclusion—that, either,
there is a helpless and irremediable necessity for
extreme and extensive want in human society,
from which, by no practicable device, can society
be protected ; or, that, if there be a specific against
this overwhelming calamity, it must be different
from any of the expedients which shall have yet
passed under our review.

2. When the agriculture of a country arrives at
its limit, there is a pressure that would not be felt,
but for the tendency of the population to increase.
But long before this limit is reached, is the pressure
felt ; because the tendency to an increase in the
population exceeds the rate of enlargement in the
agriculture. The probability, then, is, that even
emigration will not remove, will not eventually
alleviate the distresses of our land. The same
cause which outstrips the enlargement within, may
also outstrip the efflux abroad. Certain it is, that
the colonies of Britain, notwithstanding their perpetual draft on the families of the mother country,
(and many of them but too powerful absorbents for
our excess of population, from the balefulness of

their climates,) have still left us in a condition of
difficulty; scarcely, if at all lessened, by the outlet
which they afford every year to such a number of
adventurers. But this may be made a matter of
computation. The capability of increase in the
population, may be estimated with tolerable accu-
racy; and the extent of emigration requisite, for
lightening the pressure of our redundancy, may be
estimated along with it; and that, with an approximation to the truth, sufficiently near for the purposes of a practical argument.

3. Population, when permitted its full development, by an unbounded supply of the means of
subsistence, can double itself in fifteen years; and
we proceed on a computation greatly more moderate than this, when we affirm, that for an emigration, sufficient to allow an unchecked multiplication of our species in the British islands, there
behoved to be at least half a million of human beings transported annually from our shores. The
expense of so mighty a transportation, and the
magnitude of that immense flotilla, which would
need to be upheld for the business of these annual
shipments, are of themselves sufficiently startling;
and might well disabuse us of the idea, that any
very effectual relief can be ministered, by this expedient, for the wants of our population. But we
may properly add the ever-increasing difficulty of
new settlements abroad; after that the most accessible and best portions of territory had been
occupied. It is no great recommendation of a

scheme, that the longer it is prosecuted, it is always becoming more impracticable; insomuch, that every successive year must witness another augmentation both to the cost and the labour of it. Neither can we admire, as a sound or lasting expedient, for keeping right the overflowing population of one country, a process that hastens onward every other country to the same consummation. We should greatly prefer an expedient that would equally apply to all countries; and that would not lose its efficacy, even though the globe should throughout be peopled up to its capabilities; and the millennial era had arrived, at which we beheld a general fulness and prosperity in all lands. But the near, the practical consideration is, that the relief afforded even now, by all the emigration, which even the most sanguine of its advocates can count upon, is but an insignificant fraction of what a population, left to its own unchecked spontaneity, would need; and every future year, this relief would become more insignificant.

4. Now here is the evil of every partial, and at the same time, ostensible relief, against the effects of a mischief that is brought on by the general recklessness of the population. It adds to that recklessness; and so may aggravate the pressure on the one hand, more than it alleviates that pressure upon the other. This we hold to be the precise operation of a public charity, instituted for the supplies of general indigence. The power of it is overrated, greatly overrated beyond the pro-

duct of it; and so, it relaxes the economy and the providential habits of the people, to such a degree, that it falls greatly short of supplying the poverty, which itself may be said to have created. It is thus too, that, in a country, the system of whose interests and affairs is much complicated by the multiplication and variety of its resources, we should look for a more oppressive redundancy of people, than in a country of simpler economy; in Britain, for example, where the people have commerce and colonies, and the demands of various and lucrative professions to count upon, than in Norway, where the necessary limit of population is not so obscured by complexity; and which limit, therefore, in consequence of being more distinctly seen, is more decisively acted upon. It is thus that the growth and enlargement of towns, though powerful absorbents for the population bred in country parishes, has not relieved, has, we think, on the contrary, augmented the pressure that is felt in the country; and, it is thus also, that the rise of colonies, the demand from both the Indies for men from Britain, has excited, we do believe, a greater overflow of population, that it can possibly draw away from us. And we have just as little faith in the virtue of emigration. We dread, that any vacancies left behind it, would not only be filled, and that immediately; but filled, in a greater degree of compression than before. It would form just another of those resources, which, by adding to the general delusion, might aggravate the general distress. A very slight relaxation in the providential habits of the people—and, more especially in their habit of providential marriages—would suffice for this. And though the spontaneous emigration of families should be left to itself, we do fear, that a public, a proclaimed, a national system of emigration, would but enhance the evil it was devised to remedy.

5. Whenever emigration prevails, it is the evidence of a country, where the population presses on the means of subsistence, from which pressure it seeks to be relieved by successive discharges. We believe that a regular system of emigration would certainly bring on and perpetuate such a state; and surely, far more desirable, than that a people should thus press on the limit of their own home resources, were it, that they kept comfortably and somewhat largely within the limit. The effect of emigration has been compared to that of a safety-valve. But a safety-valve in the boiler, implies a great force of distension within; and surely, it were better for every land, that the distension were prevented, than that it were only relieved, and kept down to a certain maximum, which cannot be sustained, without a strongly felt violence and discomfort within the borders of the territory. The alternative may be stated within a short compass. It were better that the population should not be carried up to the extreme of what the country can bear, by the recklessness of the people; than that it should be kept down to that point by

emigration.   We may be sure that every country
is throughout in a suffering condition, which requires to be disgorged, from year to year, of its
redundant families.   There may be a few spirits,
alive to the charms and the romance of adventure,
to whom emigration would prove a lure rather than
a terror.   But, averagely speaking, there must be
a great experience of distress and destitution, to
account for the voluntary exile of thousands from
the land of their forefathers.   It must be no light
evil from which they are making their escape,
when, in the act of doing so, they forego all the
recollections of their boyhood, the scene and the
dwelling-place of their dearest intimacies.   Now,
in respect of the economic condition of a people,
it may be said with peculiar justness, that if one
member suffer, all the members suffer along with
it.   The destitution which forces a certain number, though it should be a proportionally small one,
from the land of their nativity; is the symptom of
a general destitution and distress through the
country at large, or at least in the profession to
which they belong.   And rather, infinitely rather
than a system of things, which encourages a population up to the necessity of emigrating, would we
prefer, that, in virtue of smaller numbers, the population fell somewhat beneath the employment
which remunerates, or the food that sustains them.

6. We believe it to be strictly demonstrable,
that wherever a sure and systematic, and withal, a
permanent and generally known provision is made

for the excess of labourers in a land; this, of itself, must depress the condition and circumstances of the whole body. This it does, through intervention of the principle of population; by which, it sustains in perpetual being, the very overplus which it is its object to dispose of. For, mark the effect on general wages of the mere existence of such an overplus. We believe that no where can the provision in question be so comfortable, as would be a situation of well-paid industry in any of the regular trades or employments. Ere the former, then, will be sought after, there must be an excessive, and so a disappointed or defeated competition for the latter; a competition which, though proceeding from a very small surplus of labourers, must, by an infallible law, effect a very great reduction in the price of labour. It is easy to present a beautiful sketch of home colonization, and tell, for example, of the thousands who in this way have found a harbour and an establishment in Holland. But the real question by which the policy of such an institution is determined, is, whether it has operated any sensible relief on the mass of society, or does not rather tend to bring down tens and hundreds of thousands to that minimum state, in which they are hardly detained at their own occupation; and that, by but a hairbreadth of preference over the state of a pauper agriculturist. In like manner, the system of English charity has encouraged an overflow of population, who fill up the asylum provided for them

in their numerous poor-houses; but not without
first inflicting a sore degradation on the price of
labour, and, what is worse, continuing to overhang
as by a perpetual load the labour-market; thus
depressing, and that permanently, the comfort and
sufficiency of the whole body of labourers. And
the very same, we predict, would be the consequence of a regular and extensive plan of emigration. It would at all times encourage into being,
a certain fractional excess of people, beyond the
number who can be accommodated in decent sufficiency within the borders of their own land. And
so the alternative would need to be entertained,
whether they will prefer an exile abroad, or the
pittance of a scanty remuneration for their industry
at home. But it is an alternative not confined to
them. There are not two rates of wages; one for
the overplus, whom, indeed, it were impossible
specifically and individually to single out; and
another for the general mass of the operatives
in society. All are brought down equally; and,
as in the other instances, this attempt regularly
and systematically to provide for a small aliquot
part, ends in the infliction of a universal calamity.
So utterly powerless, or rather so positively mischievous, is every expedient for the amelioration
of the people, that but adds, through the medium
of their own improvidence, to the excess of their
numbers. The high road to their collective comfort and independence, and there is no other, is
their collective virtue, and intelligence, and worth.

Off from this, both they and the patriots, or philanthropists who care for them, will find themselves alike helpless and bewildered. They may institute a thousand devices—schemes of benignant promise—smiling charities of goodly pretension and gracious aspect. They will all terminate in nothing, or worse than nothing. They smile but to betray.

7. We feel quite assured then, that the country is in a distempered condition, which is in the state of a vessel constantly running over. Rather than this, it should be in a state somewhat short of fulness. That policy must be very questionable which provides an egress, but at the same time encourages an ingress, that will certainly equal, and even tends to overpass it. In other words, emigration is any thing rather than a specific for the wants of a country; and just because it stimulates population. The abstracting process will yield no relief, if the replacing process be more than proportionally excited thereby. And amid the general impotency of this and all the former expedients, for the permanent comfort and well-being of the population, we feel shut up as to our only specific, to the operation of that moral check which regulates and restrains the increase of our species.

8. Yet though emigration, absolutely and of itself, can do no permanent good, but the contrary, there are, however, certain transition states in the history of a nation, and certain processes of domestic and economical reform, which, perhaps, it

may subserve as a temporary expedient. Certain
it is, that no scheme of emigration holds out such
an incentive to population, as does the scheme of
public charity which obtains in England; and we
have sometimes thought, that if the more innocent
of the two schemes could, for a time, be rendered
subsidiary to the abolition of the more hurtful one,
it might be the fit subject of a great national experiment.*　Emigration, though futile and ineffective
of itself, may still, as subsidiary to other schemes,
be worthy of all the attention of government.　It
is well to discriminate between those purposes to
which it is utterly incompetent, and those to which
it may at least act as an important auxiliary.　When
advocated on the former ground, it lies open to a
precipitate rejection; while, if viewed on the latter
ground, it may recommend itself even to our
soundest economists, as a great and beneficent
scheme of national policy.　When considered separately, and as a mere expedient for taking off an
excess of population, we deem it to be utterly insignificant and useless.　But not so, when conjoined with other schemes of internal or domestic
economy; and rightly adjusted, not to the impracticable object of clearing away the excess of our

* We are sensible that, by this allusion to pauperism, we anticipate the regular progress of our subjects; but we feel that
it might be done without violence, seeing that the majority of
our readers must be already enough occupied with the evils of
the system.　Furthermore, our remarks on pauperism, in the
next chapter, will be but succinct and general, it being a topic
on which we have sufficiently dilated in former publications.

people by yearly abstractions, but to the higher
and more hopeful object of preventing that excess.

9. It is thus that it might be brought to bear,
in England, on the reformation of their pauperism.
There can be no doubt, that the provision held out
by this system of charity, has slackened the operation of the preventive check all over the country.
It has multiplied and precipitated marriages in
every part of the land. It has superseded the
prudence and economy of the people; and such is
the relaxation of these habits, that a fearful burden,
both of vice and wretchedness, now lies upon the
commonwealth, with little prospect indeed of any
alleviation. The legislature, as if hopeless of all
remedy, seems afraid to look at it. The spreading
and deepening still further of a great popular cor-
ruption, is the inevitable result of letting it alone;
and yet the attempt to meddle with it, appears to
carry along with it the tremendous hazard of a
great popular violence.

10. We think that the pauperism of England,
even in its mildest, and some contend, its original
form, has done great mischief. To have vested
with a legal claim of relief, even the impotent and
the aged, must have had its effect in creating a
more reckless and improvident peasantry, and so
speeding unnaturally onward the rate of population. But the more recently admitted claim of the
able-bodied to relief, has had a still more direct
and obvious tendency the same way. It, in truth,
acts as an immediate bounty upon marriage. It is

no restraint upon the parties, in this step, that they are without wages. In many of the English counties, they have recourse upon the poor-rates, and obtain an allowance from it for each member of the household. In these circumstances, we are not to wonder at the immense number of juvenile marriages in England. The merest striplings have been known to enter into this alliance. They even threaten the parish vestries, that, if not more liberal in their dispensations of relief, they will marry, and bring upon them the additional burden of their wives and families. In some instances, the vestries have felt themselves obliged to rent, and even to furnish houses, for the reception of the newly-married couple. Who can question the effects of such a system? The whole of English pauperism may be regarded as a system of artificial incentives to population. But that part of it, more especially, which consists in the maintenance of able-bodied labourers without employment, and which, therefore, acts as an encouragement to the guilt of both sexes in the land, supplies the most direct and powerful of these incentives.

11. For ourselves, we do not approve of the late partial attempts which have been made for the reformation of English pauperism, by separating the question of a legal relief for the able-bodied, from the question of a legal relief for the impotent poor; since we hold that there is a practicable method for gradually getting rid of the whole. In either way, however, emigration might be of powerful

avail as an auxiliary; and may, in particular, be adapted in a way peculiarly beneficial to the case of those able-bodied poor who make application to the vestry, either because they are without employment, or because they receive for it inadequate wages. It were well could the alternative of emigration be offered to all such applicants; in which case, the legislature might be less scrupulous in repealing, even *instanter*, the application of the poor's fund to the relief of able-bodied labourers. Or, if they choose to go more gradually to work, it were still an important enactment, that all new applicants from among the able-bodied, all who made application for the first time, should be thus dealt with—that is, should be refused parish relief, but should, at the same time, be met by the offer of certain facilities for emigration.

12. When a scheme of emigration is thus tacked, as it were, to a scheme for the reformation of pauperism, it changes altogether its character and tendency. It, by itself, would stimulate population even beyond the relief which it could effectuate. But, when thus conjoined, it might help to restore the preventive check to its proper force; and do a great deal more, by its salutary influence on the habits of our people at home, than by all its successive shipments of the redundant families abroad. Even the latter service, however, is important in this view, that by it are chiefly carried off the breeders of the future generation—the parents of incipient families, who at present make application

because of their increasing numbers—or the young men, who meditate, and even menace the parish vestries with an impending marriage, that they might make good a larger claim upon the poor's rate. Every cargo of these effectuates not only a certain present, but a great prospective relief to the land—a relief which can only be neutralized by a still further relaxation in the prudential habits of those who are left behind, even that relaxation for which the system of pauperism is so deeply responsible, but which every encroachment upon the system must at least serve to diminish, if not to do away.

13. It is, therefore, to its wholesome re-action on the prevalent and popular habit in regard to matrimony, that we should look for the chief benefit of any such compound arrangement as is now contemplated. Emigration, separately, would cause no such re-action; but emigration, coupled with the abolition of all right or claim to parish relief at home, would operate, and that instantly, as a check to those juvenile marriages which are now so frequent in England. A young couple often will marry, though altogether without means of their own, on the prospect of immediate accommodation, however scanty, being provided for them by the parish at home. But it is utterly a mistake to imagine, that there is aught half so alluring to their eyes, in the prospect of a fearful ocean and an unknown wilderness beyond it. Of the ten who would marry, in the certainty of its being followed

up by a parish allowance, we feel confident that
there are nine who would not do the same thing,
with no other prospect than that of having to renounce for ever the land of their childhood.   They
would pause, and cast about, and wait the means
of their own independent maintenance, ere they
should throw themselves upon a necessity so re-
volting to nature.   In other words, they would feel
compelled to a postponement of the matrimonial
alliance, or to that measure which, after all, is the
great, nay, the only step, by which to resolve the
problem of relief for the miseries of an over-peopled
land.   The refusal of parochial aid to the able-
bodied, might safely be coupled with the alternative
offer of assistance for their emigration ; for, in the
vast majority of instances, the alternative would
not be taken: and so the people, committed to
their own expedients, and their own capabilities,
would simply be restored to that state, in which
we behold the workmen and the peasantry of every
other country in Europe.   The labour-market of
England, freed from the disturbing force of its present artificial pauperism, would henceforth be left
to the operation of natural principles ; and, in a
few years, not by the drainage without of emigration, but by a resurrection within of prudential
habits, it would cease to be so oppressed and overladen by the number of labourers.   It is when thus
adjusted to other, and greater schemes of reform
in our domestic economy, that the scheme of emigration becomes really hopeful.   While viewed

barely as an expedient for taking off the redundant families of our land, we fear that it can only be looked upon with distrust; and that all those who are most enlightened in the philosophy of public and political affairs, can have no value for it.   But it instantly acquires a character of worth and of importance, when adapted to the object of beneficial legislation upon so high an interest as the pauperism of England; and if it should serve to reconcile both parliament and the public to such enactments as would mitigate, if not do away, the evils of a system, that has proved so hurtful to the comfort and the moral habits of the population. However slight our estimate may be of the absolute relief which emigration can afford, yet, regarded as subsidiary to the amendment of English pauperism, we should be sorry if the scheme were to be altogether lost sight of; it being possessed of those capabilities, and susceptible of those bearings, which make it altogether worthy of being entertained as a great and comprehensive scheme of national policy.

14. For, *first,* however desirable the enactment may be, which should abolish the application of the poor's fund to the able-bodied, yet there is an apparent harshness or inhumanity in the proceeding, fitted to revolt both a generous public and a generous parliament.   Now, emigration is fitted to remove this moral barrier in the way of a most salutary reform.   The men who are thus discarded from their wonted resource, are not thrown into a

state of absolute helplessness. They have emigration between them and entire want. There is something given, or rather, something offered, for that which is taken away. It is not by a deprivation, but by a compromise, that they are dealt with. There are many of our legislators who would never have consented to the deprivation, yet may, perhaps, agree to the compromise. And this scheme of emigration will have effected a high service, if it shall but speed onward a right and a wise legislation, in a matter that ranks among the very highest of our national questions, and than which there is none wherein the strength and prosperity of the kingdom are more vitally interested.

15. And, *secondly*, there is nothing which should very much startle us, in this scheme, on the score of its expense. We believe that the number who will emigrate is greatly overrated. We are not to form our estimate upon this subject, by the number of those who have enlisted themselves as the members of Emigration Societies. Many even of these, however zealous and active now in their applications to government, would feel the preponderant attraction of home, when the outfit, and the voyage, and the everlasting leave of their native land, all looked at them in good earnest. It is true, that necessity will force men to any sacrifice; and we can scarcely imagine a better test of such necessity, than this offer of emigration. It will be found, then, we predict, that a great many of those who are now most clamorous for this relief, will not avail them-

selves of it; and that the vast majority of those able-bodied in England, who, at this moment, are receiving parish allowances, would discover some other method of finding for themselves, rather than encounter the peril of an untried enterprise, and the pain of an eternal separation from the country which gave them birth. On these accounts, government might, with all safety, meet the expense of such a scheme; and it is an expense that every year would lessen. For the colonies abroad, in proportion as their richer and more accessible territory was occupied, will hold out continually weaker allurements to emigration; and the country at home, in proportion as it was lightened of its surplus families, (not by abstraction, however, but by non-production, as we have already explained,) will have stronger attractions, in the ameliorated state of the people, for detaining them within its own shores. It is thus that the number of applications, so great, perhaps, at the first, as to appear quite formidable, would perpetually decline; and it would be found, that all the expense incurred, if indeed subservient to the proposed amendment in the system of pauperism, were the cheap purchase of so mighty a reformation.

16. But, *thirdly*, the expense might not be defrayed by government at all. It might be advanced by government on the security of the land, and repaid, after a period of years, by the emigrants themselves. Or it might be paid by the parishes from which the families do emigrate; and turn

out, after all, a cheap substitute for the far heavier expense of supporting these families at home. Still, however, we hold the chief recommendation of the scheme to lie, not in any primary or absolute virtue which it possesses of itself, but in the important function which belongs to it, as the auxiliary of another scheme for ridding the country of its greatest moral and political nuisance. We think, that, if only adapted to this object, the government might refrain from all that awkward legislation, by which it is proposed to save the country from the recurrence of that excessive population under which it labours. There is no doubt, that, so long as pauperism holds out an artificial encouragement to marriage, the gap which any emigration, however large, may leave behind it, will speedily be filled, and followed up, by as great an overflow as before. But the way to correct this, is not to lay restraint on the erection of cottages—not to neutralize the artificial encouragement by an artificial prohibition —not to counteract the violent or unnatural legis- lation in one direction, by the opposing force of a legislation as violent and as unnatural in another direction. The way to get rid of this whole com- plication, is to abolish the one, and refrain from the others. By simply doing away the application of the poor's fund to the support of able-bodied labourers, you restore the preventive check to its own proper and original energy; after which the case may fearlessly be confided to the workings of liberty and nature.

CHAPTER XIV.

ON A COMPULSORY PROVISION FOR THE INDIGENT.*

1. THE last topic which we propose to discuss, in this catalogue of expedients for the removal of want from the human family, and the secure establishment of a general prosperity and abundance in its place—is a legal and compulsory provision for the poor. It stands distinguished from all the former expedients, in one important particular. Its object is, not the creation, but the division, of wealth. Its proposal, unless in so far as it seeks

* In excuse for the very rapid survey of pauperism here, we beg to state, that elsewhere the subject has been treated by us at much greater length and detail. The following are the titles of the various publications—" The Christian and Civic Economy of Large Towns "—" Speech before the General Assembly of the Church of Scotland, explanatory of the measures which have been successfully prosecuted in St. John's Parish, Glasgow, for the extinction of its compulsory Pauperism"—" Evidence given, by us, before the Select Committee of the House of Commons in 1830, on the State of the Poor in Ireland "—" Influence of Bible Societies on the Temporal Necessities of the Poor." But, perhaps, the most complete view of our principles and methods in regard to the management of the poor, and with the least expense of time or labour on the part of the reader, may be had in a pamphlet entitled, " Statement in regard to the Pauperism of Glasgow, from the Experience of Eight Years."

employment for the poor, is, not to create additional produce, but to share the existent produce of the land more equally.   It opens up no new resources; neither does it stimulate nor impart greater fertility to the old ones.   It proceeds, not in the way of production, but in the way of partition; and, without enlarging the country's stock, would part it differently from before.   We have tried to demonstrate the futility of all the other schemes, when taken by themselves, for the economic amelioration of the species—on the ground that, without the moral check by which to restrain the numbers of mankind, the addition made to human subsistence would speedily be overtaken, or swallowed up, in the tide of an advancing population.   But, in the scheme now under review, we behold no addition made to the stock of subsistence; and it may well discharge us from the obligation of an instant faith in its efficacy, when we, moreover, think that, of all the expedients, it is the most fitted to destroy the moral check, and so to call forth an augmented population, without the benefit of any augmented produce, by which to meet the new demands itself had created.

2. It is evident, that every levy upon property for the support of the indigent, trenches on the means of its owners for the employment and maintenance of the disposable population.   There is no new provision created under such an economy.   A part of the old provision is simply transferred, or withdrawn, from the sustenance of one class to the

sustenance of another class. Every additional impost that is laid upon me in the shape of poor's
rate, lessens my ability to support those industrious
who are remunerated for their services by my expenditure. Supplies are provided for the destitute
in one quarter of society, at the expense, not of my
enjoyments alone, but of privations to those who
minister these enjoyments in another quarter of
society. And, accordingly, it has been well observed, that, for all the visible relief effected by a
poor's tax, there is as much of real though unseen
poverty created among those, who have not yet
entered within the territory of pauperism, but
stand, a countless and untold multitude, around
the very margin of it. The distress is not swept
off from the face of the community. It is only
shifted to another, and generally a far more de-
serving class of sufferers—to a mass of respectable
families on the verge of destitution; struggling
against the hard necessity of descending amongst
the throng of sturdy applicants for a legalized
charity; and all the more hopeless of relief, that
the springs of gratuitous benevolence have been
well nigh dried up, by the heavy impositions which
the artificial or compulsory system has laid on the
upper classes of society. It is thus, that, by a sort
of festering and spreading operation, the sphere of
destitution is constantly widening in every parish,
where the benevolence of love has been superseded
by the benevolence of law. Generally speaking,
every year, or at least every decade of years, the

pauperism, like a moral leprosy, makes a wider sweep among the families than before.

3. We are not to wonder at such an effect, when we advert to the mighty stimulus which this system of public charity gives to population. It releases the people from all care or concern about the consequences of their precipitate matrimony. This step is not delayed, as in other countries, till the necessary outfit and preparation for a family establishment shall have been completed. All restraint is taken off, in the way of early marriages; and the people, abandoned to improvidence, multiply without limit, and beyond the capacity of the parish to find them in profitable employment. And the principle, on which a small excess in the number of labourers works a great reduction in the price of labour, then comes into sure operation. It is the same principle with that on which the price of necessaries fluctuates more largely, with minuter variations in their supply, than the price of luxuries. A man can more easily give up a fraction of his wonted allowance in the latter, than in the former. He can more easily slacken his demand for the one, upon any short-coming in the supply, and so prevent an inordinate rise of price. But he cannot so well slacken his demand for the other; and so, in virtue of the more intense competition, there will be a disproportional rise in the price of the more important, because essential commodities. The price of bread will rise greatly more than a tenth, perhaps a third, though the crops should be defi-

cient only by a tenth. And thus it is, though in a reverse way, that the price of labour falls greatly beyond any increase which may have taken place in the number of labourers. The demand for employment, when like to be deficient, is just as intense as is the demand for necessaries, when these are like to be deficient. Employment, in fact, is the great vehicle through which the people arrive at the necessaries of life; and when, by the superabundant supply of labour, there is a relative deficiency of employment, its wages will oscillate as largely in consequence, as does the price of the first necessaries of existence. A very slight overplus of workmen, will create a very sensible and general reduction in the price paid for their work; and thus, by the connexion which obtains between a system of pauperism, and an increase, even though it should be small, in the numbers of the people, is pauperism responsible for a very sore depression in the condition and circumstances of the whole body.*

4. There is no such effect to be apprehended from the ministrations of spontaneous and individual benevolence; injudicious, though it occasion-

* And as a small increase in the numbers of the people might operate a large depression in their circumstances, so might a small reduction in their numbers operate a large relief. An improvement in their moral and prudential habits, would very speedily effect an improvement in their economic condition; when, with not much fewer people than before, we should behold this change in the distribution of them—a larger secondary, and a smaller disposable class of labourers.

ally be, in its objects and its doings. There is no such system or certainty in its operations, as would lead to the same general dependence that is now felt in England, on the allowances of a legal charity. Individual charity can withdraw itself at pleasure, and will naturally decline the protection and encouragement of the worthless. But worth-lessness, and that too of the grossest description, can compel, in its own behalf, the dispensations of the legal charity, and cast upon it the burden of all its own extravagance and folly. We have no such consequence to fear, from the fortuitous and free gratuities of the philanthropist, as from the regu-lated ministrations of the parish vestry, which are conducted irrespective of character, and require no other qualification than the actual indigence of the applicant. In the concerns of private benevolence, there is a delicacy felt on the one side, and a dis-crimination exercised upon the other; which, con-fined withal to incidental cases, form effectual guar-antees against any general relaxation of moral or providential habits, as the fruit of its liberalities. But the benevolence of law holds out a wholesale bounty and temptation to improvidence. It has changed the timid supplications of want, into so many stout and resolute demands for justice. The cry of the distressed few for pity, has been strangely transformed by it, into the cry of a whole popula-tion for the redress and rectification of their griev-ances. All the tenderness of charity on the one hand, and all its delicacy on the other, have been put to flight, by this metamorphosis of a matter of love, into a matter of angry litigation ; and we now behold the formidable array of a multitude, fired with a sense of oppression against the upper classes of society, when, in fact, it is the oppression of their own numbers that has sunk them into a state of abject prostration, from which, while the present system continues, no wisdom and no benevolence of man can save them.

5. This system of legal charity is replete with all sorts of mischief. In the first place, by a direct tendency to multiply its objects, there is more of unprovided want in every region it lights upon, than there would have been without its ministra-tions. Beyond the margin of its operations, there is a far greater mass of unreached and unrelieved misery, than we should have had *in toto*, had no such system been instituted. In other words, public charity, so far from narrowing the territory of human wretchedness, has widened and extended it ; and thus left a greater field than it·at first en-tered on, for the exercise of that private charity, which it has at the same time weakened, both in its means and in its motives. It has deadened, as is patent to all observation, the charity of relatives, the charity of immediate neighbours, the charity of the affluent. It has therefore wrought a double mischief, creating a greater amount of indigence than before ; and congealing the sources, whence, in a natural and undisturbed state of things, this indigence would have looked for its relief, and not

been disappointed. By every step it moves in advance, instead of approaching its primary and professed object, which was to curtail the sufferings of the poor, and if possible overtake them, it recedes to a greater and more hopeless distance away from it. In its economic design, which was to lessen or altogether remove the wants of the population, it has been foiled, and that most signally—so much, that, in very proportion to the largeness of its dispensations, do we behold a more straitened and distressed, and withal, a greatly more dissatisfied peasantry.

6. But if it have deviated from the true economic interest, it has more widely deviated from a still higher object of patriotism, even the moral interest of society. So intimately blended, indeed, are these two elements, that in every step of that degenerating process, which a compulsory provision for the poor never fails to originate, the economic and the moral deterioration go hand in hand. For how is it that indigence has been so multiplied under this system? Not alone by the imprudence which it has generated; as may be seen in the reckless marriages, and in the relaxed industry and economy of the people. But also in the vice which it has generated; the low and loathsome dissipation; the profligacy of both sexes; with all the mischief which proceeds from idleness, and through which the pauperism of England has become so deeply responsible for its immoralities and its crimes. And how is it, again, that charity has

waxed cold? Because law has endeavoured, however unsuccessfully, to cut off the occasions and
the calls which nature had provided for its exercise.   Hence the abandonment of children by
their parents, and the desertion of parents by their
children back again.   Hence the frequent spectacle, in every parish, of run-away husbands, and of
nearest relatives alienated in affection, because re-
leased from the obligations of duty to each other.
And not only have the ties of relationship been
broken, but the ties and sympathies of neighbourhood.   The charity of law has superseded the
charities both of home and neighbourhood.   By ab-
solving the people from all mutual care, it has well
nigh stifled within them all the feelings of mutual
kindness.   " Am I my brother's keeper?" is the
question practically put by those whom nature de-
signed to be the guardians and the helps of each
other ; it being a question prompted by the lying
promises of the system under which they live, and
which has undertaken, though it never can fulfil,
the guardianship of them all.   And it has not
only weakened the cement which binds together
the contiguous parts of the social edifice, but it
has effected a menacing disruption or rent between
the higher and the lower divisions of it.   There
is in England a gulf of separation between the
rich and the poor, exemplified, we believe, in no
other land ; where the parties regard each other as
natural enemies—the one challenging what they
feel to be their rightful allowances ; the other re-

sisting what they fear to be interminable, and at
length ruinous demands. The barriers of property have given way before the tide of an unre-
strained population ; and there is now a close and
fierce conflict, between a sense of rightful possession on the one side, and the unappeased urgencies and wants of an ever-increasing multitude
upon the other. The poor look to the rich as
hard-hearted oppressors, detaining with stern gripe
what nature and humanity pronounce to be theirs ;
the rich look to the poor as so many poachers
on their domain. Compassion on the one side,
and gratitude on the other, are alike unknown.
The golden line of life, reaching from the apex of
society to its basement, is dissevered ; nor can we
imagine, in consequence, a state of greater precariousness than that into which this system of
public charity has brought us ; or one that bodes
more fearfully for the good order, or rather the
stability of the commonwealth. It has, in fact,
vitiated and distempered the whole breath of
society in England. There now sits an unnatural
scowl on the aspect of the population, a resolved
sturdiness in their attitude and gait ; and, whether
we look to the profane recklessness of their habits,
or to the deep and settled hatred that rankles in their
hearts, we cannot but read, in these moral characteristics of this land, the omens of some great and
impending overthrow.

7. And it adds to our hopelessness, that the
growing disposition on the part of rulers, is not to

retrace this sore evil, but rather to rivet and extend it. In the face of all the English experience, Ireland, we fear, is about to welcome the footsteps of this most baleful pestilence ; the worst visitor, in the midst of all her grievances and wrongs, that ever lighted on her shores. It is in those counties of England where public charity has done its uttermost, that distress lifts the most appalling outcry; and yet is this the very specific, which, with their eyes open, our statesmen are on the eve of administering, as their infallible remedy for the distress of Ireland. What has led to outrages of greatest atrocity in the one land, is to be transferred, and that with the design of quelling and allaying for ever, all outrage and discontent in the other land. The mightiest known stimulant of population, is now being brought to bear on the most over-peopled country in Europe. And to organize a nation yet in the wildness of its infancy, that system is to be introduced, which is evidently breaking up the frame-work of a society, where law, and civilization, and order, have had their abode for centuries. It is often by impulse, and not by reason, that public sentiment is drifted along; causing a tide in the affairs of men, which no wisdom, no experience can stem. There seems, at times, a blind and headlong necessity even in the moral world, which can no more be withstood than the currents of the ocean ; transitions in the history of nations, during which, man, as if struck by impotency, stands in passive and trembling abeyance, till the hurricane have blown over him; till the sweeping anarchy, resistless as the onset of the elements, have spent its violence, and the high ordinations of Providence are fulfilled.

8. In the treatment of this controversy, romance and reality have been confounded together; and the lessons of sober experience have been as little regarded, as if they were the reveries of unsubstantial imagination.   What truth, for example, of firmer and homelier cast, or more remote from the visions of fairy land, than the strength of the parental and relative affections?   Or what admits of being more familiarly verified, than the promptitude of that mutual sympathy and aid, which obtain in every neighbourhood, when some signal visitation of distress has come upon any of the families?   It is by stifling the exercise of these principles, and laying arrest on these undoubted and universal processes, that a public and legalized provision for the poor, has wrought one of its deadliest inflictions on the cause of humanity, by closing far kindlier and more effectual sources of relief than itself has opened.   Yet this plain statement, capable though it most decisively be, both of arithmetical and observational proof, is ridiculed and resisted, just as if it were a fond or high-coloured illusion, drawn from some fictitious region of Arcadia.   Shall we refrain, it is asked, from a tax on the Irish absentees, that scope and opportunity might be left for some rare or romantic elevation of virtue among the Irish peasantry?   Now, the virtue for which we

contend, in our opposition to a poor's law, is neither rare nor romantic. We object not to any amount of taxation on the landed absentees of Ireland, if the produce of it shall be usefully, or even innocently applied. But, if applied in a legal and public way to the relief of indigence, we affirm, on the known laws of human nature, and on the grounds of a manifold experience, that—multiplying, with the one hand, the objects of destitution, and intercepting, with the other, those numerous, though unseen supplies, which circulate, at the bidding of nature, among the households, and throughout all the vicinities of the land—it will act, by a sort of two-edged malignity, in aggravating the individual distress, and, along with it, the moral and political distempers of Ireland.

9. Moreover, the influence of a poor's law on the state of general comfort in a land, is complicated with many other influences; and this has thickened still more the difficulties of the question. The common people of England stand palpably higher in the scale of enjoyment than those of Ireland; and this is enough for an impatient or immediate decision, with minds which have only room or comprehension for but one idea. It is forgotten, that, irrespective either of the want or presence of a poor's law, the people of England and Ireland admit as little of being compared together, and differ as widely in their circumstances, as the peasantry of Norway do from the straggling hordes of Kamschatka. The law, the commerce, the in-

dustry, the Protestantism, the advanced civilization of England, have elevated the habits and state
of the general community there; and would have
done so still higher, had it not been for the depressing and counteracting influence of their poor's
laws. The misgovernment, the yet untutored
rudeness, the want of humanizing intercourse between the higher and lower classes, the dark and
degrading Popery, which obtain in Ireland—have
kept down the tastes and comforts of the general
community there; and these would have sunk still
lower, had a poor's law been superadded to the
other causes of a people's degradation. The way
to escape from the bewildering influence of this
complexity, is to look to England singly, and compare the different parts of it; or to Ireland singly,
and compare the different parts of it. In the one
country, a poor's rate is universal; and where do
we find the most distressed and dissatisfied peasantry? Just in the southern counties, where the
levies and the expenditure of public charity are the
largest—proving, that the genuine effect of the
system is to depress, and not to elevate. In the
other country, the want of a poor's rate is universal; and where, again, do we find the least distress
and the lightest burden of mendicity? Just in
those northern counties, where a Protestant education, and Protestant habits, are to be found—
proving, on the other hand, the omnipotence of
moral causes, and that, after all, the true sources
of a nation's well-being lie deeply seated in the
mind and character of the population.

10. Could one divest himself of all philanthropy and patriotism, and place every human feeling in abeyance, save a mere philosophical interest in the question—he might hail the experiment of a poor's law in Ireland. But there were a cruelty in this; like that of the cold-blooded physiologist, who, in his experiments on animated nature, could inflict every species of torture for the verification of a doctrine. We believe the attempt, whenever it is made, will be a most instructive one—but at the fearful expense of greatly augmented distress, and, at length, of entire and uncontrollable anarchy to the land. With the consequent insecurity and fall of property, one of the greatest holds of social order will be broken; and in the scramble which must ensue, we can perceive no other result, than the confusion, and the conflicts, and withal, the growing penury and straitness, which attach to a state of unlimited agrarianism. There will be a rapid equalization of fortunes—terminating, if not anticipated by some great political explosion, in the equality of a common and overwhelming wretchedness. Had England, in this goodly endeavour to assimilate Ireland to herself, but laboured to impart of her real and substantial blessings, and given to her sister island the light, and the liberty, and the industrious habits, of her own population—this had been some atonement for the misrule of centuries. But, instead of this, she presents her with the virus of that moral gangrene wherewith herself is infected; she deposits the seeds of that disease under

which she is now ebbing onward to dissolution ; and, in the dotage of her own expiring weakness, holds out, to the willing acceptance of a deceived people, that which, under the semblance of a benefit and a boon, is laden with the misery of future generations.*

11. But to return from this digression. So long as a compulsory provision for the poor is the established system of any country, the great, the only specific for its economic well-being is kept completely at abeyance. It is the sure and rapid advance of population which gives such powerless-

---

* Some have assimilated an endowment for the relief of indigence, to an endowment for the support of literary or Christian instruction. The two cases, so far from being at all like in principle, stand in direct and diametric opposition to each other. We desiderate the latter endowment, because of the languor of the intellectual or spiritual appetency; insomuch that men, left to themselves, seldom, or never, originate a movement towards learning. We deprecate the former endowment, because, in the strength of the physical appetency, we have the surest guarantee that men will do their uttermost for food; and a public charity, having this for its object, by lessening the industry and forethought that would have been otherwise put forth in the cause, both adds to the wants, and detracts from the real worth and virtue of the species. And, besides, there is no such strength of compassion for the sufferings of the moral or spiritual, that there is for those of physical destitution. An endowment for education may be necessary to supplement the one, while an endowment for charity may do the greatest moral and economic mischief, by superseding the other. Relatives and neighbours could bear to see a man ignorant, or even vicious. They could not bear to see him starve.

ness, or leaves such a short-lived efficacy to every other expedient. No augmentation of resources from without, can keep head against the stimulated over-growth of this all-devouring energy from within. There may be perpetual accessions to the bulk, but none whatever to the comfort of society. A more unfortunate device could not have been imagined, by which to neutralize the good of all possible enlargements, from whatever quarter they may be afforded to us. No enriching process, whether by agriculture, or by home and foreign trade, or by the removal of existing burdens, will countervail that process, by which, under the system of a bounty for the multiplication of the species, one and all of them must be so speedily overtaken. The pressure may, for a time, be slackened; or a few short respites of felt ease and enlargement may mark our successive advancements, towards the state of a greater community than before. But the tide of population, and more especially when urged forward by pauperism, that arch-destroyer of all prudence and principle among the families, will keep us permanently sure of at least one unchanged and unchangeable element—and that is, as wretched a community as before. If, in virtue of a moral restraint, consequent on the growing taste and education of our people, their numbers could be kept sufficiently within the limit of their means; this, of itself, would be the unfailing guarantee of a general and wide-spread abundance, whether with, or without, any external augmentation. But, with the utter recklessness engendered by a poor's law, all such hopes must be given to the wind. And, whatever reforms may take place, whether in the political or economical systems of our land, let all taxes, and tithes, and monopolies, and inequalities of right or privilege, be done away, with the continuance of this single law, the power and promise of all these expedients will utterly come to nought ; and we shall have no other prospect before us, than one of helpless and ever-increasing deterioration.

12. But the full effects of such a system will be anticipated by its own violent overthrow. From its very nature it cannot last ; containing, as it does, within itself, the sure seeds of dissolution. The radical error of a poor's law consists, in its assigning the same treatment to an indeterminate, which is proper only to a determinate virtue. The virtue of humanity ought never to have been legalized, but left to the spontaneous workings of man's own willing and compassionate nature. Justice, with its precise boundary and well-defined rights, is the fit subject for the enactments of the statute-book ; but nothing can be more hurtful and heterogeneous, than thus to bring the terms, or the ministrations of benevolence, under the bidding of authority. This fatal mistake involves in it a great deal more than a mere scholastic incongruity ; or, but the commission of violence on an abstract principle. So nicely adapted is the me-

chanism of human society, to the axioms of the
most deeply, if but soundly philosophical juris-
prudence, that any law which contravenes these,
will soon betray the flaw in its principle, by the
palpable mischief which it works on the face of
the commonwealth.   The claims of justice are
definite and precise, and withal, strictly accordant
to the natural sense of morality ; so that the law
which enforces these, while it compels the observance of certain intelligible limits and lines of de-
marcation, is acquiesced in by the general mind of
society.   But the law which would enforce charity
can fix no limits, either to the ever-increasing wants
of a poverty which itself hath created, or to the
insatiable desires and demands of a population,
whom itself hath corrupted and led astray.   Under
this system, all is lax, and precarious, and indefinite.
The holders of property can see no end to the exactions of pauperism.   And the nurslings of pauperism, with their constantly-increasing number
and necessities, will overpass every limit in their
aggressions upon property.   The growing alarm
on the one side, the growing distress upon the
other, form the sure elements of an interminable
warfare, which, if not prevented by timely reformation, must at length effervesce into an anarchy,
that will alike sweep off all the good and evil of present institutions, and make room on the desolated
void for the foundations of a new-modelled commonwealth.

13. We should most gladly abjure this whole

argument, could we think that the charity of law at all lessened the amount of human suffering, or that distress was not far more effectually, as well as kindly met by the charity of spontaneous nature. Could the ministrations of relief have been provided for by law and justice, then compassion may have been dispensed with as a superfluous part of the human constitution; whereas the very insertion of such a feeling or tendency within us, is proof in itself, of a something separate and additional for it to do; of a distinct province in human affairs, within which this fine sensibility of the heart met with its appropriate objects, and, by its right acquittal of them, fulfilled the design which nature had in so endowing us. But by this unfortunate transmutation, this metamorphosis of a thing of love into a thing of law, this invasion by justice beyond its own proper domain on the field of humanity—nature has been traversed in her arrangements, and the office of one human faculty has been awkwardly and mischievously transferred to another. And the effect is just what might be always anticipated, when the laws and adaptations of divine wisdom are contravened by the short-sighted policy of man. Justice should have been left to do the things of justice; and humanity to do the things of humanity. But by the aggression of the one upon the other, this beautiful and beneficent order has been thwarted, and the consequence has been a very sore aggravation to the ills of society. By the interference of law with the business of charity, a two-fold mischief has been wrought. Human distress has been multiplied, and human compassion, its natural protector, has been weakened and paralyzed. And by the truly unfortunate meeting of these two consequences, there has been left, as the compound and aggravated result of both, a ten-fold burden of *unrelieved* suffering upon the community. We say not, that the charity of compassion would have overtaken all the distress. But we say, that the charity of compulsion has fallen many times short of it, beside the bitterness and the poison which it infuses into the *morale* of society; lighting up a thousand jealousies and heart-burnings between the poor and the rich; and converting an interchange of good-will on the one side, and gratitude on the other, into a conflict of fierce and rancorous antipathies between these two great parties in the commonwealth.

14. It forms no exception to our principle, but is rather its legitimate consequence, that, while we deprecate a legal and compulsory provision for indigence, there is a certain species of public charity that we advocate to the uttermost. There are certain distresses incidental to humanity, the inflictions of necessity and nature, which cannot be too openly or too liberally provided for. There is all the difference that can be imagined, in point both of principle and effect, between an institution for the relief of want, and an institution for the relief of disease. The one multiplies its objects.

Not so the other. The one enlists the human will on its side. The other will ever remain the object of painful reluctance and revolt to all the feelings of our sentient nature. Open a door of admission for the indigent, and we shall behold a crowd of applicants increasing every year, because lured thitherward by the inviting path of indolence or dissipation. Open a door for the admission of the diseased, and we shall only have a definite number of applicants. Men will become voluntarily poor, but they will not become voluntarily blind or deaf, or maimed or lunatic. It is thus, that while an asylum for want creates more objects than it can satisfy; an asylum for disease creates none, but may meet all and satisfy all. Public charity has been profuse where it ought not, and it has also been niggardly where it ought not. It is a disgrace to our philanthropic age, if infirmaries, or dispensaries, or asylums, whether for the cure of mental and bodily disease, or for the keeping of that which is incurable, are left to languish from want of support, or compelled to stop short, ere the necessity for which they were instituted has been fully and finally overtaken.

CHAPTER XV.

ON THE CHRISTIAN EDUCATION OF THE PEOPLE.

1. WE are now drawing towards that great conclusion, for the sake of.which we have described
the very lengthened course of our by-gone argument. We have laboured to demonstrate the futility of every expedient, which a mere political
economy can suggest for the permanent well-being
of a community. At best, they but tend to enlarge the absolute wealth of a country, without enlarging the relative comfort of the people who live
in it. They may conduct to a larger, but not, on
that account, to a happier society. They may tell
on the condition of families, during those brief and
evanescent seasons, when the population is somewhat in rear of the wealth; but, on the moment
that this distance is overtaken, there will be the
same straitness and discomfort as before. In new
countries, there might be a career of sensible advancement for centuries to come. But in old
countries, if we count only on external resources,
or the increase of means for the support of a population, leaving their numbers to proceed as they
may, there is positively nothing which can save us
from the habitual state of felt insufficiency and
narrowness. There may be gleams of prosperity

during the fluctuations, or the few short and successive stretches of enlargement which are yet in
reserve for us.   But all round, and in every possible direction, there is a besetting limit, which the
mighty tide of an advancing population tends to
overpass, and which, being impassable, throws the
tide back again upon general society; charged, as
it were, with a distress and a disorder that are ex-
tensively felt throughout the old countries of the
civilized world.   The only question remains then,
Is there no way by which the tide can be arrested,
before it comes into contact and collision with the
barrier that repels it?   Or, can the redundancy
be prevented by a moral and pacific influence, rather than checked by the evils of extreme poverty,
or that destroying turbulence which so often results from the distress and destitution of an over-
peopled land?

2. The high road, then, to a stable sufficiency and
comfort among the people, is through the medium
of their character; and this effectuated by other
lessons altogether than those of political economy.
We object not to the utmost possible illumination
of the popular mind; nor do we share in the antipathies of those who would refuse science to the
multitude.   It is not, however, by the instructions
of the economic, but by those of a higher school,
that the best economic condition of society will at
length be realized.   It is possible for men to bear
an essential part in the workings of a mechanism,
of whose principles and whose theory they are

altogether unconscious—just as the planetary masses are unconscious of the magnificent regularity to which their own movements have given rise. The moving force, that is to advance the general multitude to a better and higher condition than they now occupy, will not be brought to bear upon them by the demonstrations, however just, of any theory; and, in fact, the right impulse, and the right habit, have often been exemplified, and by large classes of peasantry, before the theory of population was ever heard of. It is so in Norway; and, most assuredly, without any innoculation of principle from the school of Malthus. It was so in Scotland, long before the promulgation of his doctrines. In both countries, they realized, in practice, what, in system and philosophy, they did not understand. A moral and intelligent peasantry, imbued with a taste for the respectabilities of life, mixing prudence and foresight with every great practical step in the history of their doings, holding it discreditable to enter upon marriage without the likelihood of provision for a family—such a peasantry have more than once been exhibited in the annals of the world, and may be made to re-appear. If, by any means, the elements of such a character can again be put together, and made general in society, we should behold the exemplification of the Malthusian doctrine, with or without the comprehension of its principles. It is not, most assuredly, the study of these principles that will germinate the character; and it is from another quarter altogether, than the demonstrations of political economy, that we are to obtain the fulfilment of those blessings to society, which the science can only point out, without being able to realize.

3. On no other subject does Christianity more evince its immense importance to the well-being of society. In the first place, it is quite palpable that they are its earnest and devoted teachers, who have the greatest power in drawing the multitude to their lessons, and establishing for themselves that most secure and deeply-seated of all popularity, which is grounded on the sacredness of their office, and on the subserviency of its faithful ministrations to the comfort, and the virtue, and the dearest interests of families. The mere disciples of a general literature or politics, little reflect on the prodigious force of that moral ascendancy which is possessed by a parish clergyman, who superadds, to the attraction of his pulpit, the charm and the efficacy of his household services; and who, by the countless attentions of an unwearied Christian benevolence, has ingratiated both his person and his cause with the hearts of those among whom he expatiates. His direct aim is neither to purchase a reputation for himself, nor even to advance the temporal comfort of his people. It is to prepare them for immortality; yet, in the single-hearted prosecution of this object, he becomes the all-powerful, though, perhaps, the unconscious instrument of those secondary, those subordinate blessings, which form the only ones that a mere worldly

philanthropist cares for. The truth is, that the
lessons of the gospel which he teaches, are all on
the side of reflection, and sobriety, and that lofti-
ness of character which consists in the predominance of the moral over the animal nature of man.
A disciple of the New Testament, whose views are
sublimed by its doctrines and its hopes, has gotten
a superiority over the passions; a certain nobility
of soul; a reach of perspective to distant consequences, whether on this, or the other side of the
.grave; an ascendancy of sentiment over sense;
and, withal, a refinement and elevation of taste,
which, though caught at first from converse with
spiritual and eternal things, still adheres to him,
even when busied with the interests and concerns
of the present life: and these, altogether, form the
best guarantees against that impetuous appetency,
which first leads to early marriages, and afterwards
lands in squalid destitution, the teeming families
that spring from them. And, besides, in that book
there are so many pointed admonitions, that each
should provide for himself, and for his own household; such a preference for the single state, when
the married endangers a man's Christianity, or his
performance of its duties; such great examples, as
well as precepts of independence—especially by
Paul, who says, that " if a man will not work,
neither should he eat," and who himself laboured,
with his own hands, for the supply of his own necessities, rather than be burdensome; that, as the
undoubted effect upon the whole, the honest and

frequent perusal of Scripture by a Christian people, does associate, in their minds, both the present and the prospective cares of a family with the solemn duties of religion. This is not a picture, but a reality, often exemplified in the abode of a cottage patriarch—where, along with his Christianity, we may witness a sufficiency, and a cast of elevation, not to be found in the houses of the irreligious and the unholy. The very library of old and favourite authors upon his shelves, is but in keeping with the general fulness of a tenement, usually better stocked and provided than that of any of his fellows. The Christianity of the man has engendered a wisdom, and a consistency, and a self-command, that led him to begin well in his entrance upon a family; and so to build up a respectable sufficiency, which, with a reckless and precipitate commencement, he could never have attained. An individual Christian is generally in better comfort and condition than other men. A whole parish of Christians would be a parish of well-conditioned families.

4. But here it is of importance to remark, that, for the production of a general economic effect, we have not to wait the production of a general Christianity. When expatiating on the connection between these two elements, we have often to encounter a certain shrewd incredulity, as if an expectation of a more elevated state for the majority hung on the fulfilment of a prior expectation, which is in itself Utopian—even that the majority shall be

converted. The imagination is, that, for the purpose of any great or sensible effect in this way, the religious character must be of co-extensive magnitude with the economic improvement; whereas there is no truth, of which the most faithful and experienced of our clergymen have a firmer, though it be a melancholy assurance, than the exceeding rarity of conversion—there being many streets in our cities, many parishes in our land, where, in the high sense and significancy of the term, the number of real Christians might not reach to one in fifty. And the question therefore is, How can we anticipate either a general economic, or a general moral effect, through the medium of a Christianity, which, in respect of its saving and spiritual influence, makes such little way among the families? But here it is not adverted to—and we admit it is indispensable to the force of our argument—that the secondary influence of Christianity goes a great way farther than its primary or direct influence. For every individual whom it converts, it may, by its reflex operation, civilize a hundred. We have the palpable exemplification of this in Sabbath-schools, where, in a few weeks from their commencement, we may perceive a decency, and a docility, and an improved habit of cleanliness and order, long before there is ground for the assurance, that even so much as one of the pupils has yet been Christianized. And what is true of children in a school, is alike true of grown-up people in a parish—where the regularities of Sabbath ob-

servation, and the humanizing influence of ministe-
rial attentions, and the general recognition of what
is right, and reputable, and seemly, have all been
in force, perhaps a century ago, and been handed
down, with increasing effect, from generation to
generation.   It is of the utmost argumentative
value upon this subject, that one·man of decided
piety, in a little vicinage, will impress, if not his
own piety, at least the respectability of his habits
and appearance, on the greater number of its families.   They can admire, and even imitate, the
graces of his character; they can aspire after, and
even realize, the decencies of his condition; without so much as comprehending, or far less sharing,
the unseen principle which has germinated them
all.   It is thus that Christianity has elevated the
general standard of morals; and so spread a beneficent influence, far and wide, among the many,
beyond the limit of its own proper and peculiar
influence upon the few.   It is this which gives it
the property of a purifying and preserving salt in
every community of human beings; and that, not
merely in respect of those virtues which enter into
the moral character, but also in respect of those
virtues which are essential to the economic well-
being of a people.   Ten righteous men among the
thousands of Sodom would have saved that city
from destruction; and a like proportion would, in
our modern day, save the thousands of general
society from that utter debasement of profligacy
and wretchedness, into which, without the presence

of Christianity in the midst of them, they will in-
evitably fall.*

* We are aware of no country which presents a more interesting field for observation than Holland—because none, perhaps, so close upon the extreme limit of its natural resources;
and, therefore, none so dependent on the moral habits of its
population for their economic well-being.   We have great value for a recent communication from that part of the world,
which appeared in the Sunday-School Teacher's Magazine;
and from which we present a few extracts:—

" I have spent five months, since last September, in Holland; living, for the most part, in an inland town, whence I
could extend my walks into the rural and fishing villages
around me; seeing much of the outward manifestations of
character among the people.   But in Holland, such is the
public provision for the instruction of the lower orders, that
every child is within reach of a good day-school, of which few
do not actually enjoy the advantage.   These schools, moreover, though themselves rather of a general, than purely religious nature, are not meant to supersede, but to harmonize
and co-operate with the catechetical instructions of the
churches throughout the provinces.   Thus, religious knowledge is widely diffused; though, in respect to it, much, of
course, depends on the comparative purity of doctrine and
discipline, as well as on the comparative degrees of vital god-
liness, which are found in the different communions and con-
gregations to which the parents may belong.   Not only so,
but although the public day-schools have had far more attention paid to them of late years than at any former period, still
education has, for a long time, been so common and so cheap,
that almost all old persons are found able to read.

" Thus, what your readers and their friends are striving to
effect for their dear *mother-country*, our Dutch neighbours
have already, through the good providence of God, actually
accomplished for what they call their beloved *father-land*.
Surely, then, it must be interesting to the former, to know what,

5. But we must here remark, that, for the purpose of a general economic improvement, to be

if nothing more, are the outward and obvious results of such a
measure of success in their own favourite enterprise—an enterprise so intimately affecting the character and happiness of
the millions that now people Great Britain and Ireland."

" The first feature, in the lower ranks, which strikes a Briton,
on coming amongst the Hollanders, is the almost universal
decency of manners and dress which prevails amongst them;
and that in spite of the extent of poverty which is found in these
once flourishing, but now much-decayed provinces.   Your
readers will ask, why there should be so much poverty?—the
reply to which is easily furnished out of history."—" We must
not therefore impute it to education, that there are many thousands of poor families and individuals in Holland; but ought
rather to investigate what the effects of that peculiarity have
been, on a people among whom this grievous extent of poverty
has been the inevitable result of quite different circumstances.

" I am now referring to the external manners and appearance of the lower ranks in Holland.   It is remarkable, that
persons, travelling there about sixty years ago, represent the
lower classes as very boorish in their manners, and as intem-
perate in the use of ardent spirits.   But I found them invari-
ably respectful, and willing to oblige me; while, as to intem-
perance, if it was to be found at all, it must have been very
much hid from public notice, for I could not perceive either
drunkards or brawlers in any quarter, either in town or country, during my whole residence among them.   That they are
universally sober, I dare not affirm; strong liquors, of various
kinds, were very common, and very cheap; the damp nature
of their climate, and the sea-faring habits of many of the
people, present a kind of apology for drinking; yet, in spite of
all this, I must again affirm, that they are very far superior, at
present, to the British in this respect.

" But to what are we to ascribe this change for the better,
in the course of the last sixty years?   Not certainly," &c.—
" May we not rather cite the following causes?   First, The

brought about by the means of Christian education, a gradual abolition of the compulsory provi-

extension and improvement of daily schools, which began just
about sixty years ago, and which have been continued, under
all the changes of government, up to the present day. Secondly, To the awakening effects of public calamities, and the
humbling influence of foreign domination on the members of
the Presbyterian, and other Protestant churches, to which
about two-thirds of the people are professedly attached. The
Dutch, like the Israelites of old, were the children of many
prayers, and the heirs of many privileges; but they, also, in the
pride of their hearts, forgot God: he, therefore, in mercy,
visited them with the rod of his chastisement. They were
brought low, and were, many of them, led to cry unto the
Lord in their distresses; and the Lord has had pity on them,
and made his own work revive in the midst of them.

" The outward decency, I might rather say, the respectability of the lower ranks, included a very remarkable observance
of the Lord's day; such, indeed, as I did not expect to find on
any part of the continent of Europe," &c.

" I cannot conclude without remarking, that the absence of
the poor's laws seems to be one of the chief blessings of Holland. By having no compulsory assessments, the virtues of
liberality and active benevolence are called out far more abundantly; and, by constant exercise, acquire a far higher degree
of real practical vigour, than they could otherwise do amongst
the rich; whilst the poor are grateful, frugal, and industrious.
In short, all the lovely fruits of mutual Christian love and respect seem thus to be fostered, which might otherwise be injured or destroyed. I was particularly pleased with the mild
and contented looks of many of the aged poor, and with the
care and good housewifery shown in the apparel both of adults
and children belonging to that class. I need not add, that in
their food they are equally simple and contented.

" Such, then, are the remarks I find myself compelled to
make, with respect to perhaps the best educated poor in
Europe," &c.

sion for indigence, which now obtains in England,
and hangs menacingly over Ireland, seems to us
indispensable.   We can anticipate no rise of wages,
no elevation in the state and sufficiency of the
working classes, from any efforts to instruct and
Christianize them, however strenuous, if the pauperism and the education are to go on contemporaneously.   We, in the first place, feel quite assured,
from the moral influences of this public charity,
that it operates as a dead weight on the ministrations of the clergymen, and stands most grievously
in the way of their success.   But, in the second
place, however vigorous and effective his exertions
may be, at the most, and while the present system of
poor's laws continues, we shall have two distinct populations, each marked by opposite extremes of
character.   The clergyman, on the one hand, may
reclaim hundreds to principle and sobriety, who
shall form a wholesome and better class of peasantry.
But the parish vestry, on the other, remains an
attractive nucleus, around which there will gather
and settle, in every little district of the land, a
depraved and improvident class, whom the temptation of this legal charity has called into being,
and who will bid inveterate defiance to all the
moral energy which might be brought to bear upon
them.   The very presence of such a class, even
though but a fraction of the community, will, with
their reckless habits, depress and overbear the
general condition of labourers.   A very few supernumeraries, we have seen, will suffice for this effect.

So that whether the temptation to improvidence operates on all the people, or only on part of them, still that redundancy is generated which tells so adversely on the general rate of wages, and so on the comfort and circumstances of the population at large. Education will make head against mendicity. It will make head against poverty in any other form than that of being fixed and legalized, and invested with the power of challenging, as its right at the bar of justice, that relief which should have been left to the willing sympathies of nature. But shielded and encouraged as it is in the parishes of England, it will stand its ground, against every attempt to dislodge it from those innumerable fastnesses which it now occupies; and in spite of every counteractive, whether by the Christian or literary education of the people, will it remain an incubus on the prosperity and comfort of the lower orders.*

* The following is an extract from my evidence before a Committee of the House of Commons on the subject of Irish Poor's Laws.

"It is a most important question for Ireland, whether you will submit for a time to its mendicity, or exchange that mendicity for a regular and compulsory pauperism. Now, on many accounts, I would prefer the former to the latter alternative; and one of my reasons is, that education will at length quell the one, but not the other. It may be difficult to furnish the Committee with a satisfactory analysis of this matter. I feel assured that so it is, however much I may fail in expounding how it is. One thing is abundantly obvious, that the act of becoming a mendicant is one of unmixed degradation, and the self-respect inspired by education stands directly and diame-

6. And we have further to remark, that as we look for no sensible improvement in the condition of the lower orders in England, while their present system of pauperism remains ; we as little look for any sensible or general improvement in their character, by the means of education, if that is merely to be the education of letters, and not the education of principle. It is not scholarship alone, but scholarship impregnated with religion, that tells on the great mass of society. We have no faith in the

trically opposed to it. It is not so with the act of becoming a pauper; a state sanctioned by law, and in entering upon which, the consciousness of right, and the resolute assertion of it, awaken feelings that serve to temper the humiliations of charity. I think that this admits of historical illustration. The mendicity of Scotland gave way in a few years to its education. The pauperism and education of England have for many years advanced contemporaneously. I do not believe that the most efficient system of education which can be possibly devised, will ever make head against the pauperism of England; at the very most, it would but give rise to two populations, distinguished from each other by opposite extremes of character. I should therefore be exceedingly sorry, if Irish mendicity were exchanged for English pauperism. I think that the floating mendicity of Ireland will fall, under the operation of those moral causes which might be brought to bear upon it; but if, in order to escape from this, you establish a law of pauperism, you will in fact establish so many parochial fixtures, or a nucleus in every parish, around which your worst population will gather, and from which you will find it impossible to dislodge them. I should exceedingly regret, if under the influence of an impatience to be delivered from this evil of mendicity, you should, in getting quit of that which is conquerable by education, precipitate yourselves into that which is unconquerable by education."

efficacy of mechanic institutes, or even of primary and elementary schools, for building up a virtuous and well-conditioned peasantry, so long as they stand dissevered from the lessons of Christian piety. There is a charm ascribed to the scholastic system of Scotland ; and the sanguine imagination is, that by importing its machinery into England and Ireland, it will work the same marvellous transformation there, on the character of their people, that was experienced amongst ourselves.   But it is forgotten, that a warm and earnest Christianity, was the animating spirit of all our peculiar institutions, for generations after they were framed ; and that, wanting this, they can no more perform the function of moralizing the people, than skeletons can perform the functions, or put forth the faculties of living men.   The scholastic is incorporated with the ecclesiastical system of Scotland ; and that, not for the purposes of intolerance and exclusion, but for the purpose of sanctifying education, and plying the boyhood of our land with the lessons of the Bible.   The scholarship of mere letters, might, to a certain extent, have diffused intelligence amongst the people ; but, it is mainly to the presence and power of the religious ingredient, that the moral greatness of our peasantry is owing.

7. A common-place politician is mainly ignorant of the connection which obtains, between the religion of a people, and the various civil and economical blessings which follow in its train.   This single lesson, if but prized and proceeded on as it

ought, were to him the greatest enlargement of political wisdom; and numerous are the practical corollaries which flow from it. More especially, would it lead him to uphold an ecclesiastical establishment; but on very different grounds from those on which, in the spirit either of high state toryism, or of high church intolerance, it is so often contended for. There is with a class of thinkers, whom we have now in our eye, the vague imagination of a certain security derived from the connection between church and state; insomuch, that, if this connection were dissolved, they would apprehend the immediate downfal of all our social institutions. And we have no doubt, that, if any of the church establishments in our empire is to be exterminated, it will be in the spirit of a general undirected frenzy, that will not be satiated on any terms short of a wasteful and wide-spread overthrow. They will share in a common fate, because the objects of a common hostility. But this still leaves unexplained, the precise connection, in the way of cause and consequence, between the existence of a religious establishment, and the stability of the general order of things. It is not because, through the lordly dispensation of its patronage, the higher orders are conciliated; or because, through the hereditary veneration of which it is the object, the lower orders are conciliated. These will be found but frail securities, on a day of wild and lawless innovation; and, without the revival of a diffused Christianity in our land, that day will speedily overtake us. It is thus that a religious establishment is of no value, but as an instrument of Christian good; and it is this, and this alone, which should recommend it, either to the politician or the patriot. It is simply, as the best machine for the extensive Christianization of the families of a land, that it is at all worthy of being upholden; and, it is obvious, that, to this effect, a reckless, unprincipled, and unholy patronage, makes it altogether useless, perhaps worse than use-less. It is our conscientious belief, that an establish-ment is an indispensable safeguard against a desola-ting flood of irreligion, but only in as far as that esta-blishment is virtuously patronized. In other words, without the demolition of our existing machinery, but through its means, and provided that right and efficient men be appointed to work it, we hold that the country may still be saved. And, hu-manly speaking, its Christian instructors will be its only saviours. These reformers of our national morality will be the only reformers that will do us good. This is the great specific for the people's well-being; and, however derided by the liberalism of our age, or undervalued in the estimation of a merely secular politics; still, it is with the Chris-tianity of our towns and parishes that the country is to stand or fall.

8. Our ecclesiastics are too little versant, and have therefore too little respect for the importance of political economy. And our economists stand at fully as wide a distance from things ecclesias-

tical. Both seem alike unconscious of the strong
intermediate link that is between them, seeing that
the chief objects of the one can only be accomplished through the successful exertions of the
other. It was for the economists to have discovered the connection between a virtuous peasantry,
and, through the consequent effect on population
and wages, the greater sufficiency of their means,
and their higher status in the commonwealth. But,
while it was for them to perceive and point out
this connection; it is for the practical educationists alone, and, pre-eminently for the Christian
educationists, to make it good. The one may demonstrate what the essential condition is, on which
the economic well-being of the common people
turns; but it is for the others, and for them only,
to realize the condition. It is for them principally, or rather for them exclusively, to supply that
element, wanting which, there is an utter impotency and failure, in all the doings and all the
devisings of our politicians, either to bring about
or to uphold a prosperous society. No enlargement in the means of subsistence can be of any
possible avail, if so rapidly followed up as heretofore, and still more if exceeded by the irrepressible
advances of the population. At this rate, a larger
community would be but a larger mass of wretchedness, a wider field of heartless and sickening contemplation to every lover of the species. What
he longs to rest and regale his eye upon, is the
joyous spectacle, not of overcrowded, but, through

the medium of cheerful because well-paid industry, of comfortable families, substantially fed, respectably attired, and as respectably lodged in their snug and decent habitations.   There is room, and there are resources in the country, not for an indefinite, but for a certain, and that a very large, yea, for a constantly though not a quickly increasing number of such families.   Beyond this number, we have no taste for mere multitude, for a swarm of human creatures, for a reckless and ragamuffin crew, overborne by that most grievous of all oppressions, the oppression of their own redundancy. If such be the general *morale* of the working classes, it is vain to look either for peace or plenty within our borders.   The object will bid defiance to all agriculture and all commerce.   At most, these can but stretch out the wealth of a country, but, without any sensible enlargement, if there be a stretching out of the population proportionably thereto. Each successive expansion will, in this case, be but a temporary shift, a brief postponement of the evil day, the support or suspension, for a moment, by some frail tenicle, ere the nation is precipitated into a gulph of wretchedness or anarchy.   It would seem to argue a growing sense of desperation among our public men, that their schemes of patriotism and philanthropy are so thickening of late upon us; while, but a semblance of relief, or, at the best, a short-lived respite will be all the result of them.   It is by the efficacy of moral means, working a moral transformation, and by that alone, that our deliverance will be effected ; and little do the mere advocates of retrenchment, and coloniza- tion, and public works, and poor-laws, and other merely political expedients for the amelioration of the people—little do they know, how utterly power- less all these enterprises are, while the Christianity of the land is unprovided for, and its Christian in- stitutions are left inoperative, from the want of zealous and energetic labourers to fill them.

9. And perhaps this indifference or incredulity, on the part of politicians and political economists, lies much deeper than we have yet ventured to say. It may be something still more hopeless than ignorance. We fear, that with many of them, it may be dis- taste and antipathy. There is a certain style of Christianity, a lifeless, inert, and meagre style of it, which is tolerated in general society. But when it comes to be Christianity in earnest, the Chris- tianity that speaketh urgently and importunately to the consciences of men, the uncompromising Christianity that enjoins the holiness of the New Testament in all its spirituality and extent, and asserts the doctrine of the New Testament in all its depth and all its peculiarity ; such a Christianity has been very generally denounced as fanaticism ; and its faithful evangelical expounders have very generally had a stigma affixed to them, and been outcasts from the patronage of the state. And yet this is the only Christianity that will either attract or moralize the population ; and that, not because of its deceitful adaptation to vulgar prejudices,

but, because of its truly divine adaptation to the actual workings of the human mind, and the felt necessities of human nature. While this enmity to the truth as it is in Jesus operates in the hearts of our rulers, it is perhaps a vain expectation, that the civil and political importance of its being sounded forth from the pulpits of our land shall come to be recognised by them. On this subject, they may have been struck with judicial blindness; and ere Christianity shall manifest its power to regenerate our social condition, and overspread the land with prosperous and contented families; perhaps it will first vindicate itself on our ungodly nation, in the utter dissolution of an economy which disowns it, in the vengeance of some fearful overthrow.

10. But however blind our mere earthly politicians may be to the rationale of that process, by which man is regenerated into a new moral character, they clearly apprehend the connection, between the existence of such a character, and the economic well-being either of the country or of the individual who possesses it. Grant but the general ascendancy of principle—and, along with this, you will have a prudence, and a prospective caution, and a superiority to mere animal or constitutional impulses, which must necessarily ensure the habit of later marriages, and so, of smaller families. And then, of itself, by a law of political economy, which can no more be contravened than a law of nature, the state of the common people

will necessarily be raised. There are only two ways in which to augment the price of labour— either by a diminution of the supply, or by an increase of the effective demand for it. But the whole of our preceding argument goes to prove, that this demand for labour cannot be carried beyond a certain limit. There is a necessary limit to agricultural produce, or, in other words, to the maintenance of labour, without which there can be no effective demand for it. Consequent to this, or rather almost identical with this, there is a limit to that employment, for the produce of which, there might be obtained in return the subsistence of the labourers. There is a limit to the extension of that capital, the accumulation of which has been regarded by many as the grand specific for the indefinite employment and maintenance of the labouring classes. There is a limit to the extension of foreign trade, which has been imagined to afford a field for the profitable industry of our workmen, as unbounded as are the resources and magnitude of the globe. There is a limit to any brief or temporary enlargement, which might ensue on the commutation of taxes and tithes. We would not say that there is a limit to the enlargement, for we hold, that no enlargement whatever of the means of subsistence would accrue to the community, from the abolition of the law of primogeniture. So that we should hold it utterly hopeless to obtain a secure and permanent elevation in the state of the working classes, by a mere increase in one term of the proportion; that is, in the effective demand for their labour. The proportion will remain as unfavourable to them as before, should there be a like contemporaneous increase in the other term of it—that is, in the supply of labour, or in the number of labourers. It is because the rate of advancing population may outstrip the rate of enlargement in any one of the resources now specified, or in all of them put together—that in every stage of the progress of society, there might be felt a continued pressure on the means of subsistence. But it is in the latter stages, it is in old countries, where all the barriers recede most slowly, because nearest to the place of their extreme and ultimate attainment, and where, at the same time, the power and tendency of increase on the part of the population are as great as ever—it is there where the pressure is felt most strongly; more in Britain than in America, for example; more in the Netherlands or in France than in Russia. It is this increase in the supply of labour, up to, and often beyond the increase in its demand; it is this rapid occupation, or rather overflow by the one of every enlargement that is made in the other; it is this which sustains, under every possible advancement in the resources of the land, the pressure of the population on the food, and makes the problem of their secure and permanent comfort so very baffling, and as yet, so very hopeless.

11. In the futility of every attempt permanently to relieve the wants, or to raise the comforts of

the people, by means of an increase on one term of the proportion—the effective demand for labour—we are shut up, as our only refuge, to a diminution of the other term—that is, the supply of labour. The only expedient which we have yet considered, and which proceeds by an operation on this second term, is that of emigration. We have tried to demonstrate, how impotent and ineffectual this expedient is; and how utterly unable we are, by all the successive drafts or transformations of families that we shall ever make, to prevent the fulness, even to a distension, of people in the land. We feel assured, that it is not by drawing off the redundancy of the population, after it is formed, that we can uphold a well-conditioned state of society—but by preventing the formation of that redundancy. In the whole round of expedients, we are persuaded that this is the only one which, however obnoxious to sentimentalists, can avail for the solution of a problem otherwise irreducible. It has been the theme, sometimes of ridicule, and sometimes even of a virtuous, though, surely, a misplaced indignation; its distinctive excellence being, that it harmonizes the moral and economic interests of a community, and, indeed, can only take effect in proportion to the worth and wisdom of our people.

12. In the political economy of Dr. Smith, society is prosperous only when in progress. He confines his view only to one term—an increase in the demand for labour, or in the means of its sup-

port. He adverts not to the general prosperity that might ensue by a mere operation on the other term, or by a moderation in the supply of labour. He looks only to the augmentation of physical means; and perceives not, that, when these are stationary, it is still in the power of moral causes to uphold, what he terms, a hearty state of the commonwealth. It was not otherwise to be expected; for his work, great and enlightened though it be, was long prior to the clear and convincing expositions of Malthus on the subject of population. And, accordingly, he makes the condition of the labourer to depend *entirely* on the state of society, in regard to the progress which it is making in wealth—that if this be on the increase, the condition is prosperous; if stationary, dull; if declining, miserable. According to him, the wages of labour must be higher in an advancing, than in an advanced state of society; insomuch that, after the wealth of a country has attained to its maximum, its industrious classes, comprising the large mass of the population, are worse off than when the country was only proceeding to the maximum. Now, this were necessarily and universally true, if wages depended only on one element—that is, the extent of the effective demand for it. When the means for the maintenance of labour increase, and so, for the time being, are somewhat ahead of the population, the competition is in favour of the workmen—who receive larger offers, and a larger maintenance, in this state of relative plenty. But should the population be encouraged by this state of things, the absolute plenty may remain, but the relative plenty is at an end; so that, with a population again pressing on the means of subsistence, the competition is against the workmen—each glad to find employment, though with but an inferior and scanty remuneration. This process has been repeatedly exemplified in the history of states; and it would seem to warrant the apprehension of some stern and mysterious necessity for the hopeless, the irrecoverable degradation of the lower orders—whose prosperity would thus appear to be in the inverse proportion of the country's abundance; insomuch, that to reach the extreme wealth of a land, might be to reach the extreme of depression and despondency for the great bulk of its inhabitants: as in China, the teeming productiveness of whose soil forms no guarantee against the constant want and wretchedness of its common people, or even the periodical starvation of millions.

13. Such instances speak strongly for the utter inefficacy, in the long run, of all those expedients which go but to enlarge the maintenance of labour, and so, the effective demand for it. That there have been many such successive enlargements, and that there are more still in reserve, even for the oldest and most civilized countries of the world, may be most readily admitted. Yet they form no security against either a continuous pressure all along, or a severe ultimate pressure, augmenting, perhaps, and becoming more intense and intoler-

able, with every approach that is made to the extreme limit of the country's resources. There is not yet a state in the world, where the actual capabilities, for the maintenance of a population, do not fall short of the potential capabilities; and, with every new advance of the former upon the latter, there will, of course, be a slackening, as it were, of the pressure—a certain relief from that feeling of straitness, to which, in almost every stage of its progress, the population of a country is exposed. Yet this may be just a putting off of the evil day; and it does afford but a gloomy perspective to the lover of his species, when, as he looks forward on the economic advancement of society, he perceives an ultimate barrier, beyond which there can be no enlargement, and no possibility of mitigation. We confess that our anticipations are greatly more cheering; believing as we do, that, even in regard to earthly prospects, and earthly prosperity, a much brighter destination is in reserve for humanity. We admit, that there is a necessary and impassable limit to the extension of the physical resources of the globe; so that if the enlargement of these were our only confidence, as it seems the confidence of most of our economists, we should give up, in despair, a permanent amelioration in the state and circumstances of our general population. Our confidence, then, is not in the enlargement of those physical resources, from whence we are to count on an increase in the effective demand for labour—it is chiefly, I might almost say exclu-

sively, in the efficacy of a moral cause, from whence
we are to look for moderation in the supply of it.
When this is brought into operation, we shall find,
that the wages of labour do not necessarily sink
with the cessation of a country's advancement in
wealth; that, even through the latest stages of this
advancement, wages may indefinitely rise; and,
after the stationary ultimatum shall have been
reached in all the countries of the earth, still there
will remain a way by which the industrious classes
might be upheld in higher prosperity and comfort,
than at any by-gone period of the world's history
they had ever realized.

14. The two expedients then, of pauperism and
education, stand very broadly and discernibly con-
trasted with each other, in the influence they re-
spectively have on that proportion which we have
now dwelt upon. By the one, the proportion is
turned against, and by the other on the side of, the
population. The one increases, the other lessens,
the ratio of the numbers to the food. There is no
withstanding of this operation; and there is no
withstanding of its consequence. And the adoption of both expedients together were most grievous impolicy. The one would neutralize, or, rather, the one, like the rod of Aaron, would swallow
up, would absorb the other; and be itself of paramount influence, at least on the economic state of
the lower orders. The pauperism which enlisted
all the sordid and sensual appetencies of our nature
on the side of improvidence, would prevail in the

struggle, over all the moral counteractives of any
system of education, however wise, and however
energetic.   The contest between a good and an
evil principle, should no more be sanctioned or set
agoing, by the reigning power of the state, than
it is, by the reigning power of the universe.   In
Scotland, they ordained education for the people;
and in all those parishes, which stand sufficiently
aloof from the contagious neighbourhood of England, do we behold a peasantry sustained in comparative comfort and virtuous independence.   In
England, they ordained a poor-law; and the cry of
distress and discontent is just the louder, in proportion to the lavishness of its ministrations.   In
Ireland, they propose to ordain both education and
a poor-law.   This were the Manicheism of human
government, and a frightful disorder will be the
result of it.   Did the evil barely neutralize the
good, so as to make on the whole an innocent composition of the two ingredients, it might be viewed
with less alarm.   But it will be found not to be an
innocent, but a mischievous composition.   Burke
had the sagacity shrewdly and instantly to perceive
this.   His was the wisdom of intuition, so that,
without formal developement, or the aid of any
logical process, he often, by a single glance, made
the discovery of a great principle; and, by a single
word, memorably and felicitously expressed it.
That education is the cheap defence of nations, is
one of the weightiest of those sentences, or oracular
sayings, which have ever fallen from any of the

seers or sages of our land.   And he characterized, with no less force and justness, the other expedient for the amelioration of his country, when he pronounced, of a legal charity for the relief of indigence, bearing on its forehead the smile and promise of a benevolence which is never realized—that it was downright fraud.

CHAPTER XVI.

CONCLUSION.

1. POLITICAL economy has had great influence on the politics of the world. The two are distinct from each other in themselves—nevertheless, in practice, they are so intimately blended, that if the former were but well understood and consistently acted upon, the results in the latter department would be quite invaluable.

2. One palpable example of this, is the effect of an enlightened political economy, in doing away the commercial jealousy of nations. The objects of that jealousy were, in the general, altogether meaningless; the preservation of a monopoly or of a colonial dependence, or of some exclusive privilege, which, when wrested from the state, that had lavished in their defence an enormous amount both of blood and treasure, was found after all to have been of no real or intrinsic worth to the country that possessed them. It is thus that empires and states have entered fiercely into contest for interests which were altogether illusory. We do not happen to think that the system of free trade will lead to any sensible enlargement of wealth in almost any land; and that they who calculated upon this, did not advert to the existence, or at

least to the proximity of a natural limit, lying a very little way beyond the artificial one, and by which all commerce as well as all agriculture is bounded. Nevertheless, and however disappointed and defeated in their sanguine anticipations many may have been as to the economical effects of the system, its moral effects, in that it cancels a topic of ever-recurring controversy, and by which the peace and brotherhood of nations were kept in perpetual hazard, give an importance and a value to the policy of the free-trade system, which are beyond all computation.

3. Now, what is true of foreign, is alike true of home politics. An enlightened political economy would not only do away much of the jealousy which springs up among different nations; but would do away much of the jealousy and hostile feeling which are still so prevalent between the different orders of a state. For example, if the real incidence of the taxes be upon land, what a world of misconception and of malignant passion would be saved, were taxes laid ostensibly as well as virtually upon the landlords. Or, if not prepared to act on a conclusion still so remote from all the ordinary notions upon the subject, what a practical reconciliation it would effect between the wealthier and the poorer classes, were taxes universally removed from the necessaries of life, and universally laid on income or on unquestionable luxuries. We believe, that though the whole of our public revenue were raised by means of a territorial impost, it would ultimately

add nothing to the burden which now lies on the proprietors of the land; and that they, when fighting against such a commutation, are fighting in defence of an imaginary interest. We believe that the same observation applies to the abolition of the corn laws; and that, if both the commercial and the financial reforms were gradually, but at length completely and conclusively effected, the lords of the soil would find their wealth unimpaired, and their influence prodigiously raised by it. When once divested altogether of the character of monopolists, and, still more, when declaredly and obviously the only tax-payers in the kingdom; we can scarcely imagine the vast moral ascendancy which they would henceforth acquire in all the affairs and deliberations of the commonwealth. Such would be their substantial gain, and we honestly think without the deduction of one farthing from their revenues, though they should both quit the monopoly, and take upon themselves the whole burden of the taxes. And what a death-blow would be thus inflicted on the vocation of demagogues! What a sweetening influence it would have on British society, after the false medium was dissipated, through which the high and the low now look on each other as natural enemies! Such a political economy as this, had it preceded, would also have superseded all those tempestuous politics which are now in agitation. Parliamentary reform, left without any ulterior object, would have been felt as if uncalled for; or at least the rancour, the exasperation, and bitterness, now connected with the prosecution of it, would have been completely done away.

4. The landed aristocracy have partly brought this upon themselves, by their blind resistance to all innovation, and by their tenacious adherence to what they imagine, but falsely imagine, to be their own indispensable interest. Had they paid all taxes, and left all trade unfettered, there would have no political sacrifice been required of them; and they would have remained in the undisturbed possession of their natural, their rightful inheritance, as lords of the commonwealth. But the democracy of England, fired by a sense of injury, have now made head against them; and may, perhaps, wrest from them, by force, that which ought to have been freely and willingly conceded in the spirit of an enlightened policy. We should rejoice in such a compromise between the two parties, as that both a full commutation of the taxes, and the full establishment of commercial liberty, unshackled by impositions or restraints of any sort, were at length effected, but effected gradually. What we fear in the present spirit of reform, is its impetuosity, and that it may not only, without the necessary delay, precipitate right changes, but, without the necessary discrimination, may hurry a new legislature into wrong changes. There lies a noble field of improvement before them, in rightly shifting the burden of taxes; in emancipating trade, and that without reserve or limitation; above all,

in providing, amply and liberally providing, both for the Christian and literary education of the people.   But there is a waywardness of innovation which might carry ruin and overthrow in its train, and of this they will have to beware.   They should meddle not with the national debt, save in an equitable adjustment of the taxes ; else they will pass a sentence of confiscation on one set of proprietors to the enrichment of another set of proprietors, and these are exclusively the proprietors of the land. They should meddle not with the church, save to commute its tithes, and virtuously to control its patronage ; else they will inflict an irreparable blow on the moral and literary wealth of the nation ; and that to the relief and enlargement of no one class, but still of the landed proprietors.   They should meddle not with the law of primogeniture ; else they will institute a process, under which the state must wax feeble, and even our commercial greatness must disappear ; our towns dwindling away, both in prosperity and in magnitude, and a numerous, but finally a wretched agrarian population rising up in their room.   Lastly, they should meddle not, either with the monarchy or the peerage ; for both a vigorous executive, and a certain *vis inertiæ* of hereditary prejudice, are as indispensable to a right politics, as both the helm and ballast of a vessel are indispensable to a right navigation.   In a word, instead of demolishing the framework of any of our existent machinery, we would have them but to guide and to animate its movements. And it is precisely because we stand in dread, lest, through the stages of our future history, the sail should predominate over the ballast, so as to make the vessel of the state veer and vacillate with every wind of speculation, that we feel as if the national security were bound up, in our having more of an agrarian, and less of a mercantile parliament.

5. Still it is all important to remark, that the internal changes which we have ventured to point out, will no more open up an indefinite career of economic enlargement and prosperity, than free trade can. They will afford a certain stretch for a somewhat larger population, but they will do no more; when we shall at length find a natural limit far more hopeless and impracticable than the artificial one, there being no reserve beyond it. In these circumstances—that is, when the means cannot be made larger for the population, it becomes abundantly obvious, that nothing can save us from the miseries of a straitened condition, but a population small enough for the means. The highway to this is education. And this is a precious use of the enlargements which are still before us, and by which the families of the land are translated for a time from extreme misery, into a state of comparative ease. They then become fitter subjects for education, than when sunk in the distress and desperation of abject poverty. When viewed in the light of absolute or ultimate resources, we have no great value, either for the removal of prohibitions from

the corn trade, or for the removal of tithes and taxes from agriculture, or finally for emigration. But when these expedients are viewed in the relation of subserviency to the education of the people, (because they afford a temporary lightening of the pressure that is now upon their families; and along with this, a spirit, and a leisure, and a means for their moral and literary culture,) in this light they may prove of incalculable service to the good of humanity. But still the position remains, that it is education, and that only, wherein the whole positive efficiency lies for a permanent amelioration in the state of the lower orders. Education is the specific; and the other expedients are at best but the circumstances for a more fit and powerful ministration of it. But the whole effect of these expedients, when once put into operation, will speedily be exhausted. The favourable opportunities which they afford, last but for a season only. They are opportunities which cannot be recalled; and if not improved for the purposes of a general education, they will leave the state of the population more irrecoverable than before.

6. We cannot bid adieu to our argument, without making the strenuous avowal, that all our wishes, and all our partialities, are on the side of the common people. We should rejoice in a larger secondary, and a smaller disposable population; or, which is tantamount to this, in higher wages to the labourers, and lower rents to the landlords. But this cannot be effected, save by the people them-

selves—and that, not with violence on their part,
or by any assertion, however successful, of a political equality with the other orders of the state.
There is no other way of achieving for them a better
economical condition, than by means of a more
advantageous proportion between the food of the
country and the number of its inhabitants; and no
other way of securing this proportion, than by the
growth of prudence and principle among themselves. It will be the aggregate effect of a higher
taste, a higher intelligence, and, above all, a wide-
spread Christianity, throughout the mass of the
population; and thus, the most efficient ministers
of that gospel which opens to them the door of
heaven, will be also the most efficient ministers of
their temporal comfort and prosperity upon earth.
Next to the salvation of their souls, one of our
fondest aspirations in behalf of the general peasantry is, that they shall be admitted to a larger
share of this world's abundance than now falls to
their lot. But we feel assured that there is no
method by which this can be wrested from the
hands of the wealthier classes. It can only be
won from them by the insensible growth of their
own virtue. The triumph will be a glorious, but,
to be effectual and enduring, it must be a pacific
one; achieved, not on the field of blood, or amid
the uproar of a furious and discordant politics. It
will be a sure, but a silent victory—the fruit of a
moral warfare, whose weapons are not carnal, but
spiritual; and which shall at length come to a

prosperous termination, not in strife and anarchy and commotion, but in showers of grace from on high upon the prayers and labours of the good. Each several clergyman, who labours piously and conscientiously in the home-walk of his own parish, helps forward this great consummation, till, by means of a universal blessing, peace and plenty will become alike universal throughout the families of a regenerated world.

APPENDIX.

(A. page 41.)—*On the Rent of Land.*

It is a signal error in a recent theory of rent, that the difference of quality in soils is the efficient cause of it. The difference between the produce returned for the same labour from a superior soil, and from the one last entered upon, is but the measure, and not the cause of rent. Had there been no gradation of soils, but had all been of the same uniform fertility with any given land which now affords rent, that land would have afforded rent still, and the same rent which it does at present. That land may yield rent, all which is necessary is, that, with the price obtained for its produce, the occupier can more than pay the wages of the labour and the profits of the capital bestowed upon it. It is the overplus which constitutes the rent of this land; and which would have been paid though there had been no land inferior to itself in existence. In affirming that it is the existence of

this inferior land which originates the rent, there
is a total misapprehension of what may be termed
the real dynamics of the subject.

The process is this :—On land of a given quality,
and anterior to its being rented, the produce, or
its price, is shared between the workmen who laboured it, and the capitalist by whom it is occupied.
But there are two reasons why this state of things
might not be stationary—the one connected with
the taste and choice of the workmen; the other,
with the taste and choice of the capitalist. The
workmen may be willing, rather than forego the
pleasures of matrimony, to part with some other of
their personal enjoyments, by entering soon upon
this alliance; even though it should be so soon as
that, through the medium of an increased population, they shall have at length to work for less
wages than they might have otherwise preserved.
And the capitalists may be willing, rather than
forego the pleasures of accumulation, to part with
some of their personal enjoyments, by sparing what
they might have spent, and vesting the produce of
their parsimony in business—even though, through
the medium of an increased capital, they shall have
to trade for less profit than they might otherwise
have been able to sustain. Thus, the increase of
capital, and the increase of population, are the real
impellent causes, why the wages and profit, which
wont to absorb the whole produce of land of a
given quality, do not now absorb it. The competition between the labourers, now in greater num-

ber, on the one hand, and the more numerous or greater capitalists, on the other, is such, that less than the whole produce is now shared between them, and the difference, wherever land is appropriated, goes to rent. Farmers, in the existing state of profit, and wages, and cultivation, are willing to pay this rent, for leave to settle on a land which formerly paid none; and should it so happen, that there exists inferior land beside that which is rented, and whose produce is just less than that of the other by the difference of the rent, farmers will be equally willing to settle on this inferior land, paying no rent at all. But, most assuredly, it was not the existence of the inferior, which originated a rent for the superior soil. It is not because farmers had descended to a worse land, that they are willing to pay rent for a better—but because they were willing to pay rent for the better, if they could have got it, they descended to the worse. The existence of the worse land, so far from originating a rent upon the better, prevented it from rising so rapidly as it would have done—because it afforded an outlet for the excess of population and capital; and thus slackened, for a time, their competition on the better land. The real cause of the rent, is this more strenuous competition of labourers and capitalists, now more numerous than before; and this cause, assigned by Dr. Smith, ought not to be superseded, as if it were a distinct and different cause, by that which, in fact, is but a consequence from itself. This in-

version of the truth, has led to vicious conclusions
in political economy; and, as is the effect of every
false principle, it has mystified the science.

Rent is not a creation by the will of the landlords, but a creation by the collective will of the
capitalists and labourers. Wherever there is property in land, it is the unavoidable result of the
one class choosing to multiply, and the other choosing to accumulate, beyond the capacity of the
higher soils to sustain them. It can only be done
away with by the abolition of that property; or,
in other words, by turning the country into a large
common, and dissociating all the activities of individual interest and hope from the business of cultivation. Labour would cease to attach itself to
any given portion of the territory, if there were
no fence of property by which the fruits of this
labour might be guarded. This property has been
termed monopoly, and all the odium which attaches
to monopoly has been cast upon its holders. But
the truth is, that the landlords are altogether innocent of the rent, which has flowed in upon them
ab extra, not at their own bidding, but at the bidding of those who complain of its oppressiveness.
The employer of labour would have had his workmen at a higher wage; but another stepped forward
and implored to be taken in at a lower wage, who,
if refused, would have been in fact the more ag-
grieved sufferer, or at least the more helpless out-
cast of the two. The owner of the land would
have let his farm at a lower rent; but, in the im-

portunity of capitalists, higher rents were offered ;
and he, by refusing these, would in fact have disappointed the most eager among the competitors.
The landlord is passive under this operation. He
is the subject, and not the agent in it. The primary and the moving forces lie with the labourers
on the one hand, and with the capitalists on the
other ; the former, through the medium of an increased population, having brought on a lower wage
than otherwise, by a necessity as irreversible as
any law of nature; and the latter, through the medium of an increased capital, having by the same
necessity brought on a lower profit than otherwise.
The difference goes to rent. The complainers of
it are themselves the makers of it. That the ori-
gination of rent should be rightly understood, is a
thing of far mightier interest to the commonwealth,
than the mere intellectual comprehension of a process. It is an incalculable loss to the working
classes, when the real cause of their sufferings is
misconceived. It bewilders the friends of humanity from the path of amelioration. And, besides,
it provokes a thousand undeserved antipathies—
being the fruitful cause of those many heart-burnings and jealousies by which society is so grievously
distempered.

Rent is inseparable from property in land, and
can only be abolished by all the fences and land-
marks of property being swept away from our borders. The effect would be as instant as inevitable.
The cultivation of the fields would be abandoned.

The population would be broken up into straggling bands,—each prowling in quest of a share in the remaining subsistence for themselves; and, in the mutual contests of rapacity, they would anticipate, by deaths of violence, those still crueller deaths that would ensue in the fearful destitution which awaited them. Yet many would be left whom the sword had spared, but whom famine would not spare—that overwhelming calamity under which a whole nation might ultimately disappear. But a few miserable survivors would dispute the spontaneous fruits of the earth with the beasts of the field, who now multiplied and overran that land which had been desolated of its people. And so by a series, every step of which was marked with increasing wretchedness, the transition would at length be made to a thinly-scattered tribe of hunters, on what before had been a peopled territory of industrious and cultivated men. Thus, on the abolition of this single law, the fairest and most civilized region of the globe, which at present sustains its millions of families, out of a fertility that now waves over its cultivated, because its appropriated acres, would, on the simple tie of appropriation being broken, lapse in a very few years into a frightful solitude, or, if not bereft of humanity altogether, would at last become as desolate and dreary as a North American wilderness.

We may here advert to a distinction between the produce of agriculture, and that of manufactures; or, as some would say, of all other manu-

factures than the manufacture of food. We think
that it will go far to explain the peculiarity of rent,
and repel at once the imputations which have been
grounded thereupon, both against land and against
landlords.

To assimilate the two, and confound all distinction between them, it is said that land is as much
a machine, and the preparation of food as much a
manufacture, as are the machines and the prepa-
rations of any other commodity. Now, without
objecting to this, as being a thing of mere nomenclature, there remains one important reality by
which to distinguish them. Food is the first necessary; other commodities are but second necessaries, or the luxuries of life. The increase of
food will surely be followed up by an increase of
population. The increase of luxuries or even of
second necessaries, will not always, will not necessarily be so followed up. Should corn become
permanently more abundant than before, it would
in the first instance fall in price; and a fall in such
a large and essential branch of family expenditure,
would, by translating men so much sooner into
circumstances of ease and plenty, multiply and
hasten on the marriages of labourers. A fall in
the price of mere luxuries, such as carpets or pic-
tures or expensive wines, would have no such
effect : and even a fall in the price of second necessaries, as of stockings for example, would have
scarcely any effect, excepting through the medium
of agriculture, and by its influence on cultivation

in the way that we have already explained.* This
is the reason why food cannot permanently remain
as a drug in the market. It in fact creates a market for itself, which other manufactures do not.
The peculiarity of the former commodity lies here,
that though its supply may be overdone for a year
or two, it cannot be overdone permanently, because there is a virtue in the commodity to extend,
and that indefinitely, the demand for itself; so
that, let the supply be kept up and augmented as
it may, there will, in the necessity of things, spring
up an equivalent demand by which to uphold its
price in the market. The same thing cannot be
said of other manufactured commodities—not even
of second necessaries. The supply of shoes may
be overdone year after year, greatly beyond the
number of feet that wear them; because there is
almost nothing in the mere production of these
shoes to multiply the feet. But the supply of
loaves cannot be so overdone year after year, because greatly beyond the number of mouths to eat
them; for there is every thing in the production
and increase of these loaves to multiply the mouths.
It is true, that on that event the feet will be multiplied too; and with the increase of demand for
food, there will also be an increase of demand for
other things, or the products of other manufactures. But these manufactures have to wait the
progress of agriculture, which itself has to wait for
nothing but the development of its own energies

* Chap. I. Sect. 9.

and means. Agriculture has the command of both
the terms which enter into the determination of
price—immediately of the supply, and mediately,
while rapidly, of the demand. Manufactures have
but the command of one term ; and they, by out-
doing its progress, are exposed to the perpetual
check of gluts, and bankruptcies, and losing speculations.

Now the rent of land is ascribed by Ricardo and
others, to a blemish, whereof air and water are
altogether free, and which, in consequence, yield
no rent. In land there is a descending gradation
in the quality of its soils ; and the last of these
which has been reclaimed, and which is the least
fitted for the production of food, is alleged to be
the cause of rent upon all the rest. But there is
no such descending gradation in the quality of air ;
no difference, for example, in the strength of its
atmospherical pressure at different places, if on the
same level, so as to make it more powerful at one
place than another for giving impulse to machinery.
And hence, according to the advocates of the new
theory, there is no air rent. But the great, and
indeed only efficient principle of rent is here overlooked. It is very true, that if, within the limits
of some square miles on the earth's surface, there
were air of ten-fold property and power, then, all
circumstances being equal, it would afford rent to
the proprietors of such a small and favoured territory ; and just because all the manufactured commodities that could be produced within limits so

narrow, did not satisfy the actual demand for them. But grant a certain definite number of these square miles, along with a right local disposition of them, and rent would cease altogether, whatever the descending gradation was in the qualities of the remaining atmosphere. The truth is, that the demand for such commodities as are wrought off through the instrumentality of steam engines, is limited by the actual numbers of mankind; and, by means of a very few square miles of the requisite atmospherical pressure, the world could be supersaturated with these commodities; so that all the air over and above this, whether of equal or inferior quality to the former, would lie a useless drug in the hands of those who should seek a rent for the use of it. Whereas, not only is the demand for those commodities which are produced by farms, or land machines, enlarged with every eventual increase in the numbers of mankind, but every addition to these commodities creates an addition to the numbers. The existence of a land, and the non-existence of an air rent, cannot, with propriety, be referred to any difference between the two elements in respect of the gradation of their qualities. The difference is altogether resolvable into the nature or virtue of their respective products: the one of limited demand, being straitened within boundaries which itself cannot enlarge; the other widening the boundaries of its demand, and in the very proportion too of every new addition which is made to its own quantity. The simple cause of

a land rent is, that the best farms, or the best
machines for the manufacture of food, work off an
excess of this commodity, over and above that
share which the capitalists and labourers employed
about it choose to put up with for themselves.
That they should so choose, is owing to the competition of other capitalists and other labourers,
whom the agriculture itself may be said to have
brought into existence, and all of whom would
be willing to occupy the best machines for the
same share, leaving the excess to go in shape of
rent to their proprietors.   And they of course
would be equally willing to be put into occupation
of the inferior machines at inferior rents, or of the
worst machine that can be wrought with a profit
at no rent at all.   Rent is not owing to a blemish,
but to a superiority in land machines over all
others.   They, in the first instance, can do what
the others cannot; not only satisfy the actual
demand of present customers for their produce,
but, by every addition to this produce, can proportionally add to the number of their customers.
And the vast majority of them can do what the
other species of machines do not—they can work off
a greater amount of their own appropriate commodity, than will remunerate the capital and labour
bestowed upon them ; and thus leave a surplus, by
which the industry is upheld that works off a thousand blessings to society.

It would remove the blemish ascribed to the
great instrument for the preparation of food by

our mercantile economists, (who have overlooked altogether the distinction, in point of virtue and effect, between the products of agriculture and those of manufactures,) could the business of the two, so unlike in their products, be likened in their processes. It is conceivable, that materials for the sustenance of human life could have been extracted, without let or limitation, by chemical manufacture, as by some treatment of decomposition and recomposition, for example, on the air which we breathe; and that the food of a differently constituted species could have been manufactured this way, in such abundance, that it would more than suffice for the alimenting of as many creatures, as the earth could accommodate with room to stand upon. This were an economy of things more suited to the taste of those who have cast reproach upon land, because of its limited capacities; and it were curious to trace the effects of it. The whole of the accessible atmosphere would come, in the course of population, to be engrossed; and then, if the air were appropriated, though with no gradation in its qualities, all that would be necessary for an air rent, were, that the food produced more than sustained the producers, and so afforded an excess that would go in the shape of revenue to its owners, and be expended by them on a disposable class of labourers. There would still be an air rent as at present. In this respect there would be no change; but there would be another and very important change, were the supposition realized of an indefinite capability in

human art, for the support of an indefinite population. Should it be absolutely and altogether without limits, the effect, however undeniable, is so very
extraordinary, that we are almost afraid to mention
it. There is a certain point, beyond which, if
human beings were multiplied, a serious inconvenience must be felt, from the mere crowding
and compression of their excessive numbers. This
is obvious enough, should it take place within the
limits of any separate locality; but it would be as
surely and severely felt, if, in virtue of a production of food *ad libitum*, it did take place over the
whole surface of the globe. The human species
would then become as sordid and miserable, as
those maggots appear to be who swarm on some
mass of hideous putrefaction. The herrings that
accumulate and condense in the western bays of
our island, are said to push the outskirts of their
shoal upon the beach. And better surely that
there should be such a limitation in the powers of
the land, and such an utter impotency in human
art to multiply beyond a certain point the means of
subsistence, than that the great human shoal should
be protruded at its extreme margin into the sea, and
serve for food to the fishes there waiting to devour
them. Rather than that this goodly earth of ours
should be turned into a human ant-hill, is it better
for man that he should have uncumbered fields—
that he should have open and spacious solitudes to
which he might make occasional escape from its
more crowded receptacles, and might, on the am-

ple domain of nature, company with nature's elements, and inhale their freshness. It is no interest, and ought to be no care of his, that the terrestrial space on which he walks, should be so over-peopled; or that, for the mere sake of numbers, human beings should multiply to suffocation. The number of His derived and dependent family, is the care of Him who sitteth on high—and most nobly hath He provided for it. He who hath the command of infinity, hath enriched its mighty tracts with innumerable worlds; and, without overburdening the one we occupy, He finds accommodation and space for the innumerable myriads of creation. Better far, than that, from the vomitories of human mechanism, there should go forth indefinite subsistence for indefinite multitudes—better far, that this should have its fixed and impassable limits; and that men, with the glorious arch of heaven above their heads, and with an ample platform beneath them, should walk forth in largeness and liberty, the privileged denizens of nature.

There is an optimism in the actual constitution of the land, as in every thing else that has proceeded from the hand of the Almighty. Had its fertility been limited to the maintenance of agrarian and secondary labourers, we should have had no disposable population; and neither science nor civilization would have arisen, to bless and to adorn the companionships of men. Had its fertility been unlimited, or could the powers of human art have extracted, without measure, the necessaries of life from any quarter of nature, the species would have lived in greater sordidness and misery still, on an earth laden by its wretched, because its over-crowded generations.

———

(B. page 74.)—*On Machinery.*

The impression against machinery has in it some-what of the same subtile delusion which we have attempted to expose in the text. There is blended with it the imagination, that employment is creative of something else beside its own products. For the apprehension of many, and that not confined to the immediate sufferers, is, that, with the intro-duction of every new method for abridging or su-perseding labour, there is the disappearance, not for a time only, but the permanent disappearance, of a resource to the labouring classes. The idea of their maintenance is strongly bound up with their occupation; and that, however remote, as in the case of buckle-makers, the product of their industry is from the materials of their food,—just as if, be-cause buckles were to be no longer fabricated, the bread, that wont to sustain the fabricators, was to be no longer forthcoming; or as if the effect of such transitions was any other than merely to change the direction of industry, without impair-ing, in the least, those stores of human aliment,

by which as great a number of industrious was sure
to be upheld in circumstances of as great sufficiency
as ever.

We dispute not the evils, though but the temporary evils, that result from those transitions of
employment which are caused by machinery.
They form a strong claim on the aid and tenderness
of the benevolent, when families, in large masses,
are, for a period, thrown out of employment; and
what were still more healthful, they form a strong
call on the manufacturing class of labourers more
particularly, to cultivate those providential habits,
by which, in virtue of their accumulations, they
might be enabled to weather the seasons of suspension and change, to which every people of mechanic
and highly artificial industry are so peculiarly exposed.   Nothing is more to be deprecated among
a people so peculiarly circumstanced, than those
institutions which discharge them from the care of
themselves, and from all prospective regard to their
own necessities—the consequence of which is, that
they are perpetually kept on the brink of destitution ; and so are landed, in total helplessness, on
those occasions when, either by a depression in
trade, or by an abandonment of old methods of
industry, thousands are reduced to a state of temporary idleness.

The vindication of machinery from the charge
of its adverse influence on the comforts of the
poor, has been made to rest upon different grounds.
It is not the true vindication, that the making of

the machines opens so great a source of employment, that the making and working of them together, take up as many hands as did the making of
the commodities without the machines ; for, in this
case, there would be no abridgment of labour, and
no advantage to master-manufacturers in setting up
the machinery.   And it is not a sufficient vindication, that, when an article is cheapened by machinery, the demand for it is so much enlarged, as
still, in spite of the abridgment in labour, to require
as many, if not more, labourers for its preparation
as before ;* for this, though true of many, perhaps
of most trades, is not true of all.   The ultimate
and substantial vindication is, that, however the
demand may vary or be lessened for particular
kinds of work, the fund, out of which the wages
come, is left unimpaired.   The maintenance abides
with us, whether the counterpart employment
abides with us or not ; and we may be very sure,
that this maintenance will continue to be discharged
on labourers, if not for the very work, at least for
some kind of work or other.   The distress and
inconvenience of the change are evils ; but they
are the only evils.

Machinery does not impair the fund out of which
industry is supported—neither does it lessen the
amount of industry, but only alters the distribution
of it, and makes it more productive than before.

* This is the chief argument, very strikingly illustrated, of
an admirable little treatise which has appeared lately, entitled,
" The Working Man's Companion."

In manufactures, the same quantity of a given article is furnished with less labour—but I continue to employ and support the same labour as before, either by extending my use of that article, or by allotting the sum which its now greater cheapness has left in my hands to the purchase of some other accommodations. The war against machinery, is a war against human enjoyments.

In agriculture, it is also the effect of machinery to have the same work accomplished with fewer hands. And this, as before, does not diminish the population, but only changes the distribution of them. It may transfer so many from the agricultural, to the disposable class. If fewer farm-labourers are required than before, proportionally to this, a larger surplus-produce will go to the landlord than before; for, just as the consumpt or expense on the farm is lessened, rent will be increased. These two effects meet and correspond—the augmentation of rent, with the augmentation in the number of the third class of labourers. One of the most important effects of agricultural improvement is, that it enlarges the disposable population.

But machinery, both in agriculture and manufactures, is attended with another effect of a still more vital character, and one on which most essentially depend the general comfort and sufficiency of our existing generation of labourers. We have already demonstrated, that the limit of cultivation is pushed forward by every invention which makes the labour of workmen, either in the agricultural

or secondary classes, more effective than before.
If, in virtue of certain machinery, all that enters
into the maintenance of an ordinary labourer, can
be prepared by fewer hands than formerly; this
opens the way to a descent among poorer soils than
formerly: and the more perfect such machinery
is, the greater is the length to which agriculture
is extended. Now, to that extreme limit the population have multiplied; and from that limit must
the agriculture again recede, if such machinery
shall be forcibly put down. It will affect the general supply of the population with food, just as a
permanent visitation of blight or barrenness would;
so that the vindication of machinery stands on much
higher ground than merely its subservience to the
enjoyments of the wealthy. It will re-act most
calamitously on the very classes who are most outrageous in this cause—it will stint the supply of
first necessaries,—if, in terror or subjection to the
tyranny of the multitude, either our farming or
manufacturing capitalists shall be forced to discon-
tinue their machines and implements of labour.*

And the reflection here occurs, that in proportion to the high and artificial state of improvement
which any country has reached, will the distress be;
should law, and security, and social order, in that
country, from whatever cause, whether by invasion

* The thrashing machine, beside helping down the agriculture to inferior soils, has a still more direct influence on the
supply of food, by the more entire separation which it effects
of the grain from the straw.

from without or by anarchy from within, come to be suspended. With every step in the progress of such improvement, has there been an onward step in the cultivation of the soil; till, corresponding to its high-wrought and extreme husbandry, the land has been filled with an extreme population. But without the utmost protection and deference to the rights of property, and confidence in distant returns on the outlays of capital, and safety from that violence which never comes in a shape so formidable to the resources of the nation, as when directed against the apparatus of our farms—such a high style of husbandry cannot possibly be upholden. The effect will be most tremendous; and far more severe than in a land of coarser husbandry, which in its days of peace has not been elaborated forward to its extreme resources, and so, in its days of warfare or misrule, will not be thrown backward upon that extreme necessity, to which every territory that is at once fully cultivated and fully peopled, would, in these circumstances, be most certainly exposed. This consideration should operate powerfully at present, in the fearful conflict that is now at work between the two elements of liberty and order. Were there to be a season of insurrectionary violence in these islands, we believe, on the principle which we have just stated, that England would suffer more than Ireland; and that, in point of intense and intolerable wretchedness throughout its families, it might then be said, " There has been no such distress in any land, or such wrath upon any people." Amid the contests of partizanship, the high and great principle should never be lost sight of on either side; that, in the preservation of justice, and authority, and good government, no country in the world has so mighty a stake as our own; and that, even by the partial relaxation, but still more by the subversion of these, will the comfort of no other people, and the prosperity of no other land, experience so calamitous an overthrow.

––––––

(C. pages 104, 150.)—*On Home Colonization.*

There are very few countries which do not present large tracts of land, on which the experiment of home colonization may be tried. The question then is, Why are they at present unoccupied? There can be no doubt, that in such a country of law, and security, and enterprise as our own, they would have been cultivated, could they, at the existing rate of profit, have remunerated the farmers. This is an object which may, with all safety, be left to the guidance of personal interest, and to the sharp-sighted intelligence of men calculating and scheming for their own individual advantage. It is not the want of capital which accounts for the non-cultivation of land in any country teeming with capital like our own; but an apprehension, either

on the part of occupiers or of money-lenders, that
if capital were embarked on the cultivation, it
would not be returned with an adequate profit,
and perhaps even be lost partially or altogether.
And if individuals would find it a losing speculation, we have no reason to believe that corpora-
tions, still less the largest corporation of all, the
government, would find it a safe one. We may
rest assured, that, down to such land as will barely
remunerate the outlay and expenses of its cultivation, the capital in the hands of individuals has not
only reached this limit, but is pressing upon it
closely, and is even wasting itself on vain attempts
to pass beyond it. And so we may safely assume,
that in any old country, which has long been in
favourable circumstances of peace, and civilization,
and order, for the development of its natural resources, if land hitherto uncultivated has been
pitched upon for the purpose of home colonization,
it is land of a lower fertility than what can repay
the expenses of its own husbandry with a fair profit to the cultivator.

But passing over the element of profit, which
forms but an inconsiderable fraction of the whole
return, it may be said of the soil which is entered
by home colonization, that it is not able to feed its
agricultural labourers with their secondaries ; and
that, therefore, a full complement of labourers cannot be applied to such land, without a lessening of
the disposable population. Not but that, in country parishes, a sufficient, an overflowing number

of agrarian workmen might be had for the enterprise; but, supported as it must be by a tax, the
produce of which formerly went to the purchase
of luxuries, there of consequence must eventually
be so many of the disposable population thrown
out of employment. Still, in spite of this circumstance, there would be a relief afforded upon the
whole by such a measure, to the general pressure
under which the community laboured from the excess of its own numbers. For the disposable labourers thrown out of employment would form but
a fraction, and in the first instance it might be a
small fraction, of the whole number enlisted in the
undertaking. If the land they began with, yielded
subsistence for nine-tenths of the essential labourers
connected with it; then, on the supposition of a
hundred men being employed, only ten would need
to be transferred from the disposable class to the
agricultural or secondary; and the return yielded,
would form a clear addition, in the food of ninety
labourers, to the previous means of subsistence in
the land. This number of idlers would be translated, not into what can rightly be termed profitable employment, but into employment, that, with
the help of a tax providing for one-tenth of their
maintenance, enables them to make out and complete the whole of it. The advantage of such a
scheme over that of all other charity-work, is quite
obvious. The forcing of a manufacture beyond its
natural limit, produces no food; and by edging
in, as it were, to a share of the pre-existent food,

so many of the superfluous population, it but condemns the whole population, each to a scantier portion than before. The forcing of agriculture beyond its natural limit, does create a clear addition to the food of the country; and if carried to a great extent, it may for a season, and before the population have had time to overtake it, yield, in the cheapening of the first necessaries of life, a sensible relief to the community at large.

This holds forth an inviting outset for the scheme; but it is well to mark its progress, and, if indefinitely carried forward, the final result of it. Once the natural limit is broken, and the *deficient* soils are entered on, the cultivation cannot proceed downwards, but by an increasing tax on the wealthy, and larger and larger drafts on the disposable population. At each successive descent, a temporary relief may be experienced; but with the same recklessness and relaxation of habit on the part of labourers, the pressure of a redundancy in our numbers will ever and anon recur with the same intensity and feeling of straitness as before. We should at length touch on the ultimate and impassable boundary of such a process, when, for the purpose of withholding it, the wealthy had to be taxed till they were reduced to the necessaries of life, and the last man of the disposable population to be withdrawn, in order to make out the requisite labour on the last, and therefore most deficient soils which had been entered on. We should then be landed in a more populous nation, yet not have a

single disposable individual within its confines.
Each would labour for his own essential maintenance; and all the interest or enjoyment connected
with the services of a disposable population, behoved to be abandoned. This is what may be
termed the extreme possibility of the system; but
it would never be realized. It would surely break
up, and that long anterior to such a consummation.
Landlords, subject to an indefinite and ever-grow-
ing taxation, would at length cease to feel an interest in the administration of their own property.
They would not continue to be the receivers of
rents, when this was so nearly tantamount to being
the mere organs of transmission, through whom the
surplus produce of the superior, found its way to
the deficient soils, and was there absorbed in the
expenses of a profitless and ungrateful cultivation.
It is fearful to contemplate the issues, after that
property had thus been undermined, and the ancient ties had been dissevered which connected the
soil with its original possessors. The occupiers of
the barren, might then turn in fierceness to the
occupiers of the fertile land, on the wonted channel of conveyance in the person of the landlord
having at length given way. A lax sense, or an
imperfect arrangement of property, in a country
yet but thinly inhabited, and of unbroken capabilities, is still so prolific of disorder, as to verify the
maxim, that a state of nature is a state of war; but
this disorder must be thickened and aggravated
ten-fold, should the same dissolution take place in

a country of teeming population, and whose very
deserts now swarmed with a host of colonized paupers that had overflown the natural limits of the
agriculture.   In the scramble that ensues, we shall
perhaps have to witness another of those dread calamities which may be awaiting us, and which we
fear nothing will avert, but a timely moral and
Christian education of the people, along with the
gradual abandonment of certain inveterate errors
which have been suffered to distemper the social
economy of our land.

   Such being the natural out-goings of the system
of home colonization, this alternative should be
carefully weighed at the commencement of it—
Whether it is better that the people should, by a
right preventive check on their own number, have
room and sufficiency within the natural limit of
the agriculture, or should be encouraged to multiply beyond that limit by a scheme, the proposal of
which has met with great acceptance from many
patriots and philanthropists in our day ?   It is utterly a vain hope, that we shall ever, by means of
such settlements, escape from the pressure of a
redundant population ; and a momentary slackening of the pressure is the most that we can expect
from it.   And this descent among the deficient
soils to make room for a surplus population, is
sure to be accompanied by a descent in the circumstances of the general population.   The very
circumstance of the soils being deficient, implies
the necessity of a charitable intervention, in order

to complete the maintenance of those who are there colonized. But, generally speaking, when the hand of charity is stretched forth, and more especially in behalf of a whole multitude, it is not for the purpose of upholding them in that state of average sufficiency which obtains among labourers, but only for the purpose of saving them from starvation; not to keep them in comfort, but to keep them in existence. These home colonists, if the system be carried to any sensible extent, will not be on the footing of independant labourers earning a respectable wage, but on the footing rather of paupers, or the dependants of a vestry, who have their supplementary allowances doled out to them, with that niggardly reluctance which usually marks the proceedings of an organized system of relief. Here then we have a population encouraged and virtually called into being, who are constrained by their situation to live beneath the par of human comfort and subsistence, and whose very presence in the land will act as an incubus with overhanging pressure on the general condition of our peasantry. They form a body of reserve, from whom masters may indefinitely draw, in every question of wages between themselves and their servants ; and by means of whom, therefore, they can, as in a market overstocked with labour, bring down indefinitely its remuneration. We hold then, in addition to every other evil of the system, that, once it is entered on and continues to be extended, the working classes will be sealed thereby to irrecoverable degradation.

It is at its outset, then, that every enlightened philanthropist should take his stand ; and at once proclaim, that nothing will serve the exigencies of a
land brought to such extremity as this, but a vigorous application of moral causes. We hold it as being
of inestimable benefit to all the classes of society,
that cultivation should stop with the last land which
yields a profit to the farmer, after having fed both
its direct and secondary labourers. The momentous question is, Shall we step beyond this limit,
or keep within it? By the former, we enter on a
headlong process of degradation, through which
we obtain, no doubt, a larger, but withal a more
wretched peasantry. By the latter, we restrict
ourselves to a smaller produce, and a smaller population, keeping the disposable class entire ; but
leaving it possible, by indefinite moral and literary
cultivation, indefinitely to raise the comfort and
condition of all the classes. There is a beautiful
harmony here, between the interest of the landed
proprietors and the interest of the general community. Landlords, on the one hand, would be
left in full possession of their rents, and in full
command of the disposable population. The general population, on the other, would be retained
within the boundaries of a soil, fully able, even at
its worst extreme, to maintain the families who
laboured it. It is a big alternative ; and the most
opposite results are suspended on it. Either the
population would be restrained within the natural
limits of the agriculture, and might be raised by

moral culture into higher and higher states of
sufficiency; in which case the rent of landlords
would be kept up, or if encroached on at all,
(and we should rejoice in such an encroachment,)
it would be by the higher wage of a now improved and independent peasantry. Or this rent
would be wrested from them by the necessities of
a pauper peasantry; in which case there would,
along with a letting down of the revenue of the
landlords, be a letting forth of the population on
deficient soils; and so, a landing both of the higher
and lower classes of society in one common degradation.

This process is as good as already entered upon
in England. The pauperism of that country may
be regarded, in certain of its modifications, as a
method of home colonization in disguise. In as
far as the wages are paid out of the poor's rate,
in so far may the farmer be induced to bring down
his agriculture among soils that cannot repay the
natural expenses of their husbandry. Of course,
he cannot afford to do this without paying a less
rent to the landlord than he could have otherwise
afforded; and indeed, in many districts of England where the redundancy of people has been
most severely felt, there has been a partial remission of the rent, for the express purpose of enabling
the farmer to take the parochial applicants into
employment. The work of his farm may by this
time have been fully engrossed up to the limit of
that agriculture which can remunerate itself. But

better it is to have a partial return from the labour
of these supernumeraries, than no return at all.
Better keep them in employment, though it should
yield but a fraction of their maintenance, than
keep them in total idleness. Now this is the virtual commencement of a scheme of home colonization, and offers indeed a distinct exemplification
of its several parts and consequences. The people who are thus admitted to country labour, can
only find occupancy among those extremes of cultivation, where the additional produce is unable to
maintain the additional men who have forced themselves into service. They cannot raise enough for
their own support, to complete which, rents are
encroached upon; or, in other words, an agrarian
population is multiplied and upheld at the expense
of the fund for the support of the disposable population. From this quarter then, from towns
where employment will languish, may we expect
an additional invasion on the already over-peopled
land; and therefore upon that part of it which lies
beyond the natural limit of cultivation. It is fearful to contemplate the result, if the present system
of England shall be longer persevered in. There
is nothing more likely to bring on a crisis, than this
unnatural accumulation of people; and nothing
more certain to aggravate its miseries and horrors,
when it shall come to be realized. If, during a
period of turbulence and disorder, the agriculture
shall be at all relaxed, (and what more likely from
the loosened and lessened interest of the adminis-

trators of landed property, in estates that become
every year less valuable and more vexatious to
them?) or if, during the same period, the now artificial economy of parish management shall be suspended, so that either the produce shall be diminished, or the existing distribution of it shall be
deranged—we cannot imagine a more fearful perspective than the famine, and the mutual ferocity,
and all the evils of anarchy, which will then be let
loose upon our suffering families. There are clearly
elements at work towards such a consummation;
and far more imperative therefore, than the necessity
for a reform in the politics, is the urgent necessity
for a reform in the economics of England. The
one opens a much higher walk than the other for
the wisdom and benevolence of true patriotism.
In younger countries there may, by an enlargement of means to the population, be a comparative
ease and tranquillity for centuries to come. In a
country, brought as ours near to the uttermost
verge of its resources, the only effectual and lasting
remedy is to check the advances of the population
upon the means. And nothing, we repeat, is competent to such an effect, but a gradual abolition of
the poor's laws, along with the instant and vigorous
application of moral causes. Village schools, and
well-served churches, and zealous parish ministrations, and a universal system of popular education,
into which the lessons of the gospel of Jesus Christ
largely and pervadingly enter,—these form the
main elements or means of our nation's peace, and
our nation's greatness.

(D. page 130.)—*On the National Debt.*

There is one conclusion from the argument in the text, which appears to us inevitable; and which, paradoxical as it may appear, we hold to be amply borne out both by reason and experience.* We can perceive no flaw in the deduction, should it only be granted that the capital displaced from business by loans is repaired, not by the parsimony of capitalists, but by the privation of customers— an inference that comes direct from the most elementary principles in political economy; and which is abundantly countenanced by the phenomena, both of the high profit that takes place in seasons of borrowing, as indicated by the low price of stocks, and by the obvious resuscitation of the withdrawn capital which must take place every year, as indicated by the unimpaired sufficiency of capital for all mercantile and agricultural concerns.

The views, then, presented in the text, on the subject of capital, have suggested to us the following important practical inference, in regard to the policy of the funding system.

* We subjoined the greater part of this argument some years ago to a former work, entitled, " The Christian and Civic Economy of Large Towns;" but the extraordinary nature of the conclusion, and its immense practical importance, if true, as being decisive, we would not only say of the vital impolicy, but of the prodigious infatuation, nay, insanity, of the funding system, have led us to insert it in this place.

The sum borrowed by government is withdrawn
from commerce and manufactures, and must, to
the extent of its power in producing commodities,
and bringing them to market, lessen the supply of
these commodities.

The price of these commodities rises in consequence, and to such a degree, too, that the sum
will be replaced; so that, in the course of a little
time, the capital, restored to what it was by the
operation of the now higher profit, will be as fully
commensurate to the business of the country as
before, when profits will again sink to their wonted
level.

But, should the same sum be borrowed next
year, the same deficiency of capital will occasion
another year of deficient supply, and of those consequent higher prices and profits which are the
unavoidable result of it. The deficiency will again
be filled up as before; and it will not be for the
want of a capital to borrow from, that government
shall be arrested in this career, however much it
may feel itself arrested by the insufficiency of the
taxes necessary to defray the interest of the increasing debt.

There might, however, be successive yearly borrowings for a considerable time; and in this way,
government has provided itself with means, over
and above its annual revenue, for defraying the
expense of our lengthened wars. If there be truth
in our reasoning on the subject of capital, this will
continue to act upon prices and profits just as long

as the practice of borrowing lasts. There will be as great a sum replaced every year, as shall both uphold the capital that is actually vested in business, and, over and above this, shall afford to government a loan, equal to that of the preceding year. But should the loan not be wanted, should the sum that government wont to absorb in this way not find its usual investiture, it will seek an investiture in trade. It will, in fact, restore the trading and manufacturing capital to the state in which it would have been, had government not made these yearly abstractions from it; and, with the now larger capital, there will be a fall of prices and profits.

The important deduction to be made from this argument is, that when government defrays any of its expenses by borrowing, it does so by a method which is doubly more burdensome to the country, than when it defrays the expense by taxes raised within the year.

Should government borrow twenty millions for the exigencies of the current year, there are, in that year, twenty millions' worth less of commodities brought to the general market than there would otherwise have been. But there is nothing in this transaction between government and so many of the capitalists of the nation, that can affect either the power or the inclination of buyers to purchase. There is as effective a demand as before, but a diminished supply—the same expenditure on the part of customers, but, on the whole, twenty millions' worth less of enjoyment in return for it.

Had government, instead of borrowing, raised the twenty millions by additional taxes, the community, no doubt, would have had twenty millions less to spend; but they would not have had the high prices to encounter, which are consequent on those abstractions of capital produced by government-loans. It is quite the same thing, whether the community shall go to market with the usual amount of money for purchases, but with prices raised to the extent of twenty millions; or shall go to market with twenty millions less of money, but with the usual prices. In either way, it suffers the loss of twenty millions' worth of enjoyment; or, in other words, it suffers no greater loss by being taxed to the extent of twenty millions, than it does by this sum being borrowed from the money-holders or capitalists of the land.

Under the borrowing system, the public are subjected, through the medium of higher prices, to the expense of repairing deficiencies, occasioned by government-loans, in the capital of the nation. The public could as easily, through the medium of higher taxes, have yielded, direct to government, the whole amount of the sums borrowed. The ability, on the part of the nation, to keep up the capital, in spite of the repeated drafts made upon it by borrowing, indicates the same ability to withstand equal drafts, if made upon it by immediate taxation. The whole sum borrowed for any year, though primarily and ostensibly raised from the money-holders, is, in fact, raised from the public—

and raised, too, *within the year.* The burden
could have been as easily borne, if the whole sum
borrowed had been raised within the year by a
direct levy. It makes no real difference, whether
bereft of a given amount of enjoyment by means
of higher prices or higher taxes.

It is thus that the national debt has all been virtually paid once, and yet remains to be paid over
again—paid, in the first instance, as it was contracted, by the high prices consequent on a deficient capital; and to be paid, in the second instance,
to the actual creditors, either by a liquidation of
the principal, or by a perpetual interest.

The hardship on the nation would not have been
greater, though all the money borrowed had been
raised by taxation, than the hardship actually borne
at the time when the loans were contracted. And
there is not a period of our by-gone history, even
though the years of profusest expenditure should
be fixed upon, in which we were not just as able
to render, in additional taxes, all the sums that
were raised by borrowing, as we were able to support the augmented prices consequent upon the
loans; and by which, in fact, the whole amount of
these loans was drawn from the community, to repair the abstractions which had been made upon
the capital.

The difference, then, between the system of
raising money by loans, and that of providing for
all the expenses by taxation, is that, while in both
ways the same pressure is made *at the time* on the

comfort of families, in the former way there is the
formation and growth of a great national mortgage, which remains to oppress and enfeeble the
country.   In either way, the state may obtain exactly the same supplies; but, in the former way,
it obtains them at a double expense to the nation.
The present burden is just as heavy in the one way
as in the other; over and above which, there is a
prospective burden equal to the present, which the
system of borrowing leaves behind it.

Notwithstanding, however, loans are more popular than taxes, and just because their double mischief is disguised.   The people do not feel that
government are taking the money out of their
pockets by borrowing, though this is virtually
done, and at the time too, in the shape of higher
prices, if not in the shape of higher taxes.   They
think that a loan only entails a distant calamity,
although the full weight of it is felt in a present
calamity.   But this is not perceived, and blindness
reconciles them to a sore infatuation.

To conclude, then; the whole sum wanted for
the service of the year should be raised by taxation, and the expedient of a loan should never be
resorted to.   Besides the economic argument for
this policy, which appears to us irresistible, we
hold the very unpopularity of it to be an additional recommendation.   It would restrain the
public appetite for war.   Government would not
enter so readily upon any rash or wanton undertaking, if the whole expense of it were not only

actually felt, but consciously felt in taxes palpably imposed for the purpose of defraying it. A more cautious and pacific spirit would thenceforth actuate the councils of the nation.

Mr. Tooke, in his able disquisition upon high and low prices, seems not to have fully adverted to the distinction in point of effect, between a war expenditure that is defrayed wholly by taxes, and a war expenditure that is defrayed partly by loans. He is right in asserting, that the money which is in the hands of capitalists, is as much spent as would be the same money in the hands of government; and that, therefore, when transferred from the one to the other, there is no greater demand thereby created to bear on the general market, and so to raise prices. But it should be considered, that though such a transference gives rise to no greater demand, it gives rise to a less supply; and that this will raise prices just as effectually. The twenty millions borrowed by government from so many of our capitalists, might all have been spent by the latter, within the year, in the outlays of their business; and so have told as effectually on general prices, as the same sum spent by government. But the borrowing has caused a cessation of this business insomuch that there are twenty millions' worth less of commodities brought to market, for the supply of the families of the land. Meanwhile, their demand for these commodities is the same, and the money which they bring to purchase them is the same; and so the price rises to such a degree, that

they must be satisfied with twenty millions' worth
less of comforts than they would have had, had no
such borrowing taken place. It would have been
no greater hardship on the community, if, taxed
to the extent of the whole loan, they had gone
with twenty millions less of money to market, when
the prices were not exposed to the influence of the
borrowing system in raising them.

That profits are raised by the government loans,
seems palpably enough indicated by the effect of
these loans on the price of stocks. It is not any apprehension for the security of government, that can
account for the whole depression of the funds, at
the period of large and frequent loans to meet the
exigencies of a war. It arises in great part from
the drafts which are made on the capital of the
nation, and from the necessary effect which the
consequent diminished supply has upon prices and
profits. The descent from 90 to 50 in the 3 per
cent. consols, during a great part of the French
wars, argues a high rate of profit throughout the
whole of that period. So long as it lasted, the
community were exposed to all the higher prices
for the various articles of comfort ; and we have
no doubt, that, by this difference of price alone,
the whole sums borrowed, enormous as they were,
actually passed from their hands to replace the deficiencies of the capital. The sum of five hundred
millions, then added to our national debt, was paid
away by the people in higher prices ; and better
far it would have been, if, instead of this, it had

been paid away by them in higher taxes. It was actually paid, yet still remains an incubus upon the nation.

And the conclusion is not essentially different, although the supplies of government should be raised, in the first instance, by the pure operation of credit, rather than by actual borrowing. Suppose, for example, that a sum so large as twenty millions should be raised within the year, in the shape of exchequer bills. There is, in this case, no abstraction of monied capital from any department of business, and therefore no raising of general prices from this cause. But there is an increase of prices, and to the same extent of twenty millions too, by another cause; that is, if not by a diminution of the money that formerly went to the side of production, at least by an increase of the money that now goes to the side of demand. The truth is, that, by the device in question, no less than an additional twenty millions are brought to bear on an aggregate produce of the same pecuniary cost as before. Through the currency and reception of these bills, a given cost of produce meets with twenty millions more in the market than it otherwise would have done, and average or general prices rise to that amount. Government brings the whole force of this extra competition to raise the price of that which cost but the same as formerly; and the effect of this extravagance on its part, is precisely the same with that of a similar extravagance on the part of landlords, who may be conceived to spend collectively, in one year, twenty millions more than their income. There is a consequent rise of prices to this amount, which goes to enrich merchants and manufacturers, and to constitute them either the creditors of government, who, in the act of funding their bills, bring a permanent mortgage upon the nation—or the creditors of landed proprietors, whose expenditure in like manner brings a mortgage upon their estates. In either case, the whole effect is a rise of prices; and not a reduction, but a rotation of property.

There is still a third way in which this matter can proceed; and it is worthy of being noticed, because of the important explanation on another subject to which it is subservient. The monied capital vested in the actual business of the country, might be rated, as before, at a hundred millions; and be returned, in ordinary times, by the sum of a hundred and ten millions. If reduced to eighty millions by a government loan, we have already seen, how, in one revolution of the economic cycle, it might be fully restored by the operation of a diminished supply upon prices. But the likelihood is, that the remaining capitalists of eighty millions may not confine their operations to what they can barely do with their own proper capital. They may superadd the power of credit to that of capital, which, in the circumstances supposed, they can do with all the greater safety, because of the large return of a hundred and ten millions to eighty millions that is now awaiting them. Let us imagine, then, that in virtue of being trusted to the extent of ten millions, they can lay out ninety instead of eighty millions on the extension of their business. This would reduce their profits for that year, from thirty to twenty millions; making, therefore, the reparation of the capital a slower process than it might otherwise have been. The sum of ten millions, by which their profits would have been augmented, has passed from them, and taken some other direction, which remains to be inquired into.

It seems obvious enough, then, that as by this device of credit they have brought ninety instead of eighty millions to bear on the outlays of their business, the money price of all which they had to purchase must have risen in this proportion. The chief of these purchases must be raw materials and labour. Confining ourselves to the latter, it may be stated as a general position—That when the operations of trade are extended by credit, the money price of labour rises. In the particular instance before us, it will do so unquestionably. The mere loan of twenty millions to government, will have no effect in this way; for though they are thereby vested with an additional command to that extent over the labour market, which they will of course make use of in adding to their naval and military establishments, yet the power of the capitalists from whom they have borrowed this sum is as much diminished; so that still, after the transaction, the joint demand of the two parties for the services of men, may be measured by the same sum, as the entire demand of the capitalists before that the borrowing took place. But should these capitalists, by means of credit, bring ninety millions instead of eighty to bear upon the market; then, with the help of the twenty millions now in the hands of government, a hundred and ten millions, in the place of a hundred, will go to the purchase of service and materials together, and so raise in that proportion the money price of both of them. And should government, by such a measure as the issuing of exchequer bills, add to the effect of these doings the operation of a pure credit on their side—there may, between the parties, be a hundred and twenty, or a hundred and thirty millions, instead of a hundred expended within the year, and that chiefly in hiring the services of men. A war, whose expenses were defrayed by taxation within the year, might have no such effect; but the various expedients so much resorted to, of loan and anticipation, have all of them the obvious and certain effect of advancing, for the time, the money price of labour.

Now this advance in the money price of labour, must, we think, tell directly on the money price of all that is purchased by labourers. More especially will it have the effect of raising the money price of grain—that being a first necessary of life. Not that it will necessarily give them a greater command over this prime article of subsistence— for, with only a given quantity of corn in the market, a mere advance of nominal wages can have no effect in sharing it out more liberally to the population. Still, however, it will have effect on the nominal or money price of corn. If all the buyers of an article have more to give for it than usual, that more will be given. There may not, in consequence, be the acquisition of a greater share by each; but there will, at least, be an endeavour after it, which is quite enough for raising the money price to all. Mr. Tooke, the able and distinguished author of the " Essay on High and Low Prices," has, we think, succeeded in showing, that the frequent scarcities of that season, go far to account for the high price of corn during the time of the French war. But we have no doubt that the war itself had a share in it. The greater waste and consumption of provisions in the shape of government stores for a navy or army, than by the same number of men in the pacific walks of life, would of itself be an item of no inconsiderable influence—particularly, as a very slight increase of demand tells more powerfully on the price of an article of main necessity, than it does in the case of all other commodities. But the chief effect of war, we apprehend, in raising the money price of agricultural produce, stands connected with the explanation which we have just given—an explanation into which we should not have entered, but for the light which it seems to cast on another interesting phenomenon that we shall now advert to with all brevity.

The question is, How comes it, that during a season of high money prices, there should always a stretch take place in the cultivation of land ? This was remarkably exemplified during the last war with France, at which time many a before out-field territory was reclaimed; and, generally speaking, a more thorough cultivation spread itself over the island at large. Now it appears to have all the certainty of an axiom, that no land can be entered on agriculturally, unless the produce yielded in return can feed the agricultural population and their secondaries, beside yielding a profit to the farmer. But we have every reason to believe, that profit was higher throughout that whole season of large borrowings and low prices of stocks, than at ordinary periods ; and, in as far as this element is concerned, the cultivation should have been straitened, rather than enlarged; whereas it was the opposite process which took place, and which calls for explanation.

Certain it is, that a higher money-price for corn can have no effect on what may be called the natural barrier of cultivation. It cannot make the land that is beyond, more fertile or less difficult to labour than before. It cannot impart to it the capacity of feeding more than its own agricultural workmen and their secondaries, if it wanted this capacity in times past; and, if it remain short of this, it is short of the possibility of being cultivated with a profit. Under all conceivable changes in the value of our denominations and our coins, there is still the stubborn necessity for the direct and indirect labourers on any given territory being, at the very least, fed from the produce of it. One can imagine a fall of substantial wages, in which case the men would either be worse fed, or be willing to put up with fewer of the second necessaries than before. This would admit a stretch in the cultivation. But it is doubtful whether, on the whole, labourers were worse off during the war than in ordinary times. With the higher prices, there were also higher money wages; and it was, in fact, a rise in the money price of labour which, partly at least, effected a rise in the money price of food. So that, with both the higher profits and the higher wages of that period—which, of themselves, ought to have contracted the agriculture, it is extraordinary, and requires explanation, that still the agriculture should have been extended.

We do not see how a high money price of corn should extend cultivation, if all the expenses of the husbandry, as estimated in money, rose in the same proportion. If the profit of agriculture kept as high, and, still more, if it rose higher than usual; and if the direct and indirect labourers obtained the same share of the produce as food to themselves —then, but for one circumstance, there does not appear the possibility of cultivation being extended, merely because money prices have risen. That one circumstance, which applies more to Britain than any other country, is taxation—and a taxation affecting, in a material degree, the expense of agri-

cultural operations. The truth is, that, in virtue
of such taxation, the last land has more to do than
merely to feed the direct and secondary labourers,
beside yielding a profit to the farmer. Over and
above these, the produce which is drawn from it
goes to feed an additional population in the employ
and service of government. It is taxation, as at
present conducted, which forces this destination
upon it. There are still taxes on many of the second necessaries of life ; and taxes which make the
implements and whole apparatus of farm labour
more expensive than otherwise. But a high money
price of corn does not add to the pecuniary amount
of these taxes ; and this alone will suffice to account
for the additional scope and outlet which that price
allows to husbandry. For the sake of illustration,
let us conceive, that, when grain is at the average
price, a hundred pounds worth, raised from the
last land, is divided in this proportion—that sixty
pounds defray the natural expenses of the husbandry, and thirty pounds more the taxes; leaving a
profit of ten pounds to the farmer. Then let the
money price rise from a hundred to a hundred and
fifty pounds, and even though the natural expenses
should rise in the same proportion, yet, with the
taxes, as estimated in money, being stationary,
there would ample encouragement be afforded for
the extension of the culture among the inferior
soils. For, on the supposition now made, the natural expenses would rise to ninety pounds, which,
with the taxes still at thirty, would leave no less

than a profit of thirty pounds—or a three times
greater profit to the farmer than usual. But he
could afford to cultivate at a profit much inferior
to this; and therefore can afford, and will feel encouraged, to enter on the cultivation of inferior
soils.

And we may now see how it is, that, in the time
of war, in as far as its expenses are defrayed, not
by taxes, but by loans, there should often be such
a general hey-day feeling of prosperity throughout
the land. The truth is, that a mere increase in his
money receipts, will give one a certain sense of
prosperity, or of getting on in the world—though,
in virtue of a proportional rise in money prices, he
may have no greater command than before over
the enjoyments of life. A general rise in money
rents and wages, and withal, in profits, will beget
the fancy, and even the sensation of prosperity,
among the three great classes of society—the feverish exhilaration of high health, without the sound
or entire possession of it. Meanwhile, and contemporaneously with this great nominal and apparent increase in the means of the general community, there must, in counterpart to the higher prices
and profits of such a season, fall a real weight of
suffering, without disguise and without palliation,
somewhere. And it is by the mere money an-
nuitants of all classes, that the pressure is chiefly
felt—who draw their stated income, and, with the
same nominal revenue as before, have to encounter
that excess of prices which we ascribe to the opera-

tion of the funding system; and by which we hold
that its immense levies are drawn, even at the time,
or within the year, in the shape of higher prices,
from the pockets of the population—as well as laid,
in the shape of a permanent mortgage, on the
country.

If our reasoning be valid on the effects that take
place during the contraction of the national debt,
it will further serve to establish the converse effects
that would take place during its repayment. By
the one process, capital was turned into expenditure; and there instantly ensued high profits and
prices to repair the deficiency. By the other process, expenditure would be turned into capital;
and there would as instantly ensue low profits, or
rather prices beneath prime cost, and consequent
losing speculations to absorb the superfluity. If,
when twenty millions were borrowed, the public
had to pay these twenty millions in higher prices;
then, should these twenty millions be repaid by a
tax, that tax would be again paid back to the public in lower prices. Should government establish
a property tax, and apply its produce wholly to the
liquidation of the national debt, it would bear far
more lightly on the community than they are at
all aware of. To them it might bear the semblance,
but not the reality of distress. The great distress
would be among merchants and manufacturers,
from the glut of capital. As by the one process,
a monied interest was formed, tantamount to the
whole value of the national debt; so, by the oppo-

site process, the whole of this immense interest
would be swept away. It would afford the most
impressive exemplification possible to all our views
on the subject of capital. Losses and bankruptcies
innumerable, would follow in the train of this great
regurgitation. The newly-created capital would
seek every where, but in vain, for a profitable investiture. It would force its way into Ireland and
more distant places; and might be the means of a
temporary relief from the pressure of our excessive
population, both by its reflux on our agriculture at
home, and by the impulse it would give to schemes
and undertakings of emigration abroad. Our landlords, the ultimate payers of taxes, are not aware
of the easy terms on which they might get quit of
the mortgage which oppresses them. It comes
upon them as a burden at the first, after they had
already borne it in high prices. They might cast
off the burden at their pleasure; and that, not by
a dishonest cancelment of the debt, but by the
literal, honest, and full repayment of it. The heavy
taxation, while it lasted, would be compensated by
the low prices; and permanent relief from the interest of the national debt would be obtained, without the expense of a sacrifice.

There is only one qualification that we can think
of, in any way affecting these conclusions on the
subject of the national debt. In as far as the money
is lent by foreigners, there is no abstraction of capital from the business of the country, and no consequent raising of prices. In as far as it is repaid

to foreigners, there is no addition made to the capital within the country, and no consequent lowering of prices. And the same may be said of all those repayments which, instead of being vested either in the home or in the return foreign trade, are carried forth of the land on any enterprise of colonization. Bating these, there would be a mighty lowering in the price of all those articles, on the production of which there was so much more of capital, and in the purchase of which there was so much less of expenditure than before—such a lowering, in fact, as would very nearly, if not fully, compensate for the extraordinary taxation, by means of which the liquidation of the debt is effected.

———

(E. page 175.)—*On Profit.*

In a recent theory of profit, the native and immediate forces by which it is determined have been lost sight of, so as to carry a mysticism into the science, in all those places of it where profit enters as an element into its reasonings.

On this subject, Dr. Smith's principle is the right one, and should have been adhered to. All other circumstances remaining the same, profit is lowered by the increase of capital, and raised by the diminution of it. It is equal to the difference between the cost and the price of commodities; between the sum laid out by one party on the production, and the sum laid out by another party in the purchase of them ; between the amount of capital employed, and the amount of its returns. Let the latter be stationary, and it is quite evident that profit will vary with the former, but in an inverse order—the profit being large when the capital is small, and small when the capital is large ; or even being extinguished, nay, converted into loss, which is a possible and frequently realized thing, when the capital is so large as either to equal or to exceed the returns which it meets with.

It had been well that both the language and reasoning of Dr. Smith had been retained upon this subject. The proper and immediate cause of a fall in profits, while the effective demand for commodities remains unaltered, is an increase of capital without a corresponding increase in the returns that are made for it. It is determined by the state of competition between capitalists, or rather between the capitals which they hold. If these increase either in number or in magnitude, without a proportional increase in the returning power, by the opening up of new lands, and the consequent increase of population ; then profits must decline with the progress of accumulated wealth in society.

Consequent on this accumulation of capital, and antecedent to this fall of profit, there must have been an extension of the business of the country, in all the various branches of its trade and manufactures. And this extension will take place in the business of agriculture, as well as in any other. The same circumstances which lead men to extend their transactions in commerce, though with the prospect of a less return than before, will lead them to extend their transactions in agriculture, with the prospect of a less return than before. In other words, land of inferior fertility and produce will, by the operation of this cause, be taken into cultivation. This concern, like every other, will fluctuate with the fluctuations of profit and interest in society. Should there be a fall of interest, and a consequent facility of borrowing, in any particular year, or period of years, farmers will be induced to attempt soils that had not been previously entered. So soon as men are satisfied with a less return, they will carry the plough to a poorer territory than before. This is one of the many phenomena that must ensue from an augmented capital, and a reduced rate of profit; and not peculiar to the affairs of husbandry, but exemplified in every other walk of enterprise and speculation.

Yet this phenomenon, but the subordinate result of a law, having a distinct principle of its own, has itself been magnified into the principle; and a controlling force has been ascribed to that which is only the determinate consequence of a prior force, determining the rate of profit. The effect has been mistaken for the efficient. The produce of the land, that is said to yield no rent, is conceived of as representing the aggregate of wages and profit. At most it is but the measure, and not the deter-

minator, of the sum of these two. The wages
of labour are not low, nor is profit either, because
land of an extremely poor quality has been taken
into cultivation; but this land has been taken into
cultivation, because wages and profit are low. If
wages be low, it is because labour, or the number
of labourers, is in excess. If profit be low, it is
because capital is in excess. But competition, the
moving force in both instances, has been well nigh
lost sight of. The land last cultivated has furnished some of our later economists with the materials of a formula—where the three elements of
rent, and profit, and wages, have been made to
enter, as symbols do into an equation, by means of
a few transpositions upon which, the whole doctrine
and philosophy of the subject have been newly cast,
and are held to have been infallibly expounded.

And it is curious to observe the proceeds of this
new mode of reasoning, through which, by a certain dexterous algebraic play, results are elicited
the most unexpected, and certainly the most opposite to all experience. One specimen may suffice. When once the produce of the last cultivated
land enters as a sort of fixed quantity into an argument; then, representing, as it does, the sum of
wages and profit, it will follow of course, that when
wages rise, it can only be at the expense of profit,
and when profit rises, it can only be at the expense
of wages—the one being high when the other is low,
and conversely. The strange conclusion educed
from this is, that by increasing the wages of labour,

we are on the high road to the underselling of our
neighbours in foreign markets; because that the
dearer the labour expended on the preparation of
export articles, the cheaper can it be afforded when
presented for sale.   And the reason of this is, that
profit being just as much lower as wages are higher,
we make a saving on the cost of the article, with
every new transfer in the course of its sales or
stages of preparation, till the ultimate price may,
in fáct, be very much reduced by the repetition of
this effect at each of the successive centages.   And
hence the paradox in question, advanced too with
a sort of axiomatic certainty.   It is a striking example of the extravagance into which men are sure
to fall, when, forsaking the obvious and real principles of a subject, they give the precedency, over
all sense and all experience, to the categories of a
school.
    We shall be saved from all such devious conclu-
sions, if we only keep in sight the proper and immediate causes by which both wages and profit are
determined.   There is a greater identity of principle between them than is commonly adverted to.
The one depends on the proportion which the
quantity of labour bears to the effective demand
for its products; and the other, also, on the proportion which the quantity of capital bears to the
effective demand for its products.   Or, just recur-
ring to the old language and style of conception
upon this subject, we should say, that the one varies with the intensity of the competition among

labourers for employment, and that the other varies with the intensity of the competition among
capitalists for business. Should there then be a
high standard of enjoyment among labourers, they
will not marry so as to overstock the country with
population ; and so, just because their taste is high,
their wages would be high ; thus landing us in the
important and delightful conclusion, that the people, collectively speaking, have their circumstances
in their own hands—it being at the bidding of their
collective will, whether the remuneration for their
work shall be a scanty or a sufficient one. The
same principle has not been extended to profit,
though it be as strictly applicable to the one element as to the other. It is for each capitalist to
determine how much of his profits he shall expend
on personal or family indulgences, or how much
of them he shall reserve for additional outlays upon
his business. Should there be a general and voluntary descent among capitalists in respect of expenditure, this of itself, by adding to the inves-
titures in trade, would produce a general fall of
profit. Whereas, by means of expenditure in this
class of society, profits might be sustained at any
given level—a level as much determined by the
standard of enjoyment, or collective will of capitalists, as wages are by the collective will of labourers. However simple and obvious this consideration may be, yet the most important, and as
yet unnoticed conclusions are deducible therefrom.
Our only inference at present is, that there is no

headlong necessity in any state of society, for either
a wretchedly low wages or a ruinously low profit.
Both, in fact, are dependent on moral causes.
There is a moral preventive check, which, if put in
steady operation throughout the labouring classes,
would keep wages high. And, however little adverted to,* there is an analogous check, which,
operating among capitalists, would keep profit high.
Instead of wages being necessarily low when profits are high, or conversely; both may rise contemporaneously, or fall contemporaneously. In
other words, there is still a highway open to us,
both for a well-conditioned peasantry, and a prosperous order of merchants and master-manufacturers in the land. There is no irreversible fatality
in that march of agriculture among the poorer soils,
which has been represented as bearing down profit
and wages. Instead of this, profit and wages may
each, in any point of the progress, make their own
resolute stand, and arrest the march of agriculture.
Let labourers, on the one hand, make a stand for
higher wages, (and this they can only do effectively,
by refraining from over-population;) and let capitalists, on the other, make a stand for higher profit,
(and this they can only do effectively, by refraining from over-speculation :) and then, so far from
their condition being overruled by the state of the
husbandry, they may jointly overrule that state;

* It is but justice to state, that this principle has been distinctly adverted to, and ingeniously illustrated, by Mr. Thos.
Perronet Thomson.

and, just by the position which they might voluntarily unite in keeping up, may they both lower
the rent of land, and somewhat limit its cultivation.
Instead of being borne down by the tide, they could
withstand and stem it; and instead of lying pros-
trate before the absorbing rent of the landlords,
they might prescribe their own bounds to the wealth
of the proprietors of the soil, which it could not
overpass.

This is the only effectual, but withal peaceful
and legitimate way, in which the other two classes
of society can make head against the landlords.
Rent, profit, and wages, have been denominated
the three ingredients of value. We confess, that
though at the expense of, and by an encroachment
on the first, we should like the two last admitted
to a larger relative share than they have at present; or, in other words, that the standard of enjoyment both among capitalists and labourers were
higher, though, as a necessary consequence, the
proprietors of the soil behoved to live less luxu-
riously, or less splendidly than before. This consummation is not to be arrived at through the medium of a contentious politics, or by the triumph
of what has been called popular rights. It will be
altogether a moral victory, which can only be gained
and perpetuated by dint of popular intelligence and
worth. Let workmen, having a proper control over
their appetite for present enjoyment, abate of their
reckless improvidence; and capitalists, having a
proper control over their appetite for gain, abate

of their reckless and excessive speculation; and we should soon witness both a higher wage and a higher profit. Instead of the action and re-action being only between these two elements, so that when the one rises, the other must necessarily fall; the action and re-action are shared among three elements, even profit, wages, and rent—so that the two first may draw indefinitely upon the last; and, with the fall of rent, profit and wages may rise, and that contemporaneously. We are aware, that, on this taking place, there might be a contraction of the agriculture; the lowest land having to yield a larger produce for the now increased remuneration of the farmer and labourers than before. But our decided preference is for a happier and more prosperous, even though it should be a somewhat more limited society.

———

(F. page 196.)—*On Free Trade.*

There is an artificial limit to the extension of trade, created by monopoly; and it is a very general conception, that, after its abolition, all let or limitation is thenceforth done away. But there is also a natural limit, which is felt, when the power to produce on the one hand, is put forth to a greater extent than can be met by the power to purchase on the other. There is palpable intimation given of this, in those glutted markets, which are the result of over-trading. Even Dr. Smith does not seem to be sufficiently aware, how closely placed the natural barrier is to the artificial one, though somewhat exterior to it. He was too intent on the destruction of the one, to have adverted much either to the existence or nearness of the other. And, accordingly, the idea most commonly suggested by the perusal of his work is, that if the wall of monopoly were only taken down, there would, thenceforth, be room for an advancement altogether indefinite, in prosperity and opulence. Hence the brilliant but unfulfilled anticipations of Canning, and Robinson, and Huskisson, on the opening up of new markets, and the removal of old fetters from the enterprise of British merchants. Hence, too, the mania communicated, as if by infection, from their speeches, and which spread itself, in a spirit of wild and ruinous adventure, over the land. The secret of that deep and general delusion which exists in the minds of men, as if the capabilities of foreign trade were perfectly inexhaustible, was fully let out, when, on the artificial check of monopoly or legal prohibition being done away, they, with an utter disregard to so much as the existence of a natural check, launched forth into all the varieties of unbridled speculation. The consequence was inevitable. On the taking down of the interior wall, they entered as if now on an indefinite career; but soon ran their heads against the exterior wall, which was situated at but a very small distance on the other side of the first. The consequent check and revulsion were felt throughout the whole commercial world. There may have ultimately taken place, a slight, but scarcely a sensible enlargement. Certain it is, that the sanguine hope of this enlargement was soon followed up, by a disappointed feeling of straitness and difficulty. And the gluts which took place, both on the abolition of the East India monopoly, and on the more general adoption of the liberal system, gave palpable evidence, how closely, though somewhat on the outside of the artificial barrier, commerce is beset with a natural barrier, beyond which she cannot overpass.

We are not, therefore, of the number of those who rate very high the economic advantages of the system of free trade. It will not much, if at all, enlarge that wealth which is in the hand of merchants, though, by its means, we may perhaps obtain a greater abundance of foreign commodities at the same cost, or obtain them cheaper than before. There will thus be a certain, though, we apprehend, a small addition to the enjoyment of consumers—which, in spite of the constant preference given by mercantile economists to the means over the end, to the benefit of producers over the benefit of customers, is really, after all, the great and only end of commerce. We can even imagine a slight extension given by means of free trade, to agriculture—in as far as we may possibly, through it, obtain at a cheaper rate, either some of the ma-

terials of husbandry, or some of those articles which
enter into the maintenance of husbandmen. Yet
notwithstanding this our humble estimate of the
advantages of free trade, in an economical point of
view, there are certain attendant moral benefits, if
we may so term them, which render the adoption of
the system one of the best and wisest achievements
of an enlightened national policy. In the first place,
it cancels a thousand heart-burnings at home. The
admission of one class to a particular trade, with
the exclusion of all others, is felt by the community
at large, to be an injustice and a wrong ; and it is
well when this, and every other rankling topic of
disaffection, are, as much as possible, done away.
Government incurs a prodigious waste of popularity, whenever its policy stands associated, in the
public imagination, with the failures and fluctuations of trade. And were it for nothing else than
to free itself from the burden of this unnecessary
odium, it were far better that it stood palpably
dissevered from the affairs of commerce altogether;
or at least that it never interfered with them, save
for the purposes of a revenue, and for the maintenance of the interests of justice. But the system is not more favourable to domestic than to
foreign tranquillity. The government which upholds it, not only stands forth in a fair and conci-
liatory aspect to its own subjects, but also to other
nations. The abolition of the restrictive system
in commerce, is, in fact, the abolition of the sorest
exasperations and jealousies which have taken place

among the states of the civilized world. There is,
therefore, a very high philanthropic interest involved in the maintenance of the opposite system.
It is on the side both of internal and external peace.
It would quiet many a discontent within our own
territory, and dry up the teeming fountain of most
of our modern wars.

Yet we are not without our fears, that the system
of free trade may retrograde, instead of advancing towards its secure and lasting establishment,
throughout the coming periods of our history. A
liberal politics forms no guarantee, but, we doubt,
the opposite, for a liberal political economy.* This

* On this subject I am happy to find that I can appeal to the
high authority of Mr. Senior, whose lucubrations on political
economy entitle him to a distinguished place among the original and enlightened thinkers of our day.

I refer to the following extracts from his work on " the Mercantile Theory of Wealth :"—

" If the unhappy prejudices that now exist on this subject
should continue, and if the extension of representative governments should increase the power of public opinion over the
policy of nations, I fear that commerce may not long be
enabled to retain even that degree of freedom that she now
enjoys."—" I have perfect reliance on the knowledge and
good intentions of our present ministers—but very little on the
knowledge possessed by the country at large. And if ministers
are unsupported by the country at large—if each class, in turn,
is to be permitted a complete or a partial monopoly, and,
bribed by this sacrifice of the general and permanent interest
of the public to its own partial and immediate advantage, to
allow others to clamour for the power to exercise a similar
oppression—if ministers are not aided by the public voice in
their struggles against individual rapacity,—we shall tread

is a subject on which the popular and the philosophical mind are not at all in harmony; and the very
admission into parliament of so large an influence
from the will of the humbler classes, may, after all,
endanger the cause of sound legislation, on every
topic where the seeming and the substantial interests of the community are at variance. We are
not afraid of any monopoly in favour of the few,
to the exclusion, from certain trades, of the many in
our own land; as the will of the many, when rendered effectual in consequence of a freer and fuller
representation, will completely overbear any partiality of this sort. But we do fear, that prejudice
and partiality may again have the ascendant in the
regulation of our commercial policy with the people

backwards, and with greater rapidity, the few steps which we
have so laboriously gained. Slowly and reluctantly, and as if
parting from our dearest friend, we have begun to withdraw
from the restrictive system. If once we begin to re-approach
it, I am justified by all experience in the fear, that, in our retrograde motion, we shall not stop at the point at which we
originally set out. It will have been an unsuccessful rebellion
against popular prejudice; and, like all unsuccessful rebellions,
strengthen and consolidate the ruling power."

" In a representative government, where each individual may
proclaim, in their utmost exaggeration, his sufferings and his
fears, where the power arbitrarily to do good is chained by
the same fetters which restrain the power arbitrarily to do evil
—where, in short, public opinion is omnipotent, and is, on
these subjects, so ill-informed, and therefore so easily misdirected,—there appears, at first sight, no limit to the extent to
which individual interest, popular prejudice, and national jealousy, might not carry the system of exclusion."

of other lands ; and that, in an assembly of mercantile legislators, there may, by mutual conni-
vance, be a protection awarded to each of the
separate trading interests, however paltry or local
it may be, against the rivalship of foreigners. We
can even imagine, that, in virtue of a more demo-
cratic government, there might be a more headlong propensity to war; and, certain it is, that the
popular mind, more especially when inflamed by
the cupidity and sensitive alarm of the trading
classes, is not always on the side of a pacific policy.
It seems all the more imperative in these circumstances, that, with every stretch of the elective
franchise, there should be a corresponding stretch
of education, and of larger intelligence among the
people ; lest, in the scramble of personal or provincial interests, that calm and comprehensive wisdom should be lost sight of, which ought to characterize the legislation of every great empire.

(G. page 237.)—*On Corn Laws.*

For the sake of its moral benefit, we know of
no achievement more urgently desirable than that
of a free corn trade. There is not a more fertile topic of clamour and burning discontent all
over the land ; and, were it but effectually set
at rest, we are aware of nothing which might

serve more to sweeten the breath of British society. The interest of cheaper food, is not the
only one concerned in the abolition of all those
restraints which have been laid upon its importation. There is, beside this, a special interest felt,
by that numerous class who are engaged in the
business of export manufactures, or export merchandise. The limit of our imports determines
the limit of our exports; so that when the one
trade comes to its *ne plus ultra*, the other must
also be brought to a dead stand. They mutually
limit and determine each other. So that the advantage to our export commerce, from a further
enlargement of our imports, opening, as it would,
a fuller and freer exportation, and telling most
favourably for this great branch of trade upon the
foreign exchanges, is really one of the most urgent
forces that is now operating on the side of an unrestricted corn trade. We shall therefore attempt
a brief exposition of what we hold to be the leading principles, and the likely results of such a
measure.

First, then, though there should, on the event
of an instant and total abolition of the corn laws,
be such a reduction of price, as would translate
the population into circumstances of larger comfort and sufficiency—we cannot imagine that this
would be more than temporary. The proportion
of the food to the population might be increased
at the commencement; but, reasoning on human
nature, and on all experience, this would soon be

followed up by the old proportion of the population
to the food. Such a regress of the ocean from our
shores, as left behind it a million of rich arable
acres, would cause an instant and large descent in
the price of grain. But no one thinks that a permanent cheapness would be the result of it. The
difference between one census and another, though
only at the distance of ten years, may well convince
us, how speedily the former balance between demand and supply, and so the former prices of food,
would be restored. Yet even still, however frequent and familiar the topic is with economical
writers, the great majority of our land-holders seem
blind to the peculiar and characteristic excellence
of that commodity in which their wealth lies. It is
a commodity which never can be so multiplied, as
permanently to glut the market. By the stimulus
which its abundance gives to population, it is very
sure, in the long run, to create a commensurate
market for itself. Unlike to other commodities,
it has the virtue of increasing the demand for itself,
just as the supply is increased. This single circumstance should help, and perhaps, above all
others, to tranquillize the fears of our landlords,
and to give them a feeling of conscious strength
and superiority over all the fluctuations to which
commerce, in every other of her departments, is
liable. They are the holders of the necessaries of
life ; and, in virtue of being so, theirs is an upper
and secure region, where they enjoy, without the
possibility of dethronement, an entire and essential

command over the services of men. They misunderstand their own situation, when they participate in the tremulous anxiety of merchants. Their wealth is as indestructible as are the laws and elements of nature; having in it that character of permanency, which belongs to the processes both of the physical and the moral world—based as it is on the capabilities of the soil, and the constitution of humanity.

But let us attempt a closer treatment of the question. We would, in the second place, remark, that there seems nothing in the freest importation of corn, which, *of itself*, should permanently contract the agriculture of our own land. The reason why the poorest of our cultivated soils has been entered on is, that still it had enough of capability for feeding its agricultural labourers and their secondaries, beside yielding a surplus to remunerate the farmer. This reason is not at all affected by the admission of foreign grain from abroad. The capability which had brought down the agriculture so far, would still remain after the abolition of all corn laws. We are aware of a possible cheapening of the article at the first, which, by translating the people into better circumstances, might raise, for a time, the quality both of their food and their secondary accommodations. While this lasted, the poorest soil which cultivation had formerly reached, might not be able to yield the now higher remuneration for labour; and there might, for some very brief season of years, be a receding of the home

agriculture, from the extreme limit to which it had
been carried. But without a permanent rise in the
popular standard of enjoyment, this could only
be temporary. The people would again multiply
to the now more abundant food; and this they
would just continue to do, till agriculture should
recover the very limit from which it had, for a short
interval, retired. When the wages, estimated in
grain, had become as low as formerly, the agriculture of our own country would then become as
large as formerly. Throughout the gradation of
soils, the same differences in respect of produce
would obtain between the superior land, and that
which is said to yield no rent. Or, in other words,
the rent of all land, *estimated in produce*, the corn
rent of all land, would, in spite of foreign competition, be just what it wont.

But it follows not, that, though rent in kind
would, after a season of disturbance, settle at the
same point which it did formerly, rent in money
would therefore do the same. And this, in the peculiar circumstances of Britain, may most severely
affect the substantial income of landlords. The
thing apprehended is, that, on the opening of our
ports for the free admission of corn from abroad,
there would be a fall in money prices—and so, a
fall in money rents. It would matter not to the
real interest of our proprietors, if this fall in money
prices extended, and in like proportion, to every
other article of enjoyment. There would then, in
spite of the declension in nominal income, be the

same real command as before over all the comforts
and conveniencies of life. Were labour, and the
products of labour, to become as much cheaper as
corn had, then the same corn rent would purchase
as great an amount as before of all that entered
into the use and maintenance of families. But
there is a special cause, in our own country, to
prevent this. Though every other ingredient in
the price of commodities should fall as much as
corn, there is an ingredient which remains, and
must remain, in a great measure stationary. There
can be no proportional remission of taxes to compensate this fall of money prices. There might,
had government nothing else to do with a revenue,
than meet the outgoings of its present expenditure;
for then it might proportionally lessen the allowance of its various functionaries; and, with a money
expenditure reduced in all its branches, maintain
the public service in as great strength and effectiveness as before. But along with its current
and actual expenses, which might fall with the
price of all other things, the revenue is also charged
with the permanent interest of an old and heavy
debt, which no retrenchment can alleviate, save
the retrenchment of a partial bankruptcy. This
is the capital reason, why, though the money price
of grain falls, the money taxes cannot be made to
fall proportionally; and it is this, chiefly, which
gives to landed proprietors a real and substantive
interest in high money rents. The great national
mortgage of our public debt has the same effect

generally, that private mortgages have on the holders of individual estates, personally and particularly.
They become substantially, as well as nominally
richer, by the augmentation of their money income;
because then the interest of their debts forms a
smaller proportion than before of their whole revenue. And the converse effect takes place on a
fall of money income. In other words, it is the
existence of our national debt which gives to the
possessors of the soil their only rational interest in
the corn laws; and the likeliest method by which
to harmonize the discordant views and feelings of
all parties upon this subject, were an adjustment
between the land and the fund holders.

We hold it impossible to effect any right adjustment between these two classes, but by means of
taxation—the topic of one of our subsequent argu-
ments; ere we have overtaken which, we can attempt no complete solution of the difficulty in question. But, meanwhile, we can state what appears
to us the likelihoods in regard to the future money
price of corn, on the event of the abolition of the
corn laws. It can be treated, we think, in no other
way than as a speculation of likelihoods; the cer-
tainties of the subject being, from the very nature
of the case, unattainable, but through the medium
of experience. Beforehand, we can only offer
hypothetical results—or the results that would ensue on certain given suppositions, which, anterior
to an actual trial, we have really no means of verifying.

We have already stated, that, with every addition to our excrescent population, there behoved to be a fresh and extended draft of corn from abroad; which, by each enlargement of the importation, would become dearer than before. There ensues a very speedy augmentation of difficulty, and so of expense, in the transport of grain, when, in consequence of the need for increased supplies, it must be fetched by inland carriage, even for small distances, from such places as are inaccessible to navigation. With every enlargement of these distances, corn would be landed dearer in our own country; and one can imagine, that, from this cause alone, the dearness, in an unrestricted state of things, may at length be equal to that dearness which is the effect of our present prohibitions. There would, on the event of a total, and, at the same time, instant abolition of our corn laws, be a desultory fall of price, to the utmost consternation of the landed proprietors. But with this abolition of the present restraint on importation, there were the abolition of a present restraint on population also—the excrescent portion of which would, from the commencement of this new era of liberty, grow to a magnitude, that, owing to the number and uncertainty of the elements concerned in the process, is at this moment undefinable. Certain it is, therefore, that there would be a recovery, to a certain extent, from the first cheapness, occasioned by an immediate abolition, if that, instead of the far wiser step of a gradual abolition, were actually resolved upon. But we hold it beyond the reach of all human anticipation, to say how far this recovery would proceed—or whether it would fully restore the money price of grain, so as to work out a full compensation to our landlords, for the loss of that protection which they at present enjoy.

For, who can compute the situation of that point, at which, in a state of perfect liberty, the underselling power of Britain will be exactly balanced, by the expense of its farthest and heaviest importation? The equipoise would at length be gained; but there are too many influences beyond the reach of precise calculation, for our being able to say when. Every augmentation, on the one hand, of our foreign manufactures, may either lessen their price in foreign markets, or add to the expense of their transit, when their superabundance is forwarded from nearer to more distant places of sale; and every consequent augmentation, on the other hand, of our imported food, enhances the dearness of it: so that the tendency, from the very first, is towards a limit, however impossible to foretell where this limit is to be, or after what increase of our excrescent population it will proceed no farther. We do not know how far, or how long, the industry and ingenuity of our own countrymen are to keep ahead of the industry and ingenuity of the people in other lands. We cannot answer for the number or extent of those regions abroad, where there shall be a constant preference of British goods to their own home manufactures, even though returns must be made for them in agricultural produce. We cannot tell the degree in which the encouragement of the industry, and the consequent increase of the numbers, of their own people, will absorb their agricultural produce, and make it an article of scarcer and dearer exportation. There is no fore-seeing what the new materials, and what the new processes of industry may be, which shall spring up in other parts of the world; so that many of our present customers may be led to seek nearer to their own doors for those articles of taste and of enjoyment, which they now fetch from our far distant island. We cannot anticipate with cer-tainty on either side of this question—neither how far the perpetual additions to British industry and skill shall extend our superiority, nor in how far the rivalship of other nations shall at length deduct from it. There are a thousand possibilities con-cerned in this matter, through which we can no more see our way, than we can through the con-tingencies of the weather. They are like the un-assignable quantities of an indeterminate equation, which lead but to a dependent or conditional re-sult. We cannot decide beforehand the proportion which, when things are left to their free course, our extrinsic shall bear to our natural population. It lies undisclosed in the womb of futurity; and both the resulting population and the resulting price, that would ensue from a free state of things, must be left to the verification of experience.

Yet, in the face of all this uncertainty, we feel

no hesitation in affirming, both the expediency and
the rightness of a free trade in corn.   That it would
land us in a larger excrescent population than we
have at this moment, is little to be doubted.   How
much larger, we have not the means of calculating.
Our own impression is, that it would not be nearly
so much larger as is commonly anticipated.   We
should not be surprised, if, in a free race of improvement among the nations, the excrescent population of Britain did not, eventually and ultimately, amount to one-tenth of its natural.   There
are certain physical inequalities, which might maintain for us a permanent superiority over other lands,
even after all the moral inequalities had subsided.
Still we cannot imagine, that, with every advantage
we have for commerce, our trade should overlap
our agriculture, so far as to extend our population
beyond a small fraction of the number maintained
by the produce of our own territory.   And even
though it should be a large, instead of a small
fraction, we would still advocate the cause of freedom.   The evils apprehended from this are two.
There might first be a considerable reduction in
the money price of food, to an extent which, if not
provided against, would depress the substantial, as
well as the nominal income of our landlords.   And,
second, there might be a precarious dependence
on supplies from abroad, which might subject us,
at times, to an aggravated suffering, on the event
of a general scarcity.   Yet we would incur both
these hazards, rather than we would the certain

and urgent evil of a dissatisfied population; who feel, and perhaps with justice too, as if defrauded of their rights, by the compulsory restraints of the legislature on the importation of food. We hold, that an immunity from this sore heart-burning were cheaply purchased, even with the risk of every evil which may have been felt or foretold as the probable consequence of liberty. It were right that it should be a gradual, but, ultimately, a complete emancipation.

It is remarkable, that the first of the apprehended evils, that is, the injury done to the landlords, would become lighter, just as the second, or the dependence of our country on foreign supplies, ever increasing with the increase of our extrinsic population, became more aggravated. It is obvious, that the greater this population became, the heavier would be the expense at which we had to fetch agricultural produce from abroad, so that the money price of corn would rise in this country; and there is no saying how nearly this might effect a full compensation to the proprietors of the soil. But though it should fall short of this, the real injury to the landlords, by a fall in the money price of corn, stands chiefly connected, as we have already remarked, with the inequality to which it would give rise between them and the fund-holders. And should this inequality be adjusted, the injury would be in a great measure repaired. Now, we can perceive how this might be brought about by a rule of conditional taxation. For the sake of example, let us imagine that all assessed taxes, and all those taxes on commodities which bore on the general enjoyments of the people, were abandoned; and that there was substituted, in their place, an income tax of 20 per cent. on land and fund holders, to be exacted equally from both classes, when the average price of wheat for the preceding year had been sixty shillings a quarter. A scale of variations in the tax could be made to quadrate with a scale of variations in the price. When wheat fell beneath sixty shillings by successive differences, there might be a series of corresponding diminutions on the income tax of landholders, and of increase on the income tax of fundholders. And the converse of this could be made to take place, when wheat rose above sixty shillings. We should thus, with all the various conceivable changes in the price of wheat, have the land-holders paying 19, or 18, or 17 per cent. and so downward in the scale in cheap years, and in dear, 21, or 22, or 23, and so upward in the scale; while the charges on the fund-holders would stand on the opposite side of par. The same rule of equity might be extended, even to private mortgagees upon land. We enter into no further details or modifications upon this plan. It is offered merely as a suggestion, and as being precisely of that character that is adapted to a measure of which the issues are uncertain. The conditional nature of the scheme meets, and is accommodated to, the uncertainty; and if it serve no other purpose, it may at least demonstrate, that

an adjustment which shall harmonize the main interests of this complicated question, is not impracticable.

The second apprehended evil we hold to be far
more serious, than most of the advocates for a free
corn trade seem disposed to allow. The dependence of a country, to any great extent, for the
subsistence of its population, on other and distant
lands, we hold to be a fearful element of insecurity
and weakness. It is this which accounts for the
ephemeral duration of many of those commercial
states, that have figured their brief and brilliant
hour in the history of the world. When their commerce abandoned them, the stamina, not of their
greatness alone, but often of their very being, abandoned them. Or, if they do abide, theirs, like
Venice, has been a shrunk and shrivelled existence;
and that, just in proportion as their now extinct
commerce did at one time overlap their agriculture.
Our comfort, in reference to Britain, is, that though
this may take place to a certain extent, it will not
do it far. An excrescence will be formed, but such
as may at any time be thrown off without impairing
the substantial wealth or greatness of our nation.
This accretion to our trade, consequent on the
abolition of the monopoly in corn, which so many
look to with triumphant anticipation, we should
look to with alarm, did we conceive that it would
effect a mighty proportional addition to our commerce—and only look to with toleration, because
of its believed and hoped-for insignificance. It is

vain to affirm that Britain, when thus extended, would rest as firmly on the motley foundation of home and foreign agriculture, as she would if, within her natural limits, she rested exclusively on her own proper basis. The advocates for freedom reason badly on this subject, when they speak of the dependence between us and other countries being reciprocal—or that they depended as much on our manufactures, as we on their food. The distinction is overlooked here, (and this is a cause of error in many other departments of political economy,) between the necessaries and conveniencies, or, still more, between the necessaries and luxuries of life. They can want our handiwork, but we, with a large surplus population, could not want their food. Our comfort is, that it will not be large. If it were, we should at times be exposed to visitations of fearful calamity—a calamity that might be alleviated, but would not be averted, by the stored and accumulated grain of former years, of which the advocates on the side of liberty conceive that it might ever be in readiness for such an emergency.

Any apprehension we have from a repeal of the corn laws, is for the country at large, and not for the landlords. There might be immediate loss to them, from a change in the power of money; but even this could be made up by an adjusted taxation. After which we see nothing else but their increasing wealth and importance, in every new addition made to the excrescent commerce and population of the land. Their estates would

rise in value, just as the contiguous land of a great
city does, with every enlargement in the number
of its houses and families.   And every season of
universal scarcity, while the cause of severest suffering to the British community, would prove a
harvest to the British landlords.   They would have
a fearful command over the services of the disposable population.   The high prices of such a period,
enhanced by such an accumulation of human beings upon our territory, would mightily enlarge
their fortunes, or clear away the debts of their former extravagance.   It may be recollected how the
famines of 1799 and 1800 redounded to the sudden
prosperity of agriculturists.   We should anticipate,
under the reformed system, a still more frequent
recurrence of like fits and intervals of prosperity.
The holders of the necessaries of life, therefore,
may well give all their apprehensions to the wind.
With the certainty that the population will increase
just as their commodity increases, from whatever
quarter it may be brought, they have nothing ultimately to fear in the consequences of an unex-
cepted freedom.   They, at all times, and amid all
changes, will be lords of the ascendant.   They
alone stand on firm vantage-ground, and should
of all men be exempted from those mercantile jealousies, by unworthily acting upon which, they
have dissevered, both from their persons and their
interests, the affections of the people.

But the most important consideration of all, or,
at least, that which harmonizes most with the gen-

eral object of our work, is, that however great the
immediate relief of a free corn trade may be, it
would at best be temporary, and, at the end of
some brief period, would at length cease to be the
minister of a greater abundance to each of the families of the land, than they at present enjoy. The
produce of our home agriculture is mightily increased within the last thirty years. Yet who will
affirm that this has secured ought like a permanent
sufficiency and comfort to the people? It has given
us a larger, but not a more prosperous commonalty
than before. And, without a change in the taste
and moral habitude of the working classes, this
will infallibly be the result of all the additional supplies that we shall ever obtain from foreign agriculture. The increase of their numbers will follow
close on the enlargement of their food; so that at
the end of the process, nay, even throughout the
process, there will scarcely be the sense and perception of any greater sufficiency than before. By
all means let the boon be granted. Let the freedom of this trade be restored perfectly, though pro-
gressively—that government may withdraw itself
from the obnoxious attitude of appearing to stand
in the way of the people's subsistence. Let this
semblance of hostility between the governors and
the governed be for ever obliterated; for, however
insignificant the material, the moral benefit that
would ensue is incalculable. The material enlargement from this, as from every other source that we
have hitherto attended to, would be but temporary

in its duration, and limited in its amount; and, after it had reached its maximum, we should only behold a larger, but in every way as straitened a population, as we do at present, or as we have done in the past stages of our history. Like all the other external capabilities of our state, it will soon be overtaken. The only sure remedy is an internal one. The people cannot, by any possibility, indefinitely provide from without, for their growing numbers. But by the moral operation of prudence and principle from within, they can accommodate their numbers to their provision. However wide the limit may be, yet, if they inconveniently press upon it, there can be no feeling of largeness. However narrow the limit may be, yet, if they keep sufficiently within it, this, of itself, as among the peasants of sterile Norway, will give the feeling of largeness. In a word, this whole argument on foreign trade, and more especially on the foreign trade in corn, but leads to one repetition more of the oft-repeated lesson—that it is not by the force of material resources, but by the force of moral restraints, we shall at length realize the spectacle of a general comfort among thriving and well-conditioned families. In other words, there is no other power than that of Christian education, which can chase away the economic or political distempers of our land; which can either conduct us at the first, or keep us permanently afterwards, in the state of a peaceful, and contented, and flourishing society.

(H. page 289.)—*On the gradual Reform of our Financial System.*

Practical men, with their contempt for theory, which almost always is a contempt for generalized truth, receive with incredulity every affirmation which relates to a state of things that greatly differs from the present state, with whose details and familiarities they are often so minutely conversant. It greatly concerns, therefore, the advocates of every change from one state to another, that the transition which they recommend should be made out in a way as gradual and safely progressive as may be ; and that, not merely for the purpose of avoiding those substantial inconveniences, which all sudden and desultory movements are sure to bring along with them, but for the purpose also, if possible, of reconciling those alarmists, whose resistance to innovation forms the great barrier in the way of all improvements.

It is the dictate of true wisdom, that nothing, save where principle or urgent necessity is involved, should be done *per saltum*—but that every thing, when possible, should be done by a process, or without violence to that great law, both of nature and of sound politics, the law of continuity. It follows not, because we recommend a complete change or a complete abolition, that we therefore want the instant change or the instant abolition of any thing. However firm our conviction of the expediency of certain measures, yet we should desire, in the act of carrying them into accomplishment, never to forget the deference which is due to existing interests, or even to existing prejudices.

On this principle we should deprecate an immediate, although we are friendly to a total abolition of the present corn laws. This should be made to take place by a gradual relaxation in fractional instalments, as of a tenth annually, whereby they might be wholly done away in ten years; at which rate, we feel confident that, before the termination of the process, all parties would be experimentally convinced, how much they had been influenced by the veriest bugbear, in their opposition to a free corn trade.

Yet there is one vestige of these restrictions, which we should feel inclined to retain—not as a relict of the old system certainly, nor yet as a protection to British landlords; but for the sake of a small addition to the public revenue, which it were most rightful and legitimate to raise from this particular source. The truth is, that these importations of grain, although exaggerated by the fancy of many, in respect to their future and eventual magnitude, will land us in a somewhat increased population, and perhaps place us in a somewhat more precarious state than we might otherwise have been. A somewhat larger establishment, both civil and military, may be required by this extension of our numbers; and it is but fair, that the excrescent population should, in some way or other, be made to defray the additional expense which their own residence amongst us shall have created. We have already stated our reasons for thinking why taxation should be shifted away from commodities altogether, and more especially from those which are in general use, whether among capitalists or labourers. But we confess, that, for the purpose of reaching the excrescent population, we should not object to a slight duty, as of five shillings a quarter on imported corn—to be remitted only in years of scarcity. So far from this being in contravention to any doctrine of ours, we hold, that not only would it be consonant with strict principle, but that the theoretic perfection of our scheme would rather be completed than impaired by it.

But neither should the general commutation of all taxes into a territorial impost be adopted immediately. It should be done by a series of particular commutations, each of which would lighten the community of some distinct burden, till the whole was, in the course of years, transferred by successive centages on the income of our landed and funded proprietors. The work of reform should begin with those taxes which bear on the essential maintenance of labourers, till every vestige of an imposition on any of their comforts was completely done away. It might then proceed to a similar relief from house, and window, and all assessed taxes. If one-third of these were taken off annually, and commuted, we should be wholly delivered

from them in three years. The reform might thus
be made to move onward from one commodity, or
object of taxation, to another—while, at each step,
the administration would gather new popularity,
and earn, at every distinct act, a fresh sentiment
of gratulation and gratitude from the country at
large.   Long before the process was consummated,
the landlords, however alarmed for the system at
the first, would have the experimental conviction
of its perfect innocence, nay, of its great positive
benefit to themselves.   At all events, did their fears
turn out to be very obstinate, or even incurable,
the process might be arrested at any given point;
when, instead of a large income tax to cover all
our present duties, they might be saddled with a
very moderate one, in lieu of the most obnoxious
of our present burdens.   It is thus, that without
endangering their own prosperity in the least, but,
we think, most materially advancing it, they have
it in their power, by successive peace-offerings, to
mollify the turbulent spirit of the age, and establish their own influence and security on a firm
basis for many generations.   We know not a more
effectual method of charming away a rancorous
politics from our nation—or a method by which
the discordant elements that are now so busily at
work in the midst of British society, could be more
readily and fully harmonized.

But it may be long before the doctrine is admitted, that all taxes fall ultimately on land, and
still longer, before it is proceeded on in the busi-

ness of legislation. The conviction that it were expedient to commute many of our most irritating taxes into a *general income tax*, may take the precedency, for many years, of the conviction that it were fair and equitable to commute all taxes whatever into a territorial impost. And we should be thankful, if the former conviction were proceeded on till the latter was fully established. It were infinitely better than the present universal system of taxation upon commodities, that there should be an income tax, although it did include the mercantile along with the landed classes. We believe the latter would pay all; but, leaving this question to be settled afterwards between these two classes, there is another question more urgent still, and demanding an immediate settlement; we mean the question between the higher and the humbler classes in society. An income tax on the former, to the ostensible relief of the latter, would wrest their most formidable weapon from the hand of demagogues. It were the grand specific, we believe, for appeasing the outcries of popular discontent, and so of warding off from the cause of public order and tranquillity, the principal danger to which, in these perilous times, it is exposed. And it were a cheap purchase of security to the payers, for it would just be making them pay openly, what, though in disguise, they now pay substantially and really.

And we would not only concede, for a time, a part of our theory, to the demand of those who prefer a general to a territorial income tax : we can even admit, that the main objects of financial reform might be achieved, although the commutation from commodities to income were not universal. There are certain establishments, as the post-office for example, which might be upheld, and continue to yield a revenue to government, though without the penalties and restraints by which it is at present guarded as a monopoly. There are even certain articles of enjoyment, as the higher wines and other undoubted luxuries, which may be taxed to any extent, without affecting the comfort of the lower classes. But sugar and tea enter far too largely into the system of their maintenance to be thus classified ; insomuch, that the abolition of the tax upon these would lead, at no great distance of time, to the cheapening of labour, and so to the extension of agriculture. This tax, therefore, should be wholly commuted ; and, in short, if ought but an income tax is to be retained, it should stand exclusively associated with the enjoyments and expenditure of the wealthy, so as not to leave even the semblance or the shadow of any hardship on the working classes of society.*

With such views, we cannot share in the patriotic enthusiasm which is felt on the subject of re-

---

* It would more fully accomplish this desirable object, if the income or property tax, instead of being levied by a centage on the whole income, were levied by a centage on the excess of that income over a certain fixed income, beneath which taxation should not be carried.

trenchment. Our patriotism and philanthropy incline us the other way. In common estimation, the demands of the public service are regarded as so many encroachments on the general comfort of society. In our estimation, they are but encroachments on the luxury of one class; and that is, the landed proprietors: and we cannot regard with complacency the abridgments which are made, either in the number or the support of national functionaries, when we believe that the only effect will be, to enlarge the means of the aristocracy, and enable them to live in greater splendour or delicacy than before. So far from taxation having been carried to its extreme limit, we believe it was never at a greater distance from the limit than at this moment; and, to substantiate the position, we make our confident appeal to the growing number of those families in the country, who are elevated above the condition of labourers, to the increased profusion of their tables, and the increased magnificence of their houses, and furniture, and equipage. In other words, there is still, with all the outcry of our being an overburdened people—there is still a larger fund for the additional imposts of government, than at any former period in British history; or, which is the same thing, a larger disposable population, who, with but the surrender of luxury on the part of private individuals, can be spared for enlarging the civil, and the military, and the educational, and all the useful or respectable establishments of the nation. When told, as we often are, that no trade can bear to be taxed any further; our reply is, that it is not the trade which furnishes the tax. Trade is but the channel, and not the fountain-head, of all the supplies which come into the treasury. It is not commerce, but its customers, who pay all taxes; and these are, mainly, the holders of the maintenance of labour. They can bear to be further taxed, so long as they indulge in articles of enjoyment which might be dispensed with; and, in giving up these, they might abridge or annihilate many a trade, yet without destroying the sustenance either of its capitalists or labourers, which, instead of being destroyed, is but transferred into the coffers of government. By this process, we but exchange the products of commerce and manufactures for public benefits; and we repeat, that, instead of stinting any goodly or desirable objects of patriotism, never was there a time when they might be more freely and bounteously extended. Having such views on the real effects and rationale of taxation, we cannot give our admiration or approval to the scurvy economics of the day. To our eye, they have the characteristics of selfishness and sordidness; and we can see nothing in these paltry savings of government, but a surrender of great public interests, that the ignoble gratifications of sense or of vanity may be left unimpaired.

One great benefit of our proposed commutation were, that it would break up the association which now obtains between lofty and high-minded pa-

triotism on the one hand, and this wretched pe-
nuriousness on the other. It might perhaps break
up too, that low arithmetical politics which has
had too long the ascendancy in the councils of the
nation. It would bring the real sides of the alternative, clearly and undisguisedly, into view; making it quite palpable, that the maintenance of the
general population was in no way affected by taxes;
so that after this element had been discharged
from the reasoning, it would become manifest as
day, that taxation and the public service might be
indefinitely extended, without one earthly interest
but that of the landlord's being made to suffer
from it.

There is one obvious effect that would ensue
from this great change in the financial system of
the country. It would lower the money price of
manufacturing labour; and so, by cheapening, it
would enlarge our exports. The taxes at present
do not neutralize; but they so far countervail the
natural advantages of British industry, as to bring
us sooner than otherwise to the limit of our exportation. By enlarging this limit, and so extending
our foreign markets, we should certainly export a
greater amount of manufactures than we do at
present; and this would seem to land us in what
we certainly do not hold to be a desirable object,
the increase of our excrescent population. It should
be recollected, however, that the same remission of
taxes which would cheapen manufacturing, would
also cheapen agricultural labour; and so, would

both let forth the agriculture upon inferior soils,
and spread a more strenuous cultivation over the
whole territory.   There would, along then with
the extension of our commerce, be an extension
of our agriculture ; so that the one might possibly
not overlap the other to a greater extent than before.   The return imports for the additional exports, need not consist of additional agricultural
produce, to feed the then larger excrescent population.   They may consist of additional foreign
luxuries, to be purchased by the landed proprietors,
whose then larger revenues, from the extension of
the agriculture, should enable them to live more
sumptuously than before.   Or they may consist of
additional second necessaries, so named, because,
though imported from abroad, they do, in fact,
form objects of demand, and so enter into the
maintenance of the general population.   We have
already adverted, and with feelings of gratulation,
to the dissimilarity between Britain and those
smaller states, whose importance and glory departed when their commerce abandoned them.
The difference lies in the amplitude of our agricultural basis, so that although commerce should
forsake our shores, we should find a resource and
a harbourage for almost all the population who are
now employed in it.   Now, whatever adds to the
agricultural basis, augments this security; and the
remission of all taxes which bear on the maintenance of labour, has clearly this effect.   It is tantamount to making the country a larger one than

before ; and the likelihood is, that with all the facilities given by this financial reform to manufacturing labour, yet, with the commensurate facilities given at the same time to agricultural labour, the excrescent population might not have a greater proportion to the natural, after the change than before it.

———

Synoptical View *of the Political Economy of this Volume.**

It has not been our object to deliver a regular system of political economy. It has been to establish the following specific proposition—That no economic enlargements in the wealth and resources of a country, can ensure ought like a permanent comfort or sufficiency to the families of the land. Followed up as these enlargements are, by a commensurate, or generally by an overpassing increase of the population—the country, while becoming richer in the aggregate, may continue to teem with as great, perhaps a greater, amount of individual distress and penury, than in the humbler and earlier days of her history. In these circumstances,

* The foot-note references to books in this article, are to former publications of the Author ; wherein some of the principles of the present work have been stated and defended.

the highway to our secure and stable prosperity is, not so much to enlarge the limit of our external means, as so to restrain the numbers of the population, that they shall not press too hard upon that limit. But the only way of rightly accomplishing this, is through the medium of a higher self-respect, and higher taste for the comforts and decencies of life among the people themselves. It is only a moral and voluntary restraint that should be aimed at, or that can be at all effectual; the fruit, not of any external or authoritative compulsion, but of their own spontaneous and collective will. This is evidently not the achievement of a day, but the slow product of education, working insensibly, yet withal steadily and surely, on the habits and inclinations of the common people; begetting a higher cast of character, and, as the unfailing consequence of this, a higher standard of enjoyment; the effect of which will be, more provident, and hence, both later and fewer marriages. Without this expedient, no possible enlargement of the general wealth can enlarge the individual comfort of families; but, as in China, we shall behold a general want and wretchedness throughout the mass of society. With this expedient, no limitation in the way of further increase to our wealth will depress the condition, though it will restrain the number of our families; but, as in Norway, we shall behold the cheerful spectacle of a thriving, independent, and respectable peasantry.

But though our main object has been to exhibit

such proofs and illustrations as may have occurred to us for the establishment of this position; and though we do not profess to have unfolded, in our volume, political economy, according to the forms, and in the nomenclature of a science; yet a political economy, such as it is, may be gathered out of it. We may not have accomplished the regular construction of a system, be it right or wrong, but we have at least furnished the materials of one; and we conclude with a brief exposition of its leading principles and peculiarities.

1. The division of the labouring population into the agricultural, the secondary, and the disposable. It presents many new and important relations in the science of political economy. No ground will be cultivated, (unless by the interference of some artificial and compulsory legislation,) that is not at least able to feed the agricultural population employed on it, and their secondaries. Hence the higher the standard of enjoyment is among the people at large, the greater will be the secondary, and the less will be the disposable class; or, corresponding to this, the greater will be the wages, and the less will be the rent, while, at the same time, the more limited will be the cultivation, because of the larger produce that will be required from the soil last entered on, to feed the larger number of secondaries.*

2. That the great aim of every enlightened phi-

---

* " Extent and Stability of National Resources."

lanthropist and patriot, is to raise the standard of enjoyment; even though it should somewhat lessen the rent, and somewhat limit the cultivation. That there must be less food raised in virtue of this narrower cultivation; and hence, a somewhat narrower society. But that this, with general comfort among the families, is vastly preferable to a more numerous society, with all the consequent miseries of an over-peopled land.

3. That there is no other method by which wages can be kept permanently high, than by the operation of the moral preventive check among the working classes of society; and that this can only be secured by elevating their standard of enjoyment, through the means both of common and Christian education.*

4. That however menacing an aspect the policy, whose object is to raise the condition of the working classes, may have on the interest of the landlords, by encroaching on the rent of land—yet they have every security for a great and growing revenue notwithstanding. Such, in the first place, is the strength of the principle of population, that there is no danger but wages will be kept sufficiently low, and cultivation be carried down among the inferior soils sufficiently far. And besides, every improvement in the methods of husbandry, by lessening the agricultural population needed for the work of farms—and every improvement in the powers of manufacturing industry, by lessening the

* " Christian and Civic Economy of Large Towns."

population needed for preparing the second necessaries of life,—will serve to increase the disposable
population who are at the service of the landlords,
and, along with this, the rent out of which this
third class of labourers is maintained. The improvements which are ever taking place in the
powers of labour, will greatly more than countervail any diminution, effected by the moral check,
on the number of labourers.   Or, in other words,
the standard of enjoyment may rise, and yet the
income of landlords rise along with it.   Human
industry, aided by human skill, is ever becoming
more productive; and, from this cause, if workmen
will only assert and make good their own proper
share of the increased produce, there are abundant
means for the comforts both of the proprietors and
of the general population being enlarged contemporaneously.*

5. That high wages are not necessarily confined
to the period when the wealth of society is in a
state of progressive increase; and neither does it
follow, that, when this wealth has attained its
maximum, and become stationary, the wages of
labour must be low.   That it remains in the collective power of labourers to sustain their wages at
as high a level in the ultimate, as in the progressive
stages of the wealth of a country.   That the moral
preventive check on population can achieve and
perpetuate this result; but that nothing else will
do it.

* " Christian and Civic Economy of Large Towns."

6. That in every country, where the laws are efficient and equitable, and the people are industrious, the cultivation of the soil will, under the guidance of personal interest and enterprise, be carried to the extreme limit of its being profitable. That, in these circumstances, to enter on a scheme of home colonization, is to extend the agriculture beyond this limit; or, in other words, to enter upon soils which will not repay the expenses of their cultivation. That such a process can only be upheld by taxation, or by turning so many of the disposable population either into agrarians or secondaries. That the process reaches its ultimatum, when the last man of the disposable population, withdrawn from the preparation of luxuries, is converted into an agricultural or secondary labourer. That this implies a state of things, when the whole rent of the land is absorbed in the expenses of a pauperism, now accumulated to the uttermost. That by the time when such a consummation is reached, and probably long before it, the landowners, loosened from all interest or care in their estates, would abandon the administration of them. That when once the tie of property was broken, there would ensue an immediate dissolution of society. That the occupiers or labourers on the inferior soils, now deprived of the essential support, which, through the medium of their proprietors, they drew from the superior ones, would turn, in violence, on the more fortunate occupiers of the better land. And finally, that, whatever temporary

respite society might obtain from a scheme of home colonization, it is a scheme which, if persisted in, must have its final upshot in the most fearful and desolating anarchy.

7. That this contemplation suggests two distinct limits—one, the extreme limit of a profitable, another, the extreme limit of a possible cultivation. That, by abstaining from schemes of pauperism, and, instead of these, giving the whole strength and wisdom of government to the best schemes of popular education, we shall keep within the former limit; and, with an untouched disposable population, whether for the luxury of proprietors, or for the public objects of a sound and enlightened patriotism, we may have, at the same time, the general population in a state of respectable comfort and sufficiency. But if, transgressing the former limit, we enter, with our home colonists, on unprofitable soils, and so make way towards the latter limit—from that moment, in thus making room for a larger, we are on the sure road to a greatly more wretched society than before; and degrade throughout the condition of the working classes, while we at once impoverish the landlords and enfeeble the state, by trenching on the disposable population.

8. That no trade or manufacture contributes more to the good of society, than the use or enjoyment which is afforded by its own commodities; hence the delusiveness of that importance which has been ascribed to them, as if they bore any creative part in augmenting the public revenue, or

as if, apart from the use of their commodities, they at all contributed to the strength or greatness of the nation; and hence, also, the futility of the common distinction between productive and un-productive labour.*

9. That although commerce re-acted most power-fully on agriculture at the termination of the middle ages, so as to introduce a new habit of expenditure among the landlords, and mightily to extend the cultivation of land—yet, now that the habit is firmly and fully established, we are not to imagine, though any given branch of trade or manufactures should be extinguished, that it will sensibly throw back the agriculture. For that no proprietor would let down the cultivation of his estate, because the failure or fluctuation of particular trades had placed beyond his reach some of his wonted enjoyments. That he would still be at no loss for objects on which to spend his income; and that, therefore, a large income would be as much his earnest aim and his felt interest as before.

10. That there is, therefore, a misplaced and exaggerated alarm connected with the decay or the loss of trade. That the destruction of a manufac-ture does not involve the destruction of the main-tenance now expended on manufacturers; and that the whole mischief incurred by such an event would be to them a change of employment, along with a change of enjoyment to their customers; after which, we should behold, in every country

* " Extent and Stability of National Resources."

subsisted by its own agricultural produce, as large a population as well maintained as before.*

11. That they are chiefly the holders of the first necessaries of life, or landed proprietors, who impress, by their taste and demand, any direction which seemeth unto them good, on the labours of the disposable population.

12. Grant but industry and protection, and then capital will be found to have in it as great an increasing and restorative power as population has; and that any policy for fostering, or any fears for the decay of the one, are as chimerical as the same policy or the same fears in reference to the other; and that capital can no more increase beyond a certain limit than population can.†

13. That the diminution of capital, occasioned by excessive expenditure, whether public or private, is not repaired so much by parsimony, as by the action of a diminished capital on profits; and that the extravagance of government or of individuals, which raises prices by the amount of that extravagance, produces only a rotation of property, without any further diminution of it, than what arises from the somewhat higher rate of profit, which an increased expenditure brings along with it; and which higher rate of profit must, to a certain extent, limit the cultivation of land.

14. That trade is liable to gluts, both general and partial; that no skilful distribution of the ca-

* " Extent and Stability of National Resources."
† " Christian and Civic Economy of Large Towns."

pital among particular trades, can save the losses which ensue from a general excess of trading; and that the result is the same, whether the undue extension has taken place by means of credit, or from an excess of capital.

15. That the rate of profit is determined by the collective will of capitalists, just as the rate of wages is by the collective will of labourers—the former, by the command which they have, through their greater or less expenditure, over the amount of capital; the latter, by the command which they have, through their later or earlier marriages, over the amount of population. That by raising or lowering, therefore, the standard of enjoyment among capitalists, profit is raised or lowered; that, in this way, both classes may encroach on the rent of land, and share its produce more equally with the landlords.

16. That when the agricultural produce of a country is equal to the subsistence of its population, its foreign trade is as much directed by the taste, and upheld by the ability, of its landed proprietors, as the home trade is.*

17. That it is not desirable that the commerce of Britain should greatly overlap its agricultural basis; and that the excrescent population, subsisted on corn from abroad, yield a very insignificant fraction to the public revenue.†

* " Extent and Stability of National Resources "—and " Christian and Civic Economy of Large Towns."
† Ibid.

18. That, nevertheless, there should be a gradual relaxation of the corn laws, and ultimately a free corn trade—with the exception of a small duty on importation, for the single purpose of a revenue to government, by which to meet the expenses to which it is subjected, from the addition made by the excrescent to the whole population.

19. That the abolition of their monopoly in corn, would not be injurious to the British landlords; saving that the increase thereby given to the value of money, might create an inequality between them and the fund-holders—which inequality, however, could be rectified, by means of an adjusted taxation.

20. That, probably, a free corn trade would not burden the country with a large excrescent population.

21. That Britain has little or nothing to apprehend from the loss of her colonies and commerce—but that a change of employment to the disposable population, and of enjoyment to their maintainers, would form the whole result of it. And that though, historically, foreign trade did, at the termination of the middle ages, stimulate agriculture, yet that now, under all the possible fluctuations of trade, there is perfect security for the cultivation of land, on to that point at which it ceases to yield any surplus produce to the landlord.

22. That, with the exception of their first brief and temporary effect on wages and the profits of circulating capital, and of their more prolonged effect on the profits of fixed capital—all taxes fall

upon land; the interest of its mortgages being included.

23. That this doctrine, though now regarded as one of the exploded errors of the French economists, should not share in the discredit attached to their school—if upheld by other reasonings, and made to rest on other principles, than those of the economists. That the grounds on which our conviction in this matter is established, were never once recognised by these economists—that is, the dependence of wages on an element over which labourers, collectively, have the entire control—we mean population; and the dependence of profit on an element over which traders, collectively, have the entire control—we mean capital.

24. That, to estimate the whole effect of taxes upon land, we should add to the effect of them, in aggravating the expenditure of landlords, the effect of them in lessening their receipts. That every tax which bears on the profit or maintenance of the agricultural capitalists, and which bears on the wages or maintenance of the agricultural, and their secondary labourers, and, generally, which enhances the expenses of farm management—creates a deduction, *pro tanto*, from the rent. That, for the commutation of all taxes into a territorial and funded impost, there would be a full equivalent to the landlords—first, in the lessened expenses of their living; and, secondly, in the enlarged rent of all the land now under cultivation. And that they, over and above, would obtain more than an equi-

valent, in the new rent which would accrue from the more extended cultivation of their land, now unburdened of all those taxes by which the cultivation had formerly been limited.

25. That the effect of tithes, in contracting the agriculture of a country, is the same with that of taxes on capitalists, or labourers, or the instruments of husbandry; and that the abolition of both would, in the first instance, enlarge the comforts of the general community; but, at last, would prove exclusively a boon and an enlargement to the landlords.

26. That tithes and taxes ought not to be abolished, but commuted, as there ought to be a more liberal provision for the various branches of the public service; and, more especially, for the support of the literary and ecclesiastical establishments, the endowment of which is indispensable to high scholarship, and to the full Christian instruction of the people.*

27. That the extreme limit of taxation is the landed rental of the kingdom; and that, were taxation carried to this limit, it would place the great bulk of the disposable population in the service of the state.

28. That the capabilities of the nation for defensive war are greatly underrated—they being at least commensurate to the extent of the disposable population.†

* " On the Use and Abuse of Literary and Ecclesiastical Endowments."

† " Extent and Stability of National Resources."

29. That the superior influence of Britain over other nations in distant parts, is due to her exports; and that if, instead of her lighter manufactures, she had to export raw produce, her power in offensive war would be lessened, while she might continue as strong in defensive war as before; and that, therefore, the balance of power is a topic of needless and misplaced anxiety on the part of British statesmen.

30. That the national debt is tantamount to a general mortgage on the land of the kingdom, and that it has occasioned no diminution of capital—the absorption of capital by the government loan of any particular year, being replaced next year by the operation of the diminished capital upon profits.

31. That if the expenses of a war are raised within the year, they do not enhance general prices; but that, in as far as they are defrayed by loans, prices rise, and so that the excess upon the whole is equal to the sum borrowed.*

32. That the national debt is therefore a double burden upon the community, having been already paid once in the excess of those higher prices which are consequent upon each loan; and to be paid a second time, either by a perpetual interest, or by the liquidation of the principal.

33. That the nation is as able to pay the expense of any war by taxes within the year, as by taxes and loans together—seeing that, in point of fact,

* " Christian and Civic Economy of Large Towns."

it does pay the loans within the year too, in the higher prices which these loans have occasioned.

34. That the law of primogeniture is essentially linked with the political strength, and other great public interests of the nation.

35. That, on the whole, no enlargement of our economical resources will suffice for the wants of a population, who are under no moral or prudential restraint on the increase of their numbers. That the effect of each successive addition to the means of our subsistence, will, in that case, be only a larger, but not a more comfortable or better-conditioned society. That however numerous, or however successful the expedients may be, for adding to the amount of national wealth—they will be nullified, in point of effect on the sensible comfort of families, by the operation of but one expedient more, which shall ensure a proportional, or beget a tendency towards greater than a proportional, addition to the national population. That a law of compulsory relief for the poor is precisely such an expedient; and that so long as it is in operation, every other device which philanthropy can suggest, or even an enlightened political economy can sanction, will turn out to be futile and abortive.*

36. That but for this disturbing force, which so unsettles the providential habits of the people, and so undermines every principle, whether of nature

* " Christian and Civic Economy of Large Towns," and Pamphlets on Pauperism, *passim.*

or Christianity, to the spontaneous operation of which the care of the poor ought always to have been confided—society might undergo a very speedy amelioration. Because that a very small excess in the number of labourers, effects a very large and disproportiônate reduction in the price of labour; and therefore, by a reverse process, it might only require a very insignificant fraction of relief from the numbers of the people, to operate a very large relief on their circumstances and comforts. That emigration for the lessening of the number, and the various other economical expedients for the enlargement of the means, will be of but slight and temporary effect, so long as the law of pauperism shall maintain the population in a state of perpetual overflow. But that, if these were related to a scheme for the gradual abolition of the pauperism, they would smooth the transition from a system of compulsory, to one of natural and gratuitous relief; after which, it were in the power of common, and more especially of Christian education, indefinitely to raise the habits and tastes, and, along with these, to raise the economical condition of the people.

FINIS.